Globalization and Resistance

Globalization and Resistance

Transnational Dimensions of Social Movements

EDITED BY JACKIE SMITH AND HANK JOHNSTON

ROWMAN & LITTLEFIELD PUBLISHERS, INC.
Lanham • Boulder • New York • Oxford

ROWMAN & LITTLEFIELD PUBLISHERS, INC.

Published in the United States of America by Rowman & Littlefield Publishers, Inc.
A Member of the Rowman & Littlefield Publishing Group
4720 Boston Way, Lanham, Maryland 20706
www.rowmanlittlefield.com

PO Box 317, Oxford, OX2 9RU, United Kingdom

Copyright © 2002 by Rowman & Littlefield Publishers, Inc.

Distributed by NATIONAL BOOK NETWORK

British Library Cataloguing in Publication Information Available

Library of Congress Cataloging-in-Publication Data

Globalization & resistance : transnational dimensions of social movements/ edited by
Jackie Smith and Hank Johnston.
    p.   cm.
 Includes bibliographical references and index.
 ISBN 0-7425-1989-9 (alk. paper) — ISBN 0-7425-1990-2 (pbk. : alk. paper)
  1. Social movements. 2. Globalization. I. Title: Globalization and resistance. II. Smith,
Jackie G., 1968– III. Johnston, Hank, 1947–

HN17.5 .G58 2002
303.48'4—dc21

                                                                2002069691

Printed in the United States of America

⊖™ The paper used in this publication meets the minimum requirements of American National Standard for Information Sciences—Permanence of Paper for Printed Library Materials, ANSI/NISO Z39.48-1992.

Errata

Due to electronic reproduction of this chapter, the following lines were erroneously deleted from the bottom of page 232:

Global Civil Society
One attempt to do so was offered by a group of scholars in the 1990s through the concept of global civil society (Falk 1995; Rosenberg 1994; Wapner 1995). That concept grew out of an earlier wave of conflict—resistance against state socialism in

Chapter 13, page 249, line 14 should read:
Rosenberg, Justin. 1994. *The Empire of Civil Society*. London: Verso.

CONTENTS

Chapter 1

GLOBALIZATION AND RESISTANCE:
AN INTRODUCTION

Jackie Smith and Hank Johnston

Several of this book's chapters originated in a panel on transnational dimensions of social movements, which took place at the 1999 American Sociological Association meetings. At the same time, one of the editors was contemplating a trip to Seattle on the hunch that something big might happen there. While the confrontations of activists and police at the World Trade Organization meeting in Seattle came as a surprise to some, this book attests to the fact that some social movement analysts have long recognized that transnational social movement mobilizations were neither novel nor transitory. For more than a decade, researchers have been providing us with evidence and theoretical tools to broaden the field of social movement studies to include global-level phenomena. By bringing together in a single binding empirically ground-breaking and theoretically innovative studies of transnational aspects of social movements, this volume seeks to clarify relationships between globalization and the ways that people organize for political and social change. Together, the chapters provide a broad look at the variety of ways that global economic and political integration affect political mobilization and contention.

Most social movement research takes the modern nation-state as the context of contemporary political contention (Tilly 1984). However, the acceleration of global integration processes in recent decades has altered our conceptualizations of the state and its capacity to influence both domestic and global processes. Such changes have crucial (if poorly understood) implications for political contention by groups promoting social change. Internally, states are increasingly constrained by an expanding web of commitments to other international actors. A growing number of intergovernmental organizations and treaties signal a more interdependent and densely integrated interstate system (Boli and Thomas 1997). This means that states have adopted limitations on their capacities for independent action in exchange for greater security and predictability in the broader system. For example, a government may agree (or be pressed by other actors) to operate within accepted human rights norms. In return, it gains some protection against the possibility of mass flows of political refugees across its borders that would result from other states' human rights violations. In the economic realm, where international monitoring and enforcement are more likely than for human rights, a state relinquishes (voluntarily or otherwise) its autonomy in the regulation of its domestic economy in exchange for both access to other states' markets and greater predictability and transparency in global economic relations.[1]

In addition to expanding trade and security regimes, globalization processes have created new transnational actors, including transnational corporations, international non-governmental organizations, transnational banks, and global criminal networks. All of these actors potentially challenge the supremacy of states as the sole or even predominant players in the global arena. Economically, the annual sales of most of the world's major corporations exceed the gross domestic products of most states (Anderson, Cavanagh and Lee 2000). Politically, prominent citizens' campaigns like those promoting an International Criminal Court or a treaty to ban land mines reveal the influence that non-state, transnational actors can have on both national and global politics (Price 1998; Johansen 2001). Finally, the recent World Trade Center bombings demonstrate dramatically how transnational criminal networks doggedly frustrate government attempts to promote their own security and control political and economic activities within their borders. In short, these observations suggest that conventional means of influence in the world system—military and economic might—are challenged by global actors that can wield influence despite their relative lack of access to these traditional resources.

This does not mean that states are irrelevant—or even less relevant—to understanding global political processes, but it does show that many contemporary, state-level political conflicts are at least partly shaped by global forces. State structures that govern policy-making processes, opportunities for public association, resource mobilization, and political expression certainly continue to define the most immediate and obvious context of political opportunities for collective action (e.g., Tarrow 2001; also see his concluding chapter in this volume); but if we accept that national polities are *nested* in an increasingly influential global polity that affects political conflicts, we cannot explain domestic political struggles without some attention to the global system in which states operate. As Doug McAdam notes in his introduction to the second edition of *Political Process and the Development of Black Insurgency*, "[b]y orienting their analysis to shifts in *domestic* opportunities, scholars in the political process tradition have generally failed to fully appreciate the multiple embeddings that shape the interpretations and actions of political actors" (1999: xxxi). Our aim in this volume is to bring together research that will help us assess the implications of globalization for political mobilization as well as identify the ways that social movement actors engage global political processes and affect change.

GLOBALIZATION AND SOCIAL MOVEMENT MOBILIZATION

A general theme in this collection is that global processes shape both *domestic* and *transnational* political mobilization. Most of the chapters offer insights about the effects of global forces on particular campaigns and organizations. In addition, two chapters theoretically explore how global forces might affect national political mobilizations. Marco Giugni's chapter offers a general framework for explaining why movements in different national contexts tend to take similar forms. He attributes movements' cross-national similarities to three global-level processes. First, globalization processes produce similar responses by movements in different contexts by structuring common transnational threats or opportunities. For example, structural adjustment loans contribute to parallel responses throughout the global South, as disaffected groups respond to similar IMF- and World Bank-imposed austerity programs (Walton and Seddon 1994; Johnston and Lio 1998).

Second, global pressures produce similar opportunity structures for collective action in different national contexts. Transnational actors become more relevant as they organize to address grievances of global character and to take advantage of parallel state-level organizations. Groups like Amnesty International or Jubilee 2000 can readily advance a common political strategy that targets multiple national governments. Social movement actors find a stronger base for building cooperative networks as their organizational counterparts in different countries increasingly assume forms that resemble their own. Common postures vis-á-vis the state and other international actors help generate shared interpretations of experiences, isomorphic organizations, and complementary activist identities.

Third, Giugni identifies diffusion processes as an explanation of cross-national movement similarities. As information and ideas about collective action flow across national boundaries, different national social movements adopt similar—though probably not identical—ideological orientations and tactics (McAdam and Rucht 1993).

Greg Maney's chapter provides an exploration of the first two of Giugni's claims about the ways globalization impacts political mobilization, namely, through the creation of globally defined targets or sources of grievances as well as through the structural affinity among states. Maney reviews world systems research on global economic trends and explores their implications for political mobilization within countries of the core and periphery.

As Giugni reminds us, the transnational diffusion is also a crucial process for explaining commonalities of ideology and tactics across different national movements. In this volume, the work of Sean Chabot analyzes diffusion processes and ideological connections between the national independence movement in India and the civil rights movement in the United States. He emphasizes that diffusion is not necessarily a spontaneous process, but rather requires substantial efforts by movement leaders to adapt ideas and meanings to diverse settings. Entrepreneurial leadership and learning, in other words, are prerequisites for the effective transnational diffusion of ideas and strategies. Nepstad's chapter reinforces this conclusion. It shows how shared cultural attributes, such as moral precepts, religious narratives, iconic figures, and action templates functioned as resources to foster transnational solidarity and shared critiques of interstate policy.

Many scholars examining transnational processes have substantiated Giugni's three processes. Kim Reimann's chapter provides additional evidence by examining influence networks relevant to Japanese citizen mobilization around the Kyoto Global Climate Change Convention. She documents how the diffusion of ideas and tactics among groups as well as structural affinity—what she calls the socialization of national leaders into the roles and practices defined by global institutions—brought legitimacy to Japanese environmental groups and strengthened their position vis-à-vis national authorities.

CONTINUITY AND CHANGE IN SOCIAL MOVEMENT MOBILIZATION

While casual observers saw the anti-WTO protests in Seattle as novel in their global orientation, any careful examination of social protest reveals that transnational political mobilization is not new. For instance, Keck and Sikkink (1998) describe nineteenth-century transnational campaigns against slavery and footbinding, and for womens' suffrage. Chatfield (1997) analyzes transnational campaigns by social change advocates to advance more peaceful international relations by promoting and shaping intergovernmental institutions such as the League of Nations and later the United Nations.

Sean Chabot's chapter develops themes of continuity and change by tracing historical connections between the African American civil rights movement and the Indian anticolonial movement and its Gandhian tactics. He describes how ideas about nonviolent collective action flowed from the Indian struggle into the U.S. civil rights movement by specifying the multigenerational network of activists who reshaped the repertoire of the Indian movement to make it applicable in their own struggle against an industrialized Western power. Michael Hanagan's examination of more than a century of transnational activism by Irish migrants challenges both the notion that transnational movement activity is new and that such activity fundamentally challenges the state. Hanagan found strong continuities in the movement networks over time, and he suggests that the benefits of today's technologies are no more significant to transnational mobilization than earlier innovations like steam ships and trans-Atlantic cable. He also found that interpersonal networks were crucial transnational conveyors of information in both the early and more recent experiences of this movement. Furthermore, challenging the notion that globalization transforms national identities, Hanagan found that transnational ties among Irish migrants did not fundamentally challenge the role of the state, and, indeed, such ties seem to have made it more relevant.

Considerations of the other instances of transnational action explored in this volume lead us to call attention to this conclusion of Hanagan's. We note that his research focuses on Irish transnational networks, where a common national identity facilitates mobilization. However, we must ask whether Hanagan's findings can be generalized to account for movements involving several *different* national groups interacting through transnational networks or within more formal transnational social movement organizations (TSMOs). It may be that these types of transnational interactions alter the relationships between challengers and traditional state structures. For instance, Franklin Daniel Rothman and Pamela Oliver examine the emergence of local-global connections in the anti-dam movement in Brazil over more than a decade. They show important changes in activists' views about the role of the state and in its vulnerability to pressures from nonstate actors and international institutions. Their research documents changing frames and strategies over the course of the movement. They begin with local church- and labor-led mobilizations around land rights and show how these eventually combine with international environmental challenges to World Bank lending policies. The combinations of activists and strategies in cooperative (and sometimes conflictual) exchanges gradually produced a *political ecology frame* that incorporated new, globally informed ideas about local grievances and their solutions. Their conclusions parallel those of other analysts of World Bank campaigns (e.g., Fox and Brown 1998), reinforcing the theme that when activists from different countries get together, their diverse experiences can translate into new understandings of global phenomena that extend beyond those bounded by national opportunity structures. The protests against expanding global trade, such as those examined in the chapters by Ayres and Smith, illustrate how the political ecology frame, along with its challenges to traditional notions of state authority, has been appropriated for a (both geographically and ideologically) broader campaign against global financial integration.

Other analyses of intensive transnational interactions among social movement activists show similar processes of dialogue, conflict, and learning as activists struggle to overcome their differences in order to advance shared goals (see Sperling, Ferree, and Risman 2001; Liebowitz 2000). The crucial conclusion of many of these studies is that activists see a need to build broad and strong alliances that can compensate for their separate weaknesses and poverty, and this demand for unity forces them to seek ways to negotiate their many important differences. Scholarship in this field needs to both document these attempts and identify the mechanisms that allow activists to build successful transnational coalitions and campaigns. In this volume, chapters by Reimann, Ayres, Nepstad, and Smith provide additional support for the claim that transnational contention involving different national groups helps shape activists' understandings of their interests in ways that can challenge the traditional roles and authority of the nation-state. Taken together, these studies reveal a rich history of transnational cooperation and/or organization that has undoubtedly shaped contemporary activist frames and organizational structures.

Considering what these studies say about continuity and change in transnational activism, we hypothesize that, while transnational social movement activities are not new, recent ones are more likely than their historical predecessors to include multiple classes of people and be more broadly based (cf. Kleidman 1993; Chatfield 1997).[2] Additionally, we hypothesize that, while transnational migrant networks have been important agents of transnational collective action in the past, as globalization processes increase communication and travel and exacerbate local problems, such networks will likely represent a smaller proportion of all transnational mobilizations.

TRANSNATIONAL TIES AND NETWORKS

Transnational ties and networks have been a central focus of globalization research, beginning with Keck and Sikkink's groundbreaking study of what they called "transnational advocacy networks" (1998). Part of the reason for saliency of ties and networks in the literature is their relatively problematic nature when compared to SMOs and mobilization networks functioning in a state system. Global grievances and transnational SMOs require focused and intentional strategies that help bridge the cultural and spatial divides between activists in different countries. Several of the chapters focus on processes of mobilizing and using transnational ties (see part IV, Transnational Networks). There seem to be two related processes that are largely overlooked in the literature: (1)

how transnational mobilization influences identity formation by bringing together activists with different political experiences; and (2) how mobilizing ideologies are worked and reworked by diffusion and innovation via transnational activist contact. Chabot's chapter sheds light on the first by tracing relations among activists as nonviolent strategies were adapted to the U.S. context. Rothman and Oliver demonstrate how ideologies diffuse through activist networks, and become resources for political movements, as well as the raw material of new frames for collective action.

Sharon Nepstad explores the question of how activists cultivate ties that can transcend national, ideological, class, and cultural differences. Such a question represents an important area for contemporary social movement scholarship. Nepstad's analysis shows that the narrative of Salvadoran martyr Archbishop Oscar Romero mobilized cultural resources of religious identity and shared moral values, and fostered solidarity across national and cultural divides. Her research raises questions about whether durable transnational ties require that activists share basic aspects of identity, and whether certain types of identities such as religious ones generate stronger foundations for long-term collective action than do others.

An important question about transnational ties that has impacts on all types of transnational movement activity is the extent to which they reflect or challenge predominant power relations in the global system. Specifically, do activists from rich, Northern states consistently dominate transnational organizations and exert disproportionate influence on transnational organizing agendas and identities? A number of studies challenge this notion that movement ideas and strategies, like other political and economic forces, flow invariably from powerful countries to weaker ones. These studies suggest that the social movement sector does not simply mimic world-system power disparities; but rather, in seeking to transform global inequalities, activists self-consciously act to change how power relations between states impinge on internal SMO relations. A question for our scholarship is how successful activists have been at overcoming structural inequities. Cases here provide some evidence related to these questions, but clearly more research is needed.

If we are to understand the broad social and political implications of rising levels of transnational activism, it is important to get a better sense of what activists are doing together transnationally. As several of our chapters show, by bringing together activists from different national backgrounds and creating opportunities for information exchange, social movement organizations encourage learning that transforms activist identities. In some instances it is the poor who instruct the relatively rich about how to challenge unjust authorities, as Rothman and Oliver's study in Brazil demonstrates. Also, both Ayres's and Smith's chapters that analyze protests against trade liberalization reveal South-to-North flows of experiences and analyses. As Northern groups faced new economic threats caused by economic liberalization, Southern activists argued explicitly that they could instruct their Northern counterparts about the anticipated effects of processes that were relatively novel in the North but all-too-familiar in the South.

But clearly the major flows of information and expertise may still be from North to South. Caniglia's and Reimann's chapters especially demonstrate that activists from core countries have important advantages, particularly in resources, language skills, technical expertise, and information access. Modeled on Western democratic structures, global political institutions reward the skillful use of techniques that are more familiar to Western activists, such as lobbying, legal analysis, and constituent mobilization. In addition, because TSMOs and the global institutions they seek to influence are geographically concentrated in the global North, they are more accessible to Northern activists.

GLOBAL POLITICAL PROCESSES

Many studies of transnational association and political contention implicitly or explicitly argue that globalization processes are creating an expanding web of interdependencies among states, thereby *nesting* national institutions within a broader, global framework of interests and obligations. These interdependent policy arenas present opportunities and constraints to would-be challengers that differ from national political arenas. National policy decisions, in short, are of interest to actors outside the domestic polity as interstate policies and institutions create new definitions of what domestic policies are acceptable. Thus, the various factors that make up the political opportunity structures of movements—splits within the elite, the presence of allies, elite repressive capacities, among others—may be altered by a whole range of dynamics that lie outside the domestic polity. Rothman and Oliver argue that the local-global anti-dam struggles they observed were products of this nested character of national and global institutions. As activists grappled with questions about how global forces affected their local predicaments and how their change efforts could effectively engage global-level processes, transnational exchanges generated mutual learning and shaped new identities and activist frames.

Although Tammy Lewis does not use this term, her study of transnational environmental SMOs illustrates the nesting of national and global political opportunities. Looking at Ecuador, Chile, and Peru, Lewis argues that transnational SMOs pursued conservation projects in countries with more open political structures and active voluntary sectors rather than in countries where preservation was most urgent for the local and/or global ecology. In other words, while global ecological and political-economic realities shaped the opportunities and strategic priorities of certain debt-for-nature swaps, national opportunity structures further narrowed the range of feasible courses of action for conservation TSMOs. Comparing her case with other transnational movement efforts, Lewis notes how the environmental and human rights movements differ. Unlike the environmental groups she studied, human rights TSMOs appear more likely to engage in struggles where domestic political opportunities are *closed*. Her study should inform future efforts to develop and test hypotheses about the ways that nested, interdependent political institutions of state and interstate systems interact to affect movement opportunities and strategic choices. Addressing such questions will require comparisons between different issue areas as well as different constellations of states and global institutions.

Beth Schaefer Caniglia's chapter explores dynamics within transnational collections of social movement actors. Her study provides insights into the logic that governs inter-governmental institutions and social movement attempts to influence them. She finds that the need to cultivate informal relationships with agencies of global institutions affects the shape of network relations among TSMOs. Those actors with effective, typically informal, ties to transnational bureaucracies serve as movement nodes, channeling crucial information and ideas between challengers and authorities. This study is an important innovation in attempts to understand power dynamics among the actors that make up transnational social movements. It also leads us to questions about how interstate institutions affect social movement dynamics and whether distinct clusters of social change proponents form both in relation to intergovernmental organizations as well as wholly (and consciously) outside those institutions.

Other chapters in this volume examine interactions between national and global institutions and processes and their effects on conflict dynamics. For instance, Ayres's study of the evolution of the Canadian campaign to oppose trade liberalization shows how activists needed to transform their strategies and expand their struggle beyond national boundaries as trade debates evolved. Reimann's focus on Japanese mobilization demonstrates the variety of global- and national- level pressures that affected both challengers' and authorities' opportunities for action. In the long-term, the mobilization around the Kyoto Climate Change Conference should have important implications for both national environmental mobilizations in Japan and for Japanese participation in future transnational environmental campaigns. Smith's examination of the protests against the World Trade Organization reveals how activists adapted national-level protest repertoires to target global arenas. It also documents multilevel strategies in which activists seek to influence the policies of one or more key governments as they simultaneously pursue a broader effort to influence global policy outcomes. As a whole, these cases present us with important clues about the workings of global political processes and the conditions that support or deter transnational social change efforts.

CONCLUSION

Globalization implies substantial changes in both the scope and character of social relations, and we should expect it therefore to affect the ways that people engage in collective political action. Global processes of cultural and economic integration and the rise of global political institutions affect how people organize, how they interpret the sources of their problems, and how they frame prospects for change. If we accept the increasingly common understanding of states *as actors within a highly interdependent and stratified state system,* we can begin to identify common, system-level influences on both national and transnational opportunities for political contention. The chapters in part I of this book present interpretations of the global system and its anticipated consequences for political mobilization in different national contexts. Two key observations emerge: (1) states' choices vis-à-vis political challengers are in fact conditioned by their relationships to other global actors; and (2) increased global integration generates potential sources of unity for political movements. These points are important foundations for future theory and research on transnational aspects of social movements.

Several of the case studies in this volume demonstrate that global activism is not novel, but rather that its frequency today stems from more than a century of diverse efforts by transnational activists to build ties, develop collective action frameworks, and share ideas about mobilizing for change. The case of early transnational mobilization by an Irish immigrant diaspora suggests that transnational movements pose little challenge to traditional notions of the state. But the mobilization in more recent times of environmental and economic justice activists against World Bank dam projects contradicts this conclusion, suggesting a need for more systematic investigation into questions of how transnational mobilizations shape state policies and actions. A second theme regarding the history of transnational mobilization, namely, Chabot's study of the transfer of ideas from the Indian nationalist movement into the U.S. civil rights movement, is that global integration may serve to expand the cultural resources available to activists. And as ideas and knowledge become more difficult for states to control in this globally integrated information economy, these may become increasingly important resources for transnational activism.

The role of ideas in cultivating and maintaining transnational ties is emphasized in Nepstad's analysis of the solidarity-building work of U.S. and Central American peace activists. Both Nepstad's and Chabot's research suggests that diffusion of ideas capable of mobilizing and uniting activists depends on the existence of favorable conditions for the successful transfer. Taken together, these two studies urge a research program that aims to further uncover the dynamics affecting the transnational transfer of ideas and the mobilization of symbolic resources for collective action. Also, future research might further specify the conditions necessary for strong and effective transnational ties.

Globalization brings with it an expanding array of political institutions that create both opportunities and constraints for activists. Chapters in parts four and five examine the global institutional architecture from a number of different perspectives. Not only do global institutions have distinct effects on activists' political strategies and opportunities, but they also shape the ways that social movement actors relate to each other. These studies provide important glimpses of the intramovement dynamics created by collective attempts to shape global policy and practice. Sidney Tarrow's final chapter offers an insightful and provocative interpretation of where the research agenda on the relationships between globalization and collective action should be headed. He identifies some important gaps in existing research and challenges scholars to both refine our concepts for analyzing globalization processes and expand the range of contentious political action we consider.

We have sought not only to orient our readers to the rich and informative analyses that follow but also to provide a set of questions that might inspire further research in this emerging field in the study of social movements and global change. Scholars of contentious politics have made some important advances in improving our theories about global integration and its effects on political contention both nationally and transnationally. But as Tarrow argues, much room remains for us to expand our theoretical tools and empirical knowledge relating to these phenomena. The chapters that follow provide important contributions to this knowledge base. And we hope that our readers will be inspired to embark on new efforts to advance a coherent research agenda that will help us better understand the connections between globalization and resistance.

NOTES

1. Consistent with world-systems theory, Northern core states tend to enjoy greater (though not total) autonomy in financial and economic policy. Southern peripheral states in the 1990s had less autonomy than prior to the international debt crisis and the implementation of Structural Adjustment lending practices by the World Bank and International Monetary Fund. International trade agreements reveal yet another way that core states have exercised their economic power at the expense of periphery states.

2. This does not mean that such movements can be expected to eliminate a middle-class bias. Rather, it observes that they incorporate a more diverse base of activists than earlier transnational mobilizations. This is largely due to the expansion of relatively inexpensive communica-

tions and transportation technologies allow greater participation by less privileged activists. It also results from the proliferation of mass mobilizing tactics within Western democratic contexts and their application to transnational policy arenas. Such wide mobilization becomes more possible as the agendas and influence of global level policy arenas expand.

REFERENCES

Anderson, Sarah, John Cavanagh, and Thea Lee. 2000. *Field Guide to the Global Economy*, New York: New Press.

Boli, John, and George Thomas. 1997. "World Culture in the World Polity." *American Sociological Review* 62: 171-190.

Chatfield, Charles. 1997. "Intergovernmental and Nongovernmental Associations to 1945." Pp. 19-41 in *Transnational Social Movements and World Politics: Solidarity beyond the State*, J. Smith, C. Chatfield, and R. Pagnucco, eds. Syracuse, N.Y.: Syracuse University Press.

Fox, Jonathan, and L. David Brown, eds. 1998. *The Struggle for Accountability: The World Bank, NGOs, and Grassroots Movements*. Cambridge, Mass.: MIT Press.

Johansen, Robert C. 2001. "Transnational Politics and Nongovernmental Organizations: Drafting a Treaty to Establish a Permanent International Criminal Court." Presented at International Studies Association Annual Meeting. Chicago.

Johnston, Hank, and Shoon Lio. 1998. "Collective Behavior and Social Movements in the Postmodern Age: Looking Backward to Look Forward." *Sociological Perspectives* 41: 453-472.

Keck, Margaret, and Kathryn Sikkink. 1998. *Activists beyond Borders*. Ithaca, N.Y.: Cornell University Press.

Kleidman, Robert. 1993. *Organizing for Peace: Neutrality, the Test Ban and the Freeze*. Syracuse, N.Y.: Syracuse University Press.

Liebowitz, Debra J. 2000. "Explaining Absences, Analyzing Change, Looking toward the Future —U.S. Women's Participation in Transnational Feminist Organizing in North America." Paper presented at International Studies Association Annual Meeting, Los Angeles.

McAdam, Doug. 1999. "Introduction to the Second Edition." Pp. vii-xlii in *Political Process and the Development of Black Insurgency 1930-1970*. Chicago: University of Chicago Press.

McAdam, Doug, and Dieter Rucht. 1993. "The Cross-National Diffusion of Movement Ideas." *The Annals of the American Academy of Political and Social Science* 528:56-74.

Price, Richard. 1998. "Reversing the Gun Sights: Transnational Civil Society Targets Land Mines." *International Organization* 52: 613-644.

Sperling, Valerie, Myra Marx Feree, and Barbara Risman. 2001. "Constructing Global Feminism: Transnational Advocacy Networks and Russian Women's Activism." *Signs: Journal of Women in Culture and Society* 26: 1155-1186.

Tilly, Charles. 1984. "Social Movements and National Politics." Pp. 297-317 in *Statemaking and Social Movements: Essays in History and Theory*, C. Bright and S. Harding, eds. Ann Arbor: University of Michigan Press.

Tarrow, Sidney. 2001. "Transnational Politics: Contention and Institutions in International Politics." *Annual Review of Political Science* 4: 1-20.

Walton, John, and David Seddon. 1994. *Free Markets and Food Riots: The Politics of Global Adjustment*. Cambridge, Mass.: Blackwell.

Part I

**Theories of Globalization and Social
Movement Mobilization**

Chapter 2

EXPLAINING CROSS-NATIONAL SIMILARITIES AMONG SOCIAL MOVEMENTS

Marco G. Giugni

Recent work on social movements and political protest stresses *differences* among single movements or movement families across countries (e.g., Kitschelt 1986; Kriesi, Koopmans, Duyvendak, and Giugni 1995; Tilly, Tilly, and Tilly 1975). Although accounting for cross-national variations is crucial in understanding how political structures affect social movements, researchers tend to overlook the striking *similarities* displayed by movements across countries. This is to some extent a matter of perception, as similarities are the reverse side of differences, and the accent can be put on either one aspect or the other. Explanations of variations so far have been the main focus of social movement research. This chapter focuses on the other side of the coin by examining the sources of similarity and resemblance within the social movement sector.

How can we account for similarities among social movements? To do so we must proceed in four steps: (1) identify similarities across nation-states, (2) look for possible explanatory factors, (3) formulate clear and testable hypotheses to explain the similarities, and (4) test the hypotheses on different movements and in different circumstances. My discussion will focus on the first and second steps and develop the third only in part. Instead of the fourth step, testing hypotheses, I will limit myself to illustrating the main arguments. Regarding possible explanations, I look at three sets of factors: (1) long-term, global, macrostructural changes, (2) similar configurations on the state level, and (3) short-term exchanges among nation-states.

Given the breadth and relative novelty of the subject matter, my goal is to explore possible relationships and suggest some useful concepts for analyzing cross-national similarities. My aim is to advance our thinking and research in two related domains. On the one hand, I hope to show that, although variation-finding comparisons are crucial to our understanding of social movements, explaining similarities deserves careful attention too. On the other hand, the concepts I propose to account for similarities should sensitize us to the increasing importance of international and transnational dynamics among social movements. To accomplish these two tasks, first I will identify those aspects of movements that tend to be shared. Second, I will propose three models that can explain movement similarities, based on three broad concepts: globalization, structural affinity, and diffusion. Third, I shall attempt to combine the three models by proposing a general model that acknowledges interactions among these concepts. Fourth, I will try to specify some mechanisms through which structure translates into action. Finally, I will illustrate the argument with the example of new social movements (NSMs) in Western Europe.

WHAT IS TO BE EXPLAINED?

To explain cross-national similarities we must first identify those aspects of movements that frequently resemble each other. To do this, it is useful to separate the long-term structural similarities from short-term conjunctural ones. Action repertoires are an example of the former. As Tilly (1986, 1995) has repeatedly shown, the repertoires of contention available to challengers for claims making have changed little during the last two centuries, after a major shift around the mid-nineteenth century. On the other hand, the almost simultaneous rise of peace movements in many Western countries in the early 1980s, principally targeting the nuclear arms race, was a more temporary contingent phenomenon. A further distinction can be made between general and particular similarity. The former concerns a movement or movement family as a whole, and refers to the rise of mobilization. The latter concerns a particular movement feature, such as a tactic or slogan. Social movement similarities range across a structural-to-conjunctural axis and across a general-to-particular axis.

A better way to identify cross-national similarities of social movements is to single out concrete items that lend themselves to empirical observation and verification. Here I distinguish among six movement characteristics.

First, social movements may address similar *issues, themes,* and *goals.* Different countries may see the rise of the same movements, such as peace, women's, and ecology movements. Also, the demands, ideology, and strategies of a particular movement in one country may reflect that of its counterparts in other countries. New social movements (NSMs) in Western Europe illustrate how movement themes and issues can resemble each other across countries. NSMs such as the women's, student, peace, ecology, and antinuclear movements all emerged at about the same time, approximately in the 1960s, and grew to become the main extrainstitutional forces in the Western world.[1] Furthermore, the goals of these movements are similar, although their size and influence may vary widely. Also, the targets of protest actions often coincide: nuclear power plants, air and water pollution, the army, nuclear weapons, and abortion rights are only some examples.

Second, movements may display similar *levels of mobilization,* that is, carry out similar numbers of protest actions and/or involve similar numbers of participants in those actions. For example, Kriesi et al. (1995) have shown that NSMs have mobilized to a roughly similar extent in Germany, the Netherlands, and Switzerland from 1975 to 1989, while in France their level of mobilization was much lower. However, this difference is less pronounced among the four countries' whole social movement sectors, as "old" movements were stronger in France than in the three other countries.

Third, the *strategies, tactics,* and *forms of action* may converge. Research on this crucial dimension has mostly focused on cross-national variations of action repertoires. The adoption of the sit-in as a specific tactic is an example. More generally, though NSMs are usually more radical in certain countries (for example, France) than in others, street demonstrations prevail everywhere.

Fourth, we may observe similar *organizational structures*, which refer to the level of resources and other organizational features (centralized/decentralized, formal/informal, integrated/isolated, and so forth). For example, at the time of their emergence, the NSMs brought to the fore nonhierarchical, participatory forms of organization, which Gerlach and Hine (1970) have called "segmented, polycentric, informal networks." Later, formalized and professional organizations emerged almost everywhere among NSMs.

Fifth, movement *cultural frames, ideas,* and *discourses* may show similar patterns (McAdam and Rucht 1993). Here we refer to the ideological and symbolic contents of mobilization. The use of similar slogans is perhaps most typical. There are numerous examples: the Marxist-Leninist and Maoist slogans of the European student movements in the 1960s, the small-is-beautiful slogan of the early ecology movement, the stress on sustainable development of the present-day global environmental movement, the nuclear-free-zone concept used by movements, and so forth.

Sixth, and perhaps most interesting, we may observe parallels in the *timing of protest*. This aspect is shared across countries both in the short and long term. Similar protest timing is illustrated by the rise of student protest in the late 1960s, mobilization against the deployment of NATO missiles in the early 1980s, and the strong opposition to communist regimes in Eastern Europe at the end of the same decade. Protest against nuclear power plants, which peaked in Germany, Italy, Switzerland, and the United States between 1975 and 1977, is another parallel in mobilization timing.

THREE MODELS OF CROSS-NATIONAL SIMILARITIES

Once we have identified movement similarities, we need to look for possible explanations. I argue in this section that those general factors used to understand differences—most notably, political opportunities—can also be used to account for resemblances. I focus on three sets of factors, summarized by the concepts of globalization, structural affinity, and diffusion. Also, I suggest that similarities among social movements across countries can be accounted for by means of three models that, when employed to explain differences, are usually portrayed as rivals. The first, the *globalization model*, points to how the increasing interconnectedness of the world stimulates transnational structures and processes which might simultaneously affect movements in different countries. The second, the *structural affinity model*, stresses the existence of similar structures in different countries that may lead to convergent patterns in movement activity. The third, the *diffusion model*, explains similarities among movements through direct (networks) or indirect (mass media) cross-national flows of information that might diffuse protest from one country to the other. Next I discuss each of these three models in more detail.

The Globalization Model

In recent years, the idea of an international system of nation-states has been challenged by the idea of a global system transcending them. The nation-state, once the uncontested leading actor on the world stage, has been challenged by processes of *globalization* that are independent of states and, therefore, must be studied in terms that do not refer to nations. According to Robertson (1992: 8), "globalization as a concept refers both to the compression of the world and the intensification of the consciousness of the world as a whole." Similarly, other authors define globalization as political processes broadening in scope and deepening in intensity (McGrew and Lewis 1992). Globalization is distinct from the mere increase in international linkages. International relations only implies relations among sovereign nation-states, whereas transnational relations—upon which the historical process of globalization is based—describes "those networks, associations or interactions which cut across national societies, creating linkages among individuals, groups, organizations and communities within different nation-states" (Modelski 1972). Globalization thus refers to the multiplicity of linkages that transcend nation-states and the increasing density of such linkages.

This process affects levels of society differently. The best known aspect refers to the creation of a global economic system under market capitalism (Wallerstein 1974, 1983) and to the rise of a distinct capitalist global society through the transnational organization of production and exchange (Sklair 1991). The late twentieth century has seen the accelerated transformation of national capitalism to transnational capitalism and the creation of an integrated global economy built on multinational corporations. But cultural globalization also occurs through a homogenized world culture, which has replaced or supplemented national or local cultures (Robertson 1992). Global cultural interdependence is mainly due to advances in telecommunications (Rosenau 1980, 1989, 1990). Finally, the world is not only globalizing through the development of markets and technology but also via political forces. Thus, from a neorealist perspective in the study of international relations, Gilpin (1981, 1987) maintains that globalization is a historically contingent process that relies upon the hegemonic states in the international system. In his view, global interdependence increases as a function of a stable world order guaranteed by the power of a hegemonic liberal state.

As a result of globalization, events in one part of the world can affect individuals and communities in far distant parts. Moreover, one event can affect simultaneously many distant individuals and communities. For these reasons, globalization has significant effects on collective action. Unlike in the past, contemporary social movements may use several leverage points. In premodern societies, local protest was the only way to bring grievances to authorities. With the expansion of the national state in the modern era—most notably during the eighteenth and nineteenth centuries— national politics gave rise to the national social movement (Tilly 1984). In a similar fashion, the growing role of transnational and global structures characterizes postmodern societies.

Thus, globalization brings about a "transnational society," a "multicentric world" of transnational organizations, problems, events, communities, and structures (Rosenau 1990). This translates into two distinct, though interrelated, implications. First, as Giddens (1990: 21) has pointed out, globalization is characterized by the disembedding of social relations, that is, by the "'lifting out' of social relations from local contexts of interaction and their restructuring across indefinite spans of time-space." As a result, contingent events that take place far away impinge on local social movements in different countries. Second, globalization processes produce transnational or supranational structures that take on increasing salience for social movements. This may bring about *transnational opportunities* for mobilization. The creation of centers of power in the European Union is a good example. Similar transnational opportunities structures should cause convergence in the emergence and behaviors of different national movements that take advantage of such opportunities.

In brief, the globalization model assumes that, in an increasingly globalizing world, national factors lose much of their explanatory power and, conversely, social movements in different contexts react to transnational opportunities in a similar fashion. The globalization model explains similarities among social movements as a product of similar movement reactions to changes occurring on the global level.

The Structural Affinity Model

While globalization is defined as the growing interdependence of the modern world, its homogenizing effects should be somewhat qualified. First, similar global processes do not necessarily lead to similar movements. For example, as Walton and Seddon (1994) have shown, reactions to economic liberalization and structural adjustment programs vary across countries according to preexisting mobilizing structures. More generally, different reactions due to varying political opportunity structures may produce divergent movement trajectories even amidst strong globalizing forces (Kriesi et al. 1995). In addition, globalization might cause reactions opposite to homogenization. For example, Europeanization has spurred countervailing forces at the regional level in many European countries (Marks and McAdam 1996).

We could say, following Rosenau (1990), that there are two global societies rather than one today: a multicentric society made of transnational links, and a state-centric society whereby the nation-state is still the dominant actor. In this chapter I stress the former, that is, transnational links that have homogenized societies and, as a result, the social movements that develop within them. In addition, I focus on movements in the Western world and for the moment place aside the impact of global market capitalism on Third World and newly industrializing countries.

Globalization has another important consequence: it contributes to the formation of what I propose to call *structural affinity*; that is, the presence of similar structures among different nations. Structural affinity can also emerge as a product of independent national developments, but globalization strongly facilitates its emergence. For instance, in a globalizing world, concepts such as democracy and capitalism tend to be shared in many national contexts, to varying degrees. Shared definitions of appropriate political and economic behaviors facilitate the emergence of movements that have comparable structures and display similar characteristics. Thus, while the globalization model refers to structural or contingent events on the transnational level, the structural affinity model focuses upon structural similarities on the national level.

Among the structural features of the political system that might affect social movements, I will look at those summarized in the concept of political opportunity structure (POS). The various aspects of POS characterize not only cross-national difference but also structural affinity in different countries, and such affinity may account for similarities among social movements in those countries. If we follow the conceptualization of POS proposed by Kriesi et al. (1995), we can highlight four aspects that can lead to cross-national similarities.

First, country-specific structure of political cleavages largely determines the mobilization capacity of social movements. These cleavages in turn are rooted in the social and cultural dividing lines of a given society. Similar cleavage or conflict structures would explain why movements with similar grievances emerge in different places and why such movements display similar levels of mobilization. In particular, as Bartolini and Mair (1990) have pointed out in relation to electoral competition, the mobilization potential of a political cleavage depends on two factors: (1) degree of closure of the social relationships it gives rise to, that is, whether one group is internally integrated and clearly segmented from others; and (2) salience in the political arena. Thus, similarly closed and salient cleavages should lead to parallels in movement emergence and mobilization.

Second, social movements are strongly constrained by the formal structure of the political system. Such structures include the state's degree of territorial centralization, the functional concentration or separation of state power, the degree of coherence of the public administration, and the presence or absence of direct democratic procedures. All these aspects characterize a state as more or less weak or strong and offer greater or fewer opportunities to challengers for access. In turn, this has an impact on social movement mobilization, in particular on strategies and tactics. Thus, similar institutional arrangements should have analogous consequences on social movements in different countries, leading to parallels in mobilization, strategies, and organization.

Third, the informal prevailing strategies political authorities use with challengers influence social movements. Such strategies can be inclusive (i.e., tolerant and facilitating) or exclusive (i.e., rigid and repressive), and coupled with the institutional structures, strongly constrain social movement mobilization and forms of action. Thus, similar prevailing strategies—that is, similar reactions of political authorities to movement actions—would strongly influence the action forms social movements adopt, which would thus tend to resemble each other across countries.

Fourth, Tarrow (1994) points out that volatile aspects of political context can influence mobilization. Kriesi et al. (1995) have summarized these aspects under the term *alliance structures*. This variable refers to short-term changes in political opportunities that may spur or discourage protest. These include increased access to participation, shifts in ruling alignments, availability of powerful allies, and conflicts within and among elites. Thus, resemblance among social movements would stem from similar alliance structures in different countries. In particular, a similar configuration of power and similar behaviors by both the alliance coalition and opponents should have analogous consequences on social movements across countries.

In brief, the specific version of the structural affinity model put forth here generalizes the POS argument by stating that similar political opportunities account for similarities among social movements across countries. Of course, more general structural affinities, such as shared social organization or culture are also relevant. In general, the fact that NSMs act within democratic societies with shared democratic values may bring them closer across countries. Here, however, I focus specifically on political-institutional affinities.

The Diffusion Model

Surely, *diffusion* is a well-studied phenomenon in social science. Yet, in the field of collective action, though scholars have often acknowledged that diffusion among social movements in different countries might occur, attempts at explanation are still quite rare (for exceptions, see Giugni 1995; McAdam and Rucht 1993; and Pitcher,

Hamblin, and Miller 1978). Diffusion is usually viewed as a residual factor that accounts for unexplained variation in different contexts. As McAdam and Rucht (1993: 58) have remarked, however, "the real challenge is not so much in demonstrating the mere fact of diffusion ... but to investigate systematically the conditions under which diffusion is likely to occur and the means by which it does." Of course, a diffusion model can be applied within countries, but here I only deal with cross-national diffusion of protest.

Diffusion theorists have produced considerable research to explain the diffusion of information and opinions (e.g., Berelson et al. 1954; Fisher 1978; Katz and Lazarsfeld 1955; Lazarsfeld et al. 1944) or the spread of innovations and techniques (e.g., Coleman, Katz, and Menzel 1966; Hagerstrand 1967; Mahajan and Peterson 1985; Rogers 1983). These studies, in general, follow a simple and straightforward definition of diffusion. Katz (1968), for instance, sees diffusion "as the acceptance of some specific item, over time, by adopting units—individuals, groups, communities—that are linked both to external channels of communication and to each other by means of both a structure of social relations and a system of values, or culture." Similarly, Rogers (1983: 14) states that there is diffusion when "an innovation is communicated through certain channels over time among the members of a social system." More recently, Michaelson (1993: 217) has defined diffusion as "the process by which an innovation (any new idea, activity, or technology) spreads through the population."

Pitcher, Hamblin, and Miller (1978) have suggested that the concept has to be modified when applied to collective action. In particular, they maintain that existing models of cultural diffusion (Dodd 1953, 1955; Griliches 1957; Coleman et al. 1966) need to take into account indirect channels of diffusion such as news media. Some authors have argued that for violent protest the probable mechanism is not direct, face-to-face communication typical of earlier diffusion studies, but rather indirect learning based on the mass media (Archer and Gartner 1976; Spilerman 1976; Pitcher et al. 1978). While it is widely recognized that mass media are crucial channels of diffusion for social movements, this could obscure the role of interpersonal networks as a source of direct diffusion. Traditional diffusion theorists were more interested in modeling the rate of diffusion of some idea, technique, or innovation than in determining the social conditions under which diffusion occurs. In my view, the latter is precisely what we need in order to explain cross-national diffusion among social movements.

More recently, Tarrow (1989, 1994) has stressed the role of diffusion processes for the spread of protest waves. In his view, protest cycles are periods of generalized disorder spurred by shifts in POS in the first place, but then develop through the diffusion of tactical innovations to other themes, groups, and locations. Competition among social movement organizations and tactical innovation shape such diffusion, which originates protest cycles. Tarrow's theory suggests that, in addition to the six foci of movement similarity mentioned earlier, two other aspects can be identified: a model of action, and the likely effects of action. On the one hand, one movement's mobilization may provide an example for other actors, groups, or movements. On the other hand, successful actions are more likely to be borrowed by movements abroad, for they increase the participants' motivations to engage in collective action.

In brief, the diffusion model maintains that similarities among social movements in different countries derive from the adoption of protest or certain protest features from abroad. Of course, preconditions for adoption are a communication channel and a flow of information between transmitters and adopters. The channels of communication can be either direct, indirect, or both.

THREE IN ONE: A GENERAL MODEL

In order to achieve a better understanding of cross-national movement similarities, I argue for the integration of all three concepts into a general model. The conceptual paths of the general model are presented in figure 2.1.

Globalization intensifies transnational linkages, with two relevant consequences for social movements. First, transnational structures such as the United Nations and the European Union form a common framework for movement activities in different countries. Although these structures are less frequent targets for social movements than nation-states, they play determining roles in such issues as the environment and international security, and are thus targeted by social movements with increasing frequency. Common international opportunities therefore open up and give rise to common social movement strategies. This implies common constraints for movements in different countries and, other things being equal, common reactions by movements to such constraints. Second, contingent events such as civil war, an accident at a nuclear plant, or a decision by a foreign government take on increasing local relevance. Events on the international, transnational, or supranational level are broadcast worldwide and, most important, people feel concerned about such events.

Globalization, conceived of as a large-scale process transforming society in the long run, has a third crucial consequence for social movements, this time an indirect one: a restructuring of the political conditions for protest. In other words, among the consequences of globalization is the creation of structural affinities in different countries. In particular, similar (though not identical) conflict structures, which correspond to existing social and cultural cleavages, are more likely to emerge in a globalizing world. As a consequence, popular protest should tend to address similar issues. For instance, labor movements have emerged in practically every contemporary Western society. Capitalist industrial relations created parallel left-right cleavages on which labor movements were based. More recently, peace, ecology, and related grievances gave rise to peace, ecology, and other new social movements in many Western countries.

Globalization also creates institutional structural affinities. Institutional resolutions of specific problems tend to resemble each other because the latter are increasingly global in scope. This produces what DiMaggio and Powell (1983) call institutional isomorphism. Similarly, institutional reactions to social movement mobilization

Figure 2.1. A General Model of Cross-national Social Movement Similarities

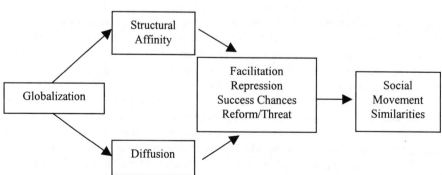

(including the mix of repression and facilitation by political authorities) should tend to resemble each other across countries, and movements adapt to their institutional environment in similar ways.

Structural affinity is a less abstract concept than globalization. Concrete aspects such as those listed under the notion of POS are more easily grasped. Furthermore, structural affinity is more subject to change, especially in the short run, than globalization. As a consequence, structural affinity has a more direct impact on social movements. However, as I will argue below, the translation of structural aspects of the political environment into concrete action becomes intelligible only if we resort to intervening microsociological factors. The same holds true for diffusion. The spread of certain protest features from one country or group of activists to the other may translate directly into resemblance among movements. Yet, the spread of information depends on a series of cultural, social, and political conditions.

Diffusion may, in turn, facilitate the creation of structural affinities. In particular, institutional parallels may result from the spread of certain practices from one country to another. For instance, a given country may adopt policing strategies by imitating those of other countries, especially if the strategies proved successful. However, the focus here is not upon the diffusion of properties that create structural affinities but rather upon the role of the latter on the likelihood of the former to generate social movement similarities.

Finally, there is the relationship between globalization and diffusion. In order to keep the model as simple as possible, I suggest viewing globalization as a macrostructural frame which creates the conditions for diffusion to take place, or at least for the intensification of diffusion processes (in addition to helping produce structural affinities). Nevertheless, globalization and diffusion should be considered as mutually related for at least two reasons. To begin with, globalization, defined as the increasing and deepening of transnational linkages, clearly sets the conditions for diffusion to occur and to intensify. At the same time, diffusion is a major factor in globalization. According to McGrew and Lewis (1992), for instance, technological innovation and its diffusion is one of four processes of globalization, the other three being great power competition, the internationalization of production and exchange, and modernization. In any event, it is difficult to disentangle these two concepts from one another, as they are part of the same process of increasing interconnectedness in the contemporary world. Nevertheless, an important link between globalization and diffusion is the role of transnational networks and diffusion in producing cross-national similarities among social movements. Certain movements, such as peace and ecology movements, have established transnational organizations and coalitions with branches in several countries which can act as channels for the spread of similar goals, tactics, and ideas. For example, organizations such as the Fellowship of Reconciliation, Pax Christi, Greenpeace, and the coalition European Nuclear Disarmament, which opposed the stationing of nuclear missiles in the early 1980s, have probably helped render peace and ecology movements more similar across countries.

To summarize, globalization is responsible for the resemblance of social movements across countries because it has helped to (1) create transnational opportunities, (2) form structural affinities in different countries, and (3) facilitate the diffusion processes. Thus, according to this model, globalization has an indirect impact on cross-national social movement similarities. Yet, while its effect on movements is mediated by structural affinity and diffusion, these are also abstract concepts that translate into action only insofar as they affect movement participants' motivations to act. Therefore, if we are to understand the processes through which globalization, structural affinity, and diffusion affect social movements, we need to turn to the microsociological mechanisms that link these three abstract concepts and movement action, thus leading to social movement similarities across countries. With no claim to be exhaustive, I will point out some of these mechanisms.

MICROMECHANISMS OF DIFFUSION

Globalization, structural affinity, and diffusion have an impact on social movements to the extent that they affect the perceptions and behavior of movement participants. Hence, we have to specify the mechanisms through which they can lead to movement similarities across countries. In other words, we need to look at the micromechanisms that translate macro-structures into social movement action. A way to do so is to introduce intermediate variables between the political *structure* and movement *action* that reflect the perception of external conditions by movement participants. In order to show how structural changes affect behavior, one should be able to build a motivational theory that specifies the links among variables in the model presented above. Here I will give only some indications for each of the three main paths in the model.

The motivational theory proposed by Koopmans (1995), drawing from Tilly (1978), identifies four mechanisms by which globalization leads to movement similarities through structural similarities. Kriesi et al. (1995) have applied the theory to NSMs in several West European countries. Koopmans identifies four concrete opportunities—motivational derivatives of POS—that interact with people's sentiments and emotions to shape movement mobilization: (1) *facilitation* refers to those actions by political authorities which lower the costs of collective action; (2) *repression* implies exactly the opposite; (3) the pair *reform/threat* refers to external responses to movement goals without any action by the movement, namely, reform if a change is favorable for the movement and threat if it is unfavorable; and (4) *success chances* refers to the likelihood that collective action will have positive results for the movement.

These four motivational factors mediate the link between structural affinity and movement similarities. While different countries in a globalizing world are more likely to present homologous structures, the impact of such structures on movement participants and activists is filtered through their perceptions and feelings. Existing POS—the political-institutional variant of structural affinity I focus upon here—affects social movements by offering them a specific set of concrete opportunities, that is, facilitation, repression, success chances, and reform/threat. Thus, one can explain variations in the levels of mobilization and the action repertoires: open systems generally provide opportunities for moderate action, while closed systems are more conducive to disruptive protest. Generalizing this argument, movements facing similar political opportunities will tend to have similar protest repertoires.

Microsociological dynamics can also help explain how globalization leads to social movement similarities through diffusion, the second path in our general model. If globalization makes cross-national diffusion easier to occur, it certainly helps explain why movements in different countries resemble each other. However, diffusion is not an automatic process. On the contrary, it occurs to the extent that movement participants establish links with their counterparts in other countries that allow them to borrow and imitate elements of protest.

I suggested earlier that organizational, political, and cultural contexts serve as intervening variables affecting the cross-national flow of information about protest events. More specifically, McAdam and Rucht (1993) focus on the cultural conditions that facilitate the spread of movement ideas. Inspired by Strang and Meyer (1993), they argue that transmitters and adopters must attribute some degree of similarity among themselves and/or their situations for diffusion to take place. This attribution of similarity creates cultural linkages among social movement participants in different countries and allows protest repertoires to spread even in the absence of direct relational ties. The attribution of similarity is made possible, or at least facilitated, by the cognitive process of "theorization." Strang and Meyer (1993) identify this as "the self-conscious development and specification of abstract categories and the formulation of patterned relationships such as chains of cause of effect." It facilitates diffusion by enabling potential adopters to define themselves as similar to transmitters, even without any direct contact.

Besides cultural conditions, however, political conditions help explain how globalization produces social movement similarities through diffusion. This brings us to the third path in our general model, the one from globalization to structural affinity and then to diffusion, ending in movement similarities. The presence of structural affinities may facilitate diffusion processes. A similar argument has been advanced by Strang and Meyer (1993) in their discussion of DiMaggio and Powell's (1983) concept of institutional isomorphism in relation to diffusion and, specifically, to culturally defined categories.

Political opportunities and their motivational derivatives can thus be seen as crucial conditions for diffusion. More generally, certain structural affinities may facilitate the diffusion of protest or of protest features, hence mediating the relationship between diffusion and social movement similarities. Even though potential adopters have established strong feelings of identity with transmitters—another kind of attribution of similarity—protest or protest elements may not spread to another country because of lack of political opportunities. For example, the adoption of civil disobedience is unlikely in a context where political authorities strongly repress illegal actions. Similarly, the use of the referendum by social movements is unlikely in countries where noninstitutional actors present important hurdles to its adoption.

In addition to favorable political opportunities in the adopters' environment, some aspects of POS in the transmitters' context may also affect diffusion. Most important is an action or a strategy's effectiveness. For example, the use of violence by social movements is more likely if it has been successful in another country. Similarly, a given movement slogan spreads to the extent that it has helped the movement to reach its goals. In both cases, political opportunities are a major factor in successful action by transmitters. Thus, diffusion also depends on opportunities in the transmitters' country or location. Of course, successful action is partially a matter of subjective appraisal, but judgment is usually made on objective criteria.

AN ILLUSTRATION: NEW SOCIAL MOVEMENTS
IN WESTERN EUROPE

In this section I illustrate the general model with a few examples drawn from NSMs in four West European countries: France, Germany, Switzerland, and the Netherlands. Given the exploratory character of this chapter, the goal is to show how the three factors described above—globalization, structural affinity, and diffusion—operated in these cases.

The first thing that catches our eye is the presence of several similar movements in all these countries. Women's, student, peace, ecology, and antinuclear movements, to mention only a few, are found throughout the Western world. However, levels of mobilization differ significantly in these countries. The figures for NSM mobilization in *unconventional actions* (demonstrations, protest marches, etc.) between 1975 and 1989 in four West European countries are as follows: 43,000 per million inhabitants in France, 168,000 in Germany, 143,000 in the Netherlands, and 101,000 in Switzerland (Kriesi et al. 1995). Such variation is related to the country-specific set of political opportunities faced by the movements. An obvious corollary is that movements confronted with similar sets of opportunities display comparable levels of mobilization. In our example, France clearly stands out from the others in that traditional cleavage structures predominate over new cleavages on which NSMs are based. The strong opposition between Socialist and Communist Parties left less space for NSM emergence.

The mobilization levels of French NSMs also stand if we consider all forms of collective action (meeting attendance, letter writing, pasting posters, etc). Drawing again from the study of Kriesi et al. (1995), NSMs have mobilized—all action forms considered—much less in France than in the other three countries: 405,000 per million inhabitants in Switzerland, 504,000 in the Netherlands, 351,000 in Germany, and only 96,000 in France.[2] Again, POS can be used to explain both variation (as the authors have done) and resemblance (as I do here). The combination of institutional structures (very closed in France and extremely open in Switzerland in the parliamentary, administrative, and electoral arenas) and prevailing strategies (exclusive in France and inclusive in Switzerland) presents two opposing sets of opportunities to movements and leads to different levels of mobilization. Conversely, similar structural settings for political mobilization in the Netherlands and Germany—that is, the presence of structural affinities—result in analogous opportunities and, consequently, less pronounced differences among social movements.

We also observe similarities in action repertoires. The action repertoires of NSMs strongly resemble each other across the four countries studied by Kriesi et al. (1995). In each country, demonstrative actions (street demonstrations, rallies, protest marches, sit-ins, and the like) are the forms of action NSMs (and movements *tout court*) most often adopt to address their demands to political authorities. For example, the authors found that of the total number of protest actions in Switzerland 58.3 percent were demonstrative actions, with 52.1 percent in the Netherlands, 61.8 percent in Germany, and 55.1 percent in France. These similarities can be attributed to structural affinity in a broader sense. In these societies, NSMs are similarly positioned in the power structure and have more or less the same degree of legitimacy. As a result, their action repertoires are similar and offer a limited range of actions to adopt.

Similarities in mobilization levels and in action repertoires are produced by structural affinities that are partly provoked by globalization processes. However, as I pointed out in the previous section, motivational factors intervene between structural affinity and social movement action. Drawing once again from the data assembled by Kriesi et al. (1995), we can see how movements that differ in focus and strategy behave in similar ways. The authors distinguish among instrumental, countercultural, and subcultural movements according to two criteria: the movement's general orientation (internal or external) and its logic of action (instrumental or identity-based). Their data show that instrumental movements display similarly high levels of mobilization, while countercultural movements mobilize much less, and subcultural movements even less. In addition, countercultural movements make wider use of confrontational actions than instrumental and, especially, subcultural movements. Thus, characteristics internal to the movements filter the impact of structural affinity on the resemblance among them.

The authors also show that parallels exist among movements that concern similar policy domains, although results here are somewhat less clear-cut. High-profile domains, such as national defense or energy, lead to lower levels of mobilization and more disruptive action repertoires than low-profile policy domains. This is because the former include more salient issues for political authorities—that is, issues concerning the core interests of the state. Movements addressing these issues threaten authorities. This makes authorities less receptive to movement demands and may even increase the likelihood of repression. In contrast, movements addressing low-profile policy domains are more likely to be accepted as legitimate and less likely to be repressed. In short, globalization contributes to structural affinity, thus leading to cross-national similarities among social movements in general. However, similar reactions of analogous movements to their environment and similar opportunities for analogous movements of a given policy domain can also account for significant parallels.

All these examples of social movement similarities refer to long-run characteristics. Nevertheless, short-run features of protest are perhaps more interesting to examine and to some extent easier to explain. Leaving aside simultaneous changes in POS as part of structural affinity, diffusion seems to play a central role in short-run similarities. For example, the use of sit-ins by various NSMs can be attributed to their spread in the United States from the civil rights movement to the student movement, then from the latter to its European counterpart, and finally from the European student movement to the NSMs. The fact that this tactic has often proven successful (at least in the eyes of movement participants, which is what counts in this respect) has certainly helped its diffusion across movements as well as across countries. Structural affinity (specifically, POS) is probably less constraining in this case, for specific protest forms or slogans adapt more easily to different contexts. In other words, they are modular (Tarrow 1994). On the other hand, certain forms of action, such as the referendum, are not always exportable because they are simply unavailable in certain countries.

Peace movement mobilization illustrates the connections of globalization, structural affinity, and diffusion to the timing of protest. Peace movements strongly mobilized in several European countries and in the United States at the beginning of the 1980s. While in the United States mobilization focused upon the nuclear weapons freeze proposal, which tried to force the U.S. government to adopt a disarmament resolution, European peace movements protested NATO's double-track decision to deploy middle-range missiles in European countries. Peace movement mobilization arose almost simultaneously in different Western European countries. Major demonstrations took place, for example, during the weekend of November 10-11, 1981, in Germany, on November 21 in the Netherlands, during the weekend of November 24-25 in Belgium, France, Great Britain, and Italy, and on December 30 in Switzerland. An even bigger international wave of peace movement protest occurred between September and December 1983, while protest in the United States peaked in December 1982 with a huge demonstration in New York. In Western Europe, NATO's decision to deploy the missiles sparked an international protest wave. In this case, the almost simultaneous mobilization of peace movements in various countries could be attributed to globalization. However, movement reactions were conditioned by national political opportunities, insofar as mobilization was particularly strong in those countries where NSMs found favorable opportunities to mobilize, such as Germany and the Netherlands. Protest arose even in Switzerland, although NATO did not concern it. In contrast, France (also not a full member of NATO) displayed lower levels of mobilization relative to its population. The French peace movement mobilized significantly only at the end of 1983, when disappointment in the Socialist government became stronger and NSMs reacted, though weakly, to government unresponsiveness. However, because of the time lag, it is very likely that, in addition to globalization, diffusion influenced the mobilization of the French movement.

Concerning the protest timing, political opportunities mediate the impact of diffusion on collective action. Far from provoking mobilization independently, I argue that diffusion takes place only where favorable political opportunities exist. To put it another way, where opportunities are unfavorable, diffusion has only a weak impact on mobilization. This perspective is, in my view, more appropriate than one that conceives of diffusion as almost automatically provoking or reinforcing mobilization. How can we otherwise explain why protest spreads rapidly to certain countries and not to other ones? Take the example of antinuclear movements in Western Europe. Antinuclear protest erupted in the first half of the 1970s when a nuclear plant in southern Germany was occupied. The German example was soon followed by Swiss antinuclear activists and a site occupation took place close to the German border. Besides site occupations, the movement displayed impressive levels of mobilization, giving rise to a wave of antinuclear protest in the border area of France, Germany, and Switzerland. What is interesting, though, is that protest did not spread as much to France because political opportunities for antinuclear opposition there were limited by the French government's strong commitment to nuclear energy. A similar process can be observed in the wave of squatter protests during the early 1980s. Protest started in Amsterdam and soon spread to Zurich and Berlin. However, given the unfavorable political opportunities for this type of protest in France after the Socialist Party seized power, mobilization remained very low there.

CONCLUSION

In this chapter, I reflected on the striking similarities that social movements often display across countries and suggested a general framework to deal with this issue. Without a sound theoretical framework, we can hardly explain why movements in different countries often resemble each other. The general model presented here is a tentative and preliminary contribution to our task of explaining similarity and resemblance in addition to difference and variation.

I have suggested that a model for the explanation of cross-national social movement similarities should take into account three basic concepts: (1) the globalization of modern societies and its consequences for collective action, (2) the presence of structural affinities in different countries, which are in part a result of globalization, and (3) diffusion processes which may provoke the spread of the protest or some of its features from one country to the other. Instead of viewing such factors as rival explanations, I have suggested that we view them as interacting factors within a general model. Furthermore, I have proposed that, in order to avoid meaningless generalizations, we distinguish among different characteristics of social movements. Here I have identified six aspects of social movements that might be similar across countries: (1) issues, themes, and goals; (2) levels of mobilization; (3) strategies, tactics, and forms of action; (4) organizational structures; (5) cultural frames, ideas, and discourses; and (6) the timing of protest.

Globalization has only an indirect impact on movement characteristics, for it forms a general structural and cultural frame with little direct relation to social movement action. Globalization, nevertheless, has two important consequences relevant to social movements: it helps produce structural affinities in different countries and it makes diffusion of movement repertoires and strategies easier. It is via these two consequences, which impinge more directly on movement participants, that globalization influences social movements. A more direct effect of globalization is transnational structures of power that may lead social movements in different countries to act in parallel ways, that is, to use similar strategies to seize the opportunities provided by these power structures. Whether it originates in globalization, diffusion, or independent country-specific developments, POS, as a specific kind of structural affinity, is crucial to understand not only variations in social movements across countries but also similarities.

In order to explain why and how social movements resemble each other across countries, we need to specify the mechanisms through which abstract concepts such as globalization, structural affinity, and diffusion influence movement participants. In other words, certain motivational factors link structural changes and people's actions. Among such factors, I have argued, those linked to political opportunities promise to shed light on this phenomenon. Thus, generalizing the POS argument, I have proposed political opportunities and their motivational derivatives as a major explanation of certain similarities in different countries, since they allow for or impede protest due to either globalization or diffusion. Unfortunately, I was at best able to illustrate my argument with the example of NSMs in four West European countries but not to operationalize the hypotheses I advanced on the basis of the proposed general model, let alone to test them systematically. These are two directions for future research.

NOTES

1. Some movements, most notably, the women's, peace, and ecology movements, were already present at the end of the nineteenth century. However, their basic characteristics and degree of politicization are largely a product of the protest wave of the sixties.

2. If we include official figures (in addition to newspaper data, from which these figures are drawn), the number of people mobilized in Switzerland rises to 872,000. All the figures reported here are the sum of participants in all actions. Because many people participated in several actions, there is no correspondence between the number of people mobilized and the total population in the country: 872,000 mobilized does not mean that nearly nine of every ten Swiss engaged in contentious politics.

REFERENCES

Archer, Dane, and Rosemary Gartner. 1976. "Violent Acts and Violent Times: A Comparative Approach to Postwar Homicide Rates." *American Sociological Review* 41: 937-962.

Bartolini, Stefano, and Peter Mair. 1980. *Identity, Competition, and Electoral Availability: The Stabilisation of European Electorates 1885 -1985.* Cambridge: Cambridge University Press.

Berelson, Bernard, Paul F. Lazarsfeld, and William McPhee. 1954. *Voting: A Study of Opinion Formation in a Presidential Campaign*. Chicago: University of Chicago Press.

Brand, Karl-Werner. 1985. "Vergleichendes Resümee." Pp. 306-334 in *Neue soziale Bewegungen in Westeuropa und den USA. Ein internationaler Vergleich*, Karl-Werner Brand, ed. Frankfurt: Campus.

Coleman, James S., Elihu Katz, and Herbert Menzel. 1966. *Medical Innovation: A Diffusion Study*. New York: Bobbs-Merrill.

DiMaggio, Paul J., and Walter W. Powell. 1983. "The Iron Cage Revisited: Institutional Isomorphism and Collective Rationality in Organizational Fields." *American Sociological Review* 48: 147-160.

Dodd, Stuart C. 1953. "Testing Message Diffusion in Controlled Experiments: Charting the Distance and Time Factors in the Interactance Hypothesis." *American Sociological Review* 18: 410-416.

——. 1955. "Diffusion Is Predictable: Testing Probability Models for Laws of Interaction." *American Sociological Review* 18: 410-416.

Fisher, Claude S. 1978. "Urban-to-Rural Diffusion of Opinions in Contemporary America." *American Journal of Sociology* 84: 151-159.

Gerlach, Luther P., and Virginia H. Hine. 1970. *People, Power, Change: Movements of Social Transformation*. Indianapolis: Bobbs-Merrill.

Giddens, Anthony. 1990. *The Consequences of Modernity*. Cambridge: Polity Press.

Gilpin, Robert. 1981. *War and Change in World Politics*. Cambridge: Cambridge University Press.

——. 1987. *The Political Economy of International Relations*. Princeton, N.J.: Princeton University Press.

Giugni, Marco. 1995. "The Cross-National Diffusion of Protest." Pp. 181-206 in *New Social Movements in Western Europe: A Comparative Analysis*, Hanspeter Kriesi, Ruud Koopmans, Jan Willem Duyvendak, and Marco Giugni, eds. Minneapolis: University of Minnesota Press.

Griliches, Zvi. 1957. "Hybrid Corn: An Exploration in the Economics of Technological Change." *Econometrics* 25: 501-522.

Hagerstrand, Torsten. 1967. *Innovation Diffusion as a Spatial Process*. Chicago: University of Chicago Press.

Katz, Elihu. 1968. "Diffusion (Interpersonal Influence)." Pp. 78-85 in *International Encyclopedia of the Social Sciences*, David L. Shils, ed. London: MacMillan and Free Press.

Katz, Elihu, and Paul F. Lazarsfeld. 1955. *Personal Influence: The Part Played by People in the Flow of Mass Communications*. New York: Free Press.

Kitschelt, Herbert. 1986. "Political Opportunity Structures and Political Protest: Anti-Nuclear Movements in Four Democracies." *British Journal of Political Science* 16: 57-85.

Koopmans, Ruud. 1993. "The Dynamics of Protest Waves: West Germany, 1965 to 1989." *American Sociological Review* 58: 637-658.

——. 1995. "The Dynamics of Protest Waves." Pp. 111-142 in *New Social Movements in Western Europe. A Comparative Analysis*, Hanspeter Kriesi, Ruud Koopmans, Jan Willem Duyvendak and Marco Giugni, eds. Minneapolis: University of Minnesota Press.

Kriesi, Hanspeter, Ruud Koopmans, Jan Willem Duyvendak, and Marco Giugni. 1995. *New Social Movements in Western Europe. A Comparative Analysis*. Minneapolis: University of Minnesota Press.

Lazarsfeld, Paul F., Bernard Berelson, and Hazel Gaudet. 1944. *The People's Choice: How the Voter Makes Up His Mind in a Presidential Campaign*. New York: Duell, Sloan, and Pearce.

Mahajan, Vijay, and Robert A. Peterson. 1985. *Models for Innovation Diffusion*. Beverly Hills, Calif.: Sage.

Marks, Gary, and Doug McAdam. 1996. "Social Movements and the Changing Structure of Political Opportunity in the European Union." *West European Politics* 19: 249-278

McAdam, Doug, and Dieter Rucht. 1993. "The Cross-National Diffusion of Movement Ideas." *The Annals of the American Academy of Political and Social Science* 528: 56-74.

McGrew, Anthony G., and Paul G. Lewis, eds. 1992. *Global Politics: Globalization and the Nation-State*. Cambridge: Polity Press.

Michaelson, Alaina G. 1993. "The Development of a Scientific Specialty as Diffusion through Social Relations: The Case of Role Analysis." *Social Networks* 15: 217-236.

Modelski, George. 1972. *Principles of World Politics*. New York: Free Press.

Pitcher, Brian L., Robert L. Hamblin, and Jerry L. L. Miller. 1978. "The Diffusion of Collective Violence." *American Sociological Review* 43: 23-35.

Piven, Frances Fox, and Richard A. Cloward. 1977. *Poor People's Movements: Why They Succeed, How They Fail*. New York: Vintage Books.

Robertson, Roland. 1992. *Globalization: Social Theory and Global Culture*. London: Sage.

Rogers, Everett M. 1983. *Diffusion of Innovations*. New York: Free Press of Glencoe.

Rosenau, James N. 1980. *The Study of Global Interdependence*. London: Frances Pinter.

——. 1989. *Interdependence and Conflict in World Politics*. Lexington, Mass.: D.C. Heath.

——. 1990. *Turbulence in World Politics*. Brighton: Harvester Wheatsheaf.

Sklair, Leslie. 1991. *Sociology of the Global System*. Brighton: Harvester Wheatsheaf.

Spilerman, Seymour. 1976. "Structural Characteristics and Severity of Racial Disorders." *American Sociological Review* 41: 771-792.

Strang, David, and John W. Meyer. 1993. "Institutional Conditions for Diffusion." *Theory and Society* 22: 487-511.

Tarrow, Sidney. 1989. *Struggle, Politics, and Reform: Collective Action, Social Movements, and Cycles of Protest*. Western Societies Program Occasional Paper Nr. 21, Ithaca, N.Y.: Cornell University.

——. 1989. *Democracy and Disorder. Protest and Politics in Italy 1965-1975*. Oxford: Clarendon Press.

——. 1994. *Power in Movement: Social Movements, Collective Action and Mass Politics*. New York: Cambridge University Press.

Tilly, Charles. 1984. "Social Movements and National Politics." Pp. 297-317 in *Statemaking and Social Movements. Essays in History and Theory*, Charles Bright and Susan Harding, ed.s. Ann Arbor: University of Michigan Press.

——. 1986. *The Contentious French: Four Centuries of Popular Struggle*. Cambridge, Mass.: Harvard University Press.

——. 1995. *Popular Contention in Great Britain, 1758-1834*. Cambridge, Mass.: Harvard University Press.

Tilly, Charles, Louise Tilly, and Richard Tilly. 1975. *The Rebellious Century, 1830-1930*. Cambridge, Mass.: Harvard University Press.

Wallerstein, Immanuel. 1974. *The Modern World-System*. New York: Academic Press.

——. 1983. *Historical Capitalism*. London: Verso.

Walton, J., and D. Seddon. 1994. *Free Markets and Food Riots*. Cambridge, Mass.: Blackwell.

Chapter 3

TRANSNATIONAL STRUCTURES AND PROTEST: LINKING THEORIES AND ASSESSING EVIDENCE

Gregory M. Maney

How do relations across national borders affect the likelihood of protest? The proliferation of international nongovernmental organizations in the 1980s and 1990s has stimulated research on transnational dimensions of social movements. Recent studies focus upon coalitions involving INGOs and the institutional opportunities at the international level (e.g., Smith 1995; Smith, Chatfield, and Pagnucco 1997; Keck and Sikkink 1998; Tarrow 2001). By providing a wide array of resources and by pressuring targeted states, transnational social movements or transnational issue networks facilitate national-level protest.

While highlighting the relevance of external actors, this body of research has generally neglected how broader patterns of economic and political relations across national borders have shaped structures of political opportunity. Perhaps because North American and Western European nongovernmental organizations play disproportionate roles in transnational mobilization, the effects upon protest of massive foreign debts in "developing" countries, increasing capital mobility, and post-Cold War shifts in alliances among states have scarcely received attention. Yet studies of development and international relations point toward these factors as key determinants of protest and rebellion (Jenkins and Schock 1992).

Can social movements research draw upon other academic fields to illuminate how transnational processes affect collective action prospects? By linking concepts from the fields of development and international relations with political process theory, I develop several propositions and evaluate them in light of case studies and cross-national statistical research. Evidence suggests that cyclical phases in the capitalist world economy, economic and political forms of dependency, and competition and conflict among states alter important dimensions of political opportunity. I focus on several forms of political opportunity identified by Tarrow (1994): (1) increasing institutional access, (2) unstable political alignments, (3) divisions among elites, (4) the emergence of support groups and influential allies, (5) diminishing repression by an authoritarian state. Although Tarrow considers repression to be a static dimension (1994: 89-96), I will treat it as variable over the long term.

Figure 3.1 illustrates how I generate propositions about these five dimensions of political opportunity from different theories of transnational economics and politics. First, I draw on world-system theory to formulate propositions about how position in the world system and cycles of the capitalist world economy affect political opportunities. Second, based on dependency theory, I suggest propositions about the effect of different forms of dependency on the constellation of political opportunities facing potential challengers. Third, I use concepts from theories of international relations to explain how competition and conflict among states shape the costs and benefits of protest. The resulting propositions are presented and enumerated in the text and summarized in table 3.1 at the end.[1]

1. INCREASING INSTITUTIONAL ACCESS

Different levels of access to political institutions alter the likelihood of protest (Kitschelt 1986). Through elections and forums for input on public policy, democratic systems reduce the need for extra-institutional action. Conversely, authoritarian regimes raise the costs of visible, large-scale mobilization. Movements challenging these regimes tend to be covert and to advocate revolutionary goals. Authoritarian-corporatist states provide official channels for pursuing grievances, but representatives are often handpicked by the state, removed from their constituencies, and susceptible to

Figure 3.1. Theories of Transnational Structures and Types of Political Opportunity

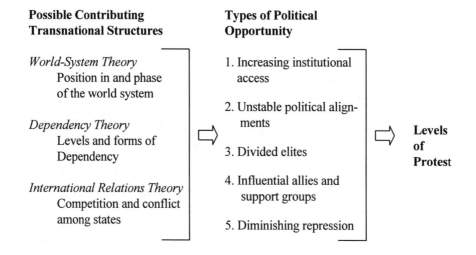

co-optation. This mixture of openness and closure makes corporatist regimes particularly vulnerable to extra-institutional challenges (Eisinger 1973).

Proposition 1.1. A country's position in the capitalist world-economy is positively related to wider access to its political institutions. The highest levels of institutional access are in core states while the lowest levels are in the periphery. Because of wealth transfers from the periphery and semiperiphery to the core, core states have considerable revenues and strong administrative capacities (Wallerstein 1979a). They use these to provide high levels of social assistance that reduce class conflict. They maintain order by giving domestic workers a greater stake in the existing system, and enhance their legitimacy through representative political institutions and relatively inclusive political processes (Chase-Dunn and Rubinson 1977; Wallerstein 1984). With higher levels of institutional access, protest is relatively infrequent and generally less disruptive.

In the periphery, international trade and core state interventions drain wealth away, which reduces administrative capacities for maintaining political and economic stability (Wallerstein 1974; Rubinson 1977; Delacroix and Ragin 1981; Grimes 2000). Combined with the coercive nature of production, peripheral states rely upon political exclusion and repression to secure accumulation. With closed polities, opportunities for mass protest, therefore, will be fewer. Regarding the semiperiphery, Jenkins and Schock (1992: 178) suggest that "these states also temper their exclusionary policies by promoting corporatist unions, neighborhood associations, and political clubs, thereby placing them in the middle range of institutional opportunities." With a mixture of openness and closure, semiperipheral states should experience higher levels of protest than states in the core or the periphery. It follows that downward mobility from the core as well as upward mobility from the periphery increase the likelihood of protest.

Assessing Evidence. In a comparative study, Rueschemeyer, Stephens, and Stephens's (1992) note a correlation between long-standing democracies and a core status. Maniruzzaman (1987) reports that on average Third World states have had military rule for most of the years between 1946 and 1984. In turn, Tilly (1990) finds that voting restrictions are more likely in military-dominated states. A regression analysis by Bollen (1983) shows peripheral and semiperipheral countries being less democratic than core countries. Consistent with the proposition, the negative effects were strongest in the periphery.

Overall, however, the available evidence fails to provide a convincing link between position in the world system and levels of institutional access. In contrast to Bollen (1983), Boswell and Dixon (1990) find no relationship between core or semiperipheral status and levels of political exclusion. Moreover, if a significant relationship existed, recent developments have undermined it. Over the last two decades, the political systems of several countries in the periphery, particularly in Latin America, have become more open and inclusive (Lipset 1994). Complicating matters further, just as states belonging to the same economic region vary in terms of their capacities, they also have very different levels of institutional access. One party, authoritarian states such as South Korea (until recently) as well as pluralistic states such as Hong Kong have managed to achieve high levels of industrialization (Koo 1987; So 1986).

While world-system theory suggests that weak state capacities are related to a country's position in the capitalist world economy, both Skocpol (1979) and Tilly (1990) provide historical examples of weak states in the core and strong states in the periphery (e.g., the weakness of the seventeenth-century Dutch state despite its strong mercantile economy). Tilly (1990) argues that both military aid and revenues from international commodity exports have enabled military-dominated states in the periphery to remain autonomous from major domestic social classes. The considerable repressive capacities of many peripheral states rather than the absence of resources and underdeveloped administrative capacities, therefore, explain any relationship between world-system position and political exclusion.[2]

Proposition 1.2. Increasing economic dependency promotes political exclusion. While world-system research emphasizes the systemic interrelationship between economic regions, dependency studies focus upon the specific transnational relations of national-level actors. Historical structuralist-oriented dependency theorists see institutional opportunities as the product of a given moment of development. In the initial stages of industrialization, the need to attract foreign direct investment (FDI) contributes to the rise of bureaucratic authoritarian states (Cardoso 1972; O'Donnell 1978; Evans 1979). Since demands for state policies to ensure better pay, limited work hours, and safe working conditions jeopardize the desirability of a country as a location for investment, labor is excluded from the polity. In some countries, opposition by local entrepreneurs to competition from multinational corporations similarly leads to their exclusion. For instance, efforts to attract FDI in countries in the Southern Cone of Latin America during the 1960s were accompanied not only by strike bans and exclusive recognition of state-run unions but also an end to elections, the disbanding of political parties, and censorship (O'Donnell 1978). Once significant FDI penetration has taken place, however, some of these regimes gradually reopen the polity. If increased dependence upon FDI promotes exclusion, then it follows that significant reductions in FDI can lead to greater institutional access as states reach out to local capital or labor to forge and implement national development policies.

Assessing Evidence. Most cross-national studies with broad samples report a positive relationship between foreign capital penetration and political exclusion (Chirot 1977; Duvall, Jackson, Russett, Snidal, and Sylvan 1981; Bollen 1983; Timberlake and Williams 1984). A more recent analysis by Boswell and Dixon (1990), however, fails to reach the same conclusion after controlling for income inequality.

Proposition. 1.3. Political dependency also contributes to institutional closure. High levels of military assistance enable authoritarian regimes to remain autonomous from major social groups (Evans 1979; Tilly 1990). Reductions in external assistance, however, encourage states to liberalize relations with civil society.

Assessing Evidence. Case studies indicate that high levels of military aid from the U.S. government contributed to the emergence of bureaucratic authoritarian states in Brazil, South Korea, and Taiwan (Evans 1979; Deyo 1989; Gold 1986).[3] Conversely, a reduction in U.S. government aid made the KMT regime in Taiwan and the military regime in Brazil more vulnerable to the demands of pro-democracy movements (So 1990; Tilly 1990). A regression analysis by Boswell and Dixon (1990) links high levels of dependence upon a single Western arms exporter with political exclusion and the denial of civil rights.

Proposition 1.4. Rise to hegemonic status in the world system creates institutional openings in less powerful states. A decline in interstate competition creates space for the relaxing of political controls and even democratic reforms in countries which once competed for influence. Because of its superior productivity, the hegemon eliminates colonial and neocolonial barriers to accessing peripheral economies (Wallerstein 1979a). Its sizable military capacities dissuade interventions by other core states (Kowalewski 1991). As a result, the hegemon can rely primarily upon its economic power and cultural influence to protect its interests abroad. During such historical moments, hegemons cultivate not only global liberalism but also global democratization (Thompson 2000).

Assessing Evidence. The preponderance of evidence supports the proposition. Historically, colonial powers have closed colonial polities to better assert and protect their interests over subjugated populations. An absence of colonization is likely to be associated with lower overall levels of political exclusion in less powerful states. Three analyses of time series data spanning centuries find that periods characterized by a "unicentric core" have lower rates of colonization (Bergesen and Schoenberg 1980; McGowan 1985; Boswell 1989).[4] Comparative historical studies of core power rivalry in the nineteenth century reach similar conclusions (Doyle 1985; McMichael 1985). Using the *New York Times* and *Times* indexes to collect event data for revolutions in thirty-four peripheral countries between 1821 and 1985, Kowalewski (1991) reports a negative relationship between hegemonic phases of world leadership (i.e., a unicentric core) and core-state interventions against revolutions in the periphery. Conversely, Tilly (1990) finds some support for the thesis that intensified geopolitical competition among powerful states has promoted the rise of military regimes in Third World countries. Nonetheless, some historical studies contradict the proposition. Both Goldfrank (1979) and Skocpol (1979) conclude that interstate competition, rather than its absence, diminishes core-state intervention in the affairs of less powerful states.

If the relaxation of external political controls increases institutional access, then higher levels of protest should occur in less powerful countries during hegemonic periods. Using data on international labor unrest from 1870 through 1990, Silver (1995) finds that annual average protest levels in the semiperiphery and periphery increased during U.S. hegemony (1951-1990) compared to the prior forty years of intense interstate rivalry.[5]

2. UNSTABLE POLITICAL ALIGNMENTS

Regardless of whether a polity is open or closed, it features a constellation of alliances and conflicts among its members. Shifting political alignments provide opportunities for the emergence of social movements demanding either inclusion in the polity or changes in the distribution of social rewards (Tilly 1978; McAdam 1982; Tarrow 1994). Jenkins (1983: 547) writes: "If the polity is closely divided, members have lost their normal coalition partners, or members find themselves in jeopardy for want of resources, the normally risky strategy of supporting the entry of a movement is more likely to be adopted."

Together, dependency and world-system concepts offer insights into transnational structural sources of political instability in "developing" countries. Beginning with Cardoso (1972), historical-structuralist dependency theorists have emphasized interactions between internal and external actors to explain industrialization in dependent countries. When class- and state-based actors share mutual interests they form alliances with one another (Cardoso and Faletto 1979), and maintain them as long as the benefits outweigh the costs. For instance, a "triple alliance" between multinational corporations, the military regime, and national privately owned businesses emerged in Brazil in the late 1960s (Evans 1979).

Proposition 2.1. Major swings in levels of transnational economic activity encourage shifts in these alliances. World-system theorists suggest that the capitalist world economy has cyclical rhythms of expansion and contraction (Wallerstein 1979b). I propose that economic expansion and contraction contribute to shifting alliances, and that protest in noncore countries should increase during transitions between phases of the world system.

Regarding expansion, dependent states seeking to industrialize can use their growing markets and/or their cheap labor to attract multinational corporations and even to negotiate more favorable terms of trade and investment (Wallerstein 1979a). Joint ventures with local companies facilitate new triple alliances. Brazil and Taiwan pursued this strategy during the 1950s and 1960s (Cardoso 1973; Evans 1983; Amsden 1985). The Manley regime in Jamaica adopted a similar program for the bauxite industry during the early 1970s (Stephens and Stephens 1985). Japan pursued a different response to world-system expansion by avoiding joint ventures and encouraging technology-licensing agreements. Japan limited access to internal markets and aggressively promoted exports by nationally owned firms (Hart 1992), thus strengthening ties between the state and local industrialists.

Regarding contraction, dependent states can respond in several ways—each again involving shifts in alliances. First, they can take advantage of weakening multinational and national corporations to forge alliances with the popular classes, as the Mexican government did during the Great Depression (Hamilton 1984). This allows states to use their greater relative power during a time of global economic crisis to strengthen their position vis-à-vis capital. Second, states can reach out to both agrarian and industrial elites and promote the national economy through protectionist policies. Several European states pursued this strategy during the global depression of the 1870s (McMichael 1985). In cases where agrarian elites have been weak or nonexistent, states have promoted national industrialization either through state-owned enterprises or through cultivating a local entrepreneurial class (Trimberger 1978; Wallerstein 1979a). Third, states can make concessions to foreign investors to avoid divestment as the Brazilian government did during the late 1970s (Evans 1983). Also states can drive down wages, slash social services, and privatize state enterprises to maintain profits and protect their revenue base as numerous states have done over the last two decades: Argentina, Bolivia, Brazil, Haiti, Jamaica, and Mexico (Walton 1989). Each of these responses to global recession generates opposition and destabilizes previous political alliances.

Assessing Evidence. Contractions and expansions in the world economy contribute to shifting alliances in dependent states, but the shapes of the alliances differ. This suggests the need to consider domestic factors as well as transnational factors. An autonomous, minimally dependent state with a commitment to economic equality can forge a popular alliance, as the Mexican case illustrates. Strategies catering to foreign actors, however, are more likely when states are heavily indebted to international lenders and rely heavily upon export earnings for hard foreign currency; when high degrees of foreign corporate penetration already exist; and when local industrial bases remain weak. This suggests it is fruitful to consider both economic and political structures on both the transnational and national levels (Evans, Reuschemeyer, and Stephens 1985). By altering the relative costs and benefits of different policies, these relations facilitate (but do not guarantee) the formation of some alliances while discouraging others. Time-series data on global market conditions and shifting political alliances would assist in further assessing this proposition.

Proposition 2.2. Direct interventions by powerful states in the affairs of less powerful states can destabilize domestic political alignments. Externally backed revolutions, coups, and campaigns to eliminate opposed political forces can dramatically change the political landscape. Foreign assistance has taken a variety of forms including troops, weaponry, military training, intelligence, money, office equipment, printing presses, vehicles, organizers, and election campaign strategists (Sims 1991; Broder 1997). In addition, the provisioning of resources by foreign states can give rise to competition among coalition partners while unifying opponents of the recipients. The political uncertainty these activities create provides opportunities for challengers to exert influence through protest.

Assessing Evidence. Since World War II, interventions by the U.S. government have contributed to regime changes in a number of countries, including Brazil, British Guyana, Chile, Costa Rica, Greece, Guatemala, Iran, Jamaica, and Nicaragua (Pierce 1991; Sims 1991; Mars 1995). Sometimes (Guatemala in particular), these changes have triggered extended periods of rebellion and political violence. Coups facilitated by covert operations increase the likelihood of rebellion, but they may decrease nonviolent, reform-oriented protest by making the state more exclusive and repressive. Through sabotaging infrastructure, encouraging dislocations in production, aiding in the arrests and murders of political opponents, bribery, and misinformation, U.S. covert operations have destabilized political systems (for recent disclosures on CIA activities, see Krauss 1999; Kornbluh 2000). Tilly (1990) suggests a curvilinear relationship between external intervention and political instability, with intermediate levels of intervention creating more instability than either the absence of intervention or military occupation.

Proposition 2.3. Shifting state alliance and conflict structures facilitate protest by stimulating domestic political realignments. Regimes faced with international isolation cultivate mass support for nationalist policies (Mars 1995). Détente, however, ends these mass nationalist mobilization and renews state coalitions with domestic and foreign elites.

Assessing Evidence. A handful of case studies support the proposition. Kraus (1979) found that efforts by the U.S. government to isolate Communist China encouraged the regime's links with peasantry and urban workers. Once the West moved toward détente, however, the Chinese state reestablished ties with formerly disenfranchised elites (So 1990). Mars (1995) reached similar conclusions about socialist regimes in Grenada and Guyana during the early 1980s. Arrighi, Hopkins, and Wallerstein (1989: 66), however, maintain that regimes born of national liberation movements demand peaceful domestic industrial relations in the name of "class struggle in the interstate system." Thus, grass-roots protest may be the cost rather than the benefit of popular alliances with the state.

3. DIVIDED ELITES AND INFLUENTIAL ALLIES

Like shifts in political alignments, heightened conflicts during times of crisis make dissenting elites more willing to support challenger movements (Piven and Cloward 1977). Elites bring legitimacy, leadership skills, and financial resources to movements. While their participation can moderate institutional transformation, it often facilitates mass mobilization (Eckstein 1989). Even if support is withheld, elite disunity translates into less coordination and fewer resources for a movement's opposition.

Proposition 3.1. By heightening social and ideological cleavages, the capitalist world economy contributes to splits among national elites and to the emergence of influential allies for social movements. Theorists suggest two ways that the modern world system divides elites. First, since World War I, the process of surplus accumulation both within and across national boundaries has given rise to socialist and national liberation movements in peripheral and semiperipheral countries while also fostering social democratic movements in many core countries (Wallerstein 1988). These movements have united around the goals of social equality and upward mobility in the world system. Once political power is gained, however, the incompatibility of these two objectives within the context of the capitalist world economy creates splits among antisystemic national elites. Growth-oriented policies, therefore, have led elites favoring internal redistribution to support challenges from below.

Second, resistance to global inequalities manifests itself not only in production-based struggles but also in ethnonationalist, women's, and student movements (Arrighi, Hopkins, and Wallerstein 1989: 35). To the extent that these "anti-systemic movements" cut across social cleavages and tap into the identities and experiences of segments of the polity, they hold the potential to create influential allies for insurgents: "Under the cover of cultural similarities, one can often weld strange alliances. Those strange alliances can take a very activist form and force the political centers to take account of them" (Wallerstein 1974: 354).

Assessing Evidence. Few researchers have systematically examined the assertion that social movements are manifestations of resistance to the modern world system. At first pass, the explanations offered for the claimed relationship appear overly general and reductionist. First, since tensions over pursuing economic growth versus social equality are endemic to the capitalist world economy as a whole, they cannot explain contrasting levels of protest either within or across the core, semiperiphery, and periphery. Second, the assertion that "status-group" movements are really class-based struggles denies race, ethnicity, and gender equal ontological standing. Just as relations of production and trade shape social relations, other relations can have equal if not greater effects on economic processes. Final judgment, however, must be suspended pending further research.

Proposition 3.2. Increasing levels of economic dependency in countries with significant national industrial bases also contribute to splits among national elites Some dependency theorists have argued that elites in dependent economies benefit from a close association with multinational corporations (Frank 1969). National elites profit from investments in foreign firms as well as patronage received in exchange for ensuring lucrative conditions of operation. The power of the multinationals in dependent economies precludes any significant local capital formation. Other dependency theorists, however, believe that a degree of industrialization can take place under conditions of dependency (Cardoso 1973; Cardoso and Falletto 1979; Evans 1979; Bradshaw 1985). Moreover, in newly industrialized countries a significant percentage of manufacturing is often locally owned and operated. In such instances, FDI creates rifts between the comprador and national fractions of the bourgeoisie. Some domestic businesses supply multinational corporations. Others, however, are forced out of business by multinationals with more advanced technologies, global sourcing, distribution, and marketing networks, superior economies of scale, and greater financial reserves (Evans 1983). As a result, disgruntled local entrepreneurs have played key roles in movements such as the democracy movement in Brazil (Alves 1989).

Austerity programs also encourage elite divisions. Within the state, some officials express concerns that IMF-mandated measures erode national sovereignty, reduce state capacities, and create instability. Austerity policies hurt the middle class by reducing spending on basic social services, slashing public employment, and devaluing the currency (triggering stagflation and a lower standard of living). Local industrialists also resent structural adjustment-mandated restrictions on the importation of intermediate capital inputs and cuts in state loans and credit; particularly when these measures are accompanied by duty-free imports in export-processing zones and lavish subsidies to attract export-oriented multinationals. As a result, anti-austerity movements frequently receive substantial support from certain segments of domestic elites.

Assessing Evidence. In a comparative historical study of rebellion in the periphery, Walton (1984) found that large inflows of FDI generated disputes among national elites. Austerity plans resulting from high levels of international debt have also provoked considerable middle-class dissent, leading to the establishment of cross-class anti-austerity alliances (Walton 1989; Walton and Ragin 1990; Walton and Seddon 1994).

Proposition 3.3. Relations between patron and client states can divide elites in client states. Increases in military aid encourage an autonomous, exclusive military that arouses the ire of civilian state agencies and local capitalists (Evans 1979; Boswell and Dixon 1990). Rapid cuts in military aid and foreign wars can also create divisions as states seek larger revenues from local elites to maintain their repressive capacities. In return for their largess, elites demand greater control over policy making. Also, counter-insurgency strategies developed by foreign state agencies can create rifts within client states. Starting with the Alliance for Progress, the U.S. government has promoted agrarian reform in the periphery to reduce support for revolutionary movements among the peasantry. Such programs have sometimes provoked strong opposition from elites negatively affected by the proposed land reform.

Assessing Evidence. The effects of military aid upon elite relations have yet to receive detailed attention beyond the handful of studies cited above. With regard to the effects of counter-insurgency strategies developed by foreign state agencies, Eckstein (1989: 40, n9) notes that: "The reformist junta in El Salvador (1979-82) . . . was divided on the issue of agrarian reform. The different military factions mobilized civilians, some in favor, others in opposition to land redistribution." In a study of the Philippines, Angeles (1999) finds that U.S.-inspired land reform policies provoked strong opposition from landed elites. However, Bredo (1986) suggests that in countries such as Japan, Taiwan, and Korea, land reform has served as an effective counter-insurgency tool.

Proposition 3.4. During periods of heightened interstate competition, powerful states frequently intervene in other states' internal affairs, either as allies or opponents of insurgents. States competing for geopolitical influence sponsor movements in rival states as well as in states that are clients of their rivals (Chase-Dunn 1978; Small and Singer 1982; Duner 1983; Kowalewski 1991). As the benefits of action (and costs of inaction) grow with increased competition, the salience of the international norm of nonintervention in other states' affairs diminishes. Violations of the norm by rival states then justify further intervention.

Assessing Evidence. Rival colonial and/or stronger neighboring states have supported revolutionary movements in the Caribbean (Small and Singer 1982). During the Cold War, the Soviet Union and Cuba supplied arms and money to socialist regimes and to insurgents in U.S. client states (Tilly 1990; Silver 1995; Black 1999). In turn, the U.S. government provided arms, money, and intelligence to these states in an effort to defeat these movements while also sponsoring armed insurgency against opposed regimes such as in Afghanistan, Cuba, Indonesia, Nicaragua, and Poland (Sims 1991; Broder 1997; Bardach and Rohter 1998; Conboy and Morrison 1999). Kowalewski (1991) finds that core states are especially likely to intervene to put down revolutions when a hegemon is in decline. Other studies, however, suggest that core states refrain from overt forms of intervention for fear of antagonizing a powerful rival (Schwarz 1970; van Wingen and Tillema 1980).

Because cross-national studies have either focused exclusively upon rebellion or have lumped together violent and non-violent forms of contention, the impact of external intervention upon protest is uncertain. At least one study suggests a positive relationship. Mars (1995: 444) estimates that during the 1980s, 39 percent of all nonviolent protests and 71 percent of all violent confrontations in Caribbean countries were "foreign related or instigated."[6]

4. DIMINISHING REPRESSION

A decline in the capacity or propensity of highly repressive states to engage in incarcerating, torturing, and murdering its political opponents increases the likelihood of protest by reducing its cost (McAdam, McCarthy, and Zald 1996).

Proposition 4.1. A higher position in the world-system hierarchy is negatively related to levels of repression. Despite core states having greater repressive capacities, most world-system theorists expect higher levels of repression in the periphery. Wider class inequalities contribute to more severe repression. If states characterized by medium levels of repression are more likely to experience protest, then protest will be highest in the semiperiphery. In the words of Boswell and Chase-Dunn (2000: 292): "While class conflict is omnipresent, open struggles proliferate in the semiperiphery, managed compromise is a hallmark of the core, and repressive class domination plagues the periphery." Thus upward mobility of a country from the periphery to the semiperiphery as well as downward mobility from the core to the semiperiphery increases the likelihood of protest.

Assessing Evidence. Surprisingly little evidence exists to evaluate the proposition. Tilly (1990:199-200) finds that while colonial powers drained their colonies of capital, they left behind highly developed repressive forces. As a result, postcolonial states have, on average, followed "coercion-intensive paths to statehood." Examining seventy-four countries of the core, semiperiphery, and periphery between 1938 and 1983, Arrighi and Drangel (1986: 60) conclude that the semiperiphery included "most of the major epicenters of political turmoil." This is consistent with the expectation that semiperipheral states engage in medium levels of repression and therefore, on average, experience the highest levels of protest.

Proposition 4.2. A contraction in the capitalist world economy contributes to an immediate increase in repression in export-dependent peripheral states, but in the long run can contribute to a decline in their repressive capacities. During a global recession, states with export-oriented economies experience a decline in revenues from international trade. With lower demand in and access to wealthy markets, export-dependent peripheral economies lower labor costs in an effort to maintain trade revenues and retain foreign direct investment (Moaddel 1994). Since these economies lack access to technologies that enhance labor productivity, per unit labor costs are primarily reduced through cutting wages, layoffs, and intensifying work. Protests resisting these changes are met with forceful state responses to minimize disruption to production. Over time, however, if revenues are already limited and drops in exports and export prices are severe, a budget crisis may force the state to reduce the size of its security forces (Moaddel 1994). Such cuts are especially likely if peripheral states receive low or reduced levels of military aid from core states. As a dependent state's ability to suppress dissent diminishes, protest increases.

Assessing Evidence. Moaddel (1994) found a positive relationship between fluctuations in the export earnings between 1975 and 1980 (a period of global recession) and "regime repressiveness" (measured by political exclusion, civil rights denial, government sanctions, and political deaths). On the other hand, Kowalewski (1991) detects a positive relationship between the expansionary A-phase of the world economy and intervention by core states to put down revolutionary movements in the periphery. Cyclical rhythms of the world economy, therefore, may have contrasting effects upon domestic and externally instigated repression in the periphery.

Proposition 4.3. Economic dependency increases state repression. Efforts by dependent states to attract and retain foreign direct investment not only result in the exclusion of national business elites and organized labor from the polity (see prop. 1.2) but also in the active suppression of protests challenging political exclusion and economic deprivation. Given the importance of political and economic stability to the dependent state's development strategy, increased resources are devoted to expanding its repressive capacities (Cardoso 1973). Foreign financial dependency further encourages repression. To continue receiving international loans, aid, and investment, debtor states must implement IMF-mandated structural adjustment measures. To ensure a steady stream of hard foreign currency to pay off debts, states must stimulate FDI in the export sector. This "stimulation" often entails union-busting and wage suppression. The absence of a mass domestic market means the state loses little in the way of economic growth or revenues by suppressing wages through repression (Boswell and Dixon 1990).

Assessing Evidence. Some, but not all, of the studies to date indicate that states with high levels of economic dependency tend to be more repressive. While Duvall et al. (1981) report that foreign capital penetration increases state repression, Timberlake and Williams (1984) fail to find a significant relationship between the two. Jackson, Russett, Snidal, and Sylvan (1978) conclude that dependent states actively involved in transforming their economies are especially likely to engage in high levels of coercion. Both Landsberg (1979) and Deyo (1989) find that multinational corporations most frequently subcontract with firms located in countries with states aggressively attacking organized labor such as South Korea, Taiwan, and Singapore. By enabling the suppression of labor costs, repression serves as both cause and effect of a country's linkages with multinational corporations. Moaddel (1994), however, failed to find a significant relationship between "peripheralization" (measured by dependence upon foreign investment and trade) and "regime repressiveness."

Proposition 4.4. Concentrated and high levels of military dependence leave dependent states vulnerable to reductions in their repressive capacities. When a state depends upon one or a few external sources for its weaponry, military training, and personnel, the elimination of these sources weakens its security forces. Sharp drops in military aid can result from fiscal crises, shifts in geopolitical strategy, or an increased emphasis on human rights by donor states. For example, the withdrawal of Soviet troops from Eastern Europe weakened the repressive capacities of these regimes, signaling the opportunity for more open forms of dissent (Tarrow 1994).

Assessing Evidence. Case studies by Rosen (1974) and Kerbo (1978) provide evidence that large cuts in military aid negatively affected the repressive capacities of client states. In Guatemala, however, massacres of villagers by national security forces actually escalated immediately after the U.S. government cut off military aid to the regime in the late 1970s (Ropp and Sikkink 1999). If the relationship holds, therefore, it may be a lagged one, where military capacities diminish after long periods of time.

Proposition 4.5. Interstate wars initially strengthen the repressive capacities of all participants, but they eventually weaken the coercive capabilities of unsuccessful contestants. As states bolster their arsenals in preparation for war, their ability to forcefully suppress domestic dissent increases (Haimson and Tilly 1989). Whether a state continues to augment its repressive capacities depends upon the course of the war. Long, intense conflicts drain weaponry and personnel, particularly those facing defeat (Tilly 1978), and forces normally engaged in domestic law enforcement are reassigned to the war effort. After demobilization, a state may have less weaponry and security personnel available than before the war, decreasing costs for challengers and increasing the likelihood of protest and rebellion.

Assessing Evidence. Evidence supports initial increases of repressive capacities and their decrease over the course of international war. Historically, the U.S. government has stepped up its repression of political dissidents during wartime (Linfield 1990). In a comparative study of revolutions in France, China, and Russia, Skocpol (1979) finds that all three states had diminished repressive capacities due to prolonged and unsuccessful military engagements. Data compiled by the Global Labor Research Working Group suggests that during the early years of World Wars I and II, labor unrest at first declined, but then it escalated during the mid-to-later war years and later peaked in the immediate aftermath (Silver 1995). The findings are consistent with the expected effects of increasing then decreasing repressive capacities. In nearly a third of the wars examined by Small and Singer (1982), the victors had higher battle fatalities than the defeated states. This suggests that major wars diminish the repressive capacities of all contestants, not just the unsuccessful ones.

The weakening of domestic repressive capacities during wartime, however, may be offset by external military intervention. Kowalewski (1991) finds a weak positive relationship between wars and core-state interventions to suppress rebellions in peripheral states. Boswell (1989) reports a five-year lagged, positive effect of global wars upon rates of colonization.

CONCLUSION

In this chapter, the concept of political opportunity structure anchors a set of propositions about the effects of various external factors on mobilization. By altering the likely costs and benefits of extra-institutional collective action, shifts in transnational relations affect the likelihood of protest. The specific effects of transnational structures depend upon a country's location in international economic and political hierarchies as well as a range of national-level factors.

Table 3.1 lists the propositions formulated by linking world-system, dependency, and international relations theories with political process theory. Insufficient research

Table 3.1. Propositions about Transnational Sources of
Political Opportunity

Institutional Access

Proposition 1.1:   A country's position in the capitalist world economy is positively related to wider access to its political institutions.

Proposition 1.2:   Increasing economic dependency promotes political exclusion.

Proposition 1.3:   Political dependency contributes to institutional closure.

Proposition 1.4:   Hegemony causes institutional openings in less powerful states.

Unstable Alignments

Proposition 2.1:   Major swings in levels of transnational economic activity encourage shifts in political alignments.

Proposition 2.2:   Direct interventions by powerful states in the affairs of less powerful states can destabilize domestic political alignments.

Proposition 2.3:   Shifting state alliance and conflict structures facilitate protest by stimulating domestic political realignments.

Elite Splits and Influential Allies

Proposition 3.1:   By heightening social and ideological cleavages, the capitalist world economy contributes to splits among national elites and to the emergence of influential allies for social movements.

Proposition 3.2:   Increasing levels of economic dependency in countries with significant national industrial bases contribute to splits among national elites.

Proposition 3.3:   Patron and client state relations can divide elites in client states.

Proposition 3.4:   During periods of heightened interstate competition, foreign states more frequently and intensively serve as both allies and opponents of insurgents.

Diminished Repression

Proposition 4.1:   A higher position in the world-system hierarchy is negatively related to levels of state repression

Proposition 4.2:   A contraction in the capitalist world economy contributes to an immediate increase in repression in export dependent peripheral states, but, in the long run, can result in a decline in their repressive capacities.

Proposition 4.3:   Economic dependency increases state repression.

Proposition 4.4:   Concentrated and high levels of military dependency leave dependent states vulnerable to reductions in their repressive capacities.

Proposition 4.5:   Interstate wars initially strengthen the repressive capacities of all participants, but they eventually weaken them in unsuccessful states.

exists to adequately assess many of the propositions. Few studies have examined the effects of either world-system position or cyclical phases of the capitalist world economy upon state repression (4.1, 4.2). Additional research is needed if we are to fully grasp the relationships between transnational processes and structures of political opportunity

The available evidence supports some expectations while calling others into question. With regard to transnational economic structures, dependency has multiple and contrasting effects upon structures of opportunity. While states with concentrated and increasing levels of economic and political dependency are more likely to experience institutional closure (1.2, 1.3), they are also more susceptible to splits among national elites (3.2, 3.3). Beyond specific relationships of dependency, shifts in the global economy hold opportunities for protest in the semiperiphery by precipitating political realignments (2.1).

Like dependency, interstate competition also has multiple and contrasting effects upon structures of political opportunity. An absence of geopolitical competition facilitates the relaxation of political controls in less powerful states (1.4). Heightened interstate competition, on the other hand, leads to the emergence of foreign states as both allies and opponents of challengers (3.4). Involvement in foreign wars eventually diminishes the repressive capacities of contestants, providing opportunities for protest and rebellion (4.5). These positive effects of war may be offset by increased core-state intervention in peripheral states during periods of international war. Both deliberately and sometimes inadvertently, interventions by powerful states have contributed to political destabilization and splits among elites in less powerful states (2.2, 3.3). While states facing international isolation have reached out to popular classes (2.3), protests aimed at the state may decrease as a consequence of such alliances.

For the sake of parsimony, I have presented propositions on economic and political relations separately, but they can be mutually constitutive and often complementary rather than competing explanations of protest. For instance, when contraction in the capitalist world economy intensifies interstate competition (Chase-Dunn and Rubinson 1979; see Kowalewski 1991 for an alternative formulation), economics and politics have mixed effects on political opportunity structures in the periphery and semiperiphery. The onset of stagnation destabilizes political alignments while geopolitical competition contributes to institutional closure.

Political process explanations of transnational protest dimensions can be strengthened by addressing cultural variations, mobilization structures, and the dynamics of organized contention. Not every political opportunity is perceived or acted upon in the same way. Whether and how they are responded to depend upon several considerations including collective identities, the structure of social networks which will be tapped into, available human and material resources, repertoires of contention, strategic innovation, levels and forms of preexisting organization, and organizational alliance and conflict structures. Specific responses to perceived political opportunities along with the responses of opposing actors, in turn, reshape the structure of opportunity organized contenders face. Some researchers have already integrated some of these components of collective action into political process frameworks (Tarrow 1994; Meyer and Staggenborg 1996; Smith, Pagnucco, Chatfield 1997). The same transnational factors shaping structures of political opportunity also affect these additional considerations and, therefore, merit greater attention in subsequent research.

NOTES

1. The extent and character of protest are not discussed in depth because of space constraints. They will depend in part on national-level factors (other than POS) and how transnational structures interact with them, such as (1) characteristics of challengers, their resources, mobilization structures, and repertoires of contention, and how these affect their ability to take advantage of favorable conditions; (2) the structure of the state, its capacities, and its policies; (3) the structure of society (e.g., social cleavages); and (4) relations between the state and society.

2. A general lack of upward or downward mobility in the modern world system has discouraged direct assessment of the relationship between mobility and institutional access. In general, more time-series studies measuring changes in transnational processes and dimensions of political opportunity are needed.

3. The international arms trade has also contributed to the rise of authoritarian regimes in Asia and the Middle East (Tanter 1984; Tilly 1990).

4. Bergesen and Schoenberg also assert that increasing incorporation of the periphery into the capitalist world economy brings shorter and less disruptive periods of competition among core states. Core states have also moved away from colonialism towards using dependencies to exert influence. Boswell (1989: 191) finds that the relationship only holds "when the new hegemon surpasses its rival after a long competitive ascent."

5. Silver attributes increased labor unrest in the periphery and semiperiphery to flows of investment from the core, strengthening the bargaining power of workers in the regions receiving the investment. It is possible that both this explanation and proposition 1.4 are valid. Greater investment increases the economic leverage of peripheral and semiperipheral workers while less interstate competition simultaneously promotes their inclusion in national polities.

6. The effects of heightened external involvement upon protest, in all likelihood, depend upon the specific forms of intervention (e.g., weapons provision, financial support to political parties, human rights advocacy) and the targets of intervention (e.g., the state or challengers).

REFERENCES

Alves, Maria Helena Moreira. 1989. "Interclass Alliances in the Opposition to the Military in Brazil: Consequences for the Transition Period." Pp. 278-298 in *Power and Popular Protest: Latin American Social Movements*, Susan Eckstein, ed. Berkeley: University of California Press.

Amsden, Alice H. 1985. "The State and Taiwan's Economic Development." In *Bringing the State Back In,* Peter Evans, Dietrich Rueschemeyer and Theda Skocpol, eds. Cambridge: Cambridge University Press.

Angeles, Leonora C. 1999. "The Political Dimension in the Agrarian Question: Strategies of Resilience and Political Entrepreneurship of Agrarian Elite Families in a Philippine Province." *Rural Sociology* 64: 667-692.

Arrighi, Giovanni, and Jessica Drangel. 1986. "The Stratification of the World-Economy: An Exploration of the Semiperipheral Zone." *Review* 10: 9-74.

Arrighi, Giovanni, Terrence Hopkins and Immanuel Wallerstein. 1989. *Antisystemic Movements*. London: Verso.

Bardach, Ann Louise, and Larry Rohter. July 13, 1998. "A Bomber's Tale: Decades of Intrigue: Life in the Shadows, Trying to Bring Down Castro." *New York Times,* 1A.

Bergesen, Albert, and Ronald Schoenberg. 1980. "Long Waves of Colonial Expansion and Contraction, 1415-1969." Pp. 231-277 in *Studies of the Modern World-System*, Albert Bergesen, ed. New York: Academic Press.

Black, David. 1999. "The Long and Winding Road: International Norms and Domestic Political Change in South Africa." Pp. 78-108 in *The Power of Human Rights: International Norms and Domestic Change*, Thomas Risse, Stephen C. Ropp, and Kathryn Sikkink, eds. New York: Cambridge University Press.

Bollen, Kenneth A. 1983. "World System Position, Dependence, and Democracy: The Cross-National Evidence." *American Sociological Review* 48: 468-479.

Boswell, Terry. 1989. "Colonial Empires and the Capitalist World-Economy: A Time Series Analysis of Colonization, 1640-1960." *American Sociological Review* 54: 180-196.

Boswell, Terry, and Christopher Chase-Dunn. 2000. "From State Socialism to Global Democracy: The Transnational Politics of the Modern World System." Pp. 289-306 in *A World-Systems Reader: New Perspectives on Gender, Urbanism, Cultures, Indigenous Peoples, and Ecology*, Thomas D. Hall, ed. New York: Rowman & Littlefield.

Boswell, Terry, and William J. Dixon. 1990. "Dependency and Rebellion: A Cross-National Analysis." *American Sociological Review* 55: 540-559.

Bradshaw, York. 1985. "Dependent Development in Black Africa: A Crossnational Study." *American Sociological Review* 50: 195-206.

Bredo, William. 1986. "U.S. Security: Potential of Land Reform Policy Support in the Third World." *Journal of Political and Military Sociology* 14: 277-290.

Broder, John M. March 31, 1997. "Political Meddling by Outsiders: Not New for US." *New York Times*, 1A.

Cardoso, Fernando H. 1972. "Dependency and Development in Latin America." *New Left Review* 74: 83-95.

————. 1973. "Associated-Dependent Development: Theoretical and Practical Implications." Pp. 142-176 in *Authoritarian Brazil*, Alfred Stepan, ed. New Haven, Conn.: Yale University Press.

Cardoso, Fernando H. and Enzo Faletto. 1979. *Dependency and Development in Latin America*. Berkeley: University of California Press.

Chase-Dunn, Christopher. 1978. "Core-Periphery Relations: The Effects of Core Competition." Pp. 159-176 in *Social Change in the Capitalist World-Economy*, Barbara Kaplan, ed. Beverly Hills, Calif.: Sage Publications.

Chase-Dunn, Christopher, and Richard Rubinson. 1977. "Toward a Structural Perspective on the World-System." *Politics and Society* 7: 453-476.

Chirot, Daniel. 1977. *Social Change in the Twentieth Century*. New York: Harcourt, Brace, and Jovanovich.

Conboy, Kenneth, and James Morrison. 1999. *Feet to the Fire: CIA Covert Operations in Indonesia, 1957-1958*. Annapolis, Md.: Naval Institute Press.

Delacroix, Jack, and Charles Ragin. 1981. "Structural Blockage: A Crossnational Study of Economic Dependency, State Efficacy, and Underdevelopment." *American Journal of Sociology* 86: 1311-1347.

Deyo, Frederic C. 1989. *Beneath the Miracle: Labor Subordination in the New Asian Industrialism*. Berkeley: University of California Press.

Doyle, Michael W. 1985. "Metropole, Periphery, and System: Empire on the Niger and the Nile." Pp. 151-192 in *States versus Markets in the World-System*, Peter Evans, Dietrich Rueschemeyer, and Evelyne Huber Stephens, eds. Beverly Hills, Calif.: Sage Publications.

Duner, Bertil. 1983. "The Many-Pronged Spear: External Military Intervention in Civil Wars in the 1970s." *Journal of Peace Research* 20: 59-72.

Duvall, Raymond, Steven Jackson, Bruce M. Russett, Duncan Snidal, and David Sylvan. 1981. "A Formal Model of 'Dependencia' Theory: Structure and Measurement." In *From National Development to Global Community*, R. Merritt and B. M. Russett, eds. London: Allen & Unwin.

Eckstein, Susan. 1989. "Power and Popular Protest in Latin America." Pp.1-60 in *Power and Popular Protest: Latin American Social Movements*, Susan Eckstein, ed. Berkeley:

University of California Press.

Eisinger, Peter K. 1973. "The Conditions of Protest Behavior in American Cities." *American Political Science Review* 67: 11-28.

Evans, Peter. 1979. *Dependent Development: The Alliance of Multinational, State and Local Capital in Brazil*. Princeton, N.J.: Princeton University Press.

———. 1983. "State, Local and Multinational Capital in Brazil: Prospects for the Stability of the 'Triple Alliance' in the Eighties." Pp.139-168 in *Latin America in the World Economy: New Perspectives*, Diane Tussie, ed. New York: St. Martin's Press.

Evans, Peter, Dietrich Rueschemeyer, and Evelyne Huber Stephens. 1985. "Introduction." Pp. 11-32 in *States versus Markets in the World-System*, Peter Evans, Dietrich Rueschemeyer, and Evelyne Huber Stephens, eds. Beverly Hills, Calif.: Sage Publications.

Frank, Andre Gunder. 1969. *Capitalism and Underdevelopment in Latin America*. New York: Monthly Review Press.

Gold, Thomas. 1986. *State and Society in the Taiwan Miracle*. New York: M.E. Sharpe.

Goldfrank, Walter L. 1979. "Theories of Revolution and Revolution without Theory: The Case of Mexico." *Theory and Society*. 7: 135-165.

Grimes, Peter. 2000. "Recent Research on World-Systems." Pp.29-58 in *A World-Systems Reader: New Perspectives on Gender, Urbanism, Cultures, Indigenous Peoples, and Ecology*, Thomas D. Hall, ed. New York: Rowman & Littlefield.

Haimson, Leopold, and Charles Tilly. 1989. "Strikes, Wars, and Revolutions in an International Perspective." In *Strike Waves in The Late Nineteenth and Early Twentieth Centuries*. New York: Cambridge University Press

Hamilton, Nora. 1984. *The Limits of State Autonomy: Post-Revolutionary Mexico*. Princeton, N.J.: Princeton University Press.

Hart, Jeffrey A. 1992. *Rival Capitalists: International Competitiveness in the United States, Japan, and Western Europe*. Ithaca, N.Y.: Cornell University Press.

Jackson, Steven, Bruce Russett, Duncan Snidal, and David Sylvan. 1978. "Conflict and Coercion in Dependent States." *Journal of Conflict Resolution* 22: 627-657.

Jenkins, J. Craig. 1983. "Resource Mobilization Theory and the Study of Social Movements." *Annual Review of Sociology* 9: 527-553.

Jenkins, J. Craig, and Kurt Schock. 1992. "Global Structures and Political Processes in the Study of Domestic Political Conflict." *Annual Review of Sociology* 18: 161-185.

Keck, Margaret, and Kathryn Sikkink. 1998. *Activists beyond Borders: Advocacy Networks in International Politics*. Ithaca, N.Y.: Cornell University Press.

Kerbo, Harold. 1978. "Foreign Involvement in the Preconditions for Political Violence: The World System and the Case of Chile." *Journal of Conflict Resolution* 22: 363-391.

Kitschelt, Herbert P. 1986. "Political Opportunity Structures and Political Protest: Anti-Nuclear Movements in Four Democracies." *British Journal of Political Science* 16: 57-85.

Koo, Hagen. 1987. "The Interplay of State, Social Class, and World System in East Asian Development: The Cases of South Korea and Taiwan." Pp. 165-180 in *The Political Economy of the East Asian Industrialization*, Frederic C. Deyo, ed. Ithaca, N.Y.: Cornell University Press.

Kornbluh, Peter. 2000. *The Pinochet File: A Declassified Dossier on Atrocity and Accountability*. New York: New Press.

Kowalewski, David. 1991. "Core Intervention and Periphery Revolution, 1821-1985." *American Journal of Sociology* 97:70-95.

Kraus, Richard Curt. 1979. "Withdrawing from the World-System: Self-Reliance and Class Structure in China." Pp. 237-259 in *The World-System of Capitalism: Past and Present*, Walter L. Goldfrank, ed. Beverly Hills, Calif.: Sage Publications.

Krauss, Clifford. March 7, 1999. "The World: The CIA and Guatemala: The Spies Who Never Came in from the Cold War." *New York Times*, section 4, p. 3.

Landsberg, Martin. 1979. "Export-Led Industrialization in the Third World: Manufacturing

Imperialism." *Review of Radical Political Economics* 11: 50-63.

Linfield, Michael. 1990. *Freedom under Fire: U.S. Civil Liberties in Times of War*. Boston, Mass.: South End Press.

Lipset, Seymour M. 1994. "The Social Requisites of Democracy Revisited." *American Sociological Review* 59:1-22.

Maniruzzaman, Talukder. 1987. *Military Withdrawal from Politics: A Comparative Study*. Cambridge, Mass.: Ballinger.

Mars, Perry. 1995. "Foreign Influence, Political Conflicts and Conflict Resolution in the Caribbean." *Journal of Peace Research*. 32: 437-451.

McAdam, Doug. 1982. *Political Process and the Development of Black Insurgency, 1930-1970*. Chicago: University of Chicago Press.

McAdam, Doug, John D. McCarthy, and Mayer N. Zald. 1996. "Introduction: Opportunities, Mobilizing Structures, and Framing Processes—Toward a Synthetic, Comparative Perspective on Social Movements." Pp.1-22 in *Comparative Perspectives on Social Movements: Political Opportunities, Mobilizing Structures, and Cultural Framings*, Doug McAdam, John D. McCarthy, and Mayer Zald, eds. New York: Cambridge University Press.

McGowan, Pat. 1985. "Pitfalls and Promise in the Quantitative Study of the World-System." *Review* 8: 477-500.

McMichael, Philip. 1985. "Britain's Hegemony in the Nineteenth-Century World-Economy." Pp. 117-150 in *States versus Markets in the World-System*, Peter Evans, Dietrich Rueschemeyer, and Evelyne Huber Stephens, eds. Beverly Hills, Calif.: Sage Publications.

Meyer, David S., and Suzanne Staggenborg. 1996. "Movements, Countermovements, and the Structure of Political Opportunity." *American Journal of Sociology* 101: 1628-1660.

Moaddel, Mansoor. 1994. "Political Conflict in the World Economy: A Cross-National Analysis of Modernization and World System Theories." *American Sociological Review* 59: 276-303.

Muller, Edward N., and Erich Weede. 1990. "Cross-National Variation in Political Violence: A Rational Actor Approach." *Journal of Conflict Resolution* 34: 624-651.

O'Donnell, Guillermo A. 1978. "Reflections on the Pattern of Change in Bureaucratic-Authoritarian State," *Latin American Review* 8:3-38.

Pierce, Jenny. 1981. *Under the Eagle: US Intervention in Central America and the Caribbean*. Boston, Mass.: South End Press.

Piven, Frances Fox, and Richard A. Cloward. 1977. *Poor People's Movements: Why They Succeed, How They Fail*. New York: Pantheon.

Rubinson, Richard. 1977. "Dependence, Government Revenue and Economic Growth, 1955-1970." *Studies in Comparative International Development* 12: 3-27.

Rueschemeyer, Dietrich, Evelyne Huber Stephens, and John D. Stephens. 1992. *Capitalist Development and Democracy*. Chicago: University of Chicago Press.

Ropp, Stephen C., and Kathryn Sikkink. 1999. "International Norms and Domestic Politics in Chile and Guatemala." Pp. 172-204 in *The Power of Human Rights: International Norms and Domestic Change*, Thomas Risse, Stephen C. Ropp, and Kathryn Sikkink, eds. New York: Cambridge University Press.

Rosen, Steven. 1974. "The Open Door Imperative and U.S. Foreign Policy." In *Testing Theories of Economic Imperialism*, Steven Rosen and J. Kurth, eds. Lexington, Mass.: Lexington Books.

Schwarz, Urs. 1970. *Confrontation and Intervention in the Modern World*. Dobbs Ferry, N.Y.: Oceana.

Silver, Beverly J. 1995. "World-Scale Patterns of Labor-Capital Conflict: Labor Unrest, Long Waves, and Cycles of World Hegemony." *Review* 18: 155-192.

Sims, Beth. 1991. *Workers of the World Undermined: American Labor's Role in U.S. Foreign Policy*. Boston: South End Press.

Skocpol, Theda. 1979. *States and Social Revolutions: A Comparative Analysis of France, Russia and China.* New York: Cambridge University Press.

Small, Melvin, and J. David Singer. 1982. *Resort to Arms: International and Civil Wars, 1816-1980.* Beverly Hills, Calif.: Sage Publications.

Smith, Jackie. 1995. "Transnational Political Processes and the Human Rights Movement." *Research in Social Movements, Conflict and Change.* 18: 185-219.

Smith, Jackie, Charles Chatfield, and Ron Pagnucco, eds. 1997. *Transnational Social Movements and Global Politics: Solidarity beyond the State.* Syracuse, N.Y.: Syracuse University Press.

Smith, Jackie, Ron Pagnucco, and Charles Chatfield. 1997. "Social Movements and World Politics: A Theoretical Framework" Pp. 59-80 in *Transnational Social Movements and Global Politics: Solidarity beyond the State,* Jackie Smith, Charles Chatfield, and Ron Pagnucco, eds. Syracuse, N.Y.: Syracuse University Press.

So, Alvin Y. 1986. "The Economic Success of Hong Kong: Insights from a World-System Perspective." *Sociological Perspectives* 29: 241-258.

———. 1990. *Social Change and Development: Modernization, Dependency, and World-System Theories.* Newbury Park, Calif.: Sage Publications.

Stephens, Evelyne Huber, and John D. Stephens. 1985. "Bauxite and Democratic Socialism in Jamaica." Pp. 33-66 in *States versus Markets in the World-System,* Peter Evans, Dietrich Rueschemeyer, and Evelyne Huber Stephens, eds. Beverly Hills, Calif.: Sage Publications.

Tanter, Richard. 1984. "Trends in Asia," *Alternatives* 10:161-191.

Tarrow, Sidney. 1994. *Power in Movement: Social Movements, Collective Action and Politics.* New York: Cambridge University Press.

———. 2001. "Transnational Politics: Contention and Institutions in International Politics." *Annual Review of Political Science* 4: 1-20.

Thompson, William R. 2000. "K-Waves, Leadership Cycles, and Global War: A Nonhyphenated Approach to World Analysis" Pp. 83-104 in *A World-Systems Reader: New Perspectives on Gender, Urbanism, Cultures, Indigenous Peoples, and Ecology,* Thomas D. Hall, ed. New York: Rowman & Littlefield.

Tilly, Charles. 1978. *From Mobilization to Revolution.* Reading, Mass.: Addison-Wesley.

———. 1990. *Coercion, Capital, and European States: AD 990-1992.* Cambridge, Mass.: Blackwell.

Timberlake, Michael, and Kirk R. Williams. 1984. "Dependence, Political Exclusion, and Government Repression: Some Cross-National Evidence." *American Sociological Review* 49: 141-146.

Trimberger, Ellen Kay. 1978. *Revolution from Above.* New Brunswick, N.J.: Transaction Books.

Van Wingen, John, and Herbert Tillema. 1980. "British Military Intervention after World War II." *Journal of Peace Research* 17: 291-303.

Wallerstein, Immanuel. 1974. *The Modern World System I: Capitalist Agriculture and the Origins of the European World Economy.* New York: Academic Press.

———. 1979a. *The Capitalist World-Economy.* New York: Cambridge University Press.

———. 1979b. "Underdevelopment Phase-B: Effect of the Seventeenth-Century Stagnation on Core and Periphery of the European World-Economy." Pp. 73-84 in *The World-System of Capitalism: Past and Present,* Walter L. Goldfrank, ed. Beverly Hills, Calif.: Sage Publications.

———. 1984. *The Politics of the Capitalist World-Economy.* New York: Cambridge University Press.

———. 1988. "Development: Lodestar or Illusion." *Economic and Political Weekly* 23: 2017-2023.

Walton, John. 1984. *Reluctant Rebels: Comparative Studies of Revolution and Underdevelopment.* New York: Columbia University Press.

———. 1989. "Debt, Protest, and the State in Latin America." Pp. 299-328 in *Power and*

    Popular Protest: Latin American Social Movements, Susan Eckstein, ed. Berkeley, Calif.: University of California Press.

Walton, John, and Charles Ragin. 1990. "Global and National Sources of Political Protest: Third World Responses to the Debt Crisis." *American Sociological Review* 55: 876-890.

Walton, John, and David Seddon. 1994. *Free Markets and Food Riots: The Politics of Global Adjustment*. Cambridge, Mass.: Blackwell.

Part II

Transnational Mobilization and National Politics

Chapter 4

IRISH TRANSNATIONAL SOCIAL MOVEMENTS, MIGRANTS, AND THE STATE SYSTEM

Michael Hanagan

Recently, much scholarly attention has focused on the globalization process and its effects on social movements and states. One dimension of globalization is the role of transnational migrants and the social movements they build. Following Basch, Schiller, and Blanc (1994: 7), "transnationalism is defined as the processes by which immigrants forge and sustain multi-stranded social relations that link together their societies of origin and settlement." The particular transnational social movements considered in this chapter are migrant-based, claims-making movements. According to scholars who study them, such movements are: (1) a new phenomenon of the modern global age, (2) a response to a modern communications revolution, and (3) a result of the weakening of modern states that further contributes to the decline of the contemporary state system through transnational outcomes of movement challenges.

A classic analysis of such a movement is *The Macedonian Conflict: Ethnic Nationalism in a Transnational World*, by anthropologist, Loring M. Danforth. He tells us that, "In this era of globalization, national communities are being 'imagined' in a new way. We are witnessing the construction of *transnational* national communities. The 'primordial sentiments' of region, ethnicity, language, and religion have become globalized" (Danforth 1995: 80). Danforth masterfully shows how individuals from Macedonia, many of whom went to Australia under Greek passports, renegotiated their identities in the fluid and multicultural climate of the diaspora. Within some families, individual members identified themselves as Macedonians while others remained firmly Greek. Danforth's depiction of the complex calculations made by individuals in deciding ethnic allegiances mocks those who insist that cultural identity is predicated on a priori cultural traits. Clearly, an array of historical, political, social, and cultural pressures influenced the construction of Macedonian or Greek identities.

Danforth's belief in the newness of transnational social movements is shared by many scholars, some of whom go further and argue that these new movements may lead to radically new political outcomes. For example, in the United States "questions of loyalty are being decentered as the construction of identities within the geography of national borders is being openly challenged by deterritorialized nation-state constructions and global racial categories" (Basch, Schiller, and Blanc 1994: 290-291). Examples of this process include Haitians in the United States fighting the Haitian military coup by making alliances with African Americans to change U.S. foreign policy, and Filipinos in the United States helping to overthrow U.S. ally Ferdinand Marcos (Blanc, Schiller and Blanc: 181-224). Sooner or later, these scholars argue, transnational movements are likely to break with the nation-state. They wonder how long "transmigrants will continue to participate in nationalist constructions that contribute to the hegemony of the dominant classes" (Schiller, Basch, and Blanc 1992: 15).

Scholars such as Arjun Appadurai agree that the territorial nation-state is in deep trouble, although he sees it as besieged on both left and right. Appadurai insists that there has been a "general rupture in the tenor of intersocietal relations in the past decades" because of mass migration and because "electronic media decisively change the wider field of mass media and other traditional media." Appadurai maintains that:

> The story of mass migrations (voluntary and forced) is hardly a new feature of human history. But when it is juxtaposed with the rapid flow of mass-mediated images, scripts, and sensations, we have a new order of instability in the production of modern subjectivities. As Turkish guest workers in Germany watch Turkish films in their German flats, as Koreans in Philadelphia watch the 1988 Olympics in Seoul through satellite feeds from Korea and as Pakistani cabdrivers in Chicago listen to cassettes of sermons recorded in mosques in Pakistan or Iran, we see moving images meet deterritorialized viewers. These create diasporic public spheres, phenomena that confound theories that depend on the continued salience of the nation-state as key arbiter of important social changes. (Appadurai 1996: 4)

Appadurai sees emigration as a space in which migrant identity can be reinvented: "deterritorialization creates new markets for film companies, impresarios, and travel agencies which thrive on the need of the relocated population for contact with the homeland." He is not optimistic about the possibilities, for "the homeland is partly invented, existing only in the imagination of the deterritorialized groups, and it can sometimes become so fantastic and one-sided that it provides the fuel for new ethnic conflicts" (Appadurai 1996: 49).

Much of the speculation about the role of transnational migration and transnational social movements in producing new political practices is based on the assumption that they are recent phenomena without a track record. Although occasional reference is made to antecedent movements, this assumption that transnational social movements have no history pervades the literature. Strangely, Danforth's study fails to demonstrate or even reflect his central claim that national communities are indeed imagined in a *new* way—for Macedonian nationalism has always been transnational. Precommunist

Macedonian nationalism seems remarkably similar to postcommunist Macedonian nationalism. After all, in the 1890s when Macedonia proper was still a part of the Turkish empire, nationalists in Bulgaria, Greece, Rumania, and Serbia all organized nationalist societies to win Macedonia's allegiance to their national cause. Founded in 1893, the Internal Macedonian Revolutionary Organization (IMRO) burst upon the scene and, for decades, was practically an independent power in the southern Balkans. In 1919, the incorporation of the bulk of Macedonia into Yugoslavia embroiled IMRO in another area of Balkan politics, and in 1923, IMRO leaders played a major role in the overthrow of Bulgarian statesman Alexander Stambuliski. Between 1923 and 1934, the organization was subsidized by the Italian government, and it practically controlled Bulgarian Macedonia adjacent to Yugoslavia, collecting taxes and enforcing its own laws (Poulton 1995, Duncan 1981). Danforth pays little attention to the divergent path followed by organized Macedonians in the United States since the 1920s. Many identified themselves with neither Greece nor an independent Macedonia but with Bulgaria! Missed here is evidence that the post-World War II period *is not the first time that Macedonian identity has been renegotiated in emigration.*

Danforth assumes that the transnational character of Macedonian nationalism is recent because he fails to consider the contemporary global transformation in the perspective of past global transformations. The last three decades have not been the first to carry out a revolution in transportation and communication that permitted "globalization"—defined by Charles Tilly as "an increase in the geographic range of locally consequential social interactions" (Tilly 1995). David Harvey cites the years between 1850 and 1930 as a major period of "time-space compression" due to the development of the steam ship and the steam locomotive (Harvey 1989). In terms of transatlantic, transnational movements, the influence of the steam ship was decisive. In 1867, it took a sailing vessel an average of forty-four days to travel between Europe and America, but a steam-powered ship could make the trip in fourteen days; by 1900 the trip was down to a week. The transportation revolution encouraged the growth of international organizations, including the Universal Postal Union (1874), International Bureau of Weights and Measures (1875), and the International Labor Office (1901). World congresses regulating industrial standards, worldwide financial transactions, and copyright laws became common occurrences (Murphey 1994).

International political organizations also multiplied in this period. The International Workingmen's Association was founded in 1864 and the International Workers Congress established the so-called Second International in 1889. Among the International's first acts was to adopt a proposal of the American AFL and call for workers to celebrate May 1 by taking off work. In 1892, there were demonstrations and work stoppages in Australia, Austria, Brazil, England, Germany, Hungary, Italy, Rumania, Russia, Russian Poland, Spain, Switzerland, and the United States (Dommanget 1972: 175-176). International reform organizations, mainly centered in Europe, such as the International League of Peace and Liberty (1867) were created; and peace societies spread throughout Europe, celebrating February 22 as International Peace Day. World congresses of feminists, social reformers, and peace activists flourished in the same period.

Meanwhile competition among carriers in the "Atlantic ferry" reduced the cost of a round trip so that workers could afford them. Italian and Spanish farm laborers even migrated seasonally to the Argentine pampas (Moch 1992: 152). In the second half of the nineteenth century, the affordability of return and seasonal migration between Europe and the United States combined with new electronic international communication to stimulate transnational migrant identities and movements. In the United States after World War I, these identities were the basis of massive political participation by ethnic groups on behalf of their native lands. The Sons of Italy, Italia Irridenta Society, Slovak League, National Alliance of Bohemian Catholics, and American Jewish Congress were all American-based organizations that asserted a "transnational identity" in championing their homelands' cause at the Versailles Conference (Vassady 1982, O'Grady 1967). In the 1920s, Afro-Caribbean migrants played a key role in the international coordination of Marcus Garvey's United Negro Improvement Association, by far the largest transnational movement in U.S. history (James 1997).

This chapter argues that transnational social movements are not new, and that while every migratory wave has its unique features, the study of past transnational movements can contribute to an understanding of contemporary ones and their outcomes. A look at the past shows that contemporary social analysts wrongly deduce transnational outcomes from transnational movements and that the conditions that determine movement emergence must be distinguished clearly from those that yield political settlements. The character of protest movements is only one of a number of important factors determining political outcomes (Meyer and Minkoff 1997).

We have been this way before. The second half of the nineteenth century and the early twentieth century witnessed the building of powerful transnational social movements. In this period, industrialization and state power were closely intertwined. Advances in transportation and communications technology and the vast wave of proletarianization that promoted mass migration were prerequisites for strong linkages between homelands and foreign-based organizations. But *trans*national social movements also required the expansion of the modern state system, first, throughout Europe and, then, through much of the world. Further, transnational social movements depended upon favorable political opportunity structures in states that were targets of emigration. Political openness and international rivalries enabled migrant groups to mobilize powerfully (McAdam 1996). But the very competitive state system that facilitated the emergence of transnational social movements made it extremely unlikely they would produce transnational outcomes.

The focus of this chapter is the transnational character of Irish nationalism over the last one hundred and fifty years. Starting in the late 1850s Irish nationalists built extraordinarily successful transnational movements. While a revolution in transportation technology was instrumental to success, the strength and enduring character of Irish nationalist organizations should remind us that these technologies have been around for a long time. Irish transnational movements resemble modern movements in that the construction of Irish identity occurred outside the patronage and framework of an existing state and that the emigrant population, at times, played an important role in formulating and redefining Irish identity. But despite genuinely transnational practices and a sense of transnational Irish identity that characterized such men as John Devoy and Michael Collins, the new state that they worked to create had no place for such practices or such identities. As a result, transnational identities merged imperceptibly into national consciousness. The concluding section compares late-twentieth-century Irish transnational movements with those of the late-nineteenth-century. It shows that, despite the development of electronic media, personal networks remain the foundation of Irish transnational movements today as in the past, and suggests that the persistence of personal ties is no anomaly.

THE IRISH REPUBLICAN BROTHERHOOD

In 1858, two Irish nationalist organizations were founded: the Fenian Brotherhood (FB) by John O'Mahony in the United States, and the Irish Republican Brotherhood (IRB) by James Stephens in Ireland. Both organizations were oath-bound, male brotherhoods. Such organizations had long histories in Ireland most recently manifested in such societies as the Defenders and the United Irishmen. O'Mahony's and Stephens's new organizations distinguished themselves by their close modeling on French conspiratorial organizations of the 1830s and 1840s (Smyth 1992). The organizations formed by Stephens and O'Mahony were part of a common project to free Ireland from British domination. In principle, the Irish-based IRB would lead an insurrection with resources provided by the U.S.-based FB.

The relationship between the IRB and the Fenian Brotherhood quickly became hopelessly entangled. Members of both organizations referred to themselves as the IRB and the entire movement became publicly known as the "Fenians" (McCaffrey 1996: 224). Over the next few decades, factional splits caused the movement to metamorphose and change its names. From 1858 to 1922, under the label of the IRB, the Fenian Brotherhood, the United Irishman, the Phoenix Society, or later, The Federation, the Irish National Brotherhood, the United Brotherhood, and the Clan na Gael, oath-bound Irish nationalist brotherhoods flourished. Many had the same leaders and appealed to the same constituencies.

Between 1858 and 1922, the IRB and related secret organizations comprised a family of transnational social movements that organized tens of thousands in both Ireland and America and carried out major intercontinental actions. The 1861 funeral of the Irish revolutionary Terence Bellew McManus tellingly illustrates the IRB's scope. McManus died and was buried in San Francisco, but California Fenians campaigned to ship his body back to Dublin. First, his coffin was sent to New York, and demonstrations were organized all along the route of the train carrying his coffin. In New York, a Fenian committee successfully lobbied Archbishop Hughes to celebrate a Solemn High Requiem Mass. In the course of his sermon the archbishop seemed to offer tacit approval of the Fenian movement. The tolerance of the U.S. Roman Catholic Church toward the Fenians was important, for in Ireland the greater part of the hierarchy, including the primate, was adamantly opposed. From New York, the IRB organized the return of his body to Dublin even though the Irish hierarchy refused permission for a church ceremony. Tens of thousands viewed his coffin and thousands more lined the route of his funeral procession (Newsinger 1994: 26-27). The McManus funeral is often portrayed as a turning point marking a revival of nationalism in Ireland.

The climax of the first wave of IRB activity was the failed Irish uprising of 1867. The attempted uprising was a desperate effort; Irish nationalists had always believed that an armed insurrection would stand a chance only when Britain was at war with a major power. Unfortunately the rapid growth of the IRB in Ireland (conservative estimates place the number of Irish members as around 54,000) combined with the availability of cheap guns and Irish-American Civil War veterans, led the more activist-oriented Irish-American leaders to decide that they must revolt alone before Britain acted against the organization (Comerford 1985: 48). But the authorities—only too well informed about the larger outlines of the scheme—moved quickly to repress the organization, which managed only a flurry of scattered insurrections.

The IRB's strategy for revolution was influenced by contemporary events such as Garibaldi and his thousand Red Shirts' landing in the Kingdom of the Two Sicilies, Narciso Lopez's efforts to liberate Cuba, William Walker's Nicaraguan expeditions, and John Brown's rising at Harper's Ferry (Comerford 1985: 48). Recruits to the IRB spent much of their time in military drilling. These drills were to prepare to meet the British army in the field, but they were also public exhibitions of strength and organization. The U.S.-based FB's major focus was on supplying IRB recruits with money, arms, and skilled military leadership. Once the insurrection had begun and an Irish republic proclaimed, IRB supporters in the British army in Ireland would join their embattled brothers and, during the actual conflict, they would recruit widely among the Irish population. They hoped a show of force would win sufficient international support to force Britain to concede independence.

In the wake of the failed Irish insurrection in 1867 and the harsh repression that followed, the organization's fortunes waned, although the extent of its decline is perhaps overestimated. In late May 1870, Michael Davitt was involved in a flourishing IRB network in England exporting Birmingham weapons to Irish Fenians (Moody 1981: 53-79). Nonetheless, a spectacular transnational action reinvigorated the movement. In 1876, U.S. Clan na Gael members, assisted by the tiny Australian IRB, rescued six Fenian convicts, British soldiers sentenced to life imprisonment in Australia for their role in the 1867 insurrection (Amos 1988). The sensational escape brought the IRB once again into prominence, encouraging its growth in both Europe and the United States.

Scholars of Irish-American history have generally written off the Fenians as ineffective and romantic, an almost comic afterthought to the grim tragedy of the famine migration. In contrast, contemporary Irish historians are more liable to lament their successes. Operating from Ireland and the United States, the IRB and related organizations played a decisive role in the struggle for Irish independence, and their successes continue to inspire the contemporary Irish Republican Army (IRA). Judged in terms of their ability to organize an insurrection that would bring national independence, the IRB and related Irish nationalist organizations were among the more successful of nineteenth-century conspiratorial brotherhoods, a group that includes such diverse organizations as the United Englishmen, the Italian Carbonari and Young Italy (Italia giovani), the French Society of the Seasons (Société des saisons), the Greek National Society (Ethnike Hetairia) and Revolution Society (Philike Hetairia), and the Serbian Union or Death (Ujedinjenje ili Smrt).

The Fenian uprising was the first chapter in the IRB's history, but not its last. The renewed IRB and Clan na Gael prepared and initiated the Easter Rebellion in Dublin in 1916, the rebellion that culminated in 1922 with the establishment of the Irish Free State. The Easter insurrection was planned along exactly the same lines as in 1867, and Britain's involvement in World War I was precisely the kind of foreign war for which Fenians had prayed in the 1860s. In 1916 from his headquarters in New York, the old Fenian, John Devoy, head of the Clan na Gael, worked with the German consul general in New York to supply guns to Irish rebels. The hard core of the revolt were sections of the Irish Volunteer Army and James Connelly's Irish Citizen Army, whose leaders had been recruited into the IRB and who met and planned the insurrection in the IRB's military committee. In the weeks preceding the insurrection, they had drilled their units intensively and publicly. In its entire history the IRB made only one official public statement, the celebrated "Proclamation of the Provisional Republic" of April 1916, which asserted:

> Having organized and trained her manhood through her secret revolutionary
> organization, the Irish Republican Brotherhood, and through her open military
> organizations, the Irish Volunteers and the Irish Citizen Army . . . and, supported by
> her exiled children in America and by gallant allies in Europe but relying in the first on
> her own strength, she [Ireland] strikes in full confidence of victory.

The 1916 insurrection and the Civil War that followed shifted control of the organization decisively to Ireland, where, in 1917, Michael Collins wrote the new IRB constitution. In early 1922 the IRB underwent its final transformation, when many of its leaders helped form the first government of the Irish Free State (Ranelagh 1988).

Meanwhile, the U.S. Clan na Gael mobilized financial and political support for the IRA and Sinn Féin. The high point of mobilization of Irish-American support for Irish rebellion came not in the 1860s with the Fenians but between 1916 and 1921, as the Irish cauldron boiled over. In both periods, transnational conspiratorial brotherhoods played a crucial role. In March 1916, a month before the Easter Rebellion, the first Irish Race Convention was convened in New York. The idea of an "Irish race" represents a crude effort at the construction of a transnational identity. This convention gave birth to an organization calling for Irish independence, the Friends of Irish Freedom (FOIF), founded by John Devoy (Tansill 1957). Under Judge Daniel F. Cohalan's leadership the FOIF used their funds to launch a nationwide campaign demanding that Woodrow Wilson intervene with Lloyd George for the cause of Irish independence. They failed, but played an important role in defeating U.S. participation in the League of Nations. In 1919 the FOIF had 275,000 members and, over the next three years, raised millions for the Irish republican cause. It raised a million dollars for a campaign to win U.S. recognition for the Irish Republic (McNickle 1996: 350-351). Ultimately, the American Association for the Recognition of the Irish Republic, organized by a rival faction of the Clan na Gael, reached over 700,000 members.

Throughout its entire history, the IRB always attempted to function as a transnational social movement, and at key junctures it succeeded in this goal. Toward the end of the IRB's active existence, its head, Michael Collins, then chairman of the provisional government of the Irish Free State, wrote to John Devoy extolling the transnational identity they had worked to create: "Our idea was to have some sort of a world-wide Irish federation, each separate part working through the government and in accordance with the laws of the country where it had its being, but all joined by common ties of blood and race" (O'Broin 1976: 197).

THE IRB: AN ENTIRELY TRANSNATIONAL SOCIAL MOVEMENT

Despite the lack of websites, fax machines, or jet planes, Irish nationalists managed to build a remarkably coherent and enduring transnational movement. Partly they were able to do so because the early Fenians benefited from the mid-nineteenth century communications' revolution; in 1858, the inception of a regular steam packet between Galway and New York brought the west of Ireland into closer communication with the United States. In 1866, a transatlantic cable permanently linked the two countries (Comerford 1985 : 48). In 1871 the American and British governments signed a postal money order agreement that greatly facilitated the sending of money overseas (Miller: 357). To understand the ability of the IRB to maintain its transnational character over seven decades, we need to look at: (1) characteristics of the migration linking Ireland and its emigrants, (2) political opportunities for republican/nationalist mobilization among emigrants, and (3) political opportunities for nationalist mobilization in Ireland. As we shall see, the emergence of an Irish transnational movement was not so much the result of transcending state borders as it was the manipulation of *interstate rivalries* and the existence of political opportunities for mobilization *within* particular states.

Crucial for our analysis is the enormous migratory wave of the 1840s and 1850s that tied Ireland to distant lands around the world, particularly the United States. By the 1840s Irish migration to the United States was already an old story. Already in the 1790s, Irish America had been a refuge for an earlier tide of Irish rebels. Theobald Wolfe Tone had resided there in 1795, and such prominent United Irishmen as Thomas Addis Emmet, James Maceven, and William Sampson migrated to the United States.

The migratory wave of the 1840s and 1850s was one of the largest in European history (see table 4.1). Moreover, it was predominantly Catholic. America was not the only destination of these migrants, many also migrated to Canada, England, Scotland, Australia, and New Zealand. Irish migration to Australia was actually larger in proportion to its population than Irish migration to the United States. Religion was a strong determinant of migrant destinations in the famine years and after. Protestant migrants were more likely to go to Canada, Scotland, and New Zealand; Catholics preferred the United States, Australia, and England. While many Irish migrants managed to retain ties to the land, the poverty that had driven them from Ireland made it difficult for most to acquire land; and in the industrializing United States and England many Irish peasants became urban dwellers. In both countries, the new migrants— particularly the Catholics—concentrated disproportionately in great cities such as London, Liverpool, Boston, New York, Philadelphia, and Chicago. They responded to the demand for unskilled manual labor. In 1855, 34 percent of the population of New York was Irish born (O'Day 1996; 193).

The concentration of the Irish Catholics in large U.S. cities promoted the growth of an organized nationalist movement. Even in largely agrarian Ireland, nationalist organization was almost always centered in urban areas (Comerford 1987). City air gave more freedom from the scrutiny of landlords and the constabulary, and the city was the site of a wage-earning proletariat who, however poorly paid, had some time and money to contribute to the patriotic cause. Also, the city offered the opportunities for the growth of a Catholic middle class that could cultivate a knowledge of Irish history and Irish politics. The existence of a large clientele of Irish laborers doubtless encouraged this new middle class to stress their Irish identity.

Table 4.1. Immigrants from Ireland to the United States, 1820 to 1979 by Decade

1820-29	51,617	1900-09	344,940
1830-39	170,672	1910-19	166,445
1840-49	656,145	1920-29	206,737
1850-59	1,029,486	1930-39	35,773
1860-69	427,419	1940-49	22,500
1870-79	422,264	1950-59	56,256
1880-89	674,061	1960-69	45,770
1890-99	405,710	1970-79	14,405

Source: Patrick Blessing, *The Irish In America: A Guide to the Literature and the Manuscript Collections.* Washington, D.C.: Catholic University of America Press, 1992. p. 289.

Organized Irish nationalism spread among all the nations of the emigration, but it did not spread everywhere equally. Outside Ireland, the United States was always the vital center, with England playing a secondary role (O'Day 1993). Communications may have been a factor in the relative weakness of Irish nationalism in Australia in the years between 1859 and 1867, but Irish nationalism had an American heart for three more fundamental reasons. First, unlike the other major countries of Irish emigration, the United States was an independent republic that, by means of violence, had thrown off successfully the British yoke. Irish-American nationalists readily appealed to the United States's revolutionary republican tradition to legitimate their own goals. Second, the country's independence and its growth as a powerful new nation between 1850 and 1870 brought the country into increased conflict with Britain and its empire. For statesmen involved in confrontations with Britain, the new Irish-Catholic immigrants were a constituency worth cultivating. Third, Irish nationalism also flourished in the United States because the high tide of Irish immigration and the formative period of republican nationalism occurred during or just in advance of a critical period of U.S. state formation, the period of the Civil War and its immediate and stormy aftermath. The crisis provided real opportunities for Irish nationalists who were sought as soldiers to fight in Union armies and as voters to participate in the bitter struggles over reconstruction.

The role of international political rivalry and internal politics in creating a favorable environment for Irish nationalism can be seen by comparing the United States and Canada. Canada was no more distant from Ireland, but the support of Irish-Catholic Canadians for republican nationalism was tepid. Because Canada belonged to the British Empire, Irish-Catholic nationalism met more determined opposition in Canada than in the United States. Irish Protestants organized into Orange lodges constituted a far larger presence in Canada. And Irish-Catholic immigrants found different kinds of political opportunity in Canada. There, Irish Catholics helped shape a new Canadian confederation by using their role as both English speakers and Catholics to mediate between French Catholics and English Protestants, but they could do so only insofar as they accepted the basis premises of a confederation tied to Britain. An ex-Fenian like Thomas D'Arcy McGee emphasized his Catholicism and renounced his republican identity. For this he was hailed as one of the fathers of the Canadian confederation. But also for this, and for his denunciation of the Fenian invasions, he was assassinated in 1868, allegedly by Fenians (Slattery 1968).

Mass Irish-Catholic immigration excited anti-Catholic prejudice throughout the English-speaking world. In the United States, such antagonism helped forge a distinctive new Irish-Catholic identity which was supportive of and influential for Irish nationalism. The transformation of migrant identity was encouraged by the growth of the Know Nothing movement in the 1840s and 1850s (Knobel 1986), which was powerful enough to inspire reactive identity formation. The Know Nothings were militant, anti-imperial republicans, but they posed fewer obstacles to Irish nationalism than imperially oriented, anti-Catholic groups in the other principal countries of the diaspora. And, most important, the Know Nothings were not strong enough to limit Irish Catholic access to the franchise. The Irish migrants who came to the United States during this period came from a variety of backgrounds, many were Gaelic speakers from the western Gaeltachtai, but most were English speakers from the east and south. Traditional rivalries between Connaught and Leinster were still alive, as were memories of faction fights at local fairs and village quarrels. To alarmed nativists they were all Irish Catholics. From U.S. nativists, immigrants acquired a keener sense of a common Catholicism and Irishness than they had at home. The creation of a U.S. Irish identity based on the equation of Irishness with Catholicism was an important element in the movement. It accelerated over the course of the nineteenth century to define Irish nationalism as Catholic. Of the Fenians' founders, O'Mahony was of mixed religious background and his secretary, Thomas Clarke Luby, the son of an Episcopalian minister. But in the United States Fenianism was dominated by Catholics.

The American Civil War made American political leaders acutely receptive to Irish Catholic opinion. To facilitate the recruitment of Irish Americans into the Union army, Lincoln's government allowed Fenian organizers such as Richard O'Sullivan Burke to establish Fenian circles within the Union army. During the Civil War, in order to acquire military expertise and to build their reputation with the U.S. government, prominent Fenians supported military recruitment. Michael Doheny, one of the founders of the FB, organized the 42nd New York. Many officers in the "Irish Brigade" (the 69th, 88th, and 63rd New York Volunteers) were alleged members of the FB, and similar claims were made about officers in the 10th Ohio, 164th New York, and 9th Massachusetts, and the Douglas Brigade from Chicago (Bagenal 1892: 138-152). Though valuable to potential insurrectionists, military experience proved costly; casualties were so high that little remained of the Irish Brigade units by the end of the war (Span 1996) Still, in 1867, many of the most important leaders of the insurrection in Ireland had been officers in the U.S. Civil War. Thomas J. Kelley, who replaced Stephens as head of the IRB and commanded the 1867 insurrection in Ireland, had been a captain in the 10th Ohio. Another leader of the rebellion, perhaps its most daring commander, was John McCafferty, who was one of Morgan's Raiders in the Confederate army.

At various points in the evolution of the Fenian movement, U.S. politicians, for diplomatic or electoral purposes, actively encouraged Irish nationalists. At the high watermark of the first wave of Fenianism in 1866-1867 Secretary of State William H. Seward met with Fenian leaders and allowed them to believe that the U.S. government was not adverse to a Fenian-led invasion of Canada (O'Broin 1971: 52-53). In the hope of provoking an Anglo-American conflict and capitalizing on U.S. indignation at Britain's tacit support for the South as well as a Confederate raid on Vermont launched from Canada, Fenians mustered armies that invaded Canada in 1866, 1870, and 1871. U.S. politicians also encouraged the Fenians as a means of wooing the Irish-Catholic vote. The elections of 1866 were expected by everyone to be close, and President Andrew Johnson pulled out all the stops to win the Irish-Catholic vote. He announced the end of all Fenian prosecutions, removed his attorney general who was detested by the Fenians for his enforcement of neutrality in confrontations between the Fenians and Canada, and interceded with Britain on behalf of the Fenian prisoners in Canada (Neidhardt 1975: 98-99).

If U.S. politicians courted Fenianism in hopes of getting the Irish-American vote, the U.S. Roman Catholic Church also tolerated Fenian activity. The church itself was an international organization administered on a national basis and, even in the late nineteenth century, in the heyday of ultramontanism, national hierarchies possessed considerable latitude. In Ireland, opponents of Fenianism headed by Cardinal Paul Cullen, the Irish primate, were in the majority. Bishop Moriarity of Kerry declared that "hell was not hot enough or eternity long enough" to punish the Fenians, but Irish-Catholic migration brought a tremendous opportunity to construct a significant Catholic presence in the United States; and the U.S. Roman Catholic Church was careful that controversies over Irish nationalism would not endanger it. Many Irish-American clergymen publicly supported the FB (Norman 1965).

Under these circumstances, a fiery Irish-American nationalism emerged at a time when political opportunities were bleak in Ireland, and Irish-Americans played a leading role in the organization of conspiratorial nationalist organizations. In part, conspiratorial organizations spread successfully in Ireland because of British repression. Ireland was subject to special laws that seriously inhibited political mobilization. For example, still in force throughout the nineteenth century was legislation forbidding the formation of Irish organizations based on elected representatives, passed in the wake of the 1798 rebellion. Police spies and packed juries which disappeared in England early in the nineteenth century were still coin of the realm in Ireland. And "coercion acts" giving the Irish administration special powers such as the suspension of habeas corpus, an extraordinary measure in Britain, were employed casually in Ireland. Between 1800 and 1921 parliament passed special powers legislation for Ireland 105 times.

Conspiratorial organizations mainly flourished after 1850 because established national movements collapsed from British intransigence, and because of the enormity of the famine catastrophe. The 1840s had witnessed the discrediting of the principal indigenous Irish nationalist movements. Daniel O'Connell's efforts to repeal the Act of Union of 1800 fell into hopeless disarray after he acceded to the authorities' threats and canceled his Clontarf demonstration in 1843; "the Liberator" himself died on his way to Rome in 1847. The ignominious failure of an attempt at rebellion in 1848 led by the Young Ireland movement similarly discredited the propagators of a new "integral" Irish nationalism, although in time their teachings influenced decisively the course of Irish nationalism. The famine of 1846-50 brought Irish politics to a standstill as demoralized tenants and laborers starved to death or fled the country.

LATER WAVES: THE NATIONAL MOVEMENT'S RECONFIGURATION

The wave of revolt in 1864-1867 was followed by two more waves of Irish protest in which the IRB and the Clan na Gael played important roles, those of 1879-1882 and 1916-1921. Although both waves of protest are interesting and important, space considerations force us to consider only the last, that of 1916-1921. The basic factors operating during the Fenian insurrection, between 1858 and 1867, also operated between 1916 and 1921. Mass migration continued to tie Ireland to America. The evolving diplomatic relationship between England and America, and different political opportunities between nations continued to shape the transnational mobilization of Irish communities. Irish nationalism became more thoroughly transnational between 1916 and 1921 when many Irish Australians, responding to the carnage of the war with a new nationalism, demanded that the United Kingdom accept Ireland's demand for self-determination (O'Farrel 1987: chapter 6). But the United States remained the center of nationalism outside Ireland and was highly sympathetic to the demand for an Irish republic. Wartime crises also strongly affected transnational mobilization. The British Empire and the United States were both at war. Political opportunities for Irish nationalist mobilization grew accordingly.

In general, after every step forward in Ireland, Irish social movements became less transnational. Later waves of nationalist protest introduced elements absent from the first. In 1879-1884 and in 1916-1922, Irish conspiratorial brotherhoods swelled and masses mobilized to win real though limited concessions from the British government. In one case they achieved serious agrarian reforms and in another an Irish Free State. While the first wave of transnational Irish protest was utterly defeated, succeeding waves allow us to see how transnationalism declined in response to nationalist advance.

The foundation of the Irish Free State provides an exemplary case. The adaptation of transnational Irish nationalist movements to the creation of a semi-autonomous Irish "state" involved the definitive abandonment of institutionalized claims to a transnational identity. Such an outcome followed from the IRB's own premises. Irish nationalists everywhere were committed to principles of democracy and to the centralized state form of organization. As the struggle for Irish independence progressed, concern centered on acquiring an electoral base and political allies in Ireland. The need to deal authoritatively with British governmental leaders meant that social movement mobilization was no longer the exclusive concern of movement leaders (who were becoming statesmen).

As a result, Irish nationalism shed its transnational character starting at the top, not the bottom. The reconfiguration of Irish nationalism, which involved the subordination of the transnational movement to elected representatives in Ireland was not due to the erosion of base-line personal contacts linking Ireland and the United States. Continued mass migration between Ireland and the United States and the continued efforts of Irish-American organizations to integrate migrants into the nationalist community allowed nationalists to maintain close ties with their native land.

As long as mass migration continued to link the nations of the Irish emigration, first-generation Irish immigrants were typically leaders of Irish-American transnational movements. The primitive tools of the mid-nineteenth century transportation revolution enabled a strong transnational movement to sustain itself. While the 1850s marked the crest of Irish emigration to the United States, it was followed by decades of mass migration larger than anything in the pre-famine period (see table 4.1). Irish-American nationalists may have been ignorant of events in Ireland but, if so, it was not due to the lack of witnesses, first-hand reports, or personal contacts. Succeeding waves of immigrants provided a rich field of recruitment for nationalist organizations and, by enlisting these newcomers, these organizations could sustain a personal network of contacts in Ireland. Irish-American migrants did not have as high a return rate as other migrant groups. Only about one in every ten migrants returned, but many maintained personal contact with kin and friends in Ireland. Between 1848 and 1900 the North American Irish sent back around $260 million dollars to Ireland: about 40 percent of this took the form of prepaid tickets to America. In the end, continually bringing over kith and kin from Ireland maintained personal ties with the homeland almost as effectively as cell phones and jet planes (Miller 1985: 357).

The integration of Irish immigrants into an American-Irish nationalist movement was strongly facilitated by fraternal organizations. The largest single Irish fraternal organization in the United States, the Ancient Order of Hibernians, originated as a Catholic mutual aid society, and long supported the cause of Irish independence. They allowed the Clan na Gael to recruit at their functions (Light 1985). In New York City, Irish immigrants often joined local organizations such as sport clubs based on the Irish county from which they came. These organizations commonly provided aid to their country of origin and kept in close contact with immigrants from the home county (Ridge 1996). With such a variety of organizations in the field and with its headquarters in New York, Clan na Gael leaders could easily ascertain political conditions or even an individual's personal credentials back in Ireland.

Irish-American nationalism represented a way of retaining ties to the old country and sometimes served as a means of advancement in America. A good example of the power of Irish nationalism in urban machine politics can be seen in Chicago in the 1880s. The city was a stronghold of a Clan na Gael faction that opposed John Devoy's New York-based organization and, in the 1890s, carried out its own bombing campaign in England. The head of the local Clan commanded community support and was a power to be dealt with. Irish politicians responded by giving the Clan serious patronage privileges. Michael F. Funchion's study of the Chicago Clan poses the question "whether the Clan in Chicago was a truly Irish nationalist organization or simply a political tool. The answer lies somewhere in between these extremes" (Funchion 1975: 9).

The election of the Democrat Woodrow Wilson as president in 1912, the U.S. declaration of war in April 1917, a year after the Easter Rebellion, and the enunciation by Woodrow Wilson of the "right to self-determination of nations" among his fourteen points suddenly gave Irish-Americans new opportunity to exert leverage. Entirely unsuccessful at Versailles, Irish-American nationalists mobilized most effectively at home to influence Irish affairs. In June 1919, Joseph Tumulty, Wilson's private secretary, warned the president that: "the Irish are united in this matter and in every large city and town are carrying on propaganda, asking that Ireland be given the right of self determination" (Tumulty 1921: 403). Wilson's failure to get the issue raised at Versailles, provoked the FOIF to campaign against Wilson's League of Nations. Many Irish nationalists rejected the League's charter, which forbade any nation to provide aid to internal revolutions in member countries. After the League's defeat, its chief opponent in the Senate, William Borah cabled the Clan na Gael leader, Daniel Cohalan, that it was the "greatest victory for country and liberty since the revolution, largely due to you" (O'Grady 1967:82).

Irish-American political concern increased in 1919 because Ireland was hovering on the edge of full-scale revolt. The postwar Irish crisis had originated in the prewar era. In 1912, the appeal to "physical force" first returned to the center of Irish politics with the Ulster Protestant Unionists, who responded to bills for home rule with threats of violence, gunrunning, and the formation of the Ulster Volunteer Force in 1913. In response, Irish nationalists organized their own volunteer organizations and their own gunrunning. In such a climate the IRB inevitably grew. Local activists played an important role in its revival, and the Clan na Gael sent Tom Clarke, one of Devoy's most trusted lieutenants, to assist in the IRB's revitalization. In 1914, the IRB had only 2,000 members but they were deployed in strategic places in all major nationalist organizations.

The pressure building up during the war in Ireland and in the wake of the Easter Rebellion of 1916 exploded in late 1918 when Sinn Féin, a party identified with the rebels of 1916 and the demand for an independent republic, triumphed. The Irish MPs elected on the Sinn Féin ticket announced that they would not participate in the British Parliament, and set up their own independent legislative body, the Dail Eireann. Claiming to represent the people of Ireland, they elected Eamon de Valera president of Ireland.

Even in Ireland, however, Irish-American political influence played an important role in promoting the republican cause. The British fear of organized Irish-American pressure weakened their campaign against Irish rebellion. Between April 1916 and April 1917, as they worked to persuade the United States to enter the war, British politicians were particularly anxious to demonstrate their moderation. Unless moderation was employed, Lloyd George, then minister of munitions, observed: "The Irish-American vote will go over to the German side, The Americans will break our blockade and force an ignominious peace on us, unless something is done even provisionally to satisfy America" (Ward 1969:113). Diarmuid Lynch, sentenced to death in 1916, was saved by his U.S. citizenship. The early release of the rank and file of combatants was also part of an effort to conciliate the United States. Releasees Harry Boland, Cathal Brugha, and Michael Collins formed the core of the restructured IRA.

Later on in 1919, with Ireland on the brink of civil war, Irish-Americans worked to convey to the Irish people the deep support that republicanism had in the United States, sometimes exaggerating their influence. In March 1919 the U.S. House of Representatives overwhelmingly passed a resolution demanding that the peace conference "consider the claims of Ireland to self-determination." Under pressure from the U.S. peace delegation, English authorities allowed representatives of the American Commission for Irish Independence to tour Ireland in April 1919. The U.S. ambassador in London reported that the delegation "missed no opportunity of stating that they represented over 20,000,000 American people, all ready to help to their utmost in assisting Ireland to achieve its objective—such as an Irish Republic" (Tansill 1957: 306, 314).

However important the Irish-American contribution to Irish revolution, the 1918 election had begun the process of reconfiguring Irish nationalist organizations and ending the partnership role of transnational organizations in the nationalist movement. IRB members had often been suspicious of electoral politics, but the establishment of an independent Irish parliament, the Dail Eireann, made abstentionism patently nonviable. In 1916, the IRB set up its own provisional government which claimed to represent the Irish people. In 1919 the Dail Eireann made the same claim. Could Irish nationalists reconcile these competing claims? The Irish Civil War that began in 1922 stemmed from some nationalists' refusal to break their republican oaths and to recognize a compromise Irish Free State, even one which had been endorsed by the Irish electorate. In 1919, as in 1922, many agreed with Ernie O'Malley who reminded his fellow republican militants "that we had never consulted the feelings of the people. If so, we would never have fired a shot. If we gave them a good strong lead, they would follow" (O'Malley 1990: 25). In 1919, in a significant political triumph, Michael Collins, head of the IRB, persuaded the Brotherhood to yield its claim to represent Ireland to the Dail (Coogan 1993: 19-20). Had Collins not been able to do so, the republican cause would have lost much support in both Ireland and America. As a result, while the IRB remained a potent force in republican politics, it was no longer as predominant. Sinn Féin and the IRA became the decisive political forces within the embryonic Irish state.

This new configuration of Irish nationalism soon made itself felt in the Irish diaspora when Irish political leaders sought to subordinate Irish-American organizations to the elected leaders of the Irish Republic. Early in his presidency, de Valera left for the United States where he spent fourteen months between October 1919 and December 1920. Although de Valera was successful in fundraising, his visit dealt a serious blow to Irish-American nationalist organizations. De Valera blundered from one political debacle to another but his ignorance of U.S. politics and inexperience were not the key issues. Fundamental was de Valera's assertion of his right, as president of the Irish Republic, to set the direction of Irish nationalism in the United States. Devoy and Cohalan resisted de Valera's claims. In the short run, the enormous prestige enjoyed by de Valera as the head of an Irish state made opposition difficult, and de Valera's supporters soon established a new Clan na Gael which accepted his leadership. In the long run, however, Devoy and Cohalan were correct that Irish Americans would not support organizations controlled by Irish politicians.

More painful for Devoy and Cohalan was the decision of the IRB to stand by de Valera's actions. In 1920, the IRB announced a break in its relationship with Devoy and Cohalan's organization. Here again, the new realities of Irish politics played a decisive role. In the midst of the Anglo-Irish Civil War, the IRB could hardly break with the elected head of the Irish state over American issues. Later, Michael Collins would disavow de Valera's claims of leadership of the American movement and regret his assertions of supremacy. But at the time, national political necessities were determinant and unity among Irish revolutionaries within Ireland was more important than unity among nationalist brotherhoods across the diaspora (Coogan 1990: 192-193).

In both the issue of the IRB's recognition of the sovereignty of the Dail Eireann and his support of de Valera's American mission, Michael Collins made political decisions that were vital to the success of the Irish revolution, but that undermined the foundations of Irish nationalism as a transnational movement. Collins's deep personal commitment to transnationalism only underlines how strong the pressures were in this direction. While the realignment of Irish nationalist organizations need not have been so brutal, transnational Irish social movements would inevitably have had to accommodate themselves to the political decisions of the Irish nation and, in some degree, subordinate themselves to national concerns as expressed by an Irish democracy.

To summarize, an examination of two waves of Irish nationalist militancy between 1858 and 1922 shows that transnational social movements and deterritorialized migrants are not recent creations, and that post-World War II communications and transportation revolutions were unnecessary for the building of strong transnational social movements. In an era of great-power rivalry and large-scale war making, transnational social movements did not threaten the state system. Not only is there no necessary connection between transnational movements and transnational outcomes but, in the case in point, Irish republican brotherhoods bitterly opposed the foundation of the League of Nations, the most important attempt to establish an international political order in that period. A look at the IRB also suggests that students of transnational movements should not concentrate singlemindedly on the "unbounded" or "borderless" character of migrant populations. However porous it may be for migrants, when a border demarcates regions of unusual political opportunity or marks the crossing into a rival state, it may still turn out to be crucial to their mobilization. Irish immigrants passed easily into Australia, Canada, Great Britain, and the United States, yet the United States was crucial to republican nationalists because of its position as a rising republican power outside the framework of the British Empire and the Commonwealth.

CONTEMPORARY IRISH TRANSNATIONAL MOVEMENTS

A quick look will show that a perspective on nineteenth- and early-twentieth-century transnational movements can help in analyzing contemporary transnational movements. In the 1970s and 1980s, Irish-Americans re-created transnational movements that helped to bring Britain to the bargaining table with Irish rebels. Basic movement dynamics changed little over the last century; in an age of electronic media, the foundation of Irish transnational social movements are rooted in the personal ties of first-generation migrants.

In the 1960s, the resurgence of protest in Northern Ireland found no serious transnational organizations in the field. Although well-known Irish political activists attempted to rally Irish-Americans and prominent Irish-American politicians voiced strong views on Irish politics, networks of obscure Irish immigrants played the predominant role in the creation of contemporary transnational movements. While the electronic media was important in keeping Irish Americans informed (and sometimes misinformed) about events in Northern Ireland, in creating sympathy for Northern Irish Catholics, and in suggesting new movement tactics, successful Irish transnational movements were built on roughly the same foundations and employed the same methods as in the nineteenth century. Electronic devices are no substitute for personal networks and intimate ties.

Media did play an important role in the revival of long-dormant Northern Irish social movements. The 1922 settlement that created an Irish Free State also established a Protestant-dominated Northern Ireland, part of the United Kingdom, with a parliament in Stormont. Irish republicans condemned both the Free State and "partition" but were defeated in a bloody civil war in 1922-1923. Although rooted in the post-World War II period, the formation in 1967 of the Northern Ireland Civil Rights Association (NICRA) to fight against job and housing discrimination, gerrymandered electoral districts, and the repressive Special Powers Acts, first attracted considerable worldwide attention. Inspired at least in part by the U.S. civil rights movement, NICRA activists sang "We Shall Overcome" and the January 1969 march from Belfast to Derry was modeled on Martin Luther King's Selma march (Purdie 1990, Ruane and Todd 1996: 274). Later in the 1960s Northern Irish activists were influenced by the student radicalism of Berkeley, Paris, and Berlin, but Irish activists had little first hand knowledge of U.S. events. In turn, early U.S. movements to support the Northern Irish civil rights' struggles had only tenuous connection to Northern Irish politics (Wilson 1975, Murray 1975).

In the 1960s and 1970s, except for rituals around St Patrick's day, Irish and Irish-American political leaders had practically no personal contact, and Irish-American political leaders had few ties to the relatively small Irish-American migrant community. Lack of coordination led to political misjudgments unthinkable in earlier generations. U.S. supporters of the Northern Irish struggle were taken unaware by the Irish movement's fast leftward evolution. Billed as a civil rights activist, Bernadette Devlin's 1969 U.S. tour was a blow to U.S. supporters of Northern Irish civil rights who were engaged in mainstream politics. Delighting members of the student movement, Devlin initially refused to meet with Chicago's powerful Mayor Daley and denounced him as a "fascist pig." She called on Irish-American workers to support a "socialist republic," courted the Black Panthers, and denounced the organizers of her tour for their hopeless conservatism. Unsurprisingly, her tour did not consolidate broad

U.S. support for a "civil rights" movement and did not radicalize the Irish-American community.

Similarly, in the early 1970s, Senator Edward Kennedy's call for immediate British withdrawal from Northern Ireland echoed traditional Irish-American political rhetoric but was no longer an option advocated by those moderates in Northern Ireland or in the Republic who were Kennedy's natural allies. Irish-Americans' demands for immediate British withdrawal from Northern Ireland, a demand modeled on that of the contemporary U.S. anti-Vietnam war movement, tingled spines in Dublin where the prospect of suddenly being given control of the six counties represented a worst-case scenario. A half-century of deindustrialization had made Northern Ireland a "workhouse economy." High unemployment, increasing poverty and the rising cost of armed occupation and repression represented a considerable drain on the British economy (£1.2 billion in 1982-83, by a conservative estimate) and an impossible one for an Irish economy (O'Malley 1990: 89).

The Irish Northern Aid Committee (NORAID), founded in 1970, the first genuinely transnational social movement of the new wave, was followed by others such as the Irish National Caucus (INC), as well as by clandestine organizations involved in gunrunning. Interestingly, Irish transnational movements were less sympathetic to the American-inspired civil rights' orientation than to traditional republican politics. NORAID leaders made little effort to "radicalize" Irish Americans but, drawing on the traditional rhetoric of Irish republicanism, publicized conditions in Northern Ireland and aided the families of those imprisoned by the British. Although NORAID leaders denied supplying the IRA weapons, it recruited from an immigrant population, some of whom turned to gunrunning in the late 1970s and early 1980s (Holland 1987).

The emergence of NORAID illustrates the crucial role of personal ties in transnational mobilization even in an age of mass media. As Sidney Tarrow has suggested, television may be successful in depicting stories of injustice but personal ties still supply the all-important context and trust (Tarrow 1998). This is doubly true if movements are engaged in illegal actions or liable to government repression. In the 1970s, Irish tourism boomed as Irish-Americans returned in search of roots, and vivid TV reports on British atrocities in Northern Ireland generated funding and political support for transnational movements. Yet the formation of a genuine transnational movement replicated the story of nineteenth-century Irish nationalism—except on a smaller scale due to the declining migrant tide (see table 4.1). Migrant communities nurtured and led both public protest groups such as NORAID and secret organizations supplying the IRA with weapons, and thus resembling the IRB or the Clan na Gael (Weintraub 1975, 1979; Wilson 1995).

As in the nineteenth century, first-generation migrants were the lifeblood of contemporary Irish transnationalism. At its inception, the key organizers of NORAID, men like Michael Flannery, were products of the last great wave of Irish migration, that of the 1920s, when many republicans, disillusioned with the Free State, had emigrated. Their reputation and continuing contacts with Irish republican veterans allowed them to serve as intermediaries. In the 1950s and 1960s, Irish emigrants relied on the same institutions as their predecessors to preserve community ties. Both public and secret transnational movements emerged within a familiar framework of migrant institutions. Organizations such as the Ancient Order of Hibernians were still in existence. Newspapers like the *Irish Echo* and the *Irish Advocate* targeted Irish immigrants. And Irish radio shows such as those on WMJM in Philadelphia and WARD in New York provided information about community-wide events. Although the American Catholic Church had become less sympathetic, in 1973 a Catholic bishop appeared publicly with Ruiairi O'Bradaigh, a spokesman for the provisional IRA. And Irish migrants generally still moved to established Irish-American neighborhoods. In New York City, this included Norwood in the northern Bronx, Woodside and Sunnyside in Queens, and Bayridge in Brooklyn. A network of neighborhood bars and construction companies helped to preserve migrants' contacts (Ridgeway and Farrelly 1994; Clark 1991). Our knowledge is fragmentary, but all accounts suggest that contemporary activists in Irish-American transnational movements are predominantly working and lower middle class, reflecting the composition of the recent migratory tide, not that of the modern Irish-American population (see interviews with NORAID supporters in Clark 1997).

A comparison of modern Irish transnational movements with past movements underlines the continuing importance of migrants' personal ties to the homeland. The migratory wave that brought sisters, brothers, nephews, and parents to the United States enabled Irish migrants to keep in touch with events via loved ones and close acquaintances. Relatively primitive communicative tools backed by mass migration sufficed to build strong transnational organizations. Certainly, in the modern world, cell phones and frequent jet-powered return trips help to renew personal contacts but, given mass chain migration and the persistence of immigrant networks, the added effect of modern technological changes may be only marginal.

CONCLUSION

A look at contemporary transnational movements and the prospects of transnational outcomes in the context of past movements indicates that deterritorialized migrants and transnational social movements are not new and that the communications revolution of the post-World War II period has had less impact on social movements than suggested. Also, in contrast to much of the contemporary globalization literature, no persuasive link can be established between transnational movements of the type discussed in this chapter and the probability of transnational outcomes. While challenging the British Empire, nineteenth- and early-twentieth-century Irish transnational movements did not challenge the competitive sovereign state system. Today in Northern Ireland, there is some reason to be more optimistic about the possibilities for a genuine transnational solution, not because of the character of social movements but because of the political environment in which they operate. If real transnational outcomes emerge in Northern Ireland, involving the fragmentation of the authority of the omnicompetent state and the creation of jurisdictions crosscutting state boundaries, it will be in the face of opposition from Irish transnational movements which seek a united sovereign Ireland. Although touching on larger issues requiring a more extended discussion, let us quickly note that the heightened possibility of transnational outcomes today derives not from the character of movements but from the evolution of the European state system. The formation of the European Union (EU), a new transnational governmental structure, and the end of military competition among European nations created a new environment in which nations are more willing to envision transnational arrangements. As in the nineteenth century, modern Irish transnational movements have been powerful forces for change in Northern Ireland. But the character of this change will be chiefly determined not by the structure of social movements, but by the character of the state system in which they exist.

REFERENCES

Amos, Keith. 1988. *The Fenians in Australia, 1865-1880*. Kensington: New South Wales University Press.

Appadurai, Arjun. 1996. *Modernity at Large: Cultural Dimensions of Globalization*. Minneapolis: University of Minnesota Press.

Bagenal, Philip H. 1892. *The American Irish and Their Influence on Irish Politics*. London: Kegan Paul, Trench & Co.

Basch, Linda, Nina Glick Schiller, and Cristina Szanton Blanc. 1994. *Nations Unbound: Transnational Projects, Postcolonial Predicaments, and Deterritorialized Nation-States*. Luxembourg: Gordon and Breach Science Publishers.

Clark, Dennis. 1991. *Erin's Heirs: Irish Bonds of Community*. Lexington: University of Kentucky Press.

———. 1997. *Irish Blood: Northern Ireland and the American Conscience*. Port Washington, N.Y.: Kenniket Press.

Comerford, R.V. 1985. *The Fenians in Contest: Irish Politics and Society 1848-82*. Dublin: Wolfhound Press.

———. 1987. "Patriotism as Pastime: The Appeal of Fenianism in the Mid-1860s." Pp. 21-32 in *Reactions to Irish Nationalism*. London: Hambledon Press.

Coogan, Tim Pat. 1990. *Michael Collins*. London: Arrow Books.

———. 1993. *The IRA, A History*. New York: Roberts Reinhart.

Danforth, Loring M. 1995. *The Macedonian Conflict: Ethnic Nationalism in a Transnational World*. Princeton, N.J.: Princeton University Press.

Dommanget, Maurice. 1972. *Histoire du premier mai*. Paris: Editions de la Tête de Feuilles.

Duncan, Perry M. 1981. "The Macedonian Cause: A Critical History of the Macedonian Revolutionary Organization," Ph.D dissertation, University of Michigan.

Funchion, Michael F. 1975. "Irish Nationalists and Chicago Politics in the 1880's." *Eire-Ireland* 10(2): 3-18.

Harvey, David. 1989. *The Condition of Postmodernity*. Oxford: Blackwell.

Holland, Jack. 1987. *The American Connection: U.S. Guns, Money, and Influence in Northern Ireland*. New York: Viking Books.

Knobel, Dale T. 1986. *Paddy and the Republic: Ethnicity and Nationality in Antebellum America*. Middletown, Conn.: Wesleyan University Press.

James, Winston. 1997. *Holding Aloft the Banner of Ethiopia: Caribbean Radicalism in America, 1900-1932*. New York: Verso.

Light, Dale B. Jr. 1985. "The Role of Irish-American Organizations in Assimilation and Community Formation." *Irish Studies* 4: 113-142.

McAdam, Doug. 1996. "Conceptual Origins, Current Problems, Future Directions." Pp. 23-40 in *Comparative Structures on Social Movements: Political Opportunities, Mobilizing Structures and Cultural Framings*, Doug McAdam, John D. McCarthy, and Mayer N. Zald, eds. Cambridge: Cambridge University Press.

McCaffrey, Lawrence J. 1996. "Forging Forward and Looking Back." Pp. 213-233 in *The New York Irish*, Ronald H. Baylor and Timothy J. Meagher, eds. Baltimore: Johns Hopkins University Press.

McNickle, Chris. 1996. "When New York Was Irish, and After." Pp. 337-356 in *The New York Irish*, Ronald H. Baylor and Timothy J. Meagher, eds. Baltimore: Johns Hopkins University Press.

Meyer, David S., and Debra Minkoff. 1997. "Operationalizing Political Opportunity." Paper presented at the Annual Meeting of the American Sociological Association.

Miller, Kerby A. 1985. *Emigrants and Exiles: Ireland and the Irish Exodus to North America*. Oxford: Oxford University Press.

Moch, Leslie Page. 1992. *Moving Europeans: Migration in Western Europe since 1650*.

Bloomington: Indiana University Press.

Moody, T.W. 1981. *Davitt and Irish Revolution 1846-1862*. Oxford: Clarendon Press.

Murphy, Craig N. 1994. *International Organization and Industrial Change: Global Governance since 1850*. New York: Oxford University Press.

Murray, Hugh T. Jr. 1975. "The Green and the Red Unblending: The National Association for Irish Freedom, 1972-1975." *Journal of Ethnic Studies* 2(2): 1-22.

Neidhardt, W. S. 1975. *Fenianism in North America*. University Park: Pennsylvania State University Press.

Newsinger, John. 1994. *Fenianism in Mid-Victorian Britain*. London: Pluto Press.

Norman, E. R. 1965. *The Catholic Church and Ireland in the Age of Rebellion, 1859-1873*. Ithaca, N.Y.: Cornell University Press.

O'Broin, Leon. 1976. *Revolutionary Underground: The Story of the Irish Republican Brotherhood, 1858-1924*. Totowa, N.J.: Rowman & Littlefield.

———. 1971. *Fenian Fever: An Anglo-American Dilemma*. New York: NYU Press.

O'Day, Alan. 1993. "The Political Representation of the Irish in Great Britain, 1850-1940." *Comparative Studies in Government and Non-Dominant Minorities* 4(11): 31-83.

———. 1996. "Revising the Diaspora." Pp. 188-215 in *The Making of Modern Irish History: Revisionism and the Revisionist Controversy*, D. George Boyce and Alan O'Day, eds. London: Routledge.

O'Farrel, Patrick. 1987. *The Irish in Australia*. Notre Dame, Ind.: University of Notre Dame Press.

O'Grady, Joseph, ed. 1967. *The Immigrants' Influence on Wilson's Peace Policies*. Lexington: University of Kentucky Press.

O'Malle, Ernie. 1992. *The Singing Flame*. Dublin: Anvil.

O'Malley, Padraig. 1990. *The Uncivil Wars: Ireland Today*. Boston: Beacon Press.

Poulton, Hugh. 1995. *Who Are the Macedonians?* Bloomington: Indiana University Press.

Purdie, Bob. 1990. *Politics in the Streets: The Origins of the Civil Rights Movement in Northern Ireland*. Belfast: Blackstafff Press.

Ranelagh, John O'Beirne. 1988. "The Irish Republican Brotherhood in the Revolutionary Period, 1879-1923." Pp. 137-156 in *The Revolution in Ireland, 1879-1923*, D. G. Boyce, ed. London: Macmillan.

Ridge, John T. 1996. "Irish County Societies in New York, 1880-1914." Pp. 275-300 in *The New York Irish*,. Ronald H. Baylor and Timothy J. Meagher, eds. Baltimore: Johns Hopkins University Press.

Ridgeway, James, and Patrick Farrelly. 1994. "The Belfast Connection; Money and Munitions from New York Are Helping the IRA Lay Siege to London: The New Triangle Trade," *Village Voice*. February 8.

Ruane, Joseph, and Jennifer Todd. 1996. *The Dynamics of Conflict in Northern Ireland: Power, Conflict and Emancipation*. Cambridge: Cambridge University Press.

Schiller, Glick, Linda Basch, and Cristina Szanton Blanc. 1992. *Towards a Transnational Perspective on Migration: Race, Class Ethnicity, and Nationalism Reconsidered*. New York: New York Academy of Sciences.

Slattery, T. P. 1968. *The Assassination of D'Arcy McGee*. Toronto: Doubleday.

Smyth, Jim. 1992. *The Men of No Property: Irish Radicals and Popular Politics in the Late Eighteenth Century*. London: Macmillan.

Spain, Edward K. 1996. "Union Green: The Irish Community and the Civil War." Pp. 193-212 in *The New York Irish*, Ronald H. Baylor and Timothy J. Meagher, eds. Baltimore: Johns Hopkins University Press.

Tansill, Charles Callan. 1957. *America and the Fight for Irish Freedom 1866-1920*. New York: Devin-Adair.

Tarrow, Sidney. 1998. "Fishnets, Internets and Catnets: Globalization and Transnational Collective Action." Pp 228-244 in *Challenging Authority: The Historical Study of Contentious Politics*. Michael Hanagan, Leslie Page Moch, and Wayne te Brake, eds.

Minneapolis: University of Minnesota Press.

Tilly, Charles. 1995. "Globalization Threatens Labor Rights." *International Labor and Working Class History* 47: 1-23.

Tumulty, Joseph. 1921. *Woodrow Wilson as I Knew Him*. Garden City, N.Y.: Doubleday.

Vassady, Bela. 1982. "The 'Homeland Cause' as Stimulant to Ethnic Unity: the Hungarian-American Response to Karolyi's 1914 American Tour." *Journal of American History* (fall): 39-66.

Ward, Alan J. 1969. *Ireland and Anglo-American Relations, 1899-1921*. London: Weidenfeld & Nicolson.

Weintraub, Bernard. 1975. "I.R.A. Aid Unit in the Bronx Linked to Flow of Arms." *New York Times* December 16, A1.

————. 1979. "Spilt among Irish-Americans Said to Cut Funds to I.R.A." *New York Times* September 7, A7.

Wilson, Andrew A. 1975. "The American Congress for Irish Freedom, 1967-1970." *Eire-Ireland* 29(1): 61-75.

————. 1995. *Irish American and the Ulster Conflict, 1968-1995*. Washington, D.C.: Catholic University of America Press.

Chapter 5

CONSERVATION TSMOs: SHAPING THE PROTECTED AREA SYSTEMS OF LESS DEVELOPED COUNTRIES

Tammy L. Lewis

Conservationists contend that biodiversity must be protected to preserve the global "heritage of mankind" (UNESCO 1972). This claim justifies the actions of transnational conservation organizations that cross political borders to promote the establishment of protected areas and national parks in less developed nations. How do transnational social movement organizations (TSMOs) choose where to pursue protection strategies? Are transnational actors effective at shaping national conservation policies? Based on a comparison of TSMOs' involvement in Ecuador, Peru, and Chile, I argue that transnational actors are most likely to mobilize efforts and influence conservation policies in nations that have open political structures and well-established nongovernmental organizations.[1]

In an age of "globalization" when faxes and e-mail ease cross-national communication, examination of social movements must move beyond the nation state as a unit of analysis to address the interactions of a growing number of transnational actors operating at the level of "global civil society" (Keck and Sikkink 1998; Lipschutz 1996; Lipschutz and Conca 1993; Princen and Finger 1994; Smith, Chatfield and Pagnucco 1997; Wapner 1996). Concepts such as political opportunity structure, which have been used to analyze the timing and outcomes of national social movement organizations' actions, are being extended to understand how the international arena shapes movements. Recent scholarship identifies the need for understanding how the global political system shapes national political opportunity structures and national social movements (Jenkins 1995; McAdam 1996; Smith 1995, 1997; Tarrow 1996).

The interaction between the international system and the national system is multidirectional. National events influence international events, and vice versa. This analysis takes a step toward understanding one piece of the complex entanglement: the way in which national political opportunity structures shape TSMOs' willingness to enter certain nations.

This study also attempts to extend the analytic concepts used in the comparative studies of movements and states to Latin America, a geographical region rich with social movement activity. Cross-national work has made considerable strides in understanding the role of the state in constraining and encouraging social movements in Europe (Jenkins and Klandermans 1995; Kitschelt 1986; McAdam, McCarthy, and Zald 1996; Rucht 1989). Studies of Latin America note that as the region shifts toward democracy, "the diversity of resistance and collective struggles has expanded dramatically" (Haber 1997: 129) to include such "new" movements as environmentalism (Eckstein 1989; Escobar and Alvarez 1992). Some Latin American states, weakened by neoliberal economic pressures and severe debt, in periods of uncertainty and instability brought about in the process of democratic transitions, may be increasingly vulnerable to the demands of national and international movement forces (see essays in O'Donnell, Schmitter, and Whitehead 1986; Pagnucco 1996).

The transnational environmental industry appears to have a different dynamic than other transnational movements, especially human rights. Smith (1997: 57) hypothesizes that "transnational movement organizations will form around issues for which national political opportunity structures are relatively closed, or for which purely national solutions are inappropriate." Case studies by DeMars (1997) on humanitarian organizations, and Coy (1997) and Pagnucco (1997) on human rights, support Smith's hypothesis. However, analysis of the transnational conservation movement, a subset of the transnational environmental movement, suggests that this claim is not valid for all transnational movement sectors. Conservation organizations can affect both state policies and the private sector through the establishment of private conservation areas. Human rights protection, by contrast, has no private dimension; it must be addressed by the state.

Transnational conservationists view their selection process as a pragmatic, rational approach to producing results. Often, political variables override biodiversity status. For example, the worst off politically (such as Democratic Republic of the Congo and Ivory Coast, both biodiversity hotspots) are bypassed in favor of assisting partners in nations that are open and contain organizations that are already working for conservation (such as Costa Rica and Botswana, neither of which are biodiversity hotspots). The consequence of this is that TSMOs may not be collaborating with partners in nations that are most in need of help from a biodiversity perspective. TSMOs engage in a form of lifeboat ethics, whereby possible "survivors" are brought on board the conservation lifeboat while other countries are left to drown. While public aid agencies have been blamed for promoting uneven development, TSMOs that follow similar patterns of interaction may be contributing to uneven conservation. Transnational human rights efforts seek to raise the bar for those at the bottom; transnational conservation actions contribute to increasing differences in biodiversity protection. If these trends continue, we can expect a growing gap between ecologically protected and ecologically depleted nations.

THE TRANSNATIONAL CONSERVATION MOVEMENT

Like transnational organizations for human rights, women's rights, and peace, transnational conservation organizations are growing both in numbers and strength (Smith 1997: 48). As an issue, conservation has generated cross-boundary concerns since the 1972 United Nations' Conference on the Human Environment in Stockholm. It has led to the establishment of transnational organizations, the enactment of three major pieces of international legislation, as well as a number of nonbinding international efforts, including the 1992 Convention on Biological Diversity.

Conservation TSMOs share the belief that the loss of biodiversity is a global problem that can be ameliorated through the protection of land. They base their actions on the work of conservation scientists who predict that biodiversity loss will be one of the greatest global problems of our era (Myers 1994). Examples of conservation TSMOs include the World Wildlife Fund (WWF), Conservation International (CI), and the Nature Conservancy (TNC). Of these, each have headquarters in the Washington, D.C. area, have partner organizations in other nations, are not for profit groups supported by private donations, and fund and implement conservation projects around the world.[2]

The dominant strategy to protect biodiversity is to establish protected areas, such as national parks, in less developed countries (LDCs) (WRI et al. 1992; IUCN 1990). Transnational organizations transfer funds to their partners in LDCs through grants and innovative mechanisms such as debt-for-nature swaps. In a swap, a transnational organization buys a portion of a developing country's debt in exchange for a commitment to environmental projects and establishing a "conservation trust fund." This reduces the developing country's foreign debt and provides funding for the conservation and management of protected areas, usually channeled through a nongovernmental organization in the developing nation. In the period from 1987 to 1992, twelve nations were the recipients of twenty-two transnational debt-for-nature swaps. Debt-for-nature swaps provide an illustration of how an aspect of the international economic condition—level of external debt—structures TSMOs opportunities for engagement. Nations that are unable to repay their debt are considered bad bets for swaps; countries that are ably paying back their debt do not appear to need assistance; those in the middle are most often targeted for swaps. McAdam (1996) suggests that research on movement opportunities needs to be more attentive to the international system in this way.

In terms of conservation interests, transnationals target LDCs because they contain many plant and animal species and high rates of endemism. This is one of the "great ironies of conservation": nations rich in biological diversity are the least able to protect it because they are poor (McNeely 1991). Eighteen "biodiversity hot spots" contain 20 percent of the planet's plant species in only 0.5 percent of the land surface of the earth (Myers 1988, 1990, 1994).

KEY COMPONENTS TO EFFECTIVENESS

This study tries to explain two aspects of TSMOs' activities: how they choose nations to work in and their levels of effectiveness. To understand effectiveness, the analysis focuses on the establishment of policies and practices that improve conservation. A rich and extensive literature differs on how to define and measure social movement "success" or "effectiveness" and why some social movements succeed while others fail (Gamson 1975; Goldstone 1980; Huberts 1989; Jenkins and Brents 1989; Jenkins and Klandermans 1995; Kitschelt 1986; McAdam et al. 1996; Rucht 1989; Smith et al. 1997; Tarrow 1989). Definitions of success range from organizational accomplishments, such as membership growth, to legitimacy issues, such as having a movement's ideas accepted into mainstream life, to political aspects, such as influencing policymakers to change policies. TSMOs have influenced domestic policies on issues such as human rights (Brysk 1993; Sikkink 1993) and indigenous rights (Brysk 1996) in Latin America. They have also succeeded in shaping the funding decisions of more developed nations for development projects (Payne 1995) and in transmitting ideas to national leaders that were "causally consequential for the end of the cold war" (Risse-Kappen 1994: 213). In the following sections, the literature that examines the broader transnational environmental movement and its role in shaping the choices of nation-states will be highlighted (Keck and Sikkink 1998; Rothman and Oliver, this volume; Schwartzmann 1991).

Both program directors of conservation TSMOs and social movement theory suggest that two variables are key to understanding TSMO engagement and effectiveness in a nation: (1) the degree of political openness, and (2) the pre-existence of conservation actors.

Transnational conservationists indicate that the most desirable nations in which to implement projects are democratic and politically stable.[3] Political criteria even outweigh biodiversity criteria. For example, one director commented that despite the Congo's tremendous biodiversity, its political instability and perceived levels of corruption would prevent his organization from working there because efforts in such countries do not yield results. This corresponds to nationally oriented social movement theories.

The multidimensional concept of "political opportunity structure" (POS) has been used to explain both of the dependent variables in this study: the entry of social movement actors into a period of engagement and levels of social movement success (Jenkins and Klandermans 1995; McAdam et al. 1996). Definitions of the concept vary among studies though most include the following four subvariables: (1) openness or closure of polity, (2) stability or instability of political alignments, (3) presence or absence of alliances, and (4) division among elites that might provide more tolerance to protest (Tarrow 1989). POS is multidimensional and captures a wide array of variation in the political system. The concept reflects conservationist concerns in choosing appropriate locations for activity.

POS has been a key framing tool for comparing national level social movements cross-nationally. In particular, the distinction between "open" and "closed" political systems has been emphasized in a number of important cross-national studies. Kitschelt's (1986) comparison of antinuclear movements in France, Sweden, the United States, and West Germany and Rucht's (1989) comparison of the environmental movement in West Germany and France both found that "political openness" contributed to social movement organizations' success. For Rucht and Kitschelt, openness is a function of how possible it is for organizations to participate formally in political procedures. Closed systems provide fewer institutionalized means for grievances to be heard. Smith et al. (1997) suggest that this national process does not translate to the mobilization of transnational organizations, though conservationists suggest it does. Another aspect of the open/closed dimension that is relevant to effectiveness is that states with open structures are usually less able to enact policy (i.e., are weaker), because of their decentralized access points, while closed states are often more able to implement policies due to their centralization of power (i.e., are stronger) (Kriesi 1995, Payne 1995, Risse-Kappen 1994).[4]

A number of theorists have been developing an expanded notion of the concept of POS to encompass international structures (Pagnucco, 1995, 1996; Smith 1995; essays in Smith et al. 1997; Tarrow 1998). Smith (1995) and Pagnucco (1995) apply POS at the international level to understand the opportunities of transnational organizations. This work differs from theirs in that, rather than try to understand the international political opportunity structure, I try to understand how transnational organizations react to the national political opportunity structures. Nonetheless, one must acknowledge that the international POS affects the national POS. TSMO research illustrates the "nested" nature of the political opportunity structure: "Local political opportunity structures are embedded in national political opportunity structures, which are in turn embedded in international political opportunity structures. These nested structures create the possibility for very complex patterns of relationships among actors" (Rothman and Oliver in this volume: 117).

Two examples from the transnational environmental movement illustrate how national governments are vulnerable to the international system. Much has been written about the successful partnership between North American and Brazilian NGOs in the creation of "extractive reserves" in Brazil for the use of rubber tappers (Keck and Sikkink 1998). The chain of activity in this and cases like it is complex: A TSMO, the Environmental Defense Fund, in collaboration with local social movement groups from Brazil, lobbied the U.S. Senate Appropriation Committee which, in turn, convinced an international lender, the Inter American Development Bank, to suspend payments on a road project in the rubber tappers' region of the Amazon until environmental conditions were met (Schwartzman 1991). Keck and Sikkink (1998) point out that part of the success of this type of strategy is that international organizations have leverage with national governments. Thus, "[T]ransnational networking help[s] to amplify local demands by resituating them in different arenas with more potential allies" (Keck and Sikkink 1998: 144; see also Tarrow 1994: 195-196). Elsewhere in Brazil, similar processes have taken place. Rothman and Oliver (this volume) demonstrate how mobilization for the anti-dam movement changed in the period from 1979 to 1992 as a result of a number of factors, including linkages between local and international groups and shifts in national politics from authoritarianism to democracy. Again, a consortium of Northern and Southern NGOs pressured both the U.S. Congress and the World Bank to temporarily withdraw loans from the Brazilian government's program to build proposed dams on the basis of their negative social and environmental consequences (Rothman and Oliver 1999). These two examples show how national governments may be more responsive to TSMO concerns when TSMOs are able to bring issues into the international arena. Conservationists have not often used this strategy.

A second key variable that transnational conservationists and movement scholars have identified to understand transnationals' engagements and their levels of success is the degree to which domestic social movement organizations already work in the issue area, with more established social movements providing better conditions for transnationals (Brysk 1993; Sikkink 1993). This corresponds with work on human rights. In a comparison of the human rights networks in Argentina and Mexico, Sikkink (1993) argues that an "international issue network" makes a difference in whether or not governments formulated and followed human rights policies, however external pressure was not enough. "Because domestic human rights NGOs are a crucial link

link in the network, where these groups are absent . . . international human rights work is severely hampered" (Sikkink 1993: 435).

Directors of conservation programs also see national NGOs as a crucial link.[5] To them, NGOs symbolize democracy and civil society. They perceived greater opportunities in Latin America than in Africa because Africa has less of an NGO tradition. When NGOs are absent, transnationals' only choice is to work with the government. They prefer not to do this. The best NGO partners were well respected with political connections. Transnational conservation organizations look for domestic NGO allies much like domestic movement organizations seek alliances in the domestic sphere (allies are one of the four subcategories in Tarrow's [1989] POS scheme).

In the empirical analysis, I evaluate the following proposition: Transnational social movement organizations are more likely to *engage* in activities and *succeed* in influencing policies and practices in nations that have open political systems and social movement actors than in nations with closed political systems and few social movement actors. Table 5.1 summarizes the expected relationships.

The relationship between the transnational organizations and domestic conservation policies and practices are explored through a comparative study of Ecuador, Chile, and Peru from the 1970s to the 1990s. These nations are similar in that they contain areas classified as biodiversity hot spots. They differ in terms of the history of their domestic policy structures, strength of domestic NGOs, conservation policies and practices, and presence of transnational conservationists. Conservation transnationals have worked most extensively in Ecuador and least extensively in Chile. However, the degree of interaction has varied in these nations over time as the domestic political structures have changed.[6] The cases illustrate the interrelationships between political openness, NGO presence, and TSMO engagement and effectiveness.

Table 5.1. **The Relationship between POS, Existence of National NGOs, and TSMO Willingness to Engage in a Nation's Politics**

Existence of National NGOs	Political Opportunity Structure	
	Closed	*Open*
Absent	TSMOs least likely to engage or succeed	TSMOs likely to foster development of NGOs
Present	TSMOs unlikely to engage; difficult for NGOs to "officially" emerge	TSMOs least likely to engage or succeed

CASE LEVEL EVIDENCE

Ecuador: High Level of Transnational Interaction

Ecuador boasts the highest percentage of land protected of any nation in the world (39 percent). Its protected area system is best known for the Galapagos National Park, established in 1959. Since that time, Ecuador's protected area system has grown tremendously through the addition of fifteen conservation units primarily in its Andean and Amazonian regions.

Domestic Political Structure. Most of the land conserved in Ecuador's protected area system was declared protected by the nationalist military government in the period from 1972 to 1979 by "inter-ministerial accord" (WCMC 1992). During this period, Freedom House rated Ecuador in the range from "partly free" to "not free."[7] On the input side, the regime was closed, but in terms of its ability to enact policies, it was strong. The military took over in 1972 to "transform oil returns into reform and development" (Anderson 1990: 35). The military's conservation actions were largely focused on the petroleum-rich region of the Amazon.[8] In Ecuador, over 50 percent of the state's budget is generated by oil extraction (EIU 1993). It is likely that the military was motivated more by economic goals than ecological ones given that these areas were not sufficiently protected.

Ecuador shifted from a closed and strong state to an open, fragmented, and weak one when the military ceded power to the civilian government in 1979 and Ecuador's status changed to "free." The fifteen parties of the constitutional, democratic government provided many points of entry, but they held limited power to establish and execute policies.

The civilian government inherited a number of "paper parks." Paper parks exist in law, but they receive little to no funding, have few guards, and lack demarcated boundaries. Illegal economic activities such as mining and logging also routinely take place in paper parks. The government is often responsible for resource extraction in parks, providing licenses for mangroves to be felled in a coastal park, and permitting oil extraction. Mining is present in five protected areas, and six of the national parks have commercial logging (WCMC 1992) despite the Forestry and Wildlife Law of 1981 which prohibits petroleum exploration and other forms of extraction within the protected area system.[9] In many cases, the policies of resource extraction agencies, such as the Ministry of Energy and Mines, are in conflict with the policies of the agency in charge of protected areas. The former agencies' policies usually take precedence (WCMC 1992), the latter having "little importance, . . . [and] virtually no power to interact and negotiate with other Government agencies" (GEF 1994: 2). In addition to the government's willing exploitation of these areas, funding was not assured to the park system because of the state's other economic priorities, including external debt. So, despite its seemingly impressive system, the military left the civilian government a protected area system that was in shambles.

NGO Presence. Social movement organizations have been influential in convincing the government to take policy actions in relation to protected areas. Fundación Natura (FN) is Ecuador's oldest, largest, and most respected conservation organization. Founded in 1978, FN received the majority of its early funding from USAID (Fundación Natura, n.d.). Since the mid-1980s, when FN was one of only a handful of environmental organizations in Ecuador, there has been tremendous institutional growth; today there are hundreds of environmental NGOs. Part of this growth is a response to local environmental damage, including oil contamination in the Amazon and deforestation in the western region of the country. However, much of the NGO growth was spurred by an influx of transnational investment in Ecuador's biodiversity.[10] This complicates the analysis since TSMOs did not respond solely to a group of organizations that had emerged without transnational support but to organizations that had been supported by conservation "network" actors, such as USAID. A second critical event that contributed to the growth of NGOs was that the government changed the rules for registering as an NGO, making it easier for organizations to be officially recognized as nonprofit groups. This legitimized NGOs and encouraged engagement in the political process.

Transnational Organizations. TSMOs have had a measurable impact on the amount of land protected and on the quality of the protection in Ecuador. Since Ecuador's military era, the international conservation network has supported NGOs and governmental agencies that work for conservation. In 1991, Ecuador ranked fifth in the world in the amount of funding it received for biological diversity research and conservation projects from public and private donors in the United States, receiving $4.5 million in that year alone (Abramovitz 1994). The private recipients of these funds have, in turn, been agents for adding areas to the protected area system and in managing the system. TSMOs have selected "competent" NGOs to work with and through, "competence" being judged in part by the organizations' prior contact with the international network. For example, in the case of FN, the conservation network— specifically USAID—had provided considerable support to build FN's institutional capacity. Prior network contacts gave NGOs legitimacy and affected TSMOs' choices. In other cases, when organizations were needed to take on tasks specifically required for international financial transfers, such as biological inventories required as part of the debt swaps, the network helped establish new organizations with these capacities. This happened with EcoCiencia, an NGO that broke off from FN shortly after the debt swap.

Two recent examples of TSMOs' interactions in Ecuador illustrate the manner in which transnational organizations have shaped and are shaping domestic conservation policies through domestic NGOs. First, in 1987 and 1989, two transnational organizations—the Nature Conservancy and World Wildlife Fund—initiated two swaps in Ecuador which generated $10 million dollars in local currency to establish and manage protected areas. Funds are channeled through the transnationals' associate, FN, for its own uses and for distribution to other domestic NGOs. The swap funds are used, in part, for protecting and managing protected areas and for acquiring small nature reserves of extraordinary biological diversity. Parks included in the program are Galapagos and Yasuní, and the Pasochoa Nature Reserve.

These swaps have two important effects: (1) they support the management of parks that had been paper parks; and (2) they contribute to shifting responsibility away from the government to private organizations by channeling funding through domestic NGOs rather than through the government agency in charge of managing protected areas. Even though the government was not taking responsibility for having a management program in all of its parks, the transnationals, by way of NGOs, shaped the government's policies by enforcing protection as a condition of the swap. The government had not been attending to protected areas; presently domestic NGOs are— with the support of transnational organizations. The transnationals are thus contributing to the "bifurcation" of political spheres discussed by Rosenau (1990).

A second example also demonstrates how TSMOs affect government policy via domestic NGOs. In 1991, the domestic NGO Fundación Antisana (FUNAN) was organized in Quito with the sole purpose of establishing a protected area around the Antisana volcano. Funding for FUNAN came almost exclusively from the Nature Conservancy. After three years of preparing scientific justifications for establishment, researching property rights, acquiring private land, and lobbying government officials, this organization succeeded in its task. In 1991, the Ecuadorian government declared Antisana an ecological reserve and FUNAN entered into a joint government-NGO agreement that allowed them to manage the area. This would not have occurred without transnational support. Current funding for the management of the reserve comes in large part from the Nature Conservancy. Domestic NGOs were again the key link between the transnationals and changes in the states' conservation actions. A consequence is that public lands are being privately managed. Another strategy of protection further contributes to the privatization of biodiversity. TSMOs are increasingly seeking the establishment of private parks, bypassing the state altogether by supporting organizations, such as Fundación Maquipucuna, which has purchased land to establish the private Reserva Maquipucuna. In cases such as this, public interest groups are taking over state functions.

The director of an umbrella organization for Ecuadorian environmental organizations stated, "The presence of international organizations is absolutely necessary in Ecuador. They obligate the government to act." Ecuador has been the recipient of a large amount of assistance from the international conservation network. TSMOs in the network have chosen well in choosing Ecuador. Its open government and strong NGO presence (supported through prior contact with the network) have contributed to transnational organizations successfully meeting their goals of establishing new protected areas (public and private) and improving the management of existing parks.

Chile: Low Level of Transnational Interaction

Chile falls at the other end of the spectrum from Ecuador. The international conservation network has not engaged in Chile in a noticeable way, nor have transnationals influenced Chilean park policies. Chile has received very little aid from the international conservation network.[11] The closed political system and the lack of conservation organizations account for much of the transnationals' distance from Chile.

Chile's protected area system has developed more autonomously than Ecuador's. The first park was established in 1907, one of the first in South America, and the system is famous for Easter Island and the national park Torres del Paine near Antarctica. Unlike the trends in Ecuador and Peru in which the majority of protected area units were established after 1972, Chile had a number of parks by this time.[12] Nonetheless, Chile's protected area system has grown in the period from 1972 to 1993: twenty new areas were added to the system (although the percentage increase of land protected was relatively small—2.4 percent, 2 million hectares). During the 1970s and 1980s, Chile was viewed as a leader in conservation; international leaders declared Chile's protected area system the "best system in Latin America" (Castro 1989: 53). Relatively speaking, Chile's parks are well managed. The protected areas are not paper parks: CONAF, the agency charged with managing parks, has a budget of around US$2.4 million annually and employs twenty-five professionals, seventy maintenance and administrative employees, and 340 guards (Ormazábal 1994: 9, 18). The parks are demarcated and have ample infrastructure, including a five star hotel in Torres del Paine.

Despite this, the system has a number of common problems. The state's commitment to the system has been inconsistent. Since the 1980s, yearly budgets for the park service has been decreasing due to macrolevel economic changes. In addition, despite Chile's prior star status, the World Conservation Monitoring Centre reports, "Infringement of protected areas by private timber and mineral companies is a major problem. . . . Areas designated for protection are often also designated for other incompatible uses by other government institutions" (WCMC 1992). Resource-led economic development has moved Chile into the economic spotlight, but at a cost to environmental conservation (Clapp 1998).

Domestic Political Structure. From 1973 to 1990, General Pinochet's military government ruled Chile. Freedom House rated Chile as "partly free" and "not free" throughout the military era.[13] During that period, Chilean citizens had limited access to the political process and were discouraged from joining together in collective action. Chile's system was "closed"—citizens did not have access to the government or the right to free speech (see Garretón 1986, Oppenheim 1993). Chile was also shut off from the international conservation dialogue that was emerging as the popularity of environmentalism grew. Conservation NGOs did not emerge during the 1980s as they did in other Latin American nations, and consequently transnational support did not follow. Another structural limitation in opportunity has been the absence of institutional incentive for philanthropy: Chile's tax structure does not encourage charitable contributions.[14]

Despite the lack of contact with the international conservation network, during the democratic years of the early 1970s prior to Pinochet's rule, Chile did receive transnational assistance to its protected area system. The UN's Food and Agriculture Organization supported a project in Chile to establish scientific management plans and establishment plans for its protected area system. The Chilean military government used its strength to follow out the FAO plan in the 1980s. The state operated autonomously, using the guidance provided by FAO's study.

NGO Presence. Political repression limited the development of NGOs and as a result, the conservation NGO sector in Chile is considerably weaker than Ecuador's or Peru's. When TSMOs explore Chile as a possible nation to work in, it does not look promising. Only one Chilean organization is focused on conservation. Comité Nacional Pro Defensa de la Fauna y Flora (CODEFF), the oldest environmental group in Chile (officially recognized in 1968), has very little influence with the government, and unlike the dominant conservation organizations in Ecuador and Peru, does not have name recognition in the general public. Even before Pinochet, Chile's civil sector was considered weak (Garretón 1986). NGOs are not afforded much respect in the Chilean political culture in general. A former director of Chile's park system described environmental NGOs as groups of "young, idealistic and opinionated students who offer no solutions, only criticisms." Unlike Ecuador where NGOs assist in park establishment and management, in Chile, the state operates autonomously.

Transnational Organizations. Chile is far less connected to the transnational conservation community than either Ecuador or Peru. Of the "big three" U.S.-based transnational conservation organizations (TNC, WWF, and CI), only WWF supports a project in Chile, and it is small. None of them have regional offices in the nation and their Washington, D.C., headquarters were unable to supply me with conservation contacts or names of Chilean NGOs. Chilean park officials comment that international funding has never been influential in Chile's park system. NGOs in Chile believe that they have been unable to get the attention of the international conservation network because the network has demonstrated a bias toward protecting tropical forests, not temperate forests (the forest type identified in Chile as a hotspot).

Another reason transnationals have looked elsewhere is that Chile appeared financially successful. Its relative success kept transnational organizations from using the debt-for-nature swap because they could not get the "biggest bang for their buck." The irony is that Chile has managed its very high debt, in part, by cutting back on government spending, including funding for protected areas, and by selling state-owned corporations. These strategies have lowered Chile's debt and improved its position in the international financial community (EIU 1994a: 40). The unintended consequence is that, unlike other South American countries that used their debt problems to broker debt-for-nature swaps, Chile could not attract potential swappers because its debt was never significantly discounted on the secondary market. Even if a swap had been financially feasible, there were few nongovernmental institutions with the capacity to manage it.

With the recent opening of the political structure, private reserves have been established through Fundación Lahuen, an NGO founded in 1991 by a group of North Americans and Chileans. Lahuen uses the Nature Conservancy's strategy of buying land and establishing private reserves. Others are also attempting to use this private strategy. Doug Tompkins, former CEO of Esprit, the clothing company, has bought 270,000 hectares of land with which he intends to create the world's largest private natural park. Though a 1994 law was written to encourage this type of action, the government has contested Tompkins's motives. The government's attack on Tompkins raises a complex question about the rights of foreigners to protect land in Chile. Interestingly, the government has not raised the same question about the rights of foreigners to extract natural resources. In the same period that Tompkins purchased his land, Trillium Corporation from Bellingham, Washington, purchased 625,000 hectares to cut trees to produce wood chips for export. The government is subsidizing Trillium with a tax holiday and subsidized workers (Larraín 1995). The juxtaposition of Tompkins and Trillium suggests that protected area policies are not just about land conservation, but they represent key resources to states concerned with economic development. Having private organizations manage state lands may be acceptable (since the state still has rights to the lands), but allowing private organizations to purchase resource-rich lands raises issues regarding the control of resources.

The transnational actors that were such a strong force for conservation in Ecuador were far weaker, and almost absent, in Chile. In Chile, international support in the 1970s built on the strengths of the existing protected area system, and FAO's plan provided a blueprint for the military government to follow in the 1980s. During the military period, domestic NGOs did not emerge. Chile's relative economic success, "tropical forest deficiency," closed political structure, and missing NGO link have kept TSMOs out of Chile in the 1980s and 1990s. This is changing, however, as the political structure opens (currently Freedom House rates Chile as "free") and as Northerners, in particular, become more involved in Chile's private parks.

Peru: Medium Level of Transnational Interaction

The case of Peru is very similar to the case of Ecuador with some notable exceptions. Both nations have received a great deal of transnational support and have witnessed growth in their environmental movement sectors in the last ten years. However, unlike Ecuador, Peru does not have a large protected area system to boast about. Transnational agents have been thwarted by the state and work even more directly with NGOs than in Ecuador. NGOs are moving into state territory, literally, in that they have taken on the management of protected areas. The responsibility has shifted markedly from the state to private citizens in "civil society." While this shift provides short-term solutions for protected area management concerns, there are no assurances of long-term support for these groups by transnationals. The conditions of support are not solely in the hands of the NGOs, but they also rely on state stability and openness, factors which are outside the control of NGOs.

Peru's protected areas system is small, and has not changed much over the last twenty years. Depending upon which sources are used, the percent of land protected ranges from 2.1 to 4.3 percent, below the South American average of 6.4 percent, and below Ecuador's 39 percent and Chile's 18 percent. It is also below average in terms of the amount of land protected in an absolute sense; Peru has protected only 4 million hectares. Its most famous areas are Machu Picchu (established in 1981), which is better known for its human history than for its biodiversity, and Manú National Park (established in 1973), in the high-biodiversity Amazonian region of the country.

The dominant feature of the state's management of the protected areas is its lack of administrative capacity. The state agency in charge of the system (INRENA) is severely underfunded. Its 1994 budget, $278,690, falls short of the $10 million operating budget recommended by a national commission (Ministerio de Agricultura 1995), and barely pays the salaries of the Lima staff (who have only three-month contracts), let alone being sufficient to hire and train park guards or build infrastructure. Like Ecuador, Peru contains a number of paper parks. Only four of Peru's national parks receive management; the other areas have no permanent management personnel (GEF 1995). Members of Peruvian NGOs underscored INRENA's lack of stability and institutional continuity by noting that INRENA calls NGOs for information, such as maps of the protected areas. As in Ecuador and Peru, the agency's staff are institutionally constrained in that resource extraction is permitted to take place in protected areas with the approval of the relevant ministries (USAID 1995).

Domestic Political Structure. Since 1968, Peru's government shifted from military rule (1968-1980, Freedom House's "not free" to "partially free"), to democratic rule (1980-1992, "free" to "partially free"), to authoritarian rule (1992, "partly free"), and back again to what observers call "pseudo-democracy" (1993-present, "partly free"). With each change came a shift in Peru's relationships with influential countries and with international financial institutions. Peru has suffered from high external debt ($21 billion in 1990) and failure to honor its debt commitments (EIU 1994b). The International Monetary Fund and private banks have repeatedly attempted to institute strategies to cut state funding (Conaghan and Malloy 1994). Peru's instability in the eyes of the international financial community shaped transnational conservation organizations' interactions in Peru (for a discussion of Peru's relationship with international banks see Cotler 1986 and essays in McClintock and Lowenthal 1983).

As in Ecuador and Chile, the military government in Peru established a large proportion of the areas protected (eight of twenty-two). A former chief of the protected area system believes the military established these areas out of a sense of pride: "They wanted to leave their mark on history. The period from 1972 to 1979 was the golden age for the establishment of protected areas. We had a strong government with a sense of patrimony, and they were efficient." The military government left its mark on paper, if not on the ground with infrastructure, boundaries, or guards. Since that time, the fiscal crisis of the state has kept Peru from effectively managing its paper park system.

NGO Presence. A number of capable conservation organizations operate out of Lima and have taken on the state's task of managing protected areas. Like Ecuador's Fundación Natura, Peru has a dominant conservation organization, ProNatura (formerly Fundación Peruana para la Conservación de la Naturaleza) which receives the majority of its funding from U.S. TSMOs. In 1994, ProNatura received more than six times INRENA's budget to manage protected lands and alone accounted for 60 percent of the public and private funding for protected areas.[15] ProNatura currently has projects in five of the nation's seven national parks. In Manú National Park, for example, ProNatura and APECO, another NGO, both have management and education programs.

Transnational Organizations. The transnational conservation network worries that Peru's biodiversity will be lost forever if it is not properly managed. From the United States alone, Peru received two million dollars in 1989 for conservation and two and a half million in 1991 (Abramovitz 1994). However, many organizations in the broader conservation network have been frustrated by their efforts to work in Peru. The World Wildlife Fund attempted a 3 million dollar debt-for-nature swap in Peru but were unable to successfully broker it because of Peru's debt problems and its poor position in the international economy. A representative from WWF commented, "At that time Peru was not exactly on great terms with the international community. So it is understandable that they would be very apprehensive. . . . As it turned out we never did a swap there because the Peruvian government could never decide on what terms they wanted to offer, then the auto-coup [the "self-coup" of President Fujimori when he dissolved the congress], and [there were] all kinds of problems. So we put our concern somewhere else." Peru's political instability was, in part, brought about by debt politics. The international political opportunity structure and domestic structure were tightly woven.

With the return to greater democratic stability, two of the leading TSMOs, WWF and CI, have now established field offices in Lima. Their efforts are focused primarily on improving the management and classification of existing areas.[16] Former chiefs of the protected area system direct both of these organizations. When transnationals fund NGOs, they are able to bypass the state bureaucracy while at the same time relying on NGO staff to know the system.

The state's reaction to the growing strength of NGOs has been negative. Jealousies exist between the state and the NGOs that have played out in some public denunciations in the media. The state is in a difficult situation. In renegotiating loans, it has agreed to cut funding of public services, including the environment. The IMF's neoliberal solution to the debt crisis has made it inevitable that, on its own, Peru cannot service its debt and effectively manage its protected areas. Large environmental NGOs, with the help of TSMOs, have filled the gap created by government "downsizing." The state views NGOs not as heroes come to save the planet, but as competitors for the same sources of funds.

In Peru, TSMOs have been thwarted from helping the state establish more protected areas since it does not currently have the capacity to manage its existing areas. Consequently, TSMOs work almost solely through NGOs by supporting their management of protected areas that already legally exist.

IMPLICATIONS

Transnational conservation organizations are most likely to enter the national politics of countries with open political structures and active nongovernmental organizations. Where they enter, they make a difference in conservation policies and practices. Transnationals have contributed to the establishment of national parks and to the management of protected areas by domestic NGOs. These NGOs are a key link in drawing transnationals. As in human rights interactions (Brysk 1993) and transnational feminist interactions (Alvarez 1997), conservation transnationals "amplify" (Brysk 1993) existing national organizations, creating the conditions for continued interactions.

TSMOs' lifeboat strategy is to assist those who have the capacity to help themselves. Conservation TSMOs would prefer to focus solely on biodiversity priorities, but when they are confronted with concrete political constraints and opportunities, they strategically react. As a result, politics often override biodiversity concerns. The unintended consequence is that while possible "survivors" are brought upon the conservation lifeboat, those nations that are biologically rich but politically closed are left to possibly "drown." As TSMOs avoid non-democratic nations, the alternatives for such nations to achieve conservation goals are limited.

In seeking a parsimonious explanation, it is tempting to conclude that TSMOs' entry into nations is dependent on national conditions (political opportunity structure and the density of NGOs). However, the situation is complicated. As is evident in the case of Peru, national POS is tightly linked to a nation's international financial status. Peru's political instability was at least in part brought on by its debt difficulties. The case of Ecuador illustrates how NGO strength is not simply reliant on the domestic factors because Fundación Natura's strength was financed by other conservation-network players such as USAID. Thus, international interactions, in part, shape national political conditions. National political conditions are the proximate, not the ultimate, cause of TSMO's entry. Prior international interaction can prevent or ease TSMO's decisions to enter.

The conservation movement contrasts sharply with the human rights movement in which TSMOs enter where abuses are worst and systems are most closed to domestic actors. Transnational human rights organizations are drawn to repressive regimes where there is "little political space" because it is unlikely that open states have poor human rights records (Coy 1997: 87). Unlike the human rights case, this research suggests that an open POS will allow for mobilization of transnational conservation actors in the same way it can permit the mobilization of local SMOs. Conservation transnationalists target states and nongovernmental actors. In open states, private actors can protect land. Smith (1997: 73) and her collaborators note, "If [TSMOs] see governments as nonresponsive or intergovernmental agencies as too complex or difficult to reach, organizers often choose alternative paths to the changes they seek," such as changing individuals' and economic actors' views and behaviors. A private system of land protection is more viable than a private system of human rights.

While open structures are more inviting to transnational conservationists, open states tend to be weak and without the resources or capacity to carry out policy mandates. Because of this, TSMOs have shifted their target from changing public policy and practices to improving the capacity of private agents to manage public land and promoting the development of private parks. Creating a system of private conservation that parallels and bypasses the state's has been effective in Ecuador, Peru, and other nations in Latin America and Africa (Langholz 1996); however, it presents many possible pitfalls. The dangers are fourfold. First, the public loses access to land and control over its use. While this is often the case even in the establishment of public parks (Akama, Lant, and Burnett 1995; Ghimire 1994; Marks 1984; West and Brechin 1991), in theory citizens can complain to the government and seek change. In private parks, locals who wish to use the land must voice concerns to private groups or individuals who have no obligation to respond to their concerns. While conservationists differ from those for-profit groups involved in privatizing other state activities in that one expects conservationists to act in the public interest, their primary concern is with the preservation of biodiversity and not with public access to land. Second, the public does not necessarily perceive parks as legitimate if they are supported by foreign sources. This may lead to poaching and other uses considered undesirable by conservationists. Related to this, movement opponents may frame parks as foreign-led initiatives even if indigenous NGOs support it. This type of argument surrounded Tompkin's park in Chile and is apparent in other Latin American nations, most notably Brazil, where there is tremendous skepticism over foreign conservation interests in the Amazon. Third, the system of private protected areas is unsustainable as long as it relies on the continuity of foreign funding since political instability may cause donors to flee. Sustainability is subject to the maintenance of a stable and an open political structure to continue receiving foreign funding. Finally, some states resist privatization because it threatens their sovereignty; they favor private management of public lands.

Unlike the transnational environmental and human rights movements, the conservation movement has not used the strategy of appealing to international agents to pressure national governments. The dominant reason is that conservationists' concerns are less threatening and their actions may actually benefit the state financially in the long run. For example, in the cases of Ecuador and Peru, the state had already enacted a policy for protected lands; conservationists' problem was that the policy was not being implemented. Rather than ask the state to make any real changes, the conservationists offered to provide state services through domestic NGOs. This differs dramatically from asking a state not to build a road or a dam. Ironically, rather than counter "economic development" plans, conservationists may be protecting land for future economic development (such as oil and timber extraction), thus doing the state a favor. In the future, conservationists may be less successful in preventing resource extraction in these areas unless states use international funding through organizations such as the World Bank.

National governments' use of international capital has made them more vulnerable to TSMO demands in general. In this chapter, the relationship between states' financial strength in the international arena and their resistance or acceptance of TSMOs' concerns has only been briefly touched upon. Historically, Ecuador and Peru have been far weaker than Chile in terms of their debt burdens and their standing with the International Monetary Fund. Ecuador and Peru's debt conditions (high debt and loan defaults) made them more vulnerable to transnational agents' entry into their politics than Chile.[17] Debt is one leverage point for transnational agents but is not the only way to examine a state's international economic power and vulnerability. Empirical research on international political opportunity structure should systematically examine the relationship between economic crises and state vulnerability to transnational movements and should identify other ways to assess international opportunities. The literature on world systems, dependency, and transitions to democracy provide useful starting points (see for examples O'Donnell 1986 et al.; Walton and Ragin 1990).

Social movement theorists recognize that national social movements are shaped by national political contexts. This study suggests that national political contexts are also a key to determining whether transnational organizations engaged in national conservation policies. It also suggests that national contexts are at least in part shaped by international conditions. Future research should continue to examine where TSMOs engage and where they do not, and to explore whether openings in the political structure trigger entrance of TSMOs in nations whose citizens' claims about their social and ecological problems (i.e., their "grievances") are constant. In an age of globalization, the degree of openness of a nation's political opportunity structure has deeper implications than in a time when states were primarily the targets of national movements. Similarities and differences between transnational movements should also be examined. National civil society is tied to global civil society. If nations in Latin America, Eastern Europe, and elsewhere continue to democratize, the role and influence of transnational organizations in national politics is bound to increase.

NOTES

1. TSMOs are organized actors with members in at least two nations that engage in efforts to promote or resist change beyond the bounds of their national citizenship (see Pagnucco and McCarthy 1992: 125).

2. These organizations work within a broader conservation "issue network" (Sikkink 1993) that also includes intergovernmental organizations and private foundations. Sikkink (1993: 415) defines an international issue network as "a set of organizations, bound by shared values and by dense exchanges of information and services, working internationally on an issue." The network conceptualization differs from that used here and by social movement theorists who problematize the interaction among TSMOs, government agencies, foundations, and elites (see for examples Pagnucco and McCarthy 1992; Smith 1995).

3. Interviews were conducted in Washington, D.C., during 1994-1995 with ten representatives from the transnationals that most actively participate in transnational conservation activity: CI, TNC, and WWF.

4. While the notions of stability/instability and elite division are not treated systematically here, literature in comparative politics suggest that this is a fruitful arena to study especially in the context of Latin America where the transitions to democracy are characterized by uncertainty and instability that may provide opportunities for social movement actors (see O'Donnell et al. 1986). Pagnucco (1996: 15) summarizes Rucht's (1990) division of political opportunity structure into two categories: "(1) formal, institutional, opportunities; and (2) conjunctural or changing opportunities." This analysis focuses on the first type. While the research shows that social movements often emerge during democratic transitions, it is likely that the content of these movements is centered on social and economic issues such as human rights and unemployment rather than environmental issues.

5. NGO and social movement organization (SMO) are used interchangeably.

6. The cases are based on field work and seventy interviews with members of the environmental and conservation organizations in Quito, Lima, Santiago, and Washington, D.C., during 1994-1995.

7. Freedom House compiles an annual report, *Freedom in the World*. A summary of this report from 1972 through 1998 was provided by Leonard R. Sussman from Freedom House.

Amazon, the state secured its control of the region.

9. An unintended consequence of this law is that boundaries to Yasuní National Park have been adjusted a number of times to open areas to oil exploration (Fundación Natura 1993, 44).

10. The amount of resources available from outside sponsors for conservation increased after the first debt-for-nature swap in 1987. This aided the rapid proliferation of environmental organizations. This is a classic example of what resource mobilization theorists would expect.

11. In the period from 1981 to 1988, Chile received only $334,275 from U.S. sponsors (Castro 1989:63). Chile's 1989 funding from the United States for conservation and biodiversity projects totaled only $222,111; and in 1991 this jumped to slightly over $1 million (Abramovitz 1991, 1994). This is meager in comparison to other biodiversity hotspots.

12. Ninety-two percent of Peru's areas and 80 percent of Ecuador's were established after 1972.

13. While the regime was largely closed, it did suffer from periods of economic crisis brought on, in part, by foreign debt. In these periods of instability, the opportunity for protest are increased (Garretón 1986). However, as I argue earlier, it is likely that during such periods, movement attention would be focused more on human rights and economic issues than on environmental ones.

14. Another possible explanation for the lack of a strong conservation movement is that CONAF, the state agency for protected lands, has had a strong and effective hand in managing the protected area system.

15. In the period from 1985 to 1994, ProNatura received almost $6 million for work in protected areas (Ministerio de Agricultura 1995). I was unable to find comparable figures for the state's system as were researchers for the German Aid Agency (GTZ), further illustrating the state's lack of capacity for basic tasks such as recordkeeping.

16. CI's staff is attempting to upgrade the status of Zona Reservada Tambopata-Candamo to national park; however, Mobil Oil has discovered oil in the region and is attempting to get a concession from the state.

17. These conditions also make it easier for profit-seeking groups, such as the IMF, to enter a nation. Based on this, one could hypothesize that a correlation exists between TSMO and IMF engagement in a nation.

REFERENCES

Abramovitz, Janet M. 1991. *Investing in Biological Diversity: U.S. Research and Conservation Efforts in Developing Countries.* World Resources Institute.
———. 1994. *Trends In Biodiversity Investments: U.S.-Based Funding for Research and Conservation in Developing Countries, 1987-1991.* World Resources Institute.
Akama, John S., Christopher L. Lant, and G. Wesley Burnett. 1995. "Conflicting Attitudes toward State Wildlife Conservation Programs in Kenya." *Society and Natural Resources* 8: 133-144.
Alvarez, Sonia. E. 1997. "'. . .And Even Fidel Can't Change That': Trans/national Feminist Advocacy Strategies and Cultural Politics in Latin America." Paper presented at the Mellon Lecture Series, Duke University, Durham, N.C.
Anderson, Joan B. 1990. *Economic Policy Alternatives for the Latin American Crisis.* New York: Taylor & Francis.
Brysk, Alison. 1993. "From Above and Below: Social Movements, the International System, and Human Rights in Argentina." *Comparative Political Studies* 26 (3): 259-285.
———. 1996. "Turning Weakness into Strength: The Internationalization of Indian Rights." *Latin American Perspectives* 23(2): 38-57.
Castro, Iván. 1989. "La Protección Del Patrimonio Ecológico." Santiago, Chile: CONAF.
Clapp, Roger Alex. 1998. "Waiting for the Forest Law: Resource-Led Development and

Environmental Politics in Chile." *Latin American Research Review* 33(2): 3-36.

Conaghan, Catherine M., and James M. Malloy. 1994. *Unsettling Statecraft: Democracy and Neoliberalism in the Central Andes*. Pittsburgh, Pa.: University of Pittsburgh Press.

Cotler, Julio. 1986. "Military Interventions and 'Transfer of Power to Civilians' in Peru." Pp. 148-172 in *Transitions from Authoritarian Rule: Latin America,* G. O'Donnell, P. C. Schmitter, and L. Whitehead, eds. Baltimore: Johns Hopkins University Press.

Coy, Patrick. 1997. "Cooperative Accompaniment and Peace Brigades International In Sri Lanka." Pp. 81-100 in *Transnational Social Movements and Global Politics*, J. Smith, C. Chatfield, and R. Pagnucco, eds. Syracuse, N.Y.: Syracuse University Press.

DeMars, William. 1997. "Contending Neutralities: Humanitarian Organizations and War in the Horn of Africa." Pp. 101-122 in *Transnational Social Movements and Global Politics*, J. Smith, C. Chatfield, and R. Pagnucco, eds. Syracuse, N.Y.: Syracuse University Press.

Eckstein, Susan, ed. 1989. *Power and Popular Protest: Latin American Social Movements*. Berkeley: University of California Press.

EIU (Economist Intelligence Unit). 1993. *Country Profile: Ecuador, 1993/94*. London: Economist Intelligence Unit.

———. 1994a. *Country Profile: Chile, 1994/95*. London: Economist Intelligence Unit.

———. 1994b. *Country Profile: Peru, 1994/95*. London: Economist Intelligence Unit.

Escobar, Arturo, and Sonia E. Alvarez, eds. 1992. *The Making of Social Movements in Latin America*. Boulder, Colo.: Westview Press.

Fundación Natura. n.d. Financiamiento de Actividades.

———. 1993. Ponencias del Ecuador Presentadas en el IV Congreso de Parques Nacionales Y Áreas Protegidas, Caracas, Febrero 1992. Quito.

Gamson, William A. 1975. *The Strategy of Social Protest*. Homewood, Ill.: Dorsey Press.

Garretón, Manuel Antonio. 1986. "The Political Evolution of the Chilean Military Regime and Problems in the Transition to Democracy." Pp. 95-122 in *Transitions from Authoritarian Rule: Latin America,* G. O'Donnell, P. C. Schmitter, and L. Whitehead, eds. Baltimore: Johns Hopkins University Press.

GEF (Global Environmental Facility). 1994. *Republic of Ecuador: Biodiversity Protection Project.* Washington, D.C.: The World Bank.

———. 1995. *Republic of Peru: National Trust Fund for Protected Areas*. Washington, D.C.: The World Bank.

Ghimire, Krishna B. 1994. "Parks and People: Livelihood Issues in National Parks Management in Thailand and Madagascar." Pp. 195-229 in *Development and Environment: Sustaining People and Nature,* D. Ghai, ed. Oxford: Blackwell Publishers/UNRISD.

Goldstone, Jack A. 1980. "The Weakness of Organization: A Look at Gamson's *The Strategy of Social Protest.*" *American Journal of Sociology* 5: 1017-1042.

Haber, Paul Lawrence. 1997. "Social Movements and Socio-Political Change in Latin America." *Current Sociology* 45(1): 121-140.

Huberts, Leo W. 1989. "The Influence of Social Movements on Government Policy." *International Social Movement Research* 2: 395-426.

IUCN. 1990. *1990 United Nations List of Parks and Protected Areas*. Gland, Switzerland: IUCN.

Jenkins, J. Craig. 1995. "Social Movements, Political Representation, and the State: An Agenda and Comparative Framework." Pp. 14-35 in *The Politics of Social Protest*, J. C. Jenkins and B. Klandermans, eds. Minneapolis: University of Minnesota Press.

Jenkins, J. Craig, and Barbara G. Brents. 1989. "Social Protest, Hegemonic Competition, and Social Reform: A Political Struggle Interpretation of the Origins of the American Welfare State." *American Sociological Review* 54:891-909.

Jenkins, J. Craig, and Bert Klandermans, eds. 1995. *The Politics of Social Protest: Comparative Perspectives on States and Social Movements*. Minneapolis: University of Minnesota Press.

Keck, Margaret E., and Kathryn Sikkink. 1998. *Activists beyond Borders: Advocacy Networks in*

International Politics. Ithaca, N.Y.: Cornell University Press.

Kitschelt, Herbert P. 1986. "Political Opportunity Structures and Political Protest: Anti-nuclear Movements in Four Democracies." *British Journal of Political Science* 16: 57-85.

Kriesi, Hanspeter. 1995. "The Political Opportunity Structure of New Social Movements: Its Impact on Their Mobilization." Pp. 167-198 in *The Politics of Social Protest,* J. C. Jenkins and B. Klandermans, eds. Minneapolis: University of Minnesota Press.

Langholz, Jeff. 1996. "Economic, Objectives, and Success of Private Nature Reserves in Sub-Saharan Africa and Latin America. *Conservation Biology* 10(1): 271-180.

Larraín, Sara. 1995. "Desarrollo sustentable...¿Para Quién?" *Ambiente y Desarrollo* XI (1): 59-62.

Lipschutz, Ronnie D. 1996. *Global Civil Society and Global Environmental Governance: The Politics of Nature from Place to Planet.* Albany: State University of New York Press.

Lipschutz, R. D., and K. Conca, eds. 1993. *The State and Social Power in Global Environmental Politics.* New York: Columbia University Press.

Marks, Stewart A. 1984. *The Imperial Lion: Human Dimensions of Wildlife Management in Central Africa.* Boulder, Colo.: Westview Press.

McAdam, Doug. 1996. "Conceptual Origins, Current Problems, Future Directions." Pp. 23-40 in *Comparative Perspectives on Social Movements,* D. McAdam, J. D. McCarthy and M. Zald, eds. Cambridge: Cambridge University Press.

McAdam, Doug, John D. McCarthy, and Mayer N. Zald, eds. 1996. *Comparative Perspectives on Social Movements.* Cambridge: Cambridge University Press.

McClintock, Cynthia, and Abraham F. Lowenthal. 1983. *The Peruvian Experiment Reconsidered.* Princeton, N.J.: Princeton University Press.

McNeely, Jeffrey A. 1991. "Bio-diversity: The Economics of Conservation and Management." Pp. 145-155 in *Development Research: The Environmental Challenge,* J. T. Winpenny, ed. London: Overseas Development Institute.

Ministerio de Agricultura (Instituto Nacional de Recursos Naturales). 1995. "Estratégia del Sistema Nacional de Áreas Naturales Protegidas Del Peru, Plan Director." Cooperación Técnica Alemana (GTZ).

Myers, Norman. 1988. "Threatened Biotas: 'Hot Spots' In Tropical Forests." *The Environmentalist* 8(3): 187-208.

———. 1990. "The Biodiversity Challenge: Expanded Hot-Spots Analysis." *The Environmentalist* 10(4): 243-256.

———. 1994. "Population and Biodiversity." In *Population: The Complex Reality,* S. F. Graham-Smith, ed. London: The Royal Society.

O'Donnell, Guillermo, Philippe C. Schmitter, and Laurence Whitehead. 1986. *Transitions from Authoritarian Rule, Latin America.* Baltimore: Johns Hopkins University Press.

Oppenheim, Lois Hecht. 1993. *Politics in Chile: Democracy, Authoritarianism, and the Search for Development.* Boulder, Colo.: Westview Press.

Ormazábal, César. 1994. "Mecanismos Financieros para Apoyo Sostenible a la Conservación de Áreas Protegidas y de Biodiversidad en Chile." Santiago, Chile.

Pagnucco, Ron. 1995. "The Comparative Study of Social Movements and Democratization: Political Interaction and Political Process Approaches." *Research in Social Movements, Conflict and Change* 18: 145-183.

———. 1996. "Social Movement Dynamics during Democratic Transition and Consolidation: A Synthesis of Political Process and Political Interactionist Theories." *Research on Democracy and Society* 3: 3-38.

———. 1997. "The Transnational Strategies of the Service for Peace and Justice in Latin America." Pp. 123-138 in *Transnational Social Movements and Global Politics,* J. Smith, C. Chatfield, and R. Pagnucco, eds. Syracuse, N.Y.: Syracuse University Press.

Pagnucco, Ronald, and John D. McCarthy. 1992. "Advocating Nonviolent Direct Action in Latin America: The Antecedents and Emergence of SERPAJ." Pp. 125-147 in *Religion and*

Politics in Comparative Perspective, B. Misztal and A. Shupe, eds. Westport, Conn.: Praeger Publishers.

Payne, Rodger A. 1995. "Nonprofit Environmental Organizations in World Politics: Domestic Structure and Transnational Relations." *Policy Studies Review* 14: 71-182.

Princen, Thomas, and Matthias Finger. 1994. *Environmental NGOs in World Politics: Linking the Local and the Global.* London: Routledge.

Risse-Kappen, Thomas. 1994. "Ideas Do Not Float Freely: Transnational Coalitions, Domestic Structures, and the End of the Cold War." *International Organization* 48(2):185-214.

Rosenau, James. 1990. *Turbulence in World Politics: A Theory of Change and Continuity.* Princeton, N.J.: Princeton University Press.

Rucht, Dieter. 1989. "Environmental Movement Organizations in West Germany and France: Structure and Interorganizational Relations." *International Social Movement Research* 2:61-94.

———. 1990. "Campaigns, Skirmishes and Battles: Anti-nuclear Movements in the USA, France and West Germany." *Industrial Crisis Quarterly* 4: 193-222.

Schwartzman, Stephan. 1991. "Deforestation and Popular Resistance in Acre: From Local Social Movement to Global Network. *The Centennial Review* 35:397-422.

Sikkink, Kathryn. 1993. "Human Rights, Principled Issue-Networks, and Sovereignty in Latin America." *International Organization* 47(3):411-441.

Smith, Jackie. 1995. "Transnational Political Processes and the Human Rights Movement." *Research in Social Movements, Conflict and Change* 18:185-219.

———. 1997. "Characteristics of the Modern Transnational Social Movement Sector." Pp. 42-58 in *Transnational Social Movements and Global Politics*, J. Smith, C. Chatfield,and R. Pagnucco, eds. Syracuse, N.Y.: Syracuse University Press.

Smith, Jackie, Charles Chatfield, and Ron Pagnucco, eds. 1997. *Transnational Social Movements and Global Politics.* Syracuse, N.Y.: Syracuse University Press.

Tarrow, Sidney. 1989. *Struggle, Politics, and Reform: Collective Action, Social Movements, and Cycles of Protest.* Ithaca, N.Y.: Cornell University Press.

———. 1994. *Power in Movement: Social Movements, Collective Action,and Mass Politics in the Modern State.* Cambridge: Cambridge University Press.

———. 1996. "States and Opportunities: The Political Structuring of Social Movements." Pp. 41-61 in *Comparative Perspectives on Social Movements,* D. McAdam, J. D. McCarthy, and M. N. Zald, eds. Cambridge: Cambridge University Press.

UNESCO. 1972. "Convention concerning the Protection of the World Cultural and Natural Heritage." Paris.

USAID. 1995. "Environmental and Natural Resource Management in Peru." USAID/Peru.

Walton, John, and Charles Ragin. 1990. "Global and National Sources of Political Protest: Third World Responses to the Debt Crisis." *American Sociological Review* 55: 876-890.

Wapner, Paul. 1996. *Environmental Activism and World Civic Politics.* Albany: State University of New York Press.

WCMC (World Conservation Monitoring Centre). 1992. *1992 Protected Areas of the World: A Review of National Systems.* Gland, Switzerland: IUCN.

West, Patrick C., and Steven R. Brechin. 1991. *Resident Peoples and National Parks: Social Dilemmas and Strategies in International Conservation.* Tucson: University of Arizona Press.

WRI (World Resources Institute), World Conservation Union (IUCN), and United Nations Environment Programme (UNEP). 1992. *Global Biodiversity Strategy.*

Part III

Transnational Diffusion and Framing Processes

Chapter 6

TRANSNATIONAL DIFFUSION AND THE AFRICAN-AMERICAN REINVENTION OF THE GANDHIAN REPERTOIRE

Sean Chabot

> The biggest job in getting any movement off the ground is to keep together the people who form it. This task requires more than a common aim: it demands a philosophy that wins and holds the people's allegiance; and it depends upon open channels of communication between the people and their leaders. All of these elements were present in Montgomery. . . . It was the Sermon on the Mount, rather than a doctrine of passive resistance, that initially inspired the Negroes of Montgomery to dignified social action. It was Jesus of Nazareth that stirred Negroes to protest with the creative weapon of love. As the days unfolded, however, the inspiration of Mahatma Gandhi began to exert its influence. . . . Nonviolent resistance had emerged as the regulating ideal. In other words, Christ furnished the spirit and motivation, while Gandhi furnished the method. (King 1958: 84-85)

With these words in *Stride toward Freedom: The Montgomery Story*, Martin Luther King, Jr. describes how the Gandhian repertoire helped turn a one-day bus boycott into the American civil rights movement. The Gandhian repertoire not only provided a method for mass protest, but it also turned the African-American community's Christian spirit of love into a force of activism. King's words, however, do not address why civil rights activists failed to adopt and implement the Gandhian repertoire on a mass scale before the Montgomery bus boycott in 1955 and 1956. Moreover, they do not indicate how transnational diffusion of the Gandhian repertoire evolved over time.

In the chapter following the above quotation, King discusses his personal "pilgrimage to nonviolence" (King 1958: chap. 6). King's intellectual odyssey, though, is only part of the answer to why and how the African-American community in

Montgomery fostered the ability to apply the Gandhian repertoire en masse. This chapter develops a more comprehensive answer by tracing American responses to the Gandhian repertoire historically, from initial awareness in 1917 to full implementation in Montgomery.

THEORETICAL FRAMEWORK FOR TRANSNATIONAL DIFFUSION

In the past several years diffusion researchers and social movement theorists have finally started to acknowledge each other's insights and apply each other's concepts. McAdam and Rucht (1993) have inspired more explicit attention to diffusion processes in the social movement literature. Following in their footsteps, Soule (1997), for instance, confirms that given the presence of mutual interests and channels of communication, the spread of innovative ideas and practices from transmitters to potential adopters depends primarily on cultural and structural similarity (see also, Strang and Meyer 1993). In particular, she argues that the shantytown tactic applied by the student divestment movement in the United States "spread among colleges and universities with similar size endowments, of roughly the same level of prestige, and of the same institutional type (Soule 1997: 955)." Focusing on the transnational dimension, Giugni (1995, 1998), among others, claims that protest diffuses across borders only if both the transmitting movement and the adopting movement face favorable political opportunity structures in their respective countries (see also, Tarrow 1989, 1994).

At the other side of the dialogue, Valente (1995) and Rogers (1995) have stimulated greater awareness for social movements among diffusion researchers. Both Valente and Rogers emphasize the relevance of concepts like critical mass (Marwell and Oliver 1993) and thresholds (Granovetter 1978) for diffusion between social movements. Responding to their cue, recent work has conscientiously incorporated social movements as essential arenas for diffusion processes. Strang and Soule (1998), for example, deliberately include case studies of social movements to illustrate the sources, structural mechanisms, and cultural processes involved in diffusion within and across geographical entities. Moreover, last year's symposium on "The Social Diffusion of Ideas and Things," edited by Lopes and Durfee (1999), contains two articles dealing specifically with social movement diffusion. Soule (1999) demonstrates that the perceptual context of protest may allow specific tactics to diffuse among social movement groups despite their lack of success and effectiveness. Ayres (1999), on his part, analyzes the impact of the Internet on the dynamics of political contention. The fact that new communication technology has accelerated the global dissemination of information, he points out, does not necessarily facilitate the emergence of sustainable social movements.

Although barriers between the two fields have crumbled, both groups of scholars still take many of the classical assumptions in diffusion theory for granted. Social movement scholars continue to presume that establishing cultural and structural similarity between transmitters and possible adopters is a *prerequisite* for diffusion within and between social movements. By doing so, they underestimate the socially constructed nature of collective identity, exclude agency from their theoretical framework, and fail to distinguish alternative types of diffusion (Snow and Benford 1999: 24-25). Snow and Benford (27-37) break new ground by avoiding some of these pitfalls and analyzing four distinct types of diffusion processes: reciprocation, accommodation, adaptation, and contagion. Yet even they do not question the five stages and two-step mechanism identified by classical diffusion theory.

Classical diffusion theory assumes that diffusion proceeds from stage to stage until an innovation is either implemented or rejected (Ryan and Gross 1943; Katz and Lazarsfeld 1944; Hägerstrand 1967; Coleman, Katz, and Menzel 1966; Rogers 1995). This fundamental assumption holds for diffusion within as well as across national borders. During the initial *knowledge stage*, the potential adopter becomes aware of an innovation for the first time, often through exposure to the mass media. The characteristics of the receiving individual or group, the perceived need for the innovation, the norms of the social system, and previous practice help determine whether initial awareness motivates the potential adopter to seek more information about the innovation in question. After gaining sufficient knowledge, the potential adopter forms either a favorable or an unfavorable attitude toward the innovation at the *persuasion stage*. During this stage, the potential adopter interacts primarily with interpersonal networks (particularly with trustworthy opinion leaders) to learn more about the innovation's positive and negative attributes.[1] On the basis of cognitive knowledge and affective perception, the potential adopter is now mentally prepared to either adopt or reject the innovation during the *decision stage*. The subsequent *implementation stage*, then, involves translating the new idea into actual practice. Applying the new idea in a different context may warrant reinvention and adaptation. And finally, at the *confirmation stage*, the adopting individual or group reevaluates whether the innovation meets expectations, and either decides to prolong or discontinue implementation (Rogers 1995: 161-185; Lionberger 1960).

Classical diffusion theory not only identifies five stages but it also posits that diffusion follows regular laws and patterns:

> At first, only a few individuals adopt the innovation in each time period (such as a year or a month, for example); these are the innovators. But soon the diffusion curve begins to climb as more and more individuals adopt in each succeeding time period. Eventually, the trajectory of adoption begins to level off, as fewer and fewer individuals remain who have not yet adopted the innovation. Finally, the S-shaped curve reaches its asymptote, and the diffusion process is finished. (Rogers 1995: 23; Tarde 1903: 127)

In other words, diffusion either proceeds incrementally until the majority of an adopting group has implemented an innovation or stops when members of the adopting group decide to reject that innovation at one of the five stages. Although recent diffusion studies recognize that adopters may reinvent or adapt an innovation to fit their particular environment, most diffusion scholars still adhere to the basic premises of the classical model (Rogers 1995: 174-180; Valente 1995; Lopes and Durfee 1999).

The classical diffusion model underlying contemporary studies of social movement diffusion is too linear and mechanistic to understand the transnational diffusion of the Gandhian repertoire. Before the African-American community in Montgomery finally implemented the Gandhian repertoire, various activist networks debated the relevance of the Gandhian repertoire for civil rights protest in the United States. Contrary to classical diffusion theory, however, initial awareness of the Gandhian repertoire actually raised obstacles against transnational diffusion instead of leading to widespread persuasion and adoption. Overcoming these obstacles depended on neither a "critical mass" a "threshold," nor established opinion leaders.[2] Rather, it came from small groups of radical activists who experimented with the Gandhian repertoire despite hostile circumstances. These collective trials helped reinvent the Gandhian repertoire and enabled its transplantation from India to the United States. But even after adaptation to American circumstances, it took more than a decade before civil rights activists fully implemented the Gandhian repertoire. Clearly, a theoretical framework for studying why and how the Gandhian repertoire traveled across time and space must account for these kinds of unexpected twists and turns in the diffusion process.

My theoretical framework for transnational diffusion among social movements acknowledges the existence of various diffusion levels, from knowledge to confirmation, but asserts that the transition from one stage to another is uncertain and nonlinear. The next section deals with specifics, for now I highlight my theoretical framework's fundamental building blocks.

In the first place, I emphasize that the knowledge stage often produces two obstacles against transnational diffusion: hyper-difference and over-likeness. Hyper-difference refers to the tendency to exaggerate cultural and environmental differences between transmitters and adopters, while over-likeness reflects the impulse to underestimate the need for adaptation and reinvention (Fox 1997). Obviously, the relevance of these obstacles depends on the particular case of transnational diffusion.

Second, overcoming these diffusion obstacles requires intellectual dislocation and practical relocation. On the one hand, adopting groups must realize, on a mental level, that the innovative repertoire is not only relevant in its original geographical and temporal setting. On the other hand, adopting groups must translate this mental realization into small-scale practical experiments with the new repertoire. During this relocation process, the adopters reinvent the repertoire of collective action to fit their own situation. Far from diluting the original repertoire, reinvention is essential to full implementation by adopting groups that face different temporal and geographical conditions from those faced by the transmitting group (Fox 1997).

And finally, the transition from partial to full implementation (and confirmation) is particularly problematic for transnational diffusion between social movements. While small groups may successfully implement a foreign repertoire on a limited basis, full implementation by a social movement demands mass participation and a favorable external environment. My framework posits that each case study must first verify empirically *that* this transition has taken place and then concentrate on *why* and *how*.

THE GANDHIAN REPERTOIRE AS INNOVATIVE DIFFUSION ITEM

Within social movement theory, the term repertoire generally refers to a limited set of collective action *forms* that a protest group learns, shares, and implements in its interactions with authorities and the public. These forms of contention emerge from previous experiences of struggle, not from abstract ideas or philosophy (Tilly 1995: 26). The Gandhian repertoire, however, did not contribute any new forms of collective action: strikes, boycotts, non-cooperation, and even civil disobedience were already familiar elements of the political landscape before Gandhi became an activist. Nevertheless, the Gandhian repertoire was innovative because it fundamentally transformed the *substance* and *meaning* of these forms of resistance (Sharp 1979).

In contrast to previous struggles, Gandhi's campaigns in South Africa and India illustrated that nonviolent action could be active and militant, instead of passive and submissive. Moreover, Gandhi emphasized that he and his associates engaged in nonviolent direct action *despite* their capacity for violent resistance, not because they were afraid or unable to use violent means. And finally, Gandhi stressed that his ideas were directly based on concrete experiences of struggle, not dogmatic ideology. The Gandhian repertoire, therefore, continuously evolved along with changes in the temporal and spatial context (Gandhi 1999, hereafter, *CWMG, Collected Works of Mahatma Gandhi*). To distinguish the Gandhian repertoire from forms of violent or passive resistance, Gandhi invented the term *satyagraha* and defined it as follows: "Truth (*Satya*) implies love, and firmness (*agraha*) engenders and therefore serves as a synonym for force. . . . [Satyagraha is] the Force which is born of Truth and Love or non-violence . . . (Gandhi 1928: 102)."

At the individual level, the Gandhian repertoire outlined a code of discipline for participants in direct action campaigns. Everyone was supposed to suffer the anger of an opponent without retaliation, avoid the use of insults or any form of violence, willingly submit to arrest or punishment, and obey the orders of group leaders (Bondurant 1971: 39-40). At the strategic and organizational level, the Gandhian repertoire emphasized self-reliance, honorable negotiation with the authorities, self-discipline, and openness in communication (Bose 1947: 175; *CWMG* 76: 4-5; *CWMG* 27: 53-56). Through his journals, books, speeches, and letters, Gandhi encouraged open discourse with followers and critics, particularly on the meaning of satyagraha. And at the most practical level, the Gandhian repertoire stressed several steps that had to precede any campaign involving nonviolent direct action. First, the satyagraha group must try to resolve the injustice through honest negotiation and arbitration. Then, the group must raise public consciousness through publicity and agitation, prepare for mass action by participating in demonstrations, and issue an ultimatum to the authorities. Finally, after these legal attempts at persuasion have failed, the group may initiate nonviolent direct action in the form of a strike, an economic boycott, mass noncooperation, or civil disobedience (Shridharani 1939; *CWMG* 76: 11-14; *CWMG* 20: 303-307).

Although other repertoires contained similar action forms or tactics, the Gandhian repertoire was the first to identify a code of discipline, organizational guidelines, and practical steps aimed at militant and nonviolent direct action on a mass scale. Moreover, the Gandhian repertoire was not only innovative in content but also in flexibility. Instead of protecting his invention, Gandhi encouraged other protest groups to experiment with the Gandhian repertoire in their own historical and geographical environment (Fox 1989). Gandhi himself helped transplant the Gandhian repertoire from the Indian minority's struggle in South Africa to the national independence movement in India. For civil rights groups in the United States, of course, transplantation of the Gandhian repertoire was not quite so simple.

MENTAL BARRIERS AT THE KNOWLEDGE STAGE

American activists became aware of Gandhi around 1917, the year he initiated the first satyagraha campaign in India. World War I provided the context for interest in Gandhi as a leader who perhaps could help save the world from the destructive menace of white imperialism. The most important diffusion channels during the knowledge stage were international correspondence,[3] sermons, speeches, and the American press (both African-American and mainstream). Although information and awareness about Gandhi and the Indian movement spread rapidly during the 1920s and 1930s, few opinion leaders believed that the Gandhian repertoire was directly relevant for the civil rights struggle (Singh 1968; Watson 1989).

Activists fascinated with Gandhi during this initial diffusion period basically divided into three major camps. One camp, represented by the influential National Association for the Advancement of Colored People (NAACP) and African-American intellectuals like W. E. B. Du Bois, admired Gandhi's courageous efforts but considered attempts to apply the Gandhian repertoire in the United States unrealistic at best. The second camp, led by the racially exclusive United Negro Improvement Association (UNIA) and its founder Marcus Garvey, saw Gandhi primarily as a powerful leader of the colored Asian masses and a close partner of the black African masses. This camp gained notoriety and a large following in the early 1920s but quickly faded away after Garvey's exile from the United States in 1927 (Franklin and Starr 1967: 108-112). The third camp, consisting of the Fellowship of Reconciliation (FOR) and religious pacifists like John Haynes Holmes, compared Gandhi to Jesus and presented him as the world's only hope in the universal struggle against injustice. Closely related to all three camps was a small group of Indian exiles, which had come to the U. S. to promote Indian independence and lobby for American pressure on the British government.

These diffusion networks, each connected to the Indian exile network, unwittingly raised two obstacles against the Gandhian repertoire's implementation in the 1920s and 1930s. Unwittingly, because while none of the civil rights networks intended to delay a Gandhian-based social movement, their interactions did exactly that. Public discourse about Gandhi's relevance for civil rights protest oscillated between two extremes, and neither was conducive to the implementation of the Gandhian repertoire in the United States.

On one side, civil rights leaders argued that Gandhi's efforts in India were psychologically important because they illustrated that subordinate groups belonging to the colored races could organize massive resistance against white supremacy.[4] At the same time, however, many of these leaders felt that *hyper-difference* between the two situations and cultures rendered adoption and implementation of the Gandhian repertoire in the United States impossible. W. E. B. Du Bois represented this paradoxical stance well. On the one hand, he greatly admired the efforts of Gandhi and other Indian nationalists.[5] On the other hand, he argued vehemently against modeling African-American resistance on the Gandhian repertoire. In one of his columns, Du Bois claimed that cultural differences between African-Americans and Indians made adoption of the Gandhian repertoire impossible. Fasting, prayer, sacrifice, and self-torture, he declared, had been "bred into the very bone of India for more than three thousand years. . . . [and] would be regarded as a joke or a bit of insanity" by African-Americans in the United States. The reason was that "our culture patterns in East and West differ so vastly, that what is sense in one world may be nonsense in the other (Du Bois 1943: 10)." Like most civil rights leaders, Du Bois believed that the NAACP repertoire of legal agitation and publicity had achieved significant progress and deserved to be continued (Broderick and Meier 1965).

On the other side, religious pacifists tended to exaggerate the similarity between Gandhian methods and Christian nonviolence, thereby underestimating the Gandhian repertoire's uniqueness and the need for reinvention. In 1921, Reverend John Haynes

Holmes delivered a sermon in New York entitled "Who Is the Greatest Man in the World To-day," in which he compared Gandhi with Jesus Christ (Muzumdar 1982). Holmes was a prominent opinion leader within the religious pacifist community, with ties to the NAACP, FOR, and Indian exiles (particularly Muzumdar).[6] Following his lead, many other activists started writing articles on Gandhi's divine personality and the Indian movement's holy war against materialist civilization (Singh 1968; Watson 1989). Although these journalistic efforts increased public awareness of Gandhi and the Indian struggle, the abstract *over-likeness* they created between Gandhi's fight against British rule and Jesus' resistance against Rome actually obstructed diffusion of the Gandhian repertoire from India to the civil rights struggle in the United States. Conscientious religious pacifists assumed that Gandhian ideas and practices applied only to their personal lives, not to mass protest. As Richard Fox observes: "For many U.S. activists in the 1930s, even Christian ones, a Christ-like Gandhi gave no political direction (Fox 1997: 72)."

CONFRONTING DIFFUSION BARRIERS THROUGH INTELLECTUAL DISLOCATION

Not all diffusion efforts during the 1920s and 1930s suffered from the dichotomy between hyper-difference and over-likeness. International travel, scholarly writing, and several organizations contributed to the *dislocation* of the Gandhian repertoire from the confines of Indian culture (hyper-difference) and abstract universalism (over-likeness). The immediate impact of these new insights and personal networks, however, was relatively limited.

Several Gandhian emissaries from India traveled to the United States to eradicate stereotypes about India and Gandhi. In 1929, for instance, C. F. Andrews, Gandhi's close friend and confidant, came for a lecture tour throughout the country. Soon after, Madeleine Slade, Vithalbhai Patel, Bhicoo Batalivala, Kamaladevi Chattopadhyaya, Vijaylakshmi Pandit, and Manilal Parekh (all coworkers of Gandhi) followed in Andrews' footsteps (Muzumdar 1962: 11-12). Toward the end of the 1930s, several African-American leaders decided to see India and Gandhi for themselves, among them Howard Thurman and Benjamin Mays. Thurman was dean of Howard University's chapel and had close ties with the FOR, while Benjamin Mays was dean of Howard University's School of Religion and active in several civil rights organizations. Both had an opportunity to meet with Gandhi in private. To Thurman, Gandhi stressed that the Gandhian repertoire was also relevant to the African-American struggle by noting: "Well, if it comes true, it may be through the Negroes that the unadulterated message of non-violence will be delivered to the world." In response to Mays's queries about mass protest in confrontation with a majority, Gandhi asserted: "I would say that a minority can do much more in the way of non-violence than a majority. . . . I had less diffidence in handling my minority in South Africa than I had here in handling a majority (*CWMG* 68: 234-238; *CWMG* 70: 261-264)." Overall, international travel laid the basis for interpersonal diffusion networks between India and the United States, while the mass media reserved ample column space for sharing the travelers' insights and experiences with a wider audience (Kapur 1992).

Another way to escape the dichotomy between hyper-difference and over-likeness during the 1920s and 1930s was through academic writing. Two books were particularly crucial in this regard. Richard Gregg's *The Power of Nonviolence*, published in 1935, clearly showed that the Gandhian repertoire was indeed applicable in the West and outlined the specific means for doing so. Gregg himself was also an important human bridge between religious pacifists in the United States and satyagrahis in India.[7] The other human bridge was Gandhian activist Krishnalal Shridharani who, in 1939, published *War without Violence, A Study of Gandhi's Method and Its Accomplishments*, a virtual handbook on how to adopt and implement the Gandhian repertoire in a Western democracy like the United States. Together with Haridas Muzumdar, Dr. Syud Hossain and Dr. Anup Singh, he was a member of the second generation of Indian exiles, establishing close interpersonal links with religious pacifists and civil rights activists in the United States (Muzumdar 1962: 13, 27-28).

Finally, several organizations during this period created fertile settings for dislocation of the Gandhian repertoire. These fertile settings included traditional organizations like the NAACP, churches, and universities, as well as less visible organizations like the Highlander Folk School (HFS), the Southern Regional Council (SRC), the American Friends Service Committee (AFSC), the War Resisters League, and the Fellowship of Reconciliation (FOR). Aldon Morris (1984) refers to these less visible organizations as "movement halfway houses," and defines them as:

> group[s] or organization[s] that are only partially integrated into the larger society because [their] participants are actively involved in efforts to bring about a desired change in society. . . . What is distinctive about movement halfway houses is their relative isolation from the larger society and the absence of a mass base. (139)

Despite their lack of mass appeal, movement halfway houses provided valuable resources to civil rights networks, including training, skilled activists, knowledge, media contacts, and experience (140).

During the 1930s, Howard University was perhaps the most important "traditional" organization that contributed to the dislocation of the Gandhian repertoire. Its president, Mordecai Johnson, was convinced that African-Americans should adopt the Gandhian repertoire, while its School of Religion (with Howard Thurman and Benjamin Mays) stimulated serious debate about Gandhi and satyagraha. Howard students responded positively to these role models, and in 1930 two of them, Martin Cotton and Vivian Coombs, put the Gandhian repertoire into practice by refusing to go to the back of the bus during their journey from Philadelphia to Washington, D.C. These personal acts of civil disobedience took place several days after the Salt March started in India (*Baltimore Afro-American* 1930: 3).

Two "halfway houses" were particularly essential for the dislocation process: Highlander Folk School (HFS) and the Fellowship of Reconciliation (FOR). Myles Horton and Don West founded HFS in 1932 as a community where workers and activists could learn about the world they lived in and apply their ideals in an interracial setting without class distinctions (Adams 1975: 35-36). Starting in the 1940s, civil rights activists regularly came to the HFS to take classes, exchange information, and encourage each other to experiment with the Gandhian repertoire. Besides providing a safe haven for civil rights activists, HFS also served as a real-life model for an integrated society (p. 122). On the basis of this model, HFS developed a mass education program that stimulated oppressed African-Americans to find their own answers to daily problems (Morris 1984: 141-157; Payne 1995).

FOR, an interracial organization of Christian pacifists, also facilitated the eventual dislocation of the Gandhian repertoire. Although most of its members initially fell into the over-likeness trap, FOR provided a positive environment for thoughtful discussion of the Gandhian repertoire. Before 1940 these discussions primarily affected individual behavior, but during World War II FOR activists started to realize that real social change depended on confrontational collective action. Due to its pacifist roots, civil rights were not FOR's primary concern. It did, however, share its personnel, knowledge, and experience with civil rights activists—particularly after the civil rights movement's emergence (Morris 1984: 157-166).

RELOCATION OF THE GANDHIAN REPERTOIRE

The rise of Nazism sparked a series of changes within FOR. After a dispute between die-hard pacifists and pragmatic realists, FOR members elected A. J. Muste as executive secretary in August 1940. The radical pacifists, led by Muste, regarded Gandhian nonviolence as a total way of life, while the realist group, which included Reinhold Niebuhr, considered nonviolence strategically irresponsible in the face of Hitler's evil empire. In September 1941, at FOR's annual conference, Muste announced three staff appointments that would have tremendous (but, at that time, unexpected) repercussions for the American civil rights struggle. He nominated James Farmer as race relations secretary, Bayard Rustin as secretary for student and general affairs, and George Houser as youth secretary (Anderson 1997: 68).

As a recent university graduate, James Farmer had already met numerous proponents of Gandhi. At a meeting of the National Negro Congress in 1937, for instance, he heard Mordecai Johnson and A. Philip Randolph speak. And from 1938 to 1940, during his undergraduate studies at Howard University's School of Religion, he established close ties with two African-American leaders imbued with Gandhian philosophy: Benjamin Mays and Howard Thurman (Farmer 1985: 134-135). Thurman became Farmer's mentor and introduced him to the study of Gandhi. He also helped Farmer land a temporary job at the New York FOR, where he explored in detail the Gandhian repertoire (Farmer 1985: 142).

As FOR secretary, Farmer tested the practical relevance of the Gandhian repertoire for civil rights activism in the United States. Disappointed by the lack of progress achieved by the traditional methods of the NAACP and the National Urban League (NUL), he argued that:

> Segregation will go on as long as we permit it to. Words are not enough; there must be action. We must withhold our support and participation from the institution of segregation in every area of American life—not an individual witness to purity of conscience, as Thoreau used it, but a coordinated movement of mass cooperation as with Gandhi. And civil disobedience when laws are involved. And jail where necessary. More than the elegant cadre of generals we now have, we also must have an army of ground troops. Like Gandhi's army, it must be nonviolent. Guns would be suicidal for us. Yes, Gandhi has the key for me to unlock the door to the American dream. (Farmer 1985: 74)

Unlike previous supporters of Gandhi, whose diffusion efforts never surpassed the persuasion stage, Farmer developed an elaborate plan for reinvention and implementation of the Gandhian repertoire. The memo to Muste outlining his specific ideas symbolized Farmer's intellectual transcendence of the hyper-difference and over-likeness barriers:

> From its inception, the Fellowship has thought in terms of developing definite, positive and effective alternatives to violence as a technique for resolving conflict. It has sought to translate love of God and man, on one hand, and hatred of injustice on the other, into specific action. Leading naturally into a study of the Gandhian movement, this quest has been served mightily by the clear analysis in Shridharani's *War without Violence* and by the work of J. Holmes Smith. New vistas have been opened, new horizons revealed. In general terms, we have spoken of the new technique as "nonviolent direct action." . . . Certain social and cultural differences between the United States and India, and certain basic differences between the problems to be dealt with in the two countries, militate strongly against an uncritical duplication of the Gandhian steps in organization and execution. The American race problem is in many ways distinctive, and must to that extent be dealt with in a distinctive manner. Using Gandhism as a base, our approach must be creative in order to be effectual. (Farmer 1985: 355-360)

This statement expressed Farmer's conviction that civil rights groups could apply the Gandhian repertoire without resorting to blind imitation.

Following the Gandhian repertoire, Farmer also proposed an organizational strategy that incorporated all levels of civil rights activism: the mass constituency, the organizers, and the army of satyagrahis (p. 357). Furthermore, as specific adaptation to the American context, Farmer identified three African-American institutions that would help maximize mass involvement in the Gandhian struggle: churches, civic associations, and universities (p. 359). In 1942, after approval of his memo, Farmer founded the interracial Congress of Racial Equality (CORE) in Chicago. Unlike FOR, which concentrated primarily on pacifist issues, CORE exclusively focused on civil rights and racial justice.

Houser and Rustin also became members of CORE, although they never relinquished their FOR membership. Prior to CORE, Houser and Rustin (like Farmer) had established ties with various pacifist, civil rights, and labor organizations (including Norman Thomas's Socialist Party and Randolph's Brotherhood of Sleeping Car Porters). After the creation of CORE, however, Houser and Farmer concentrated on organizing small-scale nonviolent direct action campaigns in Chicago,[8] while Rustin traveled across the country disseminating the Gandhian message through lectures, articles, and nonviolent workshops. Rustin never committed himself exclusively to one activist organization. Besides FOR and CORE, he was involved in Randolph's March on Washington Movement (MOWM), the American Friends Services Committee (AFSC), the War Resisters League (WRL), and various other organizations. Later, at the end of the 1950s and the start of the 1960s, Rustin shared his vast knowledge and experience with the Montgomery Improvement Association (MIA), the Southern Christian Leadership Conference (SCLC), and the Student Nonviolent Coordinating Committee (SNCC) (Anderson 1997: 111-113).

CORE was not the only civil rights organization reinventing the Gandhian repertoire during the early 1940s. In 1941, African-American labor leader A. Philip Randolph decided that the traditional methods of pressuring the American political system were outdated. In contrast to the NAACP and the NUL, he wanted to involve all segments of the African-American community from all sections of the country by initiating a mass march on the capital. He created the March on Washington

Committee as the organizing vehicle for the march and, like Gandhi, emphasized the need for self-discipline among the participants (Garfinkel 1959; Pfeffer 1990). The Roosevelt administration, fearing domestic unrest at a time of international war, eventually conceded to Randolph's demand for opening up the wartime defense industries to African-Americans by signing an executive order. Instead of disbanding his organization after the executive order, Randolph took advantage of the favorable national and international political conditions by expanding its activities in the form of the March on Washington Movement (MOWM). In September 1942, influenced by CORE's direct action campaigns and his friend A. J. Muste, Randolph announced that the MOWM would adopt the Gandhian repertoire (1942: 4-11).

Randolph dislocated the Gandhian repertoire from India by fusing it with the labor movement's familiar sit-down strike and calling it "nonviolent good-will direct action" (Randolph 1943). Moreover, Randolph's reputation as labor leader and atheist illustrated that the Gandhian repertoire was also relevant for those without religious fervor or an absolute commitment to pacifism. Randolph relocated the Gandhian repertoire by specifying the organizational and behavioral prerequisites for mass, nonviolent direct action in the United States. He organized smaller forms of direct actions to provide the African-American masses with training and discipline, and proposed "Negro mass parliaments" to discuss and act on daily problems. Moreover, like Gandhi, he stressed that negotiation would always precede direct action, and declared that every participant was pledged to nonviolence in word and deed (Pfeffer 1990: 658-60). Besides dislocation and relocation, Randolph also brought well-known American Gandhians together. At the "We Are Americans Too!" Conference in July 1943, for instance, Jay Holmes Smith and E. Stanley Jones[9] joined Randolph, Farmer, Rustin, and Houser to discuss ways of implementing the Gandhian repertoire on a mass scale.[10]

Collectively, Farmer, Houser, Rustin, and Randolph made two essential contributions to the African-American community's adoption and implementation of the Gandhian repertoire. In the first place, they enabled the relocation of the Gandhian repertoire from India to the United States. Instead of blindly copying Gandhi's precepts, they creatively reinvented his guidelines and methods by adapting them to the contemporary American context. And in the second place, they shared their expertise and practical experience with the next generation of civil rights activists. Although African-American leaders during the late 1950s and early 1960s received most of the acclaim for their application of the Gandhian repertoire, it was the core group of Gandhians in the 1940s (led by Randolph, Farmer, Rustin, and Houser) who first experimented with the Gandhian repertoire. Without this intergenerational transfer of ideas and practices, transnational diffusion of the Gandhian repertoire would have ended with the small-scale trials during the 1940s, not the civil rights movement.[11]

TRANSNATIONAL DIFFUSION IN ABEYANCE

Classical diffusion theory's S-curve predicts that more individuals will adopt an innovation in each succeeding time period, particularly after experimentation and adaptation (Rogers 1995: 23). This case study does not confirm such a prediction. Instead of more widespread adoption of the Gandhian repertoire, most civil rights activists after 1943 reverted back to the traditional repertoire of agitation and publicity without direct action (Broderick and Meier 1965). There were a few trials with the

Gandhian repertoire between 1944 and 1955, such as the FOR's Journey of Reconciliation in 1947 and Randolph's League for Non-violent Civil Disobedience, but none matched the intensity or scale of CORE and the MOWM before 1944. Largely due to the national (and international) obsession with anticommunism during this era, American activists shifted much of their attention to "safer" foreign issues like World War II, the United Nations, the Cold War, and the Korean War (Egerton 1994). Domestic civil rights activism concentrated primarily on the federal courts, because any kind of militant direct action was immediately branded communist. Within this inhospitable political climate for further experimentation with the Gandhian repertoire, CORE and MOWM declined while the NAACP achieved a string of legal victories (with, of course, the 1954 Supreme Court decision outlawing school segregation as the most significant victory).

Although transnational diffusion of the Gandhian repertoire during this period generally retreated from the implementation to the adoption stage, several actors took advantage of technological improvements in international travel, creating new diffusion networks between Gandhians in India and civil rights activists in the United States. Rustin, for instance, traveled to India in 1948, while Mordecai Johnson followed his trail the next year.[12] Some of the older activists' enthusiasm trickled down to the younger generation. James Lawson (a disciple of FOR's A. J. Muste and a veteran of Rustin's nonviolent workshops in the early 1940s), for instance, went to India in 1953 as a fraternal worker for his church and stayed out of the United States until the Montgomery bus boycott in 1956 (Branch 1988: 143; Morris 1984:162-166).

And finally, one of the Indian Gandhians to come to the United States during this period was Ram Manohar Lohia. In 1951, Lohia, who had organized his own civil disobedience campaigns in India, went on a lecture tour throughout the country.[13] In his speeches, Lohia criticized the traditional repertoire's gradualist approach and urged African-Americans to implement the Gandhian repertoire, instead of talking about it. Like the diffusion pioneers in the early 1940s, Lohia believed that hands-on experience was the only way to grasp the power of nonviolent direct action: "Education by activity in the subject to be taught, basic education we call it, is the newest way, and that is the way I suggest. Not manifestoes or speeches about non-violence, but practice!" (Wofford 1961: 86-87).

UNEXPECTED IMPLEMENTATION OF THE GANDHIAN REPERTOIRE

The emergence of the Montgomery bus boycott in 1955 brought new life to the transnational diffusion of the Gandhian repertoire. After the African-American community collectively initiated the one-day bus boycott, various pre-1944 Gandhian networks provided the knowledge and experience that allowed it to grow into a full-fledged Gandhian social movement. Although a complete account of the dense ties between the old and the new generations of Gandhian activists is beyond the scope of this chapter, let me sketch a few of the connections. These specific intergenerational connections merely scratch the surface of much broader and deeper transnational diffusion links.

Most obviously, Martin Luther King, Jr. based his knowledge of the Gandhian repertoire on A. J. Muste's classes at Crozer Theological Seminary, Mordecai

Johnson's sermon in 1950, and Benjamin Mays's friendly advice. Moreover, during the Montgomery bus boycott, King established close ties with FOR activists Reverend Glenn Smiley and Bayard Rustin (King 1958; Branch 1988). Another Montgomery civil rights leader with significant intergenerational ties was E. D. Nixon. Nixon worked for A. Philip Randolph's BSCP and, during the 1930s, had helped his friend Myles Horton organize African-American workers in the South. At the start of the 1950s, moreover, Nixon joined other African-American activists (including Rosa Parks) at HFS workshops (Morris 1984: 144-146; Adams 1975).

The impact of preexisting Gandhian networks stretched far beyond the Montgomery bus boycott. In 1957, Rustin created King's organizational vehicle, the Southern Christian Leadership Conference (SCLC), on the basis of the Gandhian repertoire (Anderson 1997). In 1961, James Lawson drafted the statement of purpose for the Student Nonviolent Coordinating Committee (SNCC), and became a major role model for student leaders like John Lewis, James Bevel, and Diane Nash. That same year, Farmer and CORE asked Lawson to train activists preparing for the Freedom Rides, which, of course, were inspired by Houser and Rustin's 1947 Journey of Reconciliation (Farmer 1985). Finally, the famous March on Washington in 1963 was clearly modeled after March on Washington plans in 1941. As a sign of gratitude toward previous generations of civil rights activists, Randolph himself was appointed director of the 1963 march and Rustin its chief organizer (Pfeffer 1990).

THEORETICAL IMPLICATIONS

Why did civil rights activists fail to fully implement the Gandhian repertoire before 1955? How did transnational diffusion of the Gandhian repertoire proceed over time? It is tempting to highlight the role of Martin Luther King, Jr. in answering these questions. Doing so, however, would seriously underestimate the diffusion efforts of civil rights activists before Montgomery. While King helped popularize the Gandhian repertoire by wrapping it in religious language that the African-American masses understood, creative reinvention of the Gandhian repertoire primarily took place at the start of the 1940s. The core group of "reinventors," in turn, relied on previous generations of Gandhian activists in the United States for knowledge, networks, favorable settings, and resources.

This chapter approaches the questions concerning why and how transnational diffusion occurred differently. On the one hand, it argues for the relevance of classical diffusion theory. On the other hand, it asserts that, in contrast to classical diffusion theory, transnational diffusion of the Gandhian repertoire did not advance sequentially from one diffusion stage to the next but experienced several unexpected twists and turns before full implementation. The case study confirms the significance of this assertion and analyzes *how* transnational diffusion evolved over time. Initial American awareness of the Gandhian repertoire did not simply lead to the persuasion and adoption stages, but raised dual barriers of hyper-difference and over-likeness. Transcending these barriers demanded intellectual dislocation and practical relocation by pioneering groups of civil rights activists, not the attainment of a "critical mass" or "threshold" (cf. Rogers 1995; Valente 1995; Marwell and Oliver 1993; Granovetter 1978). Finally, full implementation of the Gandhian repertoire did not directly follow mental adoption and partial application, as classical diffusion theory would predict, but happened unexpectedly after a "down" period of more than a decade.

The definitive answer to *why* American civil rights activists did not fully implement the Gandhian repertoire before 1955 is much less clear-cut. Social science in general is unable to paint a complete picture of the panoply of intentions and events involved in such a collective phenomenon. My case study, though, suggests at least three partial (and complementary) answers. First of all, civil rights activists were simply not prepared, in terms of knowledge and experience, to fully implement the Gandhian repertoire in the United States before the experimental trials during the early-1940s. This observation limits the unexplained period to the years between 1944 and 1955. Second, events like the race riots of 1943, anticommunist hysteria after World War II, and the NAACP's legal victory in 1954 created unfavorable political conditions for massive nonviolent direct action in the United States.[14] The end of the Cold War frenzy and the lack of concrete results after the 1954 Supreme Court decision reduced the fear and heightened the combativeness of the African-American community in Montgomery.

Relatively favorable circumstances in 1955, however, did not automatically lead to implementation on a mass scale.[15] Mass implementation of the Gandhian repertoire did not occur until *after* leaders and common people, in unison, decided to initiate a collective boycott of the Montgomery buses. The emergence of the bus boycott, in turn, impelled previous generations of Gandhian activists to share their knowledge and experience with the new generation of civil rights activists. This intergenerational transfer of knowledge and experience, the third element of my answer, explains most convincingly why full implementation of the Gandhian repertoire started in 1955 and 1956, and not earlier.

Even if my theoretical framework helps to clarify and explain transnational diffusion of the Gandhian repertoire from India to the United States, does this make it relevant to social movement theory in general? Personally, I believe that the three fundamental elements of my theoretical framework—the obstacles of hyper-difference and over-likeness, the necessity for dislocation and relocation, and the problematic transition from partial to full implementation—also apply to other cases of transnational diffusion between social movements. The only way to really test the validity of my theoretical framework, however, is by comparing my case study with various other case studies. One could, for instance, compare my case of transnational diffusion between *distinct* social movements with cases of transnational diffusion between social movements *within* a worldwide movement. One could also compare transnational diffusion of a *repertoire* of collective action with transnational diffusion of one particular collective action *routine*. In any case, this chapter will have succeeded if it inspires social movement scholars to translate mental awareness of transnational diffusion into practical application in the form of additional research.

NOTES

1. According to the classical diffusion model's *two-step flow hypothesis*, most people are directly influenced by face-to-face communication and only indirectly by mass media channels: "The first step, from media sources to opinion leaders, is mainly a transfer of *information*, whereas the second step, from opinion leaders to their followers, also involves the spread of interpersonal *influence*. This *two-step flow hypothesis* suggested that communication messages flow from a source, via mass media channels, to opinion leaders, who in turn pass them on to followers" (Rogers 1995: 285; Katz 1957).

2. "The *critical mass* occurs at the point at which enough individuals have adopted an innovation that the innovation's further rate of adoption becomes self-sustaining. . . . A *threshold* is the number of other individuals who must be engaged in an activity before a given individual will join that activity. . . . An individual is more likely to adopt an innovation if more of the other individuals in his or her personal network have adopted previously" (Rogers 1995: 333-334; see also Granovetter 1978; Marwell and Oliver 1993; and Valente 1995).

3. From about 1917 until his death, Gandhi himself corresponded with an amazing number of American opinion leaders. Reddy (1998) assembles most of these letters, which also appear in the *Collected Works of Mahatma Gandhi* (*CWMG*). About this international correspondence, P. Rama Moorthy remarks: "Gandhi's letters are the East-West commerce of minds, the East in Gandhi—or more precisely Gandhi in the East—facing the rigor of the Western critical intellect (Narasimhaiah 1969: 253)."

4. Prior to 1927, Garvey and his followers emphasized this aspect of the Gandhian movement in India without developing specific plans for implementing the Gandhian repertoire in the United States.

5. During the 1920s and 1930s, Du Bois established close ties with Indian exiles like Haridas Muzumdar and Lajpat Rai. He also met C. F. Andrews during his trip to the United States in 1929, and he published a message from Gandhi to African-Americans in the NAACP's *The Crisis* ("To the American Negro, A Message from Mahatma Gandhi," July 1929: 225).

6. Holmes also corresponded with Gandhi frequently, and he met him twice (in London in 1931 and in New Delhi in 1947). Reddy states that Gandhi and Holmes exchanged twenty-seven letters between 1926 and 1947 (1998: 160-182).

7. Gregg also corresponded extensively with Gandhi, and stayed at his ashram in 1925 and 1930. For letters, see Reddy (1998: 50-88).

8. During these initial campaigns CORE explicitly reminded participants to follow the steps in the Gandhian repertoire: "Remember technique!…Gather facts. Negotiate. Rouse public opinion, and then, if absolutely necessary, and only as a last resort, Take Direct Action" (CORE newsletter, Meier and Rudwick 1973: 13).

9. Jay Holmes Smith, who had been a missionary in India, founded the Harlem Ashram, the committee for Non-Violent Direct Action (NVDA), and the Free India Committee. E. Stanley Jones, also a missionary in India, was a friend of Gandhi and author of *Mahatma Gandhi: An Interpretation*. Jones also corresponded with Gandhi over many years: see Reddy (1998: 183-188).

10. Due to race riots before the conference, this core group of Gandhians was unable to fully implement the Gandhian repertoire between 1944 and 1955 (Sitkoff 1971).

11. I stress that collective experiments with the Gandhian repertoire, not just individual activists' insights, enabled the reinvention of the Gandhian repertoire: "Repertoires . . . do not descend from abstract philosophy or take shape as a result of political propaganda; *they emerge from struggle*" (Tilly 1995: 26; italics mine).

12. For Rustin's trip, see Anderson 1997: 130-139; Johnson describes his experiences in "Gandhi's Purity of Heart," Mordecai Wyatt Johnson Papers, Moorland-Springarn Research Center, Howard University [Box 1+: 1-2].

13. Myles Horton invited Lohia to give a speech at HFS, and accompanied him during his six-week tour through the United States (Wofford 1961).

14. After the race riots of 1943, most civil rights leaders retracted even tacit support for MOWM and CORE's confrontational protest methods. McCarthyism and fear of red-baiting only solidified the opposition to militant action (Egerton 1994). And finally, Thurgood Marshall's successful court cases during this period allowed the NAACP, and its traditional repertoire of protest, to regain an image of superiority.

15. In other words, less prohibitive national and international political opportunity structures do not adequately explain the transition to full implementation. The collective initiative to engage in mass direct action and, most important, the "older" activists' willingness to

transfer their knowledge and experience to contemporary activists made full implementation (and confirmation) of the Gandhian repertoire possible.

REFERENCES

Adams, Frank (with Myles Horton). 1975. *Unearthing Seeds of Fire: The Idea of Highlander.* Winston-Salem, N.C.: John F. Blair.

Anderson, Jervis. 1997. *Bayard Rustin: Troubles I've Seen.* New York: HarperCollins.

Ayres, Jeffrey M. 1999. "From the Streets to the Internet: The Cyber-Diffusion of Contention." *Annals of the American Academy of Political and Social Science.* 566: 132-143.

Baltimore Afro-American. 1930. "H.U. Men Refuse Jim Crow on Philadelphia." May 3.

Bondurant, Joan. 1971 [1958]. *Conquest of Violence: The Gandhian Philosophy of Conflict.* Princeton, N.J.: Princeton University Press.

Bose, N. K. 1947. *Studies in Gandhism.* Calcutta: Indian Associated Publishing.

Branch, Taylor. 1988. *Parting the Waters: America in the King Years, 1954-1963.* New York: Harper.

Broderick, Francis L., and August Meier. 1965. *Negro Protest Thought in the Twentieth Century.* Indianapolis: Bobbs-Merrill.

Coleman, James S., Elihu Katz, and Herbert Menzel. 1966. *Medical Innovation: A Diffusion Study.* Indianapolis: Bobbs-Merrill.

DuBois, W. E. B. 1943. "As the Crow Flies." *New York Amsterdam News,* March 13.

Egerton, John. 1994. *Speak Now against the Day: The Generation before the Civil Rights Movement in the South.* Chapel Hill: North Carolina University Press.

Farmer, James. 1985. *Lay Bare the Heart: An Autobiography of the Civil Rights Movement.* New York: New American Library.

Fox, Richard G. 1989. *Gandhian Utopia: Experiments with Culture.* Boston: Beacon Press.

———. 1997. "Passage from India." Pp. 65-82 in *Between Resistance and Revolution: Cultural Politics and Social Protest,* Richard G. Fox and Orin Starn, eds. New Brunswick, N.J.: Rutgers University Press.

Franklin, John Hope, and Isidore Starr, eds. 1967. *The Negro in 20th Century America.* New York: Vintage Books.

Gandhi, Mohandas K. 1928. *Satyagraha in South Africa.* Ahmedabad: Navajivan Publishing House.

———. 1999. *Collected Works of Mahatma Gandhi (CWMG)* on CD-ROM. New Delhi: Government Publications Division.

Garfinkel, Herbert. 1959. *When Negroes March: The March on Washington Movement in the Organizational Politics for FEPC.* Glencoe, Ill.: Free Press.

Giugni, Marco. 1995. "The Cross-National Diffusion of Protest." Pp. 181-206 in *New Social Movements in Western Europe: A Comparative Analysis,* Hanspeter Kriesi, Ruud Koopmans, Jan Willem Duyvendak, and Marco Giugni, eds. Minneapolis: University of Minnesota Press.

———. 1998. "The Other Side of the Coin: Explaining Crossnational Similarities between Social Movements." *Mobilization: An International Journal* 3(1): 89-105.

Granovetter, Mark. 1978. "Threshold Models of Collective Behavior." *American Journal of Sociology* 78: 1360-1380.

Gregg, Richard B. 1935. *The Power of Nonviolence.* Philadelphia: J. B. Lippincott.

Hägerstrand, Thorsten. 1967. *Innovation Diffusion as a Spatial Process.* Chicago: University of Chicago Press.

Kapur, Sudarshan. 1992. *Raising Up a Prophet: The African-American Encounter with Gandhi.* Boston: Beacon Press.

Katz, Elihu. 1957. "The Two-Step Flow of Communication: An Up-to-Date Report on an Hypothesis." *Public Opinion Quarterly* 21: 61-78.

Katz, Elihu, and Paul F. Lazarsfeld. 1944. *Personal Influence: The Part Played by People in the Flow of Mass Communications.* New York: Free Press.

King, Martin Luther, Jr. 1958. *Stride toward Freedom: The Montgomery Story.* New York: Harper.

Lionberger, Herbert F. 1960. *Adoption of New Ideas and Practices.* Ames: Iowa State University Press.

Lopes, Paul, and Mary Durfee, eds. November 1999. "The Social Diffusion of Ideas and Things." *Annals of the American Academy of Political and Social Science* 566: 8-155.

Marwell, Gerald, and Pamela Oliver. 1993. *The Critical Mass in Collective Action. A Micro-Social Theory.* Cambridge: Cambridge University Press.

McAdam, Doug, John D. McCarthy, and Mayer N. Zald, eds. 1996. *Comparative Perspectives on Social Movements: Political Opportunities, Mobilizing Structures, and Cultural Framings.* Cambridge: Cambridge University Press.

McAdam, Doug, and Dieter Rucht. July 1993. "The Cross-National Diffusion of Movement Ideas." *Annals of the American Academy of Political And Social Science* 528, 56-74.

Meier, August, and Elliott Rudwick. 1973. *CORE: A Study in the Civil Rights Movement, 1942-1968.* New York: Oxford University Press.

Morris, Aldon. 1984. *The Origins of the Civil Rights Movement: Black Communities Organizing for Change.* New York: Free Press.

Muzumdar, Haridas T. 1962. *America's Contributions to India's Freedom.* Allahabad: Central Book Depot.

―――., ed. 1982. *The Enduring Greatness of Gandhi: An American Estimate.* Ahmedabad: Navajivan Publishing House.

Narasimhaiah, C. D., ed. 1969. *Gandhi and the West.* Mysore, India: University of Mysore.

Payne, Charles. 1995. *I've Got the Light of Freedom: The Organizing Tradition and the Mississippi Freedom Struggle.* Berkeley: University of California Press.

Pfeffer, Paula F. 1990. *A. Philip Randolph, Pioneer of the Civil Rights Movement.* Baton Rouge: Louisiana State University Press.

Randolph, A. Philip. 1942. "Keynote Address to the Policy Conference of the March on Washington Movement." March on Washington Movement: Proceedings of Conference Held in Detroit, September 26-27: 4-11.

―――. 1943. "A Reply to My Critics." *Chicago Defender,* June 19 and 26.

Reddy, E. S., ed. 1998. *Mahatma Gandhi: Letters to Americans.* Mumbai: Bhavan's Book University.

Rogers, Everett. 1995. *Diffusion of Innovations,* 4th edition. New York: Free Press.

Ryan, Bryce, and Neal C. Gross. 1943. "The Diffusion of Hybrid Seed Corn in Two Iowa Communities." *Rural Sociology* 8(1): 15-24.

Sharp, Gene. 1979. *Gandhi as a Political Strategist.* Boston: Portent Sargent.

Shridharani, Krishnalal. 1939. *War without Violence.* New York: Harcourt, Brace.

Singh, Harnam. 1962. *The Indian National Movement and American Opinion.* New Delhi: Rama Krishna.

Sitkoff, Harvard. December 1971. "Racial Militancy and Interracial Violence in the Second World War." *Journal of American History* 58: 661-681.

Snow, David A., and Robert D. Benford. 1999. "Alternative Types of Cross-National Diffusion in the Social Movement Arena." Pp. 23-39 in *Social Movements in a Globalizing World,* Donatella della Porta, Hanspeter Kriesi, and Dieter Rucht, eds. London: MacMillan.

Soule, Sarah A. 1997. "The Student Divestment Movement in the United States and Tactical Diffusion: The Shantytown Protest." *Social Forces* 75(3): 855-882.

―――. 1999. "The Diffusion of an Unsuccessful Innovation." *Annals of the American Academy of Political and Social Science* 566: 120-131.

Strang, David, and John W. Meyer. 1993. "Institutional Conditions for Diffusion." *Theory and Society* 22: 487-511.

Strang, David, and Sarah A. Soule. 1998. "Diffusion in Organizations and Social Movements: From Hybrid Corn to Poison Pills." *Annual Review of Sociology* 24: 265-290.

Tarde, Gabriel. 1903. *The Laws of Imitation*. New York: Holt.

Tarrow, Sidney. 1989. *Democracy and Disorder: Protest and Politics in Italy, 1965-1975*. Oxford: Clarendon.

――――. 1994. *Power in Movement: Social Movements, Collective Action and Politics*. New York: Cambridge University Press.

Tilly, Charles. 1995. "Contentious Repertoires in Great Britain, 1758-1834." Pp. 15-42 in *Repertoires and Cycles of Collective Action*, Mark Traugott, ed. Durham, N.C.: Duke University Press.

Valente, Thomas W. 1995. *Network Models of the Diffusion of Innovations*. Creskill, N.J.: Hampton Press.

Watson, Blanche. 1989 [1923]. *Gandhi and Non-violent Resistance*. New Delhi: Anmol Publications.

Wofford, Harris, Jr. 1961. *Lohia and America Meet*. Madras: Snehalata.

Chapter 7

FROM LOCAL TO GLOBAL: THE ANTI-DAM MOVEMENT IN SOUTHERN BRAZIL, 1979-1992

Franklin Daniel Rothman and Pamela E. Oliver

The anti-dam movement in southern Brazil began in 1979 as a local mobilization to aid peasants affected by the proposed flooding of river valleys by large hydroelectric dams. Initially the movement organization was known as CRAB (*Comissão Regional de Atingidos por Barragens*, Regional Committee of Those Displaced by Dams). Framing the issue as a land struggle, local activists took advantage of early openings in a democratic transition and drew on their national and international church networks to defend those affected (or *atingidos)*. In the process, they broadened the collective identity of *atingidos* from the government's definition, namely, those owning land that was to be flooded, to those working or living on land, and then to those who would be affected in other ways. In 1987 they signed a landmark accord with ELETROSUL which met movement demands of just compensation in cash or land prior to dam construction. In the late 1980s, in the wake of the crisis in mobilization following the fall of the Berlin Wall, the defeat of the agrarian reform movement, the growing conservatism of the church, and the weakening of its chief adversary, ELETROSUL, the anti-dam movement came into contact with the international environmentalist movement, forging a new ideology which linked class and environmental concerns. In 1991, CRAB played a leading role in the First National Congress of People Affected by Dams held in Brasília, which created MAB (*Movimento Nacional de Atingidos por Barragens*, National Movement of People Affected by Dams). The national movement was divided into five regions and CRAB was renamed MAB–Sul (*Movimento Nacional dos Atingidos por Barragens–Sul*, Movement of People Affected by Dams– Southern Region).

There is growing recognition of the importance of international networks in local mobilizations, and growing theorization from an international perspective about the relation between these international networks and national social movements. This scholarship needs to be integrated with a realistic understanding of just how international and local actors interact in particular mobilizations. Local, national, and international actors each pursue their own ends. They constantly respond to situations created by others' actions, and at times align their efforts with others when it serves their purposes. Understanding these processes requires appreciation of nested political opportunity structures, a more complete theorization of external-internal movement linkages, and a recognition of the complex processes underlying frame shifts. We draw on existing social movement theory and recent work on international movement networks and use this case to illuminate the specific ways the different levels are linked.

THEORETICAL FRAMEWORK

Our work builds on the growing stream of scholarship on national and international political opportunity structures. Political opportunity was initially conceived as a unidimensional continuum in which whole societies, movements, or eras had more or less political opportunity, Political opportunity is now generally seen as a qualitative multidimensional network field in which different groups of actors, kinds of appeals, modes of protest, and forms of organization are responded to differently by the other actors in their environment, and thus have different prospects for success.[1] In this conception, particular eras or locations can be repressive for some forms of mobilization but, paradoxically, favorable for others. Recent scholarship has extended social movement theory to international movement organizations. Boli and Thomas show that there has been an enormous growth in international nongovernmental organizations (INGOs) from about 200 in 1900 to nearly 4,000 in 1980, with roughly 100 new INGOs founded annually (Boli and Thomas 1997). Several works by Smith (Smith 1995; Smith et al. 1994) document the extent and importance of transnational social movements, including the women's, environmental, and human rights movements. Keck and Sikkink (1998) provide a rich theoretical and empirical account of what they call international "advocacy networks" which are important conduits for information and influence. Their research on environmental advocacy networks (1998, chapter 4) is particularly useful in helping to understand the evolution of the anti-dam movement in southern Brazil during the period 1979-1992. Tarrow (1998) and the essays in Smith, Chatfield, and Pagnucco (1997) specifically discuss the ways in which social movement concepts can be extended to international mobilizations. Other scholars continue to expand the concept of political opportunity structures to encompass international influences and the uncertainties and instabilities which arise in democratic transitions (e.g., Pagnucco 1996; Tarrow 1998; and essays in Smith et al. 1997). Keck and Sikkink (1998) posit that international advocacy networks become important resources for national movements when there is a barrier to a movement's ability to influence its national government. Tarrow (1998) discusses the variety of relations that may hold between actors in different nations, including not only movement alliances but also diffusion and political exchanges. In particular, actors may employ their links to one set of actors to strengthen their strategic position with respect to other actors.

Nested Political Opportunity Structures

The concept of nested political opportunity structures is a useful way to think of the ways these different levels affect local action. Eisinger's (1973) original use of "political opportunity" referred to cities in the United States, and subsequent work by other scholars (e.g., Hellman 1987) confirms that municipal, state, and regional political and economic structures always provide local character and constraints to local manifestations of social movements. Local political opportunity structures are embedded in national political opportunity structures, which are in turn embedded in international political opportunity structures. These nested structures create the possibility for very complex patterns of relationships among actors.

Clarifying Relations between Internal and External

In analyzing these nested structures, it is important to clarify the relation between "external" and "internal" actors in a local struggle. If research is focused only on international actors, there is a risk of replicating the original "resource mobilization" error and assume that external resources and international advocacy efforts cause local mobilizations. However, the empirical literature on social movements seems definite that most local mobilization cycles begin with indigenous or internal insurgency which then attracts external resources (e.g., McAdam 1982; Morris 1984; Tarrow 1998; Koopmans 1993). These resources come both from the "conscience constituents" who support the movement's values and from external elites. The international advocacy networks studied by Keck and Sikkink generally parallel national conscience constituents, but many international NGOs also receive heavy funding from "elites," including national governments and large corporate foundations. The most common interpretation of resource flows from elites to movements within nations has been that external elites donate to movements for the purpose of moderating or coopting them (e.g., Haines 1984; Jenkins and Eckert 1986), but this possibility seems less often considered in international resource flows. Instead, international elites are said to channel money to local movements to undercut or circumvent national governments (Smith 1990).

Several other dimensions of internal/external relationships also need to be recognized. First, the boundary between "external" institutions and "internal" agents is often blurred, for example when the regional priests and university professors are adult children of peasants in the area. Similarly, key support for the southern civil rights movement came from African-American churches in the North (Morris 1984). Case studies repeatedly find that people with dual or complex identities are important "network bridges" between political communities and aid the flow of information and resources between them. The Gramscian "organic intellectual" remains an important feature of many local mobilizations.

Second, it is a mistake to view local activists as the passive recipients of external support and overlook their proactive fund-raising. Additionally, external-internal links are not one-way resource flows but rather two-way flows of influence and information. International networks and movements need active local groups just as much as local groups need external resources. Their interchanges are bilateral, interactive, and strategic, with both agency and reactivity occurring on both sides.

Third, it is crucial to differentiate among international actors. Some seek to foment mobilization, others to moderate it. Moreover, the international networks involved in particular local mobilizations often enter on opposite sides of the struggle. This multitude of international networks may be understood with Maney's (1998) useful extension of Klandermans's (1990) concept of alliance and conflict structures, which, in turn, is compatible with Keck and Sikkink's (1998) discussions of advocacy networks and a multidimensional network conception of political opportunity structures. International actors seek local allies as part of their international-level competition for resources and influence. In this way, local actors may forge ties with global alliance and conflict networks and bring otherwise poor and marginalized communities into contact with powerful international institutions or social movements. When these ties are in place, both sides may be proactive in seeking to influence others and pursue their goals.

Specifying How Frames and Identities Change with Opportunity Structures

Framing processes (Snow et al. 1986; Snow and Benford 1988) and collective identities (Melucci 1989, 1995) are important in this case. The framing of the anti-dam movement clearly shifted over time in southern Brazil. Initially understood as a struggle about peasants' right to land and livelihood, the anti-dam movement evolved into a land struggle that was also about the destruction of natural habitat through misguided industrialization and agricultural policies. Similarly, the collective identity *atingidos* was actively constructed and reconstructed by the local activists in the process of their struggle. These shifting frames and collective identities had important implications for political opportunity. They defined who was a member of the affected group, and who would be logical allies for the struggle. During the first phase, 1979-1987, allies were those concerned about land struggles and the plight of the poor. Since 1988, and specifically during the period under study, 1988-1992, allies were also those concerned about the environment. It is well recognized that frames and collective identities are consequential for resource flows and alliances and are tied to evolving international master frames, consistent with research in other locales (e.g., Johnston 1991; Klandermans 1997; Marullo, Pagnucco, and Smith 1996; Snow and Benford 1992; and the essays in McAdam, McCarthy, and Zald 1996).

However, in the anti-dam case and, we suspect, in most cases, it would be a gross distortion to imagine that shifts in identities and frames were made lightly, in a simple opportunistic chase after resources and allies. The case materials reveal that both the land struggle frame and the later shift to a more ecological frame were tied to deep and complex ideological understandings of the political and economic world. The shift between frames required a great deal of intellectual and ideological "work." It was not a matter of activists' simply picking a frame that would better reach out to others or resonate with others' ideologies. Instead, it involved a wholesale reworking of the activists' own understandings to reconcile core values and beliefs with new ideas. This reworking was deeply affected by the new political opportunity structure in which they found themselves. In short, it was much more like a learning process of bilateral influence than a marketing scheme. Understanding the complexity of this process is necessary to avoid facile interpretations of frame alignment processes.

METHODOLOGY

Field work in the southern states of Rio Grande do Sul and Santa Catarina was conducted by the first author from October 1992 through January 1993. A variety of data collection methods and techniques were used to provide diverse perspectives and to cross-check factual claims. Overall, approximately 100 people were interviewed, including movement leaders and participants, progressive leaders of the Catholic and Evangelical Lutheran churches, university advisers, NGO activists, a limited number of affected persons, and ELETROSUL and World Bank officials. Analysis of these interviews was cross-checked and supplemented by analysis of written documentation of various types. The analysis of CRAB's frame evolution was based on a detailed reading of CRAB files, including position papers, minutes of meetings, newsletters, and other internal documents, as well as interviews with participants. Primary data on resource flows were obtained from CRAB staff and documents, as well as from officials and documents of the Evangelical Lutheran Church of Brazil (IECLB), which served as a conduit for Bread for the World's funds to CRAB. Papers based on this research have been presented and circulated in Brazil among academics and movement activists, where its empirical claims have been widely substantiated, and a few earlier errors of fact or interpretation have been corrected.

DAM RESISTANCE AS A LAND STRUGGLE: 1979-1987

In 1979, ELETROSUL, the federal government's regional power company of the three-state region of southern Brazil, announced that it would build twenty-two hydroelectric dams in the Uruguai River Basin. By 1983, church activists, aided by professors at the regional college, rural new unionists (Keck 1989) and, by 1986, a group of new, young activists, had organized a broad mobilization in affected areas of the states of Santa Catarina and Rio Grande do Sul. This movement expanded its original aims from just compensation for those displaced by dams to outright opposition to the building of dams. By 1987, the movement in southern Brazil had achieved notable success in obtaining recognition and concessions from the electric sector, as evidenced by the signing of a major accord which, backed by popular mobilization, enabled CRAB to maintain a strong bargaining position with ELETROSUL. These initial organizers succeeded because they had network ties to other peasant movements in the area (Navarro 1996; Grzybowski 1985, 1987) and to larger national and international movements, and because recent events had created space for their mobilization. Consistent with their backgrounds and network ties, they framed the issue as part of the larger struggle of rural people for land and against the destructive forces of capitalist expansion, and they built a broad-based movement that was strongly allied with land and anti-dam struggles in other regions.

Structure of Political Opportunities, 1979-1987

The movement's backdrop was the shifting political opportunity structure in the transition from repressive authoritarianism, conventionally divided into the overlapping periods of controlled liberalization (1974-1985) and democratic transition (1983-1988). The Geisel government (1974-79) constituted the third stage of Brazil's military regime. Its policy of *distensão* was a program of careful and controlled liberalization measures which began to ease repression and grant human rights (Alves 1985). In 1979, João Figueiredo was inaugurated president and began the "opening" (*abertura*) subphase of controlled liberalization, the process of restoring political rights. The government decreed partial political amnesty, which allowed all exiles to return to Brazil and all political leaders to regain their rights. This increased the ranks of Left activists and intellectuals opposing the authoritarian regime through political parties, especially the new Worker's Party (PT), trade unions, and NGOs. Elite opposition groups, such as the National Council of Catholic Bishops (CNBB), further opened the political space.

The deterioration of the Brazilian economy in the late 1970s and early 1980s contributed to both elite fragmentation and popular protest. A combination of processes, both internal and external to Brazil, combined to create the debt crisis of 1982. In the early 1980s, as external lending contracted, the debt crisis became part of a broader economic crisis. During the period 1981 to 1983, Brazil experienced the sharpest drop in economic activity in the country's history (Navarro 1992). A growing wave of protest culminated in 1984 with the campaign for direct presidential elections, which entailed a high level of popular mobilization and . . . framed the issue of democratization from new perspectives" (Navarro 1992: 6-7).

As opposition groups were obtaining increased access to the political system, the military, economic, and political elites were becoming weaker and more fragmented. In 1981, the federal government sent military forces to repress landless peasants encamped at Encruzilhada Natalino, in the region of the anti-dam movement, but they stopped short of total repression. This relatively successful resistance of the landless took on symbolic and strategic significance, and it is considered to be the birth of the MST (*Movimento dos Trabalhadores Rurais Sem Terra*, the regional and national movement of landless rural workers). This and several other key events signaled divisions within the military and encouraged subsequent mobilization. The ascending phase of the cycle of protest benefited all movements, as they further weakened elite repression and worked in alliance with each other.

Political elites were also divided. In Rio Grande do Sul, despite the election in 1982 of a governor who supported the military regime, the state legislature provided a forum for popular groups and movements via opposition parties. In 1983 it held legislative hearings, published a report on the dams issue, and provided space for a statewide meeting of the movement. With regard to regional and local elites, although ELETROSUL courted mayors and leaders of producer cooperatives to support dam construction, most were divided or awaited further specification of ELETROSUL'S plans.

A campaign for direct elections in 1984 failed, as military and political elites negotiated a transition pact. In January of 1985 the electoral college chose Tancredo Neves, candidate of an opposition coalition, to be the first civilian president elected in twenty-one years. When Neves died in April 1985, Vice President José Sarney was sworn in as president, promising to maintain the course set by Neves. His initial priorities were to draft a National Agrarian Reform Plan (PNRA) and to gather a National Constituent Assembly to draft a new constitution. The latter was promulgated in October 1988, with widespread popular participation, and completed the process of institutional normalization and democratic transition (Moisés 1989) on course since 1983. The re-creation of formal democratic institutions and weakening of ELETROSUL contributed to demobilization and signaled CRAB's transition to a new phase in which it would need to seek new alliances.

Religious Networks and the Availability of Resources and Information

The anti-dam struggle was rooted in a religious and class understanding that poor people needed land for their livelihood. The states of Santa Catarina, Rio Grande do Sul, and Paraná comprise the southern region of Brazil. Its rural areas are populated primarily by *colonos*, who still retain their German and Italian ethnic identities and cultural and religious practices, even though they speak Portuguese and share a Brazilian national identity.[2] These peasant smallholders were severely affected by the highly selective processes of agricultural modernization and agro-industrialization during the late 1960s and 1970s, which resulted in socioeconomic differentiation and increasing economic marginalization.

Transformations in the Brazilian Catholic Church during the 1960s and 1970s led progressive priests and other pastoral agents to orient themselves toward peasants' land rights and to provide the only viable basis for mobilization. After the military coup of 1964, and especially during the period 1968-1973, when repression was most harsh, the Catholic Church became the only voice of resistance. The church developed an elaborate word-of-mouth communication system for organizing self-help projects and reacting to human rights violations. Personal and professional ties forged a strong national and international communications and resources network. In 1975 the Brazilian CPT (*Comissão Pastoral da Terra*, Pastoral Land Committee) was created from grassroots origins as an autonomous pastoral entity whose mission was to service peasants causes. The CPT was itself a product of developments in global Catholicism and the particular Brazilian experience. In the late 1970s, the CPT actively supported those peasants in southern Brazil dislocated by the giant Itaipu dam and others who would later form the MST.

International religious networks became available to the poor of southern Brazil through a complex multilateral influence process, as European churches struggled with the ideological challenges of domestic Marxism and the moral claims of the needy in developing nations. Pope Paul VI issued his most progressive statement in relation to the Third World, Populorum Progressio, in 1967. In 1968 the Medellín Conference of Latin American bishops approved a document emphasizing the need for structural change in Latin America and stimulating liberation theology, with its strong Marxian themes of class struggle and capitalist imperialism. By the late 1970s, the Brazilian church had addressed the church's conservative- progressive conflict and found internal harmony around the "preferential option for the poor." European churches created development organizations to respond to the needs of developing nations, bypassing governments to give money directly to private groups serving the poor. Some of these new organizations, such as the French Catholic Committee against Hunger and for Development (CCFD), grew in response to the Freedom from Hunger Campaign (FFHC) which had been launched by the UN Food and Agricultural Organization. In Germany, the Campaign against Hunger and Disease (MISEREOR) was established by Catholic bishops in 1958 and Bread for the World by Protestant churches in 1959 (Smith 1990: 83). These organizations tended to be staffed by left-leaning ex-missionaries eager to fund programs for structural change as well as direct relief. The large German ethnic population in southern Brazil influenced MISEREOR and Bread for the World to form a progressive alliance to support the collaborative efforts of the CPT and the Evangelical Lutheran Church.

The activists who initiated resistance to the Rio Uruguai dams project were CPT pastoral agents in collaboration with a German Evangelical Lutheran pastor, rural unionists, and leftist faculty at the regional university. These people were Gramscian "organic intellectuals" who lived in local communities while linked to international discourses and resources through the progressive church, which had close ties to unions and the emerging Worker's Party. Many of them were descendants of the original Italian or German *colonos* and valued the local ethnic customs, religious beliefs, and peasant way of life.

During the period 1979-1983, public access to information from ELETROSUL on dam construction was very limited, causing uneasiness among *colonos* about their future. However, this was not sufficient to generate mobilization. Links with external communication networks were essential for obtaining and distributing the necessary information about construction plans and resettlement options. Pastoral agents obtained information about government plans, determined which areas would be affected, and obtained testimony from other regions about government compensation and resettlement programs.

The bishop of Chapecó, Santa Catarina, Dom José Gomes, obtained crucial information through the National Conference of Bishops and placed human and material resources of the church at the disposal of the incipient movement. Several early movement leaders were former Catholic priests or seminarians. Pastors of the Evangelical Lutheran Church arranged a visit by a man affected by the giant Itaipu Dam, whose testimony, along with a videotaped documentary, dramatized the plight of dam-affected people. In addition, three radio stations in the region owned or controlled by the Catholic Church transmitted news about plans for dam construction and about CRAB activities.

The initial mobilization drew on local resources. In the very beginning, some organizers paid for gasoline themselves to attend community meetings. Local churches began to contribute small amounts to pay for CRAB expenses. Once the pastoral agents had mobilized the rural trade unions, the latter began to make small fixed annual contributions of one to five minimum-wage salaries on a monthly basis. Staff of FAPES, the regional college of Erexim, Rio Grande do Sul, channeled funds from CCFD of France and MISEREOR of Germany for research on socioeconomic problems of the dam-affected population and some costs of organization. In 1981, CRAB leaders decided they needed additional resources and drafted a project proposal which was forwarded through CPT to MISEREOR, which funded it. In the fall of 1983, CRAB successfully solicited funding from Bread for the World to expand the movement. In short, the initial activists proactively reached through their existing religious-political networks to obtain funding to build and expand their movement.

The Construction of Atingido as Involving Land and Human Dignity

CPT activists and their allies framed the dam struggle in the context of liberation theology, the linking of faith and life, and the linking of faith and politics (Secretariado Diocesano de Pastoral 1991). Biblical references were often cited to justify the church's support for peasants' access to land in a humane, Christian view of property—that the land is a gift of God and that all have equal access to it (CPT 1987). CPT's program of political pedagogy sought to raise political consciousness, create collective will, and transform viewpoints from fatalistic to assertive (Grzybowski 1985).

Building on this tradition, the church/CRAB leaders constructed a powerful discourse of "losses" which would result from the construction of the dams. According to former movement adviser Derci Pasqualotto, who had church ties and was of Italian descent, church/CRAB leaders appealed to sentimental values to mobilize the people, saying that dam construction would cause flooding of homes, churches, and cemeteries, thus creating a strong motivation to defend these community institutions.[3] The message was reinforced by knowledge of relatives or friends who had suffered similar losses from other dam projects. This discourse of losses used by church/CRAB leadership resonated with deeply held traditions and values among the *colonos* (Scherer-Warren et al. 1988). Faillace (1990) cites the importance of religion—Catholic or Evangelical Lutheran—for the *colonos* faced with loss as they looked to parish leaders for help in reconstructing their worlds. This discourse of losses both reinforced *colono* identity and contributed to an emerging political identity as *atingidos*.

From the beginning, ELETROSUL and the Regional Commission confronted one another over the meaning of the term *atingido* (Faillace 1990). For ELETROSUL, the *atingido* was the owner-operator who had legally established ties to the land. CRAB struggled with ELETROSUL over their meanings, including in its definition of *atingido* various categories of landless agriculturalists (e.g., squatters, renters, sharecroppers, indigenous populations) as well as landowners' adult children. In addition, the definition of what would affect people was also expanded. This new definition inlcuded not only water but also transmission lines, workers' living quarters, and the construction site (Faillace 1990: 38). The more inclusive definition of *atingidos* widened the mass base of the movement. CRAB estimated that 200,000 people (40,000 families) were affected, in contrast to ELETROSUL's estimate of 14,500 (Faillace 1990: 31). Faillace (1990: 38) argues that the peasants adopted the new political identity of *atingido*, molding it to characteristics of their social organization and using it to refer to salient aspects of dam construction.

Expanding the Networks, Expanding the Movement

From 1984 through 1987, CRAB continued with its class/land struggle frame and its church-linked networks. It expanded its mobilization, information generation, and alliance making with other class/land struggle movement organizations in the region. These included the new combative farmworkers unions, the landless workers movement, and the Workers' Party. They also formed new relationships with dam resistance groups elsewhere in Brazil, helping to create networks of communication and collaboration between regions.

The Worker's Party grew along with rural social movements, campaigns for direct presidential elections, and movements for agrarian reform. CRAB supported and benefited from movements responding to the Itaparica dam in northeastern Brazil, which mobilized thousands of people and forced the utility to negotiate with them about construction and resettlement plans. The growing number of political openings and the example of other protests gave popular movements leverage over their opponents, and made ELETROSUL more willing to negotiate with CRAB than it would have been in another period. The debt crisis of the mid-1980s, compounded by elite divisions within the state, crippled ELETROSUL's ability to effectively implement dam construction plans. Its inability to clearly inform and implement plans damaged its credibility and weakened its base of support. Under the combative leadership of a new union organizer in the Itá dam region and four young core activists, CRAB's organization was strengthened by forming a general assembly and holding consultations with the social base which produced a list of thirty-nine demands. A series of direct-action protests pressured ELETROSUL and maintained popular enthusiasm. By 1987, the selective use of noninstitutional and institutional actions had gained legitimacy for the movement organization, enabling it to obtain official recognition from the Ministry of Mines and Energy. In 1987, the combined factors of CRAB's stronger mobilization and organization and ELETROSUL's weaknesses led to the negotiation and signing of the landmark accord of 1987 with ELETROSUL. Among its principal provisions, the 1987 agreement conditioned ELETROSUL's purchase of *atingido* lands on its prior offering of three options to *atingidos*: (1) land of equivalent quality and value in the immediate region or one of the three southern states; (2) cash indemnification, with *atingidos'* participation in farmland and capital improvements' value; (3) inclusion of all landless *atingidos* (including adult children of *atingidos*) in resettlement projects. The accord has allowed CRAB to effectively monitor ELETROSUL's actions in the Machadinho and Itá dam projects and to manage the Itá resettlement project. It has often been cited as a model.

THE CONSTRUCTION OF NEW ALLIANCES AND IDEOLOGY: 1988-1992

The fall of the Berlin Wall, the completion of the democratic transition, and the shift in 1988 to democratic consolidation opened a new political opportunity structure. Brazilian popular movements underwent a crisis of mobilization, the alliances formed during repression broke apart, and new alliances were formed. Progressives within the Brazilian Catholic Church were weakened, which, together with the increased strength of conservatives, diminished the church's support for workers' movements. The ascending phase of the protest cycle ended with the failure of the agrarian reform movement in the 1988 constitution and the narrow defeat of the Worker's Party candidate for president in 1989. The weakness of ELETROSUL and its lesser physical presence in the region further reduced mobilization of CRAB's social base.

At the same time, the international and national environmental movements were growing in power and influence. CRAB maintained contacts with Polo Sindical, a rural trade union consortium established in the Northeast region in 1979 to coordinate the farmworkers struggle with the regional power company over the Itaparica Dam project. Through its contacts with Polo Sindical, CRAB came into contact with national and international NGOs as a transnational environmental advocacy network was being formed (Keck and Sikkink 1998:132). In this context, CRAB leadership and core activists went through a process of ideological reconstruction to integrate land struggle and ecology themes. They reframed the dams issue to ally with the newly constructed political ecology branch of the environmental movement. On CRAB's side, the product was a new synthetic ideology that positioned it to play a bridging role between the class-based rural movements and the urban-based environmental movements.

Land Struggles and Political Ecology

Prior to 1985, anti-dam struggles and ecology movements followed different paths. The former were peasant-based and focused on the land struggle, while the latter were urban-based and directed at industrial pollution. Ironically, before 1985, only the international lending agencies and, in some situations, the Brazilian electric sector considered both the ecology movement and the anti-dams movement as part of the environmentalist movement, because they both opposed "progress." In late 1983, the anti-dams movement in the Uruguai River Basin took a position of outright opposition to dam construction. It deeply questioned the need for more electric energy and thus challenged the development model, which led it to be accused of opposing progress (Vianna 1990: 6). The ecology movement, which in many instances prevented the installation of polluting industries and agro-industrial complexes, was criticized in similar fashion. For example, the tanning industry of the Rio do Sinos Valley of Rio Grande do Sul State accused the environmental NGO Union for Natural Environment Protection (UPAN) of being anti-progress.[4] Despite their common opponents, the anti-dams movement and the environmental movement did not initially form an alliance in southern Brazil, although this later became one basis for their cooperation.

CRAB's reframing of the dams issue was mediated through its ties to other land struggle movements in Brazil. Although CRAB itself remained entirely rooted in its land/imperialism frame until 1989, Brazil's ecology movement had already begun to influence other land and dam struggles in Brazil around 1985. By 1986, the ecology movement in Brazil adopted a political ecology ideology.[5]

A crucial factor in the political ecology turn in Latin America was the rubber tappers movement, which had been fighting since 1975 to guarantee land use rights and improve the living standards of Amazon forest peoples, framing themselves as a land/class movement. In the early 1980s, the rubber tappers faced increasing pressure from deforestation caused by cattle ranching and agriculture. In 1983 a small network of activists and organizations based in Washington, D.C. began to target multilateral bank lending in developing countries, choosing Brazil's Polonoroeste Project in the Amazon as one of the initial targets (Keck and Sikkink 1998: 135). In 1985, the group established contact with Chico Mendes, leader of the Acre rubber tappers. That same year a meeting was held in Brasília as a calculated effort of the Rubber Tappers to break out of regional isolation and to seek new allies nationally and internationally (Schwartzman 1991: 406). The result of the meeting was the creation of a National Council of Rubber Tappers (CNS) and the launching of the extractive reserves proposal, which called for land to be set aside for traditional sustainable land uses. This proposal allied the rubber tappers with local indigenous groups and, through them, brought ties to the ecologists. The rubber tappers movement's strategic importance and its objectives, its organizational capabilities, and its proactive characteristics attracted the support of the Environmental Defense Fund (EDF). In this way, the rubber tappers forged an alliance of their rural peasant-based struggle with urban segments of civil society, broadening the social and political base of the movement (Vianna 1990: 6). By 1988, the rubber tappers movement had explicitly adopted an ecological discourse.

A similar articulation began in 1985 between the Polo Sindical and EDF. The active mobilization of Polo Sindical attracted environmentalist attention. In the turn to political ecology, movement activists came into communication with EDF and the World Bank which, in turn, pressured the utility to provide better compensation and resettlement guarantees as conditions on a $500 million loan for Brazil's electric power sector. Polo Sindical's written public denunciation of the northeast utility was widely circulated among environmental INGOs and the World Bank and received a great deal of attention.

CRAB leaders had close ties to the Polo Sindical and were fully informed about the growing involvement of the EDF in the Itaparica struggle. Similarly, they were aware of the importance of the rubber tappers movement (Dalla Costa 1988) and its implications for broader coalitions for land struggles. However, the involvement of environmental NGOs came more slowly to the south. CRAB first met with World Bank investigators in 1986 and the negotiations for World Bank loans gave them bargaining power with ELETROSUL. But CRAB was not directly influential in the environmental movement and did not adopt ecological frames until after 1988. Their ultimate shift in frames was the result of a protracted and self-conscious process of ideology reconstruction and political education of the central leadership, core activists, and segments of their mass base.

In short, the rubber tappers movement initiated the turn to political ecology among land struggle movements in Brazil, influencing the Polo Sindical and then CRAB. Political ecology developed from the two-way interactions between international environmentalists and local activists. It involved as much the "classing" of environmentalism (that is, its need to recognize human need as part of the environment) as the "greening" of land struggle issues.

The Greening of CRAB: 1988-1992

Although CRAB was well aware of the development of political ecology in other regions, its first direct link with environmental NGOs did not occur until 1988. Young CRAB leader Luiz Dalla Costa attended an international conference in San Francisco sponsored by the International Rivers Network (IRN) about the construction of large hydroelectric dams and made additional contacts with major environmental NGOs and World Bank officials. His report to the movement on these activities emphasized the importance of building networks in Brazil (with groups such as the rubber tappers movement and environmental NGOs), building networks with other Latin American countries, and applying pressure to the multilateral banks and national governments to oppose large dams (Dalla Costa 1988). Conference participant Carlos Aveline, president of UPAN (Union for Natural Environmental Protection), was chosen to initiate contacts for the Latin American network and, in a UPAN publication, called on Latin American ecological entities to join the network as well as to support CRAB and its initiatives to organize a national anti-dams movement (Aveline and Hartman 1988). Important outcomes of this conference for CRAB were (1) the establishment of local-national-international ties, and (2) growth of the organization's capacity to help create national and transnational advocacy networks opposed to large dams.

Nevertheless, even through 1989, a CRAB publication by an important left intellectual avoided the ecology frame. It characterized large dams as a geopolitical strategy for Brazilian "subimperialism" to control rich natural resources in the interests of guaranteeing natural resource supply to U.S. transnational industries (Schilling 1989).

The reconstruction of CRAB's ideology into political ecology occurred largely in late 1989 and 1990. In October 1989, CRAB sponsored a two-day workshop on environmental legislation for *atingidos* and movement leaders, with participation by movement advisers from CEDI (Ecumenical Center for Documentation and Information), a Brazilian NGO based in Rio de Janeiro. CEDI was important for land struggle issues in Brazil and had also maintained close contacts with U.S. environmental NGOs (Schwartzman, 1991: 410). In July 1990, two days of discussions were held on ecology and the ecology movement. Consultant-adviser Aurélio Vianna of CEDI, also a graduate researcher on dam-affected people, helped prepare a working paper for didactic use in the 1989 workshop. He was also an adviser in both events and wrote an article on these training sessions (CRAB 1989, 1990; Vianna 1990). These documents reveal the process of ideological reconstruction and political education that integrated ecology and land struggle themes. They offered simple technical explanations of environmental laws (CRAB 1989), discussion of the strategic uses of the environmental legislation by the anti-dams movement and the relation between CRAB and the struggle for the land and the environment.

To summarize, first, enduring values were validated, and the grassroots struggle for the land was affirmed as the principal issue of the movement. Second, the reality of a change in the political opportunity structure was identified: the defeat of agrarian reform in the new constitution required social movements to develop new strategies to "guarantee resistance and advances in the struggle for the land" (CRAB 1989). Third, using as an example local agriculturalists' indiscriminate use of pesticides, ecology was shown to be relevant to the improvement of living conditions, and thus linked to core values. The example of the rubber tappers movement (CRAB 1990; Vianna 1990: 6) was fundamental as a precedent for linking the class-based land rights struggle with the universal values of the ecology movement. This NGO/CRAB alignment of the land struggle and ecology frames did not signify the replacement of Marxist discourse but rather its incorporation into a political ecology master frame, which could facilitate alliances with ecology movements with an urban base (Vianna 1990: 7-8).

However, frame alignment between NGOs and CRAB leadership was not sufficient. For the political ecology frame to mobilize core leaders and activists, it had to not only demonstrate its potency as a prognosis, and its motivating rationale for these leaders to take action, but also reflect their experiences. Regardless of the importance of CRAB's strategic role as a political ecology movement, CRAB's popular legitimacy, both locally and with the NGOs, depended on its mass base.

Adoption of the proposed frame by CRAB's mass base was more difficult. Reduced investment funds limited ELETROSUL's construction to the Itá dam site, reducing CRAB's mass base and mobilization principally to the Itá area and the resettlement project in Paraná State. In this context, movement leadership devised several strategies which sought to relate and adapt the *colono* way of life to an alternative development which was not environmentally destructive. First, they offered courses and publications for agriculturalists, teachers, and youth in environmental education, which obtained sustained funding from the Brazilian National Foundation for the Environment. Second, a project for the development of sustainable peasant agriculture was undertaken by a consortium of four rural unions (Sindicatos n.d.), for which funding was obtained from the NGO of Luxembourg, ASTM (*Action Solidarité Tiers Monde*, Third World Solidarity Action). Third, the resettlement project emphasized education, training, and technical assistance in agroecology, particularly for younger *colonos*. Although CRAB leadership recognized that it is impossible today to make a *colono* feel like an ecologist (CRAB 1990) by giving priority to resettlement, youth, and agroecology , the movement was attempting to integrate core values with the new ideology by investing in the reconstruction of the *colonos'* way of life, or construction of a new way of life which, maintained family and community ties with physical space and with the environment (Vianna et al. 1990: 54).

CRAB's synthesis of land struggle and class ideologies with ecology put it in an important structural position in meetings in 1991 and 1992 in preparation for the 1992 United Nations Conference on Environment and Development (UNCED or Rio-92). In these meetings, CRAB and its allies successfully persuaded environmentalist organizations to permit movement organizations lacking explicit ecological perspectives to participate in their forums, thus opening the way to links and alliances between the environmental movement and class-based organizations, including CPT, the labor unions, and the landless rural workers movements.[6]

Since 1991, CRAB has taken a leadership role in the national anti-dam organization, MAB, while achieving strategic mobilization in response to localized dam projects as the regional chapter MAB-Sul. In March 1997, MAB and MAB-Sul and the International Rivers Network played leading roles in convening representatives from twenty countries at the First International Meeting of People Affected by Dams in Curitiba, the capital city of Paraná State. In 1998, MAB and MAB-Sul were involved in plans for public hearings in Brazil in 1999 by the recently created World Commission on Dams.

CONCLUSION

The story of the anti-dam movement in southern Brazil illustrates several general processes important in forming linkages between local mobilizations and international social movements. First, the evolving and multidimensional local and national political opportunity structures were always important. Dam resistance was affected by the particular social and economic structures in each locale, by the overall repressiveness of the government in different phases of authoritarianism and democratization, by the phase of a cycle of protest, by economic and political factors which affected the efficiency and strength of the electrical utility, and by international processes and events which affected the availability of loans to support major hydroelectric projects.

Second, local struggles never occurred in a vacuum, but they drew on what we have come to call the "preexisting" organizational structures and ideologies, that is, the structures and ideologies inherited from previous events and experiences. In southern Brazil, the local people who could respond to the threat of dam construction were those with external communication network ties. These ties gave them access to information about plans for dams and other communities' bad experiences with compensation and resettlement. Similarly, local activists' embeddedness as organic intellectuals in the international religious/political networks of the progressive church helped them interpret their communities' needs and address those needs through protest and resistance. Finally, their location in the social networks of the international progressive church gave them access to the resources necessary to pursue their program.

Third, the initiative for protest and resistance always began with local people, as did the initiative to seek external resources. External agents were reactive, responding to requests or proposals, or entering an area after the disruption had started.

Fourth, and related, interchange among activists and international organizations and movements was always two-way. The master ideologies of liberation theology and later political ecology certainly affected the thinking of local people. But also the struggles and needs of poor peasants influenced the international movement of the progressive church toward liberation theology and, later, the shift of the international environmental movement toward political ecology. Local activists needed support and resources from outsiders to help them in their struggles with local elites, but the progressive church and the international NGOs had just as much need for the active grassroots participation and innovations of local groups.

Fifth, these local-national-international ties, first to the progressive church on the land struggle and later to the ecology movement, constituted the formation of transnational advocacy networks which provided leverage in negotiations with the Brazilian government. Finally, frame alignment processes were inextricably linked to the construction and reconstruction of social networks and complex ideologies, and the depth of these processes needs to be fully acknowledged if it is to be understood. Opponents of movements often point to apparent inconsistencies or changes in movement ideologies as evidence of their superficiality, but this is rarely a fair characterization of the actual belief systems of committed activists in any movement. In this case, the earlier construction of liberation theology was itself a deep process of ideological reconstruction involving multiplex influence networks between the needs and struggles of the world's poor and Latin American and European religious leaders. By constructing dam resistance as a land struggle, the early CRAB and CPT activists drew on their core values and beliefs in the ideology and resources of the progressive church and positioned the anti-dam movement in alliance with other rural land struggles. For eight years, this ideology sustained a growing and active mobilization. When the political opportunity structure changed at the end of the democratic transition, activists needed ways to find new allies, and the shift to a political ecology frame provided the basis for land defense movements to obtain resourceful urban and international allies. However, this change could not be, and was not, casual or superficial. It required a deep examination and integration of core values into the new ideology so that it could justify the actions of central leaders and core activists. Several years of discussions were necessary, and the new ideology was a synthesis that held to the core values and imperatives of the old class- and Bible-based defense of land while encompassing the new ecology-based defense of land. This new ideology, in turn, influenced the international actors in contact with local activists and became the basis for new networks and alliance structures.

Each specific case is, of course, unique, and no claim is made that the specific configuration of events found in this case will be replicated in all cases. But the case materials point to the ways in which we may expect to see agency, initiative, and influence among local actors, even as they are embedded in, and influenced by, larger transnational movement networks and political opportunity structures.

NOTES

1.   Space does not permit a detailed review of the enormous literature on political opportunity. For recent reviews, see Tarrow (1998) and the essays in McAdam, McCarthy, and Zald (1996).

2.   Originally the term *colonos* described the largely Protestant German, and largely Catholic Italian and Polish immigrants who arrived in several waves in the nineteenth century. These immigrants acquired small tracts of land in government or private-sponsored colonization projects in the region and maintained commercial as well as subsistence agricultural production. Today, the term *colonos* refers to the several types of agricultural smallholders whose production is based on family labor: small owner-operators, sharecroppers, renters, squatters (Grzybowski 1985: 250), within a diversified cash-crop system.

3.   Derci Pasqualotto interview, October 26, 1992, Florianópolis.

4.   Carlos Aveline telephone interview, December 22, 1998, Brasília.

5.   See Viola (1987) for a detailed discussion of political ecology in the context of the evolution of the ecology movement in Brazil. It differs from earlier preservationist and

conservationists ideologies in its focus on the human and social dimensions of nature-society relations, particularly social injustice. For the Brazilian Left, political ecology represented the classing of ecology (Waldman 1988).

    6. Aurélio Vianna interview, October 21, 1992, Rio de Janeiro.

REFERENCES

Alves, Maria Helena Moreira. 1985. *State and Opposition in Military Brazil.* Austin: University of Texas Press.

Aveline, Carlos C., and Angela Hartmann. 1988. "Por uma Ação Conjunta em Defesa dos Rios." São Leopoldo-RS: União Protetora do Ambiente Natural-UPAN.

Benford, Robert D. 1993. "Frame Disputes within the Nuclear Disarmament Movement." *Social Forces* 71: 677-701.

Boli, John, and George M. Thomas. 1997. "World Culture in the World Polity: A Century of International Non-governmental Organization." *American Sociological Review* 622: 171-190.

CPT. 1987. *Comissão Pastoral da Terra: Seu Compromisso Eclesial e Político.* 2a ed. Goiania: CPT. 1988: 4-5.

CRAB (Movimento dos Atingidos por Barragens). 1989. "Curso sobre legislação ambiental." Erechim, RS, October 16-17, 1989.

———. 1990. "Relatório sobre debate da questão ecológica e os diversos movimentos sociais." July 28, 1990. Erechim, RS.

Dalla Costa, Luiz A. 1988. "Relatório de atividades e avaliação da viagem aos Estados Unidos." Erechim, RS: CRAB.

Eisinger, Peter K. 1973. "The Conditions of Protest Behavior in American Cities."*American Political Science Review* 67: 11-28.

Faillace Sandra Tosta. 1990. "Comunidade, Etnia e Religião: um Estudo de Caso na Barragem de Itá (RS/SC)." Master's thesis, Universidade Federal do Rio de Janeiro, Museu Nacional.

Gerhards, Jurgen, and Dieter Rucht. 1992. "Mesomobilization: Organizing and Framing in Two Protest Campaigns in West Germany." *American Journal of Sociology* 983: 555-595.

Grzybowski, Cândido. 1985. "Comissão Pastoral da Terra e os Colonos do Sul do Brasil." Pp. 248-273 in *Igreja e Questão Agrária,* Vanilda Paiva, ed. São Paulo: Edições Loyola.

———. 1987. Caminhos e Descaminhos dos Movimentos Sociais no Campo. Petrópolis: Vozes/FASE.

Haines, Herbert H. 1984. "Black Radicalization and the Funding of Civil Rights: 1957-1970." *Social Problems* 321: 31-43.

Hellma, Judith A. 1987. *Journeys among Women: Feminism in Five Italian Cities.* New York: Oxford University Press.

Jenkins, J. Craig, and Craig M. Eckert. 1986. "Channeling Black Insurgency: Elite Patronage and Professional Social Movement Organizations in the Development of the Black Movement." *American Sociological Review* 51: 812-829.

Jenkins, J. Craig, and Kurt Schock. 1992. "Global Structures and Political Processes in the Study of Domestic Political Conflict." *American Review of Sociology* 18:161-185.

Johnston, Hank. 1991. "Antecedents of Coalition: Frame Alignment and Utilitarian Unity in the Catalan Anti-Francoist Opposition." *Research in Social Movements, Conflicts and Change* 13: 241-259.

Keck, Margaret E. 1989. "The New Unionism in the Brazilian Transition." Pp. 252-296 in *Democratizing Brazil,* Alfred Stepan, ed. New York: Oxford University Press.

Keck, Margaret E., and Kathryn Sikkink. 1998. *Activists beyond Borders: Advocacy Networks in International Politics.* Ithaca, N.Y.: Cornell University Press.

Klandermans, Bert. 1990. "Linking the 'Old' and the 'New' Movement Networks in the Nether-
    lands." Pp. 122-136 in *Challenging the Political Order*, R. J. Dalton and M. Kuechler, eds.
    New York: Oxford University Press.
————. 1997. *The Social Psychology of Protest*. Oxford: Blackwell.
Koopmans, Ruud. 1993. "The Dynamics of Protest Waves: West Germany, 1965 to 1989."
    American Sociological Review 585: 637-658.
Mainwaring, Scott. 1986. *The Catholic Church and Politics in Brazil, 1916-85*. Stanford, Calif.:
    Stanford University Press.
Maney, Gregory. 1998. "Rival Transnational Networks and Intersecting Dependencies: The
    Yanomami and Kuna Indigenous." Unpublished manuscript. University of Wisconsin,
    Madison.
Marullo, Sam, Ron Pagnucco, and Jackie Smith. 1996. "Frame Changes and Social Movement
    Contraction: U. S. Peace Movement Framing after the Cold War." *Sociological Inquiry*
    661: 1-28.
McAdam, Doug. 1982. *The Political Process and the Development of Black Insurgency*. Chi-
    cago: University of Chicago Press.
McAdam, Doug, John D. McCarthy, and Mayer N. Zald, eds. 1996. *Comparative Perspectives
    on Social Movements*. New York: Cambridge University Press.
Melucci, Alberto. 1989. *Nomads of the Present: Social Movements and Individual Needs in Con-
    temporary Society*, John Keane and Paul Mier, eds. Philadelphia: Temple University Press.
————. 1995. "The Process of Collective Identity." Pp. 41-63 in *Social Movements and Culture*.
    Hank Johnston and Bert Klandermans, eds. Minneapolis: University of Minnesota Press.
Moisés, José Álvaro. 1989. "Dilemas da Consolidação Democrática no Brasil." *Lua Nova* 16:
    47-86.
Morris, Aldon. 1984. *The Origins of the Civil Rights Movement: Black Communities Organizing
    for Change*. New York: Free Press.
Navarro, Zander. 1992. "Democracy, Citizenship, and Representation: Rural Social Movements
    in Southern Brazil, 1978-1990." Cambridge, Mass.: MIT Center for International Studies,
    Working Paper C92/3.
————. 1996. *Política, Protesto e Cidadania no Campo: as Lutas Sociais dos Colonos e dos
    Trabalhadores Rurais no Rio Grande do Sul*. Porto Alegre: Editora da Universi-
    dade/UFRGS.
O'Donnell, Guillermo, Philippe Schmitter, and Laurence Whitehead, eds. 1987. *Transitions from
    Authoritarian Rule: Latin America. 2nd ed.* Baltimore: Johns Hopkins University Press.
Pagnucco, Ron. 1996. "Social Movement Dynamics during Democratic Transition: A Synthesis
    of Political Process and Interactionist Theories." *Research on Democracy and Society*, 3:
    3-38.
Rothman, Franklin Daniel. 1996. "Emergência do Movimento dos Atingidos pelas Barragens da
    Bacia do Rio Uruguai, 1979-1983." Pp. 106-136 in *Política, Protesto e Cidadania no
    Campo: As Lutas Sociais dos Colonos e dos Trabalhadores Rurais no Rio Grande do Sul.*,
    Z. Navarro, ed. Porto Alegre: Editora da Universidade/UFRGS.
Scherer-Warren, Ilse et. al. 1988. "A Implantação das Barragens na Bacia do Rio Uruguai e suas
    Implicações Sociais: O Movimento das Barragens e os Camponeses da Região de Lages
    SC." Relatório final. Florianopólis: Universidade Federal de Santa Catarina.
Schilling, Paulo. 1989. "A Política Hidrelétrica Brasileira: O Homem, a Ecologia, a Soberania e
    o Desenvolvimento." Paper presented at Seminário de Discussão do Projeto Cone Sul. Ere-
    chim, February 22- 23, 1989.
Schwartzman, Stephen. 1991. "Deforestation and Popular Resistance in Acre: From Local Social
    Movement to Global Network." *Centennial Review* 35: 397-422.
Secretariado Diocesano de Pastoral. 1991. Fé e Política. Chapecó, Sindicatos dos Trabalhadores
    Rurais de Porto Lucena, Porto Xavier, Pirapó and Dezesseis de Novembro. n.d. "Um tra-
    balho sindical para a defesa do meio ambiente."

Smith, Brian H. 1990. *More than Altruism: The Politics of Private Foreign Aid*. Princeton, N.J.: Princeton University Press.

Smith, Jackie. 1995. "Transnational Political Processes and the Human Rights Movement." *Research in Social Movements, Conflicts and Change* 18: 185-219.

Smith, Jackie, Charles Chatfield, and Ron Pagnucco. 1997. *Transnational Social Movements and Global Politics: Solidarity beyond the State*. Syracuse, N.Y.: Syracuse University Press.

Smith, Jackie, Ron Pagnucco, and Winnie Romeril. 1994. "Transnational Social Movement Organisations in the Global Political Arena." *Voluntas* 52: 121-154.

Snow, David A., and Robert Benford. 1988. "Ideology, Frame Resonance and Participant Mobilization." Pp. 197-217 in *From Structure to Action: Comparing Social Movement Research Across Cultures,* Bert Klandermans, Hans-Peter Kriesi, and Sidney Tarrow, eds. Greenwich, Conn.: JAI Press.

Snow, David A., and Robert D. Benford. 1992. "Master Frames and Cycles of Protest." Pp. 133-155 in *Frontiers in Social Movement Theory*, Aldon Morris and Carol McClurg Mueller, eds. New Haven, Conn.: Yale University Press.

Snow, David A., E. Burke Rochford, Jr., Steven K. Worden, Robert D. Benford. 1986. "Frame Alignment Processes, Micro-Mobilization, and Movement Participation." *American Sociological Review* 51:464-81.

Switkes, Glenn. 1998. "Brazil Dam Moves Forward despite Outstanding Social and Environmental Concerns." *World Rivers Review* 13: 5, 4.

Tarrow, Sidney. 1998. *Power in Movement: Social Movements, Collective Action and Mass Politics in the Modern State*. 2nd ed. Cambridge: Cambridge University Press.

Vianna, Aurélio. 1990. "O Movimento de Atingidos por Barragens e a Questão Ambiental." *Proposta* 46: 5-8.

Vianna, Aurélio et al. 1990. "Lutas de Resistência ou Lutas por um Novo Modelo de Sociedade." *Proposta* 46: 56.

Viola, Eduardo J. 1987. "O Movimento Ecológico no Brasil 1974-1986: do Ambientalismo à Ecopolítica." *Revista Brasileira de Ciências Sociais* 3: 5-26.

Waldman, Maurício. "Ecologia na Perspectiva dos Trabalhadores." *Tempo e Presenca*. Maio, 1988: 4-5.

Chapter 8

CREATING TRANSNATIONAL SOLIDARITY: THE USE OF NARRATIVE IN THE U.S.-CENTRAL AMERICA PEACE MOVEMENT

Sharon Erickson Nepstad

Increasingly, social problems are expanding beyond national borders. A shift in one country's economy can have profound effects on the international market and economic health of other nations. The proliferation of nuclear and biological weapons threatens the security of all countries and global warming affects the entire earth. As problems are becoming more transnational, so too are movements for social change. Activists are stretching beyond state boundaries to work in solidarity with those with whom they identify in distant countries (Keck and Sikkink 1998; Smith, Chatfield, and Pagnucco 1997). Although there is growing academic interest in such "transnational social movements," there are few empirical studies that draw out the theoretical implications of the formation and dynamics of these movements.

Toward this end, I add another case to the literature on transnational movement emergence through an examination of the U.S.-Central America peace movement. This was a movement of U.S. citizens who, throughout the 1980s, proclaimed solidarity with the poor in El Salvador, Nicaragua, and Guatemala in their efforts to establish new societies based on the principles of social justice. Activists also attempted to constrain American military influence in the region and change U.S. foreign policy toward Central America. The movement was primarily composed of numerous local and regional groups that undertook a wide array of actions, including vigils to remember the casualties in Central America's wars, campaign work to defeat aid to the Nicaraguan Contras, clothing and medicine shipments to refugees, and picketing the military base that houses the School of the Americas where Latin American military officers are trained (Nepstad 2000; Smith 1996). A few organizations coordinated large-scale national campaigns. Witness for Peace led more than 4,000 North Americans on delegations to the war zones of Nicaragua to gain first-hand experience of the effects of the Contra War. The Sanctuary effort mobilized over 70,000 U.S. citizens to aid Central American refugees by breaking federal immigration laws (Golden and McConnell 1986). The "Pledge of Resistance" committed over 80,000 Americans to civil disobedience if the United States engaged in acts of aggression toward Central America (Smith 1996: 60).

These are only a few examples of the thousands of actions undertaken in the U.S.-Central America peace movement. Given the amount of transnational collective action that occurred, a number of questions arise: Why did U.S. citizens organize around El Salvador, Nicaragua, and Guatemala but not other countries that were suffering from social injustices and human rights abuses? How were activists able to overcome the racial, class, ethnic, linguistic, national, and ideological differences to form transnational links? What contributed to the solidarity that emerged between this group of North and Central Americans? I propose that answers to these questions can be found in the collective identity that progressive Christians in both regions shared.[1] However, these Christians did not initially hold a similar understanding of the values, beliefs, and practices that this identity represents and therefore this collective identity had to be constructed. The aim of this chapter is to elucidate the factors that facilitated this process. To do so, I draw upon qualitative in-depth interviews that I conducted with thirty-two Central America solidarity activists. A theoretical sample (Glaser and Strauss 1967) was employed to ensure a diverse representation of geographic regions, age range, gender, and levels of participation within the movement.[2]

TRANSNATIONAL SOCIAL MOVEMENTS
AND COLLECTIVE IDENTITY

The globalization of social problems and emergence of numerous cross-national and transnational social movements has generated a few studies that provide a starting point for examining the U.S.-Central America peace movement. For instance, research on cross-national movements—referring to movements that begin in one nation and are imitated or diffused to another—indicates that three factors are important. First, the object of diffusion must be of interest and use to both the originating movement and the adopting group. Second, both movements must possess a number of similar cultural and/or structural characteristics that provide the basis for mutual identification. Finally, both movements must be linked together through relational ties and social networks and/or through nonrelational ties such as the media (McAdam and Rucht 1993; Morris 1981; Oberschall 1989; Tarrow 1994). In other words, the more these movements hold shared interests and are similar on a number of social, cultural, or institutional dimensions, the more likely that diffusion will occur.

Such similarities may not be a prerequisite for the emergence of transnational social movements. These movements emerge semi-independently in various countries, rather than being intentionally transmitted from one to another, but they share common goals and mobilize action against similar targets (Tarrow 1994). In a study of first wave international feminists, Rupp and Taylor (1999) note that there were conflicting interests, goals, and ideas among the various organizations that were part of this transnational feminist movement. There was no consensus on what feminism means, nor was there a single, unitary ideology or political strategy. Yet they argue these divisions were surmountable because feminists embraced a collective identity of "international sisterhood" that united them. Collective identity is typically understood as a "shorthand designation announcing a status—a set of attitudes, commitments, and rules for behavior—that those who assume the identity can be expected to subscribe to" (Friedman and McAdam 1992: 157). These identities are frequently a reflection of ascribed characteristics—such as race, class, gender, or sexual orientation—but they can also reflect beliefs, ideologies, or loyalties. In the case of the international feminist movement, a transnational collective identity was constructed from their ascribed gender status and shared social location. On the broadest level, feminists accentuated the boundaries between men and women to generate this sense of "we-ness." They drew upon the shared experience (or potential) of motherhood and women's vulnerability to sexual violence as another means of fostering feminist identity. This simultaneously allowed for differences in tactics and strategies while unifying feminists around their commonalties as women.

Although a collective identity may enable activists within a transnational movement to transcend their internal differences, we must also study how activists deal with the external pressures and challenges of competing interests and identities. Like all people, activists seldom possess a single identity. And, as Gamson notes, "however much we identify with a movement, we have other subidentities built around other social roles. Inevitably, we may face conflicts between how we as movement members feel called upon to act and the actions called for by these other role identities" (1991: 45). As movements become more international, activists will undoubtedly face potential contradictions between their identities as activists and as citizens of particular nations. Yet we have little knowledge of how activists deal with opposing identities and the factors that lead them to prioritize one over the others.

If Rupp and Taylor are correct that collective identity may be crucial for transnational movements, then we need a greater understanding of how such identities are formed. Moreover, we need to learn why some identities are granted precedence over competing identities and loyalties. By exploring the construction of a collective Christian identity in the U.S.-Central America peace movement, I aim to enhance our understanding of these processes, thereby providing some answers to these questions. I expand upon Rupp and Taylor's work by examining another transnational movement in which participants did not share a common understanding of the beliefs and behavior associated with a particular identity. But, unlike the international feminist movement, Christians in the United States and in Central America had no common social location or ascribed traits that could provide the basis for the construction of a collective identity. In fact, they faced race, class, linguistic, and ideological differences and shared only a Christian faith. I posit that one strategy for building a collective identity that could overcome these obstacles was the use of a symbolic narrative.

NARRATIVES AND SOCIAL MOVEMENTS

There has been a surge of interest in the cultural dimensions of movements, resulting in an abundant literature on framing, identity, ideology, and rhetoric. Only a handful of scholars, however, have examined how movement stories inspire or sustain activism. Specifically, Benford (1994) demonstrates how narratives operated as frames that fostered collective action in the anti-nuclear movement. Hunt and Benford's (1994) study of the peace and justice movement indicates that stories help align personal and collective identities. Polletta (1998) argues that storytelling can contribute to a movement organization's ability to withstand setbacks and influence mainstream politics. And Fine (1995) has categorized the types of narratives commonly told by activists into "horror stories" that raise awareness of injustices and compel action, "war stories" that relay participants' experiences within the movement, and "happy endings" that boost morale by revealing the unexpected rewards of activism. Somers calls attention to the social epistemology and ontology of narratives:

> Scholars are postulating something much more substantive about narrative: namely, that social life is itself *storied* and that narrative is an *ontological condition of social life*. Their research is showing that stories guide action; that people construct identities (however multiple and changing) by locating themselves or being located within a repertoire of emplotted stories; that "experience" is constituted through narratives; that people make sense of what has happened . . . by attempting to assemble or in some way integrate these happenings within one or more narratives; and that people are guided to act in certain ways, and not others, on the basis of the projections, expectations, and memories derived from a multiplicity but ultimately limited repertoire of available social, public and cultural narratives. (1994: 613-614)

In this context, stories are told to help make sense of the social world, define who we are, and guide behavior. Narratives are more than an embodiment of movement frames or ideological beliefs; they are an independent cultural resource that can serve unique purposes. Consequently, they should be examined as a distinct phenomenon since "subsuming narrative under the broader category of frame [or other cultural dimensions] obscures differences . . . in how they organize and represent reality, their relation to collective identities, how they engage audiences, and their criteria of intelligibility" (Polletta 1998: 421).

An overview of the traits that distinguish narratives from other cultural dimensions, namely, collective action frames, can clarify these differences. The first characteristic is that narratives have a heuristic plot that reveals a moral or grand purpose, which helps to make sense of unusual or disturbing circumstances (Polletta 1998). In contrast, frames are persuasive devices employed by movement leaders to convince an audience that a situation is unjust and that change is both possible and imperative. In other words, narratives make a situation intelligible; frames recruit people to do something about it. Second, narratives employ three points of view: the protagonist, the narrator, and the audience (Polletta 1998). An effective narrative fosters the audience's identification with the protagonist who embodies the values of the movement. Yet unlike framing—which is inherently dialogical and interactive (Snow and Benford 2000)—narratives are unidirectional. The narrator tells the story to an audience who listens or dismisses it, but typically does not challenge the plot. Framing, on the other hand, reflects ideological maneuvering and debate on the part of movement leaders, opponents, and the targeted recruitment pool. Finally, narratives are based in a limited number of plot lines or canon. Although there is no consensus on the number of plots or the extent of their universality, "there is agreement that stories not conforming to a cultural stock of plots typically are either not stories or are unintelligible" (Polletta 1998: 424). To be effective, frames must also be compatible with the values and beliefs of the targeted audience. However, frame resonance is not dependent on canonical familiarity. Multiple frames are possible and leaders use marketing skills to compose frames for the intended population and gather evidence to underscore their validity.

Like frames, however, not all narratives are equal in their mobilizing capabilities. What factors make a story powerful enough to create a collective identity, inspire action, and build international solidarity? Blain (1994) argues that effective movement narratives must "constitute a field of knowledge" for the audience by persuasively presenting information about unjust conditions, key issues, and the central parties in the struggle. Particularly for transnational efforts like the Central America peace movement, Stoll (1999) proposes that stories are more effective at educating a distant audience than the dissemination of facts and statistics. For example, he believes that Nobel Laureate Rigoberta Menchú's story of life as an indigenous woman under Guatemala's military dictatorship helped draw attention to a conflict that could have otherwise been easily ignored. Her personal account garnered international support because it provided a human face to the victims of repression and economic exploitation that was rampant in Guatemala. Individual life stories can personalize distant or abstract issues by embodying broader injustices, thereby enabling the audience to experience the situation vicariously.

Yet Blain and Stoll both emphasize that these personalized accounts only mobilize action when conveyed melodramatically.[3] Drawing on Kenneth Burke, Blain argues that melodramas are effective because they employ victimage rhetoric that vilifies opponents, generates moral outrage at the violation of the innocent, and calls upon people to join the heroes in redemptive action to defeat the wicked. In other words, they portray a simplified but clear moral struggle between good and evil and invite activists to cast their lot with the oppressed in a redemptive struggle to overcome the villainous powers. Stoll suggests that such moral clarity is essential in building transnational solidarity movements since European and North American audiences will not make an emotional investment in a distant conflict unless there is a despicable enemy who commits egregious offenses against innocent victims:

> Solidarity imagery is a desperate bid for the attention of foreigners who have little at stake but whose governments can have an impact. . . . If they perceive much ambiguity, such as a contest between equally sordid factions, the only response is a check to a relief agency, if that. What they are most likely to embrace is a well-defined cause with moral credibility. . . . One of the simplifying functions of solidarity imagery is that it offers a single platform to support. . . . What happens without the illusion of a single platform is illustrated by Peru and Colombia. In Peru the Shining Path guerrillas made no effort to conceal their terrorism against non-combatants. . . . In Colombia the guerrillas split into murderous factions, undermining the claim to be a representative political force. As a result, North Americans who care about these countries have not had a single, plausible movement like the Sandinistas or the URNG to support. Instead, they face many-sided conflicts between elected governments, social democratic oppositions, left-wing terrorists, right-wing terrorists, and drug mafia. Even though the death tolls in these countries have approached Central American levels, little has developed in the way of solidarity organizing to change U.S. policy. (1999: 235-236)

Yet not all melodramas mobilize collective action. Benford and Hunt (1992) suggest that such stories only work if the antagonists are easily vilified and the heroes are likable. Moreover, Snow and Benford (1988) propose that if we want to understand the failure or success of movement narratives, the audience's interpretation must be taken into account. This is affected by several factors. First, the story must have "empirical credibility" to be believable. Second, a narrative is always perceived through an interpretive screen that is shaped by personal experience and biographical influences. Some stories may simply be too far removed from the reality and experience of audience members that they cannot identify with the heroes or empathize with the victims. Third, narratives have greater mobilizing potential if they symbolically mirror the cultural heritage of the audience—that is, "ontological narratives" that provide values, beliefs, and a worldview. A story must resonate, as Jasper (1997: 274) puts it, with "a god term or other theme that is widely honored."

NARRATIVES IN THE U.S.-CENTRAL AMERICA PEACE MOVEMENT

One of the most powerful narratives in the U.S.-Central America peace movement is the story of Oscar Romero, the archbishop of San Salvador. Many of the respondents in my research mentioned that this story strongly influenced their decision to join the movement. For instance, one North American activist described how Romero so transformed and radicalized his own faith that he abandoned his seminary training to join the Salvadoran guerrilla forces. Part of his responsibility was to develop international solidarity by telling El Salvador's story, including the narrative of Archbishop Romero. He reflected:

> Personally, I can't even begin to talk about the effect that Romero had. Not only on Central America, but the whole world. . . . Romero's words were so powerful, prophetic, revolutionary. The greatest thing about El Salvador is the word got out and built solidarity like it's never been organized before. . . . I was at a socialist conference in Cuba and people from all over the world were there. They were amazed at the level of solidarity that Central America has been able to gain and it's because we got in from the beginning. We worked very closely with people from other countries and *people told the story.* We didn't rely on the New York Times to tell our stories. It's been person to person, and that's the best thing we've ever done. (italics mine)

I contend that Romero's life story effectively contributed to the emergence of transnational solidarity for several reasons. First, it offers an emotionally engaging, personalized account of the injustices committed during El Salvador's civil war, thereby educating the international audience about the situation. Second, it possesses all the traits of a melodrama including a villainous military regime that committed horrible atrocities against morally credible victims, and a likeable hero with whom the audience could identify. Third, this identification was strengthened because Romero's life symbolically reflected and resonated with the ontological narrative of Christianity. This provided the foundation upon which a transnational collective identity between progressive North and Central American Christians could be constructed. Finally, Romero provided a model of action for all who claimed this identity, namely, speaking out against injustices in Central America and choosing the side of the poor in their struggle for liberation. To support these assertions, I turn to a closer examination of the "plot" of Romero's life and activists' accounts of how it influenced them.

Archbishop Oscar Romero

In 1977, when Romero was appointed archbishop, El Salvador was deeply embroiled in civil war. Tensions had been simmering for centuries as economic and political problems increased due to a shortage of land, dependence on coffee as the main export crop, and white domination. These conditions benefited an oligarchy who amassed wealth and fortune while the vast majority of the population fell further into poverty. A significant incident that preceded the war occurred in 1932 when the army overthrew a recently elected reformist president and replaced him with a military dictator. A small group revolted but was quickly subdued by the army, who took revenge by executing between 10,000 and 30,000 people, most of whom had not been involved in the rebellion (Anderson 1971). This incident profoundly shaped the mentality of the military government, particularly during the 1970s and 1980s, when "some of the oligarchy's paid political statements in newspapers hinted that something like 1932 might be necessary again" (Berryman 1984: 95).

A series of military regimes reigned throughout the next decades, all of which kept the unequal socioeconomic structures intact. Conditions worsened in the 1960s and 1970s and the landless population grew from 11.8 to 40.9 percent of rural families, leaving 90 percent of these households with insufficient income to provide basic nutrition (Peterson 1997: 29). With a military government protecting the interests of the elite, the impoverished masses turned to grassroots organizing as the only available means of social change. As a result, numerous peasant and labor groups were formed in the 1970s, primarily under the direction of Catholic activists who had gained their organizing and leadership skills from participation in base Christian communities and other pastoral programs.

Such programs were the result of a renewal movement within the Catholic Church, inspired by the Vatican II Council (1962-1965) and the Latin American Bishops Conference in Medellín, Colombia, in 1968. Pope John XXIII significantly altered the role of the church during Vatican II by proclaiming that all have the right to a decent standard of living, education, and political participation. Moreover, he emphasized that the church is and should be involved in *this world* and should not focus exclusively on otherworldly, spiritual matters. The Medellín documents stated that justice would be obtained through organization and action by the popular sectors of society. Consequently, the Catholic Church created a number of projects in which poor people could meet, study the church's social doctrine, discuss their grievances and goals, and plan a course of action to change their circumstances (Peterson 1997; Smith 1991). While these programs instigated tremendous church renewal in the poorest regions, the relationship between Catholic projects and oppositional politics was unsettling for some church leaders. A division grew between the "campesino priests," who worked among the poor and advocated social change, and many within the church hierarchy who felt that the popular church was too closely aligned with particular political interests and parties.

Just as the popular church saw many of its members gaining confidence and becoming active in community organizations, state repression increased. So-called death squads were formed in the 1970s. Dressed in civilian clothes, these paramilitary groups would abduct their victims from their homes, cars, or at work. They would be tortured and executed, and their corpses left in one of the infamous "body dumps" or a symbolic location, such as the steps of a liberation oriented church. The intention was to create such a climate of terror that people would be too frightened to continue organizing. Because of the effectiveness of their projects, the "campesino priests" were specifically targeted. By the late 1970s, one of the most notorious death squads—the White Warriors—began circulating fliers urging people to "Be a patriot! Kill a priest!" (Lernoux 1980).

This was the context in which Romero began his tenure as archbishop. The church was divided, economic conditions—already abysmal—were further exacerbated by the civil war, and priests were being tortured and killed. Given the tense circumstances, the choice to appoint Romero was strategic. He was considered quite conservative, emphasizing prayer and personal salvation—not social change. One priest described him as "churchy, a lover of rules and clerical discipline, a friend of liturgical laws

[who] suffered from nervous tension . . . and showed signs of delicate health" (Erdozaín 1980: 6, 8). The liberation-oriented priests wondered if he would have the courage to denounce the repression against the church. In short, Romero was not expected to make any changes in the institutional church's status quo-preserving position nor did anyone anticipate that his health would withstand the pressures of the position. Nevertheless, he was respected by all as a man of deep honesty and integrity. Thus, the campesino priests were hopeful but skeptical of Romero.

Ultimately, Romero turned out to be much more than the popular church hoped for; he became not merely a supporter of the poor, but the most outspoken "voice of the voiceless." His transformation is often referred to as a "conversion," a key theme in the narrative of Christianity. A Jesuit in El Salvador describes the change in Romero:

> Romero was altogether aware, from the outset, that he had been the candidate of the right. He had known the cajolery of the powerful from the start. . . . Thus not only were the powers cheated of their hopes for a nice, pliable ecclesiastical puppet, but the new archbishop was actually going to oppose them. In store for him . . . was the wrath of the mighty—the oligarchy, the government, the political parties, the army, the security forces, and later, the majority of his bishop brothers, various Vatican offices, and even the U.S. government. . . . Romero had in his favor a group of priests and nuns, and, especially, the hope of a whole people . . . If Archbishop Romero set out on new paths, at his age [59], in his place at the pinnacle of the institution, and against such odds, then his conversion must have been very real. (Sobrino 1990: 8-9)

Most consider the assassination of Father Rutilio Grande as the epiphanal point in the archbishop's conversion. Romero had held Grande in the highest regard and considered him a friend although he disapproved of his pastoral work, which he considered dangerously close to revolutionary ideas. A mere three weeks after Romero's inauguration, Father Grande was murdered on his way to mass. This profoundly affected the archbishop, who claimed that it "gave me the impetus to put into practice the principles of Vatican II and Medellín which call for solidarity with the suffering masses and the poor and encourage priests to live independent of the powers that be" (quoted in Peterson 1997: 61).

The violence against the church escalated and more priests were arrested, expelled, and killed. Roughly three months after Grande was murdered, the White Warriors announced that the remaining Jesuits had thirty days to leave the country or they would be systematically eliminated (Lernoux 1980). Romero was pushed to defend the progressive clergy and condemn government and military repression. As he visited base Christian communities throughout the country and heard stories of torture, disappearances, and murder, he became more emphatic in his denunciations of the violence and his calls for social change. He began to discuss the inherent problems of the economic system. During one interview, Romero bluntly proclaimed: "The situation of injustice is so bad that the faith itself has been perverted; the faith is being used to defend the financial interests of the oligarchy" (quoted in Erdozaín 1980: 74). The archbishop also called upon soldiers to refuse orders. On March 23, 1980, Romero addressed them in a homily that was transmitted throughout the country during his weekly radio broadcast:

> Brothers, you belong to our people. You are killing your own brothers and sisters in the peasants. God's law, which says, "Thou shalt not kill," should prevail over any order given by a man. No soldier is obliged to obey an order against God's law. No one has to carry out an immoral law. It is time to recover your conscience and obey it

rather than orders given in sin. . . . In the name of God, and in the name of this long-suffering people whose cries rise ever more thunderously to heaven, I beg you, I order you, in the name of God: stop the repression. (quoted in Berryman 1984: 150)

Romero had come a long way within three years. No longer was he considered the "safe" person to head the Salvadoran church; in fact, in the eyes of the military regime and its wealthy constituents, he was a serious threat.

As a result of Romero's "option for the poor," he was denounced as a subversive and began receiving death threats. When people suggested that he hire security guards, he refused, stating that he would accept the same risks that the Salvadoran people faced. He was keenly aware that he might be killed but he remained undeterred, knowing that his death would only strengthen the cause of the people. In the last interview he gave, just two weeks before he was murdered, he prophetically reflected:

> I have frequently been threatened with death. I must say that, as a Christian, I do not believe in death but in the resurrection. If they kill me, I shall rise again in the Salvadoran people. . . . If they manage to carry out their threats, I shall be offering my blood for the redemption and resurrection of El Salvador. Martyrdom is a grace from God that I do not believe I have earned. But if God accepts the sacrifice of my life, then may my blood be the seed of liberty, and a sign of the hope that will soon become a reality. May my death . . . be for the liberation of my people. . . . You can tell them, if they succeed in killing me, that I pardon them, and I bless those who carry out the killing. But I wish they could realize that they are wasting their time. A bishop will die, but the church of God—the people—will never die. (quoted in Sobrino 1990: 99-100)

On March 24, 1980, while conducting a memorial mass, an assassin shot Romero through the heart. Although his physical life ended, he was indeed resurrected in the Salvadoran struggle. His image and words were frequently recalled, eulogized, incorporated into songs, poems, and artwork, and his story told repeatedly, throughout Latin America as well as in the United States.

Fostering a Transnational Collective Identity and Solidarity

Romero's narrative found a receptive audience among progressive U.S. Christians, both Catholics and Protestants alike. Yet why was his story so powerful when countless other Salvadoran martyrs were not able to evoke a response? Why did Anglo, middle-class North Americans identify with a Latino born into a poor, Third World family? How did this story facilitate a collective identity when U.S. Christians lived thousands of miles away and the vast majority had no first-hand experience of civil war, violent persecution, or martyrdom? There are several reasons why his narrative was effective.

Personalized Account. One reason why Romero's story fostered international solidarity is because it provided a personalized account that reflected the broader injustices in El Salvador. Seventy thousand people died in this civil war but to North Americans inundated by almost daily news reports of atrocities throughout the world, this could have easily become just another sad statistic. Romero put a human face to this conflict and his story educated U.S citizens about the human rights abuses that the Salvadoran military was inflicting on the civilian population. Just as "the concrete experience of Anne Frank conveys the meaning of the Holocaust in an experiential mode that no amount of factual information on the six million Jewish victims of Nazi death camps can convey" (Gamson 1995: 104-105), Romero's story offered an emotionally engaging means of understanding the reality of the Salvadoran civil war.

Moral Clarity and a Sympathetic Hero. In addition, the story presented the Salvadoran conflict with moral clarity, avoiding ideological justifications or obfuscation. Romero's life melodramatically depicts a struggle of good against evil, in which morally repugnant villains commit unconscionable crimes against morally respectable victims. The violence that the military inflicted on the church was abominable; the most sacred spheres of life were profaned in horrific ways. Church catechists were kidnapped, priests were tortured, missioners were raped and murdered, and a bishop was shot while celebrating the Eucharist. The fact that many victims were church workers devoted to improving the lives of the poor granted them moral authority while the military was perceived as violently preserving an economic and political system built on exploitation. The moral clarity of this narrative, along with the brutality of the repression against the church, generated indignation and created a "moral shock" (Jasper 1997) that caught the attention of progressive faith communities in the United States. In fact, Blain argues that a crucial reason that melodramas elaborate the details of violations is to "amplify the level of moral outrage . . . [because] once aroused, these emotions can then be transformed into a campaign to fight the villains" (1994: 820, 822).

Not only was the Salvadoran military regime easily vilified but Romero was a sympathetic hero with whom the progressive Christian audience could identify. Undoubtedly, part of his appeal was due to the fact that he was very human and made mistakes, including his early misunderstandings of the liberation orientation of the popular church. And much like the audience, he was initially unaware of the injustices and human rights abuses occurring in El Salvador but was willing to listen, learn, and allow God to transform him. He was not spouting extremist ideological rhetoric; he was a man of deep faith and integrity, which called him into relationship with those who suffered from the economic and political conditions in his country. Many U.S. Christians may not have been able to connect with the ideology of the Farabundo Martí National Liberation Front or with a figure such as Che Guevara. Yet, they could identify with Romero because in him "that which is Christian and that which is human is very present" (Sobrino quoted in Dennis, Golden, and Wright 2000: 116).

Ontological Resonance. Snow and Benford (1988) remind us that melodramas with admirable heroes can still fail to create solidarity or inspire action if they are too far removed from the cultural heritage and life experience of the audience. Somers (1994) concurs, stating that we evaluate the importance of narratives by assessing how well they match our fundamental beliefs and values. Therefore, the more closely a movement story reflects the plot and theme of a mobilizing pool's ontological narrative, the more likely it is to engage potential recruits. Not surprisingly, progressive Christians resonated with the story of Romero because the "plot" of his life parallels the life of Christ. For example, both Jesus and Romero were born into families of modest means who were not politically or socially prominent. Each man devoted his life to spiritual pursuits, giving up family, wealth, and security. Both stood up to the religious authorities of their times. Jesus challenged the hypocrisy of the Pharisees; Romero criticized the church hierarchy for collaborating with and condoning the actions of the Salvadoran army. Each called for radical social transformations. Jesus interacted with Samaritans, who were ostracized by society, told the rich to sell their possessions, and overturned the tables of moneylenders in the market when their exorbitant interest rates oppressed the poor. Romero denounced the economic system that benefited a few while impoverishing the masses. Such actions created enemies for both men. Each had an impending sense of his death but was willing to sacrifice his life for a greater cause and was able to forgive those who took his life. Although Jesus and Romero were assassinated, both were resurrected in the sense that their undeserving deaths amplified and spread their messages, which are still remembered today. The similarities between the two were so clear that it has been said that, "The secret of Monseñor Romero is simply that he resembled Jesus" (quoted in Dennis et al. 2000: 107).

Model for Action. The familiar "plot" of Romero's story not only helped progressive North American Christians identify with the story, it also imparted valuable lessons. One moral is told through Romero's "conversion" to the poor. This familiar Christian concept of conversion takes on a new, politicized meaning in Romero's story. Recall that at the time of his appointment, Archbishop Romero was considered a moderate conservative who would keep the church out of the intense political conflict brewing in El Salvador. But as his priests were murdered for their advocacy of the oppressed, he became convinced that the church must take a "preferential option for the poor" and work for their liberation. He stated,

> This is the commitment of being a Christian: to follow Christ in his incarnation. If Christ, the God of majesty, became a lowly human and lived with the poor and even died on a cross like a slave, our Christian faith should also be lived in the same way. The Christian who does not want to live this commitment of solidarity with the poor is not worthy to be called Christian. (Romero 1989: 191)

This lesson planted the seeds of solidarity by inviting North American Christians to also begin a process of conversion that reveals the political implications of faith and calls for identification with the poor of Central America. Comments from activists indicate that the lesson was heard:

> The witness of the martyrs—the four North American churchwomen and Romero— was so compelling. They were living out their love and following Jesus in ways that knowingly led them to their death. The church in El Salvador believed that it was to serve the poor and they knew it was deadly to do so, but they carried on. So those of us in the church in this country, seeing that, could not help but learn from them and be deepened in our own faith.

Another lesson of Romero's story is that faith requires action. Fine (1995) argues that narratives can contribute to movement mobilization by fostering identification with key characters, who provide a model of appropriate action. Romero unequivocally denounced the repression and exploitation of the poor and began to demand changes. He was untiring in his efforts to address the root causes of the poverty and violence. He called upon the rich to end the feudal system and implement economic reform, he asked President Carter to stop sending military aid, and he called upon soldiers to refuse to follow orders to torture and kill. Sympathizing with the plight of the poor was not enough; Christians must actively work to change the conditions that create this suffering. One activist echoes this moral:

> The witness of Oscar Romero was very important. . . . He didn't just say people have the right to bread. He said people have the right to organize, to freely march and communicate with others. . . . So all of this was washing up on our shores—sort of like the Word coming from Palestine to Rome and converting Rome. . . . So all of that was

happening and then Romero was killed in such a brutal, deliberate, transparent way. This reverberated shock waves throughout the faith community in this country. . . . And the fact is that once that happens, the organizing happens and you have to do something. You have to take the next step. . . . Actions follow on hearing the intolerable.

A successful movement narrative should also provide motivation to persist even in the face of danger or defeat. Once again, Romero's story provides a model of faithful perseverance. Despite the intention of his assassins—who hoped his murder would deter such outspoken criticism—Romero's example encouraged people to continue the struggle despite the risks. For instance, one activist who worked in El Salvador during the war, observed how Romero unequivocally denounced injustices, even though he knew it could cost him his life. Romero's example and belief in the resurrection gave him the courage to continue in his work. He reflected: "At the end of his life, Romero knows he's going to be killed and yet he doesn't stop saying what he's been saying. Right before he dies, he says to the rich, 'Take off your ring before they come for your hand.' And I thought, if we have his promise [of resurrection], if we really believe it, then why are we afraid to die?" By following Romero's example, which is ultimately following Jesus' example, one serves a higher purpose that transcends even death.

The narrative of Romero fostered a collective identity because it draws upon and resonates with the ontological narrative of Christianity. By emphasizing the essential values and beliefs that Christians share regardless of their race, class, or nationality, the life of Romero helped to accentuate a sense of "we-ness." One activist articulated this sense of a shared identity: "We connected to Central America because of our common Christian faith. There was a theological and spiritual dimension to it. They were our 'lesser brothers and sisters,' if you will, in Matthew 25." Moreover, as progressive Christians in El Salvador and in the United States identified with Romero as the protagonist of this story, they jointly opposed the antagonists: the Salvadoran military and the U.S. administration that supported them. Thus Romero became an icon that served a very important unifying function:

> An icon [is] a symbol that resolves painful contradictions by transcending them with a healing image. . . . For white, middle class audiences, icons such as Rigoberta [Menchú], Martin Luther King Jr., and Nelson Mandela bridge the gap between privilege and its opposite. They create identity by pointing to a common enemy—the Guatemalan army, segregation, apartheid—against whom privileged and unprivileged can be on the same side. Such images . . . are probably necessary to pull together any movement. (Stoll 1999: 245-246)

Romero not only embodied the values of Christianity but also united people of faith in redemptive action against a common opponent.

Competing Identities

By reflecting the ontological narrative of Christianity, Romero's story reminded progressive American Christians of their beliefs and priorities. This was important because they, like all people, had multiple identities; they were not only Christians but also U.S. citizens. As they learned about the violence and repression that took the life of Romero and many others, U.S. Christians were forced to face the contradictions between their support for the persecuted church of Central America and the actions of their government, which was sponsoring the groups responsible for this suffering. The Reagan administration argued that Central American regimes needed U.S. assistance in their battle against Soviet aggression (Nepstad 1997; Smith 1996). Since Marxism was considered a serious threat to religious freedom, many people of faith might have concluded that supporting the Salvadoran military regime was a necessary evil in the greater goal of eradicating the communist menace. The assassination of Romero could, from this perspective, be perceived as a tragic casualty in a just war. Faced with these competing identities, North American Christians had to decide whether they would support their government's position on Central America or place their solidarity with the Christians suffering under these regimes.

Despite the familiarity of the Cold War theme, many people of faith prioritized their religious identity over their national allegiance. I propose that two factors contributed to this decision: the qualities of the narrators and the institutional context in which the story was told. Narrators are not neutral; on the contrary, the audience's perception of the narrator can strongly influence the authority and authenticity of the story. The context of storytelling is also important since people's attitudes are profoundly shaped by the institutions they participate in and cherish. Thus, "Stories are differently intelligible, salient, available, and authoritative depending on who tells them, when, for what purpose, and in what institutional context" (Polletta 1998: 425).

Narrator Qualities. Based on his analysis of Martin Luther King Jr., a master storyteller, Morris (1984) provides insight into the qualities that make narrators effective. First, King had undeniable charisma that emotionally drew the audience into the story. Second, as a Christian minister and a southerner, black churches regarded him as a trusted insider. This enabled him to shape their religious views in support of civil rights. As Morris notes, "It would surely be difficult for an 'outsider' to tamper with the sacred religious beliefs and practices of a people" (1984: 98). Third, King had credibility because he practiced what he preached. King set an example by going to jail rather than submitting to unjust laws, by boldly and nonviolently confronting racists without hatred. In the Central America peace movement, U.S. communities of faith heard Romero's story from North American priests, nuns, and church workers who had served as missioners in Latin America during the violent period of the 1960s through the 1980s. Like King, these narrators were trusted insiders. Although not all were charismatic, many missioners were skilled public speakers who had years of experience presenting sermons and homilies. They also possessed moral credibility since they had given up wealth and security to commit their lives to the church, and they had no apparent ulterior motives. Moreover, the missioners had "empirical credibility" (Snow and Benford 1988) because they had lived among the poor of Central America and therefore had first-hand accounts of the suffering. In contrast, political leaders had little credibility or public trust, particularly after the Watergate scandal and the Vietnam War.

Institutional Context. The setting in which an audience hears a narrative is also important. An institutional context may foster identification with the key characters by physically and symbolically reminding individuals of the values and beliefs the institution and the protagonist represent. It is not surprising that Romero's story was strengthened by the fact that it was often told in churches and religiously affiliated settings. This underscored the similarities between Romero and Christ since images and cultural artifacts that reflect the narrative of Christianity surrounded the audience. For instance, a crucifix symbolizes the sacrifice and resurrection of Christ, which is echoed in the murder of Romero and his resurrection in the Salvadoran people. Additionally, "people's attitudes are heavily shaped by . . . such institutions as schools and churches, whose primary purpose is to interpret social reality and make moral pronouncements regarding the 'right' relationship for people with the world around them" (Morris 1984: 96). Thus, a narrative told in church may be interpreted as having implicit institutional endorsement and therefore representing a morally correct view. Sitting in a familiar and cherished institution, church members were likely open to a trusted and credible narrator's story and message. Of course, the institutional context can also have tremendous structural value for the dissemination of a narrative and the potential for mass action. The pre-existing networks of churches allowed for rapid transmission of the narrative, bloc recruitment, and the availability of financial and human resources (Morris 1984; Nepstad 1997; Smith 1996).

Yet, not all Christians in the United States proclaimed solidarity with Central Americans and joined the movement to change U.S. foreign policy toward the region. In fact, the Christian Right strongly supported the Reagan administration's position. If Romero's story resonated with the ontological narrative of Christianity, why did it not engage all Christians? Although this question merits greater attention than can be devoted in this chapter, a brief answer lies in the fact that people of the same faith will accentuate different elements of religious teachings and consequently socialize members of their tradition to emphasize certain values and beliefs over others. These socialization influences form a cognitive filter that determines whether we "morally focus" on an issue, ignore it as irrelevant, or even take notice of it (Zerubavel 1997).

In essence, conservative or progressive religious socialization functioned as an "interpretive screen" (Snow and Benford 1988) through which the audience perceives movement stories. Those in the Historic Peace Churches, liberal Protestant denominations, or the progressive tradition in the Catholic Church were socialized to focus on justice, peace, and the plight of the poor and oppressed. For instance, the mainline Protestant commitment to social justice dates back to nineteenth-century efforts to abolish slavery; this tradition continued into the twentieth century with progressive social gospel advocates who preached reforms of urban industrial America according to Christian principles of equality and love. The Historic Peace Churches— the Quakers, Mennonites, and Church of the Brethren—have a 500-year-old theological tradition of peace and justice. Catholic social ethics can be traced to the 1891 publication of Pope Leo XIII's encyclical, "The Condition of the Working Classes." Succeeding encyclicals have built upon this foundational work, taking more progressive stands on the right of laborers to fair wages, the need for an equitable distribution of wealth, an end to economic exploitation, and the priority of communal well-being over the right to private property (Smith 1996). In contrast, evangelicals, fundamentalists, and other conservative denominations have traditionally focused on personal piety, salvation, and evangelism. Therefore, the central emphases of Romero's story may have been too far removed from the moral focus of conservative Christians.

For those missioners who were appealing to the progressive tradition of Christianity, they drew upon these church teachings to accentuate the Christian nature of this movement, thereby diminishing the accusations that it was leftist propaganda. Romero himself was careful to articulate the needs of the Central American poor in a manner that would connect with the interpretive screen or moral focus of the audience (as quoted in Dennis et al. 200: 39):

> The church is concerned about the rights of people . . . and life that is at risk. . . . The church is concerned about those who cannot speak, those who suffer, those who are tortured, those who are silenced. This is not getting involved in politics. But when politics begins to "touch the altar," the church has the right to speak. Let this be clear:

when the church preaches social justice, equality, and the dignity of those who suffer and are assaulted, this is not subversion; this is not Marxism. This is the authentic teaching of the church.

CONCLUSION

As globalization continues, activists building transnational ties will face increasing challenges posed by race, class, and cultural and ideological differences. Like Rupp and Taylor (1999), my research confirms that a collective identity can contribute to a sense of solidarity that enables movement participants to transcend these barriers. Unlike the international feminist movement, however, progressive Christians in North and Central America did not share a common social location or ascribed traits. Therefore, the narrative of Archbishop Romero helped accentuate their shared religious beliefs and values and identify a common enemy that both groups of Christians could oppose. Romero humanized a distant conflict, reminded Christians of their moral obligations, and provided a model of action. Yet Romero could not have become such an inspiring icon if he did not resemble Christ, whose narrative formed the ontological foundation of the Christian audience's core values and beliefs. Furthermore, if the narrators had not been credible, Romero's story would have lost its validity.

Symbolic narratives serve a variety of functions within social movements yet they remain curiously neglected. We ought to pay greater attention to narratives as an independent cultural resource rather than merely an expression of collective action frames or ideology. Future research could expand our knowledge of how people prioritize competing identities and why some narratives are effective in mobilizing action while others fail to even arouse interest in their targeted audience. Finally, problems are likely to arise when the key characters are transformed into sacrosanct icons and melodramatic stories oversimplify a conflict, offering an interpretation that does not accurately represent the moral complexity of the situation. The advantages as well as the drawbacks of using symbolic narratives in social movements deserve greater academic attention.

NOTES

1. As Smith (1996) documents, Christians constituted a significant portion of the U.S.-Central America peace movement. There was also a secular segment of the movement that was primarily influenced by socialist values. While participation of secular groups and individuals was important, the central focus of this chapter is on the mobilization of "progressive Christians." I use this term to denote an ecumenical group that is predominantly comprised of members of the Historic Peace Churches, mainline Protestant denominations, and progressive Catholics.

2. Due to FBI harassment and repression, many solidarity organizations were not willing to give out their membership or mailing lists; therefore, I was unable to randomly construct a sample. Instead, I contacted several national Central America organizations and developed a "theoretical sample" (Glaser and Strauss 1967) that was guided by several criteria: an equitable representation of gender, age, levels of participation in the movement, geographic regions, and secular as well as religious groups. My sample included seventeen women and fifteen men who ranged in age from thirty-two to seventy-five years old. Participants included movement leaders as well as rank-and-file activists.

148   *Sharon Erickson Nepstad*

3. I am not using the term "melodrama" in the colloquial sense of an exaggerated or intentionally distorted drama. In this context, it simply refers to a narrative that depicts a situation in morally clear terms and evokes heightened emotions because of the degree of victimization.

REFERENCES

Anderson, Thomas. 1971. *Matanza: El Salvador's Communist Revolt of 1932.* Lincoln: University of Nebraska Press.
Benford, Robert. 1993. "'You Could Be the Hundredth Monkey': Collective Action Frames and Vocabularies of Motive within the Nuclear Disarmament Movement." *Sociological Quarterly* 34(2): 195-216.
Benford, Robert, and Scott Hunt. 1992. "Dramaturgy and Social Movements: The Social Construction and Communication of Power." *Sociological Inquiry* 62(1): 36-55.
Berryman, Phillip. 1984. *The Religious Roots of Rebellion: Christians in the Central American Revolutions.* Maryknoll, N.Y.: Orbis Books.
Blain, Michael. 1994. "Power, War, and Melodrama in the Discourses of Political Movements." *Theory and Society* 23: 805-837.
Dennis, Marie, Renny Golden, and Scott Wright. 2000. *Oscar Romero: Reflections on His Life and Writings.* Maryknoll, N.Y.: Orbis.
Erdozaín, Plácido. 1980. *Archbishop Romero: Martyr of Salvador.* Maryknoll, N.Y.: Orbis.
Fine, Gary Alan. 1995. "Public Narration and Group Culture: Discerning Discourse in Social Movements." Pp. 127-143 in *Social Movements and Culture*, Hank Johnston and Bert Klandermans, eds. Minneapolis: University of Minnesota Press.
Friedman, Debra, and Doug McAdam. 1992. "Collective Identity and Activism: Networks, Choices, and the Life of a Social Movement." Pp. 156-173 in *Frontiers in Social Movement Theory*, Aldon D. Morris and Carol McClurg Mueller, eds. New Haven, Conn.: Yale University Press.
Gamson, William. 1991. "Commitment and Agency in Social Movements." *Sociological Forum* 6 (1): 27-50.
———. 1995. "Constructing Social Protest." Pp. 85-106 in *Social Movements and Culture*, Hank Johnston and Bert Klandermans, eds. Minneapolis: University of Minnesota Press.
Glaser, Barney, and Anselm Strauss. 1967. *The Discovery of Grounded Theory: Strategies for Qualitative Research.* Chicago: Aldine.
Golden, Renny, and Michael McConnell. 1986. *Sanctuary: The New Underground Railroad.* Maryknoll, N.Y.: Orbis Books.
Hunt, Scott, and Robert Benford. 1993. "Identity Talk in the Peace and Justice Movement." *Journal of Contemporary Ethnography* 22(4): 488-517.
Jasper, James. 1997. *The Art of Moral Protest: Culture, Biography, and Creativity in Social Movements.* Chicago: University of Chicago Press.
Keck, Margaret E., and Kathryn Sikkink. 1998. *Activists beyond Borders: Advocacy Networks in International Politics.* Ithaca, N.Y.: Cornell University Press.
Lernoux, Penny. 1980. *Cry of the People.* New York: Penguin Books.
McAdam, Doug, and Dieter Rucht. 1993. "Cross-national Diffusion of Social Movement Ideas." *The Annals of the American Academy of Political and Social Science* 528: 56-74.
Morris, Aldon. 1981."Black Southern Student Sit-in Movement: An Analysis of Internal Organization." *American Sociological Review* 46: 744-767.
———. 1984. *The Origin of the Civil Rights Movement: Black Communities Organizing for Change.* New York: Free Press.
Nepstad, Sharon Erickson. 1997. "The Process of Cognitive Liberation: Cultural Synapses, Links, and Frame Contradictions in the U.S.-Central America Peace Movement."

Sociological Inquiry 67: 470-487.

———. 2000. "School of the Americas Watch and Transitional Justice in Latin America." *Peace Review* 12(1): 67-72.

Oberschall, Anthony. 1989. "The 1960 Sit-ins: Protest Diffusion and Movement Take-Off." Pp. 31-54 in *Research in Social Movements, Conflicts and Change*, vol. 1, Louis Kriesberg, ed. Greenwich, Conn.: JAI Press.

Polletta, Francesca. 1998. "Contending Stories: Narrative in Social Movements." *Qualitative Sociology* 21(4): 419-446.

Peterson Anna. 1997. *Martyrdom and the Politics of Religion: Progressive Catholicism in El Salvador's Civil War.* Albany: State University of New York Press.

Romero, Oscar. 1998. *The Violence of Love.* Farmington, Pa.: Plough Publishing House.

Rupp, Leila, and Verta Taylor. 1999. "Forging Feminist Identity in an International Movement: A Collective Identity Approach to Twentieth-Century Feminism." *Signs* 24(2): 363-386.

Smith, Christian. 1991. *The Emergence of Liberation Theology: Radical Religion and Social Movement Theory.* Chicago: University of Chicago Press.

———. 1996. *Resisting Reagan: The U.S.-Central America Peace Movement.* Chicago: University of Chicago Press.

Smith, Jackie, Charles Chatfield, and Ron Pagnucco. 1997. *Transnational Social Movements and Global Politics: Solidarity beyond the State.* Syracuse, N.Y.: Syracuse University Press.

Snow, David, and Robert Benford. 1988. "Ideology, Frame Resonance and Participant Mobilization." *International Social Movement Research* 1: 197-217.

———. 2000. "Clarifying the Relationship between Framing and Ideology." *Mobilization* 5(1): 55-60.

Sobrino, Jon. 1990. *Archbishop Romero: Memories and Reflections.* Maryknoll, N.Y.: Orbis Books.

Somers, Margaret. 1994. "The Narrative Constitution of Identity: A Relational and Network Approach." *Theory and Society* 23: 605-649.

Stoll, David. 1999. *Rigoberta Menchú and the Story of All Poor Guatemalans.* Boulder, Colo.: Westview Press.

Tarrow, Sidney. 1994. *Power in Movement: Social Movements, Collective Action and Politics.* Cambridge: Cambridge University Press.

Zerubavel, Eviatar. 1997. *Social Mindscapes: An Invitation to Cognitive Sociology.* Cambridge, Mass.: Harvard University Press.

Part IV

Transnational Networks

Chapter 9

ELITE ALLIANCES AND TRANSNATIONAL ENVIRONMENTAL MOVEMENT ORGANIZATIONS

Beth Schaefer Caniglia

The expanding international environmental agenda has contributed to social movement efforts to influence global environmental policy making. Movement tactics range from banner hangings and meeting blockades to legal analysis and lobbying of government delegates at international meetings. Greenpeace is a prominent example of a transnational social movement organization (TSMO) that engages in both confrontational, disruptive actions as well as very conventional, lobbying strategies at most international environmental meetings. While some Greenpeace activists engage in dramatic and obstructive antics such as dumping toxic wastes or burning genetically modified food crops in front of international conference halls, others produce slick, informative background sheets on issues under negotiation. Such background documents seek to shape global media discourse, and they also serve as tools for teams of Greenpeace lobbyists who work the halls inside global environmental meetings. Lobbyist teams often use their connections with officials to obtain inside information that can be strategically used by their colleagues outside the meeting hall.

Reflecting these realities, recent discussions indicate that our theoretical understanding of elite-movement relationships needs revision to account for the variety of ways that movement actors relate to economic and political decision makers (Diani 2000; Klandermans 2000; Zald 2000). In his recent *Mobilization* essay, Mayer Zald (2000) argued that we should spread "the social movement net deeper into routine politics" and classify some activities of the political elite as movement behavior, based on the organizing concept of ideologically structured action (ISA). In response, Diani (2000) and Klandermans (2000) suggested that, while ISA might not be the answer, movement scholars would certainly benefit from further clarification regarding the relationship between movements and institutional political actors. In particular, Diani (2000) suggests we focus our attention on social networks. I support Diani's call and argue that a network focus has serious implications for how stratification among movements and political elites is conceptualized. We must exercise caution when defining the boundaries of social movement networks.

For example, Margaret Keck and Kathryn Sikkink have introduced the concept of "transnational advocacy networks," which include actors such as international and domestic nongovernmental research and advocacy organizations, local social movements, foundations, the media, churches, trade unions, consumer organizations, and intellectuals, parts of regional and international intergovernmental organizations, and parts of the executive and/or parliamentary branches of governments (1998: 9). Such a definition pays no heed to stratification, social distance, or power. I see these dimensions as central aspects of the relationship between elites and movements. I agree with Zald (2000) that political elites and movements frequently share similar ideologies regarding social change; and I agree that movement actors vary in the extent they should be considered political "outsiders." However, I do not believe we can reasonably argue that stratification between political elites and movement actors has disappeared. Instead, the blurring boundaries between movements and institutional politics challenges us to develop new tools for conceptualizing and measuring stratification and power among movement participants and political elites.

In this chapter I reconceptualize one dimension of the political opportunity structure—elite alliances—in a way that incorporates both Zald's (2000) recognition that ideology frequently links movements and elites and Diani's (2000) call to use movement networks as the unit of analysis. I trace the role of political elites first as conscience constituents in resource mobilization theory and then in terms of elite alliances in the political opportunity theory. Elite alliances are most commonly conceptualized as a macrostructural dimension of the political opportunity structure, implying they will exert an overarching effect on entire social movements. While recognizing the macrostructural impact of elite allies, I argue that we should widen our conceptual lens and analyze elite alliances as diadic ties between political elites and movement actors. Such ties affect individual movement actors differently, depending upon the nature and number of ties they cultivate with elites. I then demonstrate the utility of this framework by presenting and analyzing a model designed to measure the relationship between environmental TSMO ties with elite political organizations, measured as United Nations and other intergovernmental organizations (IGOs), and the social network positions of these TSMOs.

TRANSNATIONAL ELITES AND MOVEMENT OPPORTUNITIES

According to McAdam, the political opportunity concept includes the following dimensions: "(1) the relative openness or closure of the institutionalized political system; (2) the stability or instability of that broad set of elite alignments that typically undergird a polity; (3) the presence or absence of elite allies; [or] (4) the state's capacity and propensity for repression" (1996: 27). These dimensions are used to explain a variety of movement outcomes (McAdam 1996). For example, Nelkin and Pollack (1982) find evidence that Germany's open political apparatus gives the antinuclear power movement there more opportunities to protest than in France. The authors attribute the German movement's greater success to more avenues of political access. Gale (1986) observes that sympathetic state agencies facilitated mobilization of the U.S. environmental movement. In the transnational arena, Smith (1995) identifies how social movements help determine citizen organizations' access to global institutions as well as the general parameters of human rights debates. She also links the expansion of transnational environmental movement organizations with a series of UN conferences and documents, suggesting that the expansion was related to new openings for movement organizations at the UN (Smith 1997).

These and other studies illustrate how the political opportunity structure framework helps explain social movement outcomes. Nonetheless, a great deal of work remains to be done regarding how particular dimensions of the political opportunity structure are linked to movement outcomes (McAdam 1996). In particular, very little research focuses on how elite allies affect movement outcomes.

Political Elites and Social Movements

POS theory proposes that elite allies can affect movement characteristics, such as tactical repertoires, mobilization, and success rates. When sympathetic elites are present, the likelihood of success increases; when they are absent, success is less likely (Piven and Cloward 1977; Smith 1997; Zald and McCarthy 1987). Connected to this is the resource mobilization argument that social movement actors use protest and media strategies to influence elites and attract the sympathy of other "reference publics" (Lipsky 1968), turning them into *conscience constituents* (Zald and McCarthy 1987). Certainly not all conscience constituents are elites, but those that are can use their positions to raise awareness of a movement's grievances and place its demands more prominently on the public agenda. Several studies confirm these insights. Jenkins and Perrow (1977) found that the support of liberal organizations outside the farm workers' movement was a critical component of the United Farm Worker (UFW) success. Piven and Cloward (1977) highlighted the central role elites played in facilitating or blocking the progress of poor peoples' movements. Edwards and Marullo stressed the importance of alliances as a source of "external legitimacy," which was associated with the survival of peace movement organizations (1995: 923).

Nonetheless, it seems that many studies of the elite-movement relationship are limited in two ways. First, many assume that the political arena is closed to the direct participation of social movement actors (Zald 2000), despite the fact that the POS framework holds the "relative openness or closure of the institutionalized political structure" as a key variable. This misconception stems from the insistence among the vast majority of social movement scholars that movements are strictly comprised of political "outsiders" (Zald 2000).

Second, it is assumed that social movements are comprised exclusively of nonelites, and that political elites do not personally share movement grievances. This implies that the only way these elites can be mobilized on behalf of social movements is to evoke their sympathy or to threaten their chances for reelection. Such reasoning makes sense with reference to many social movements of the 1960s and earlier, since many were waged by the dispossessed and/or powerless in hopes of gaining wider participation and more collective goods (e.g. Jenkins and Perrow 1977; Piven and Cloward 1977). However, in recent years, the lines between movement adherents and political elites have become blurred (Zald 2000; Meyer and Tarrow 1998; Neidhardt and Rucht 1993; Klandermans 2000).

As a result, this view of the social movements-elite relationship has simply outlived reality. Proponents of the new social movements framework and feminist scholars have illustrated that postmodern social movement grievances have diversified to include identity and quality-of-life issues, in addition to class-based grievances (Jenkins and Eckert 1986; Buechler 1996; Taylor and Whittier 1996). Jenkins and Eckert (1986: 814) point out that movements seeking "collective goods for the general public lack a natural community for mobilization, such as consumer rights and environmental protection (in which, strictly speaking, there is no conscience constituency; all citizens are purportedly direct beneficiaries)." In light of this, social, economic, and political elites can become personally invested in social movement outcomes.

It is not uncommon to find political elites at the forefront of movement activities. Al Gore champions the environmental movement. Similarly, Zald evokes Ronald Reagan, asking "Does anyone believe that Ronald Reagan was part of the conservative movement before he ran for the presidency and not after?" (Zald 2000: 10). Zald continues:

> It is common, especially among proponents of the political process approach, to argue that political movements are politics by another means, or that social movements represent a vehicle for access when formal institutions deny access; one turns to movements when access to routine politics is denied, or when one cannot achieve one's objectives there. But the converse is less often argued—*routine politics are often an extension of social movement ideologies by other means.* (10, emphasis added)

In other words, Zald is advocating an approach to social movements which incorporates a messy reality where movement activists and political elites frequently share similar beliefs and interests. "Bureaucrats, legislators, jurists, and executives identify with movements and share ideologies with those we label activists" (10). But elites are often limited regarding how they can advance movement goals. Because the power of elites is legitimated via the institutions whose leadership roles they fill, elites must not violate the behavioral norms of their institutions (Weber 1947; Collins 1979). Zald states that "[t]he logics of action in a dedicated SMO, or in an informal network of activists will be different than the logics of action in a party or a legislature"(2000: 10). For example, since Vice President Al Gore is a politician, there is an expectation that he will use politically legitimate strategies to facilitate the protection of the environment. It is unlikely that he will climb a water tower to hang Greenpeace banners or perform street theater donning a chemical suit.

Furthermore, there is pressure for elites to place institutional allegiance above their movement interests. If a conflict emerges, political elites are faced with difficult decisions of whom to support. As Zald states, "[a] legislator with deep concern about movement goals, but little commitment to maintaining the party in a governmental coalition, is going to face very different decisional conflicts and career choices than a legislator with a pragmatic orientation or one with a commitment to a political career" (2000: 11).

Due to these conflicts, relationships among nonelite movement actors and elite sympathizers are uniquely constrained. These institutionally legitimized patterns of behavior demarcate political elites from actors in SMOs, although elites may consider themselves movement adherents and advocates of social change (Zald 2000). Therefore, political elites should not be conceptualized exactly the same as movement participants, even if those elites dedicate much of their time to a movement's cause. Because they are political representatives, they possess authority that nongovernmental movement participants do not. Thus, while movement actors and political elites share similar ideologies and often communicate with each other, the fact remains that political elites are more powerful actors in policy-making arenas.

Social Movements as Social Networks

Mario Diani claims that "it will serve us best if we get rid of the Holy Trinity of 'parties, interest groups and movements' and locate the distinctiveness of movements in social networks" (2000: 22). He argues that social movements are loosely coupled collections of actors who share common beliefs about the need for social and/or political change. And while the extent of cooperation and competition among specific movement actors may vary over time (Zald and McCarthy 1987), the structure of relations *at any given time* profoundly affects each organization within the sector. Regarding the role of elites in these networks *boundary specification* is an important methodological consideration. It entails setting systematic criteria for determining which actors will be included as members of the population or network (Laumann et al. 1983; Aldrich and Whetten 1981; Marsden 1990). Network scholars typically utilize either a *realist* or a *nominalist* criterion for boundary specification (Laumann et al. 1983). When a realist framework is applied, participation in similar events and/or activities is the primary criterion for inclusion. "The network is treated as a social fact only in that it is consciously experienced as such by the actors composing it" (Laumann et al. 1983). Two recent examples of the realist framework are Laumann and Knoke's (1987) analysis of the energy and health policy domains in the United States and Keck and Sikkink's (1998) study of transnational advocacy networks.

Laumann and Knoke (1987) did not separate policy-making agencies from social movement organizations, corporations, or other actors involved in the health or energy policy domains when determining what organizations should be included in the same policy network. All actors were considered as potentially equal participants in their policy domain—a null hypothesis to be empirically tested via the network analysis. They used a multifaceted strategy of boundary specification, first compiling a list of domain participants from meeting attendance records, newspapers, and other sources of media; and then interviewing participants from this list to determine if key organizations had been left out.

Keck and Sikkink (1998) used a similar technique to define transnational advocacy network participants. They did not compile comprehensive lists of organizations, but rather spent considerable time with campaign participants in order to identify important ones. They included in their networks those organizations and people instrumental in advocating the network's principles and who actively participated in network campaigns. Actors that had an opportunity or propensity to participate, yet did not, were not considered in both Laumann and Knoke's (1987) and Keck and Sikkink's (1998) analyses.

While it is appealing to demarcate network boundaries according to joint participation and awareness among network members, this approach more closely describes what Aldrich and Whetten (1981) define as "action-sets" rather than network structures. Action-sets are comprised of groups of actors—most frequently organizations—purposefully, though temporarily, "joining together to carry out a project no single organization could accomplish" (387). In other words, action-sets are akin to coalitions. Aldrich and Whetten (1981: 387) state that "a network is defined as the totality of all the units connected by a certain type of relationship," and it is the responsibility of the researcher to carefully consider the "type of relationship" that unifies network members.

The nominalist approach to boundary specification allows us to demarcate the network of *all* environmental TSMOs, as opposed to the action-set of TSMOs that commonly works together. This approach is superior to the realist approach because it enables us to analyze the entire network, including organizations that are not actively engaged in coalitions. By applying a nominalist approach we are able to learn something about coalition *potential*, along with the understanding of existing coalitions.

My approach is more *nominalist* than Keck and Sikkink (1998) or Laumann and Knoke (1987). It uses Smith's (1997) list of environmental TSMOs to delineate the social network and considers all TSMOs as status equals within the international environmental policy-making arena. Network analysis is used to untangle the web of relations that connects them to each other. Whether they are, in fact, equals becomes an empirical question—just as it was in Laumann and Knoke's study; however, my approach assumes that policy-making elites are more powerful than environmental TSMOs and, thus, excludes these actors from the network analysis. Following Zald (2000), I base this decision on the fact that political elites and social movement actors face conflicts of interest when working toward movement goals—conflicts of interest that result from their institutional roles. Thus, movement actors and political elites do not comprise a sets of equal domain participants, and they should not be included as participants in the same network.

Zald also observes that policy-making elites and movement participants interact more directly today than in the past. This has implications for social movement participants—above and beyond the movement as a whole. Distinct movement organizations have the opportunity to seek out, build, and maintain relationships with policy-making elites. One of the central questions of my research is how stratification among members of the transnational environmental movement (measured as network centrality) is affected by direct ties between political elites and specific movement organizations. By specifying network boundaries as I have, I am able to answer this question. It also provides for a full network to be delineated, rather than including only those actors actively engage in sector activity.

DATA AND METHODS

I employ a model that analyzes how elite alliances affect the structural positions within TSMO networks. Using data from the *Yearbook of International Organizations*, I also address whether formal alliances with elite agencies (e.g., UN agencies and IGOs) affect TSMO network positions differently than informal ties.

My analysis is based on a data set which was assembled by Smith (1997) from entries in the 1993 *Yearbook of International Organizations* (Union of International Associations). This yearbook is published annually by the Union of International Associations (UIA) and is considered the definitive source of international nongovernmental organization (NGO) data (Boli and Thomas 1997).[1] Smith coded founding dates, aims, membership information, and several indicators of interorganizational ties for those organizations defined as transnational social movement organizations (TSMOs). Her data set includes all TSMOs, including those active in such diverse areas as human rights, women's issues, development, and environmental issues (Smith 1997).

For the current study, TSMOs were selected for inclusion if their specific goals (or "aims" under the *Yearbook* heading) indicated that the organization worked for political change related to environmental issues. Environmental issues were defined to include: wildlife, development, population, animal rights, nuclear power, as well as any of these in combination with other aims. Out of approximately 15,000 international organizations included in the 1993 *Yearbook*, Smith identified 631 TSMOs, of which 163 were environmental TSMOs. The current study begins with all members of this population and eventually focuses on sixty cases for which complete data are available.

Dependent Variables: Simple Count and Betweenness Centrality

I expanded Smith's data set to include information about connections among the members of the environmental movement network. The *Yearbook* asked each organization to list nongovernmental organizations (NGOs) with which they were connected. A matrix was constructed by listing members of the environmental TSMO network along the rows and columns in identical order. A zero was inserted in the matrix if no relation was specified by either organization, and a one was entered if either organization listed the other as a contact. This is a symmetrical matrix, which assumes a relationship exists if only one actor lists the other as a contact (see Wasserman and Faust, 1994: 165).

This matrix was analyzed using *UCINET* network analysis software to calculate TSMO network positions (Borgotti, Everett, and Freeman 1992). First, Freeman's centrality measure was computed. This measure indicates the number of ties each organization has to others within the network, expressed as a percentage of all ties present in the network (Freeman 1979). The organization with the highest percentage of ties is the most "central" in the network. This measure of *simple count centrality* represents a TSMO's involvement relative to others within the network.[2] Connections provide opportunities for the organization to influence others and to obtain access to crucial resources (Laumann and Knoke 1987; Knoke 1990).

The second measure used in these analyses is called *betweenness centrality*. This measure indicates the number of times a given organization is located between two otherwise unconnected organizations. This is a measure of the number of relations within the network where a particular TSMO can act as a broker of information or resources between two other organizations. Such brokering relationships are important in advocacy networks for three reasons. First, broker organizations are frequently connected to many others in their network and serve as efficient information sources for organizations that do not maintain contact with many others. Second, broker organizations can link disconnected organizations when a policy debate transcends traditional boundaries within the network. Third, brokers have the capacity to withhold, share, or distort information in their possession, making them extremely powerful players (Fernandez and Gould, 1994). Each organization's centrality was then entered into SPSS to create two ratio-level dependent variables. Models designed to explain TSMO centrality were then estimated using OLS regression techniques.

Independent Variables: Elite Alliances

In these analyses I use two measures of alliances between TSMOs and elite agencies.[3] The variable measuring formal, institutional ties indicates the number of UN agencies and IGOs with which the TSMO holds "consultative status." Consultative status is obtained by TSMOs through a formal application process and by meeting specific criteria established by the UN General Assembly (Willetts 1996). Organizations with consultative status may send representatives to UN and IGO meetings, and they may submit position papers. Hundreds of NGO representatives attend UN and IGO meetings, making the UN Plaza and other IGO headquarters prime locations for TSMO networking. This variable allows us to analyze whether organizations with consultative status with many UN agencies occupy more central positions than those holding consultative status with few or no UN agencies.

Institutionalized ties are expected to affect TSMO centrality for a number of reasons. As stated, consultative status allows organizations to send representatives to the meetings of UN agencies and IGOs. This provides TSMOs opportunities to interact with other advocacy organizations and with government and intergovernmental officials by increasing likelihood of cooperation with them (Wasserman and Faust, 1994: 293). Other benefits of consultative status include access to official documents and authorization to submit policy reports and statements for review by state representatives. Accredited nongovernmental organizations can act as conduits of policy information—both from elite agencies to other TSMOs and the other way around. Given this, we derive the following hypothesis.

H_1: TSMOs holding consultative status with numerous IGOs and UN agencies will be more central in the environmental TSMO network than those holding consultative status with none or with fewer IGOs and/or UN agencies.

The second elite-alliance variable is a measure of informal connections with UN agencies. This variable considers the number of TSMO contacts with UN agencies and/or IGOs, but it excludes organizations with which the TSMO holds consultative status. These informal ties are not governed by strict, politically moderated guidelines imposed by an institution. Rather, they are relationships based on reputation, trust, shared goals, and reciprocity.[4] Because some of these relationships are close and informal, they can be resources for acquiring up-to-date and even "privileged" information (Caniglia 2000). Such information is critical to social movement groups—especially those that attempt to influence international policy—because it enables them to act quickly. This variable assesses whether TSMOs that maintain informal ties with UN agency or IGO personnel are more densely connected to other TSMOs.

We would expect this to be the case for several reasons. First, TSMOs with many informal ties with elite policy-making bodies can be information sources for TSMOs without elite ties. Organizations unable to secure information on their own seek out relationships with those who have it. Second, many TSMOs with insider information see it as their duty to share it with others. In fact, while there is an unspoken rule that TSMOs protect the identity of their sources, UN and IGO personnel often give information to their TSMO partners in the hope that they will rally either support or opposition to policy issues being decided. According to one TSMO leader:

I think most NGOs don't get insider information. Which is another reason why they hate [her organization's name]; they hate [another large NGO], because [this NGO] is very well-connected, too. But what we always try to do when we get that information is somehow package it or . . . just get it around somehow to a few key people who are also in a position to do something about it. We don't get a lot, and then we get used by those people who are giving us the privileged information often, because they want *us*. We sort of have to gauge whether they want us to be a conduit to a few other key people with that information. So, somebody from their organization will say to me "we've heard rumors that these three countries are close to ratifying the fish docks agreement; they need a push from the NGOs." We use them, they use us. [emphasis added] (Interview A)

These sentiments were echoed by the co-chair of a Southern NGO network:

Most of the time when you get information and it's supposed to be secret, they somehow indicate that. So, we just use the information without attributing where we got it from. That is our job, to get it out, which is why they gave it to us in the first place. (Interview B)[5]

Thus, TSMOs that have informal relationships with elite members of global governing bodies frequently find themselves in very powerful positions. They can choose to keep the information to themselves, in hopes of capitalizing on it for their own aims. They can use the information to draw attention to their ability to acquire it. And, they can use it to mobilize their TSMO colleagues into a coalition. Stemming from this, the following hypothesis will be tested:

H_2: TSMOs with informal connections to numerous IGOs and/or UN agencies will have higher centrality in the environmental TSMO network than those informally connected to fewer or no IGOs or UN agencies.

As we see in table 9.1, most TSMOs in the environmental movement sector do not hold consultative status with any UN agencies or other intergovernmental bodies. Only 40 percent of the TSMOs in this population reported formal, consultative ties. In contrast, most of the environmental TSMOs do have informal ties with UN agencies or other intergovernmental organizations. Twenty-one percent of the environmental TSMOs in this population have informal ties with at least one UN agency or intergovernmental organization (IGO), and 57 percent report informal ties with one or more UN agencies or IGOs.

Table 9.1.   Summary of Social Ties Variables: Elite Alliances and Centrality Measures

Variable	0 Ties	1-5 Ties	6 and more Ties
Elite Alliances			
Consultative Status	75.5% (123)	22.0% (36)	2.5% (4)
Informal Ties	42.8% (79)	43.4% (60)	13.8% (44)
TSMO Network Position			
Simple Count Centrality	48.5% (79)	46.6% (76)	5.0% (8)
Betweenness Centrality	77.3% (126)	3.7% (6)	19.0% (31)

A crosstabs analysis explored the overlap between TSMOs with consultative status and those with informal ties with IGOs. Among the 138 organizations for which we had data on these variables, 40 percent (55 organizations) had neither consultative status nor informal ties. Thirty-one percent (43 organizations) did not have formal consultative status, but they did have one or more informal ties with IGOs. However, only four organizations held consultative status and claimed no informal ties with IGOs. The remaining 26 percent (36 TSMOs) reported some combination of consultative status and informal ties with IGOs.

A similar pattern emerged when we looked at the social network positions held by members of this population of environmental TSMOs. Close to 52 percent (46.6% + 5% = 51.6%) of the organizations were connected to at least one other environmental TSMO in this population, while 48.5 percent were isolates—reporting no ties with other environmental TSMOs. In other words, half of the TSMOs working on environmental issues in 1993 were not actively engaged in coalitions. Regarding betweenness centrality—where the TSMO is in a structural position to broker and/or control information and other resources—most organizations in our population did not find themselves in this powerful structural position. While fewer than half of the environmental TSMOs in this population were totally isolated from their peers, only 22.7 percent (3.7% + 19%) were in a structural position to broker between two otherwise unconnected organizations.

Control Variables: Organizational Characteristics

Because TSMOs vary along several dimensions, aside from whether they hold consultative status or have informal connections with UN agencies or IGOs, the regression models include the following variables to control for the influence of particular organizational characteristics. These variables were chosen from those available in Smith's (1997) data set because they are potentially related to centrality, and because they may help to distinguish which organizations gain central positions.

Age of the TSMO was calculated by subtracting an organization's founding date from 1993. This variable was included because it is possible that older organizations are more central because they have been active in a sector longer. Over time, members of one activist organization often join forces with other similar organizations (Diani 1995). Being active in sectors can lead to opportunities for joint campaigns. Also, an overlapping labor market in the advocacy community can lead by itself to connections among different organizations (Keck and Sikkink 1998). Conversely, since transnational networking is relatively new among social movement organizations, it is possible that younger organizations have mastered the technique more than older organizations. This stems from Stinchcombe's (1965) theory regarding birth cohort effects on organizational behavior. Thus, while it remains an empirical question whether older TSMOs in the environmental population will be more, less, or equally central, there are theoretical reasons to control for its possible systematic effect.

NGO membership was also included in the model. Because the network we are interested in stems from connections with other TSMOs, this variable controls for the possibility that having nongovernmental organization (and other TSMO) members may contribute to centrality. TSMOs that allow other NGOs to join their organization may have devised specific marketing (or mobilizing) techniques to build alliances with other organizations. In other words, they may be professional "networkers." At the very least, TSMOs that allow other NGOs and/or TSMOs to join their organizations express an appreciation for the value of cooperative activities and might be more likely to seek out alliances with other like-minded organizations.

Size of organizational membership may also affect structural position because TSMOs can make more contacts with members of their network.[6] Large organizations frequently have more "slack" or "fluid" resources that can be used to build and maintain connections with other environmental TSMOs. Because the actual number of members was not available for most organizations in the population, the number of countries in which the organization had members was included to account for this possible effect. This variable was used exactly as it appeared in Smith's original data set.

Similarly, *TSMO headquarters location* may affect centrality. If a TSMO has its headquarters in a place like Washington, D.C. or Paris, where many similar organization headquarters can be found, its personnel have more opportunities and fewer barriers to interact with like-minded organizations. Two variables were constructed to control for headquarters location. The first was based on a table in the *Yearbook of International Organizations* that summarizes how many international organizations in the volume have headquarters in each city. I then coded the number of international organization branches present in each TSMO's headquarters city. These included all organizations listed in the *Yearbook*—TSMOs, international NGOs and intergovernmental organizations. The presence of other branches provides general networking possibilities, and therefore they should be controlled for in the model.

The second headquarters location variable is more specific and indicates how many of the 163 environmental TSMOs have their headquarters in the same city. One would assume that two environmental TSMOs that have headquarters in the same city would be more likely to be connected to each other than to TSMOs outside their headquarters city. Using *Yearbook* entries, each environmental TSMO in our population was assigned a number representing how many other TSMOs from this population had their headquarters in their city.

RESULTS

Initial regression analyses indicated that just over 100 of the cases were eliminated due to missing data, leaving sixty cases to analyze. Closer inspection of each variable's distribution revealed that the majority of missing data could not be attributed to one or two variables; however, the control variables as a group were leading to the elimination of 75 percent of the lost cases. Because several cases had missing data on the control variables, a missing data variable was coded. Those environmental TSMOs without missing data on any of the control variables was given a zero on this missing data variable, and those with missing data on any of the control variables was coded a one. An independent samples t-test was run to determine if there was any significant bias between those organizations that were excluded due to missing data. The elite alliance measures—holding consultative status and having informal ties—and both centrality measures were included in this analysis.

Comparing the samples did not indicate significant bias for three of the four variables between those with and without missing data. However, a slight bias was found related to simple count centrality. Those excluded due to missing data

Table 9.2. OLS Estimates of the Regression of Freeman's Centrality Measure on Organizational Characteristics and Indicators of Alliances with UN Agencies

Variables	Model 1	Model 2	Model 3 Full Model	Model 4	Model 5
Organization Characteristics					
Age	.02232		-.04581	-.04394	-.03539
	(.095)		(-.194)	(-.184)	(-.150)
Number of member countries	-.000954		-.001986	-.001975	-.001384
	(-.055)		(-.115)	(-.114)	(-.080)
Density of I.O. branches in H.Q. city	-.001270		-.001014	-.001038	-.0007734
	(-.154)		(-.123)	(-.126)	(-.094)
Number of other pop. members in H.Q. city	.228		.249	.253	.167
	(.223)		(.244)	(.247)	(.163)
NGO Members	.240		.964	.964	.402
	(.032)		(.131)	(.131)	(.054)
Alliance Indicators					
Consultative status		-.251	.04751		.879*
		(-.109)	(.021)		(.380)
Informal alliances		.500‡	.537‡	.543‡	
		(.626)	(.673)	(.681)	
N	60	60	60	60	60
F	.324	12.998‡	4.733‡	4.638‡	2.727*
R^2	.03	.32	.39	.39	.34

Note: Numbers in parenthesis are standardized regression coefficients. Estimates are unstandardized regression coefficients. $*P<.05$ $‡p<.01$

Table 9.3. OLS Estimates of the Regression of Betweenness Centrality on Organizational Characteristics and Indicators of Alliances with UN Agencies

Variables	Model 1	Model 2	Model 3 Full Model	Model 4	Model 5
Organization Characteristics					
Age	1.624		-3.095	-1.351	-2.713
	(.140)		(-.267)	(-.116)	(-.234)
Number member countries	-.01247		-.06683	-.05865	-.04475
	(-.015)		(-.078)	(-.069)	(-.053)
Density of I.O. branches in H.Q. city	-.05967		-.03117	-.04920	-.02236
	(-.147)		(-.077)	(-.121)	(-.055)
Number of other Pop. Members in H.Q. City	12.038		10.508	13.188	7.494
	(.239)		(.209)	(.262)	(.149)
NGO members	-15.958		10.832	16.803	-3.765
	(-.044)		(.046)	(.046)	(-.010)
Alliance Indicators					
Consultative status		17.295	35.639		66.1‡
		(.152)	(.313)		(.581)
Informal alliances		18.026‡	19.663‡	24.573‡	
		(.731)	(.501)	(.626)	
N	60	60	60	60	60
F	.453	12.665‡	4.730‡	4.638‡	2.727*
R^2	.04	.32	.39	.34	.24

Note: Numbers in parenthesis are standardized regression coefficients. Estimates are unstandardized regression coefficients. $*P<.05$ $‡p<.01$

systematically tended to be less central than those included in the analyses—on average exhibiting 1.26 fewer ties than those without missing data. The findings should be interpreted accordingly. Nonetheless, there is reason to believe that the findings related to the effect of elite alliances on simple count centrality are still valid and generalizable to the excluded organizations. As we will discuss below, the pattern of significant effects that results when simple count centrality is the dependent variable is identical to those that result when betweenness centrality—an unbiased centrality measure—is the dependent variable.[7]

To test the hypotheses mentioned above, OLS regression was employed. Two full models were specified: one analyzing the effects of the independent and control variables on simple count centrality and one analyzing their effects on betweenness centrality. Table 9.2 shows the results when simple count centrality is the dependent variable. In model 1, Freeman's simple count centrality measure was regressed onto all control variables. This model explained 3 percent of the variance in simple count centrality, and none of the organizational characteristics obtained significance. In model 2, simple count centrality was regressed onto the elite alliance variables: consultative status and informal ties. These variables explained 32 percent of the variance in simple count centrality, and informal alliances were strong, statistically significant predictors of simple count centrality.

In model 3, simple count centrality was regressed onto all independent and control variables. This model explained 39 percent of the variance—a slight increase over the inclusion of only the alliance variables. Formal consultative ties are positive, although their effect remains statistically insignificant; in fact, the coefficient indicates a negligible increase in centrality per consultative tie. Informal ties remains the only statistically significant variable in the model and indicates that, for every two informal political elite ties held by a TSMO, that TSMO will have just over one additional tie with other TSMOs. Although the organizational characteristics still do not reach significance, the higher R2 suggests that some variance is explained indirectly via consultative status or informal ties.

Table 3 shows the results when the same models are run with *betweenness centrality* or "brokerage capacity" as the dependent variable. In model 1, betweenness centrality is regressed onto all control variables. Similar to model 1 in table 9.2, this model explains 4 percent of the variance in betweenness centrality, and none of the organizational characteristics obtains statistical significance in the model. Model 2 regressed betweenness centrality onto only the two elite alliance indicators: formal consultative ties and informal ties with UN agencies/IGOs. Consultative ties are positively associated with betweenness centrality, but not statistically significant. Informal ties are the critical predictor—just as we saw in model 2 in table 9.2. These two alliance variables predict 32 percent of the variance in betweenness centrality/brokerage capacity.

Model 3 in table 9.3 shows the results when betweenness centrality is regressed onto all control and elite-alliance variables. This full model explains 39 percent of the variance in betweenness centrality and exhibits the same predictive pattern we observed in the full model for simple count centrality. Informal ties with elite organizations are the primary predictor of a TSMO being in a position to broker between two otherwise unconnected TSMOs. Formal consultative ties predict in the same direction but do not obtain statistical significance.

Models 4 and 5 were run for each dependent variable to analyze how the coefficients might change when one of the alliance variables was removed. Again, a similar pattern emerges for both dependent variables. When formal consultative ties are removed in model 4 only a slight decrease in variance is explained. All coefficients remain relatively consistent, suggesting that very little unique variance is explained by formal consultative ties. In other words, groups with consultative status that are effective movement networkers or brokers are also engaged in substantial informal relations with IGO officials.

Informal ties with IGOs are removed in model 5. This time, the effects differ for betweenness centrality and simple count centrality. In the case of simple count centrality (table 2), there is a slight drop in overall variance explained when informal ties are removed from the model. Consultative ties are now significant positive predictors of the dependent variable; and the coefficient suggests that for an increase of approximately one consultative tie the TSMO will gain one additional tie with other TSMOs. In contrast, when we remove informal ties in model 5 for betweenness centrality, approximately 15 percent less variance is explained by the model. This suggests that informal ties are much stronger predictors of betweenness centrality than they are for simple count centrality.

DISCUSSION AND CONCLUSION

This study was designed to offer a means to reconceptualize and measure the effects of political elites and their ties with movement actors. It allows us to assess the relationship between elite alliances and the network positions obtained by organizations in social movement networks. By analyzing the effects of elite alliances on network positions, we can begin to understand how the formation and maintenance of ties with political elites affect stratification among social movement organizations.

Only hypotheses related to how informal connections with UN agencies would affect centrality were supported in these analyses. Formal ties, measured by consultative status, did not significantly contribute to our understanding of TSMO network positions. Instead, those organizations with more informal connections with IGOs and UN agencies were the most central in the 1993 environmental TSMO network.

There are several possible explanations for these findings. Although TSMOs have been in consultative status with the UN Economic and Social Council (ECOSOC) since the very early years of the UN, until recently most TSMOs have been excluded by strict criteria (Willetts 1996). In spite of their formal exclusion, TSMOs have developed strong, informal links to UN agency personnel as a means for influencing political change (Donini 1996). One explanation for this is that UN personnel rely on NGOs to legitimize and subsidize their activities (Boutros-Ghali 1996). It is not unusual for TSMOs to cosponsor events with United Nations agencies. UN agencies often straddle governments and NGOs as a means to insure their success and survival, especially in light of constant budget cutting at the UN.

This account still does not adequately explain the difference between the influence of formal, consultative ties and informal ties. In table 9.4, I summarize information gathered from fieldwork. This information is based on three sources: (1) participant observation of a UN General Assembly Session reviewing the Commission on Sustainable Development (CSD); (2) official documents about rights accorded to consultative-status TSMOs; and (3) one question asked of respondents during the CSD's sixth session. The table summarizes the official benefits granted to consultative-

Table 9.4.   Interview Responses on the Benefits of Consultative Status
and Informal IGO Ties

Benefits of Consultative Status	Benefits of Informal Relationships
Receipt of UN documents	Interpretation of UN documents
Distribution of position papers	Feedback on position papers
Access to UN meetings	Insight into country delegation position and
Guidelines for agency accreditation	political context
and meeting participation	Insight into other UN agencies and personnel
	Consideration when opportunities arise
	Information and introductions regarding other
	organizations with similar projects
	Funding opportunities
	Inside, "privileged" information

status TSMOs and contrasts those benefits with those cited by TSMO leaders as stemming from informal ties with IGOs and UN agencies. Because I have already elaborated the official benefits of consultative status, I focus here on the findings regarding the benefits of informal ties between TSMOs and IGOs, drawing comparisons when useful.

According to the ten TSMO leaders I interviewed, informal relationships with UN agencies and other IGOs afforded paramount opportunities and insights. For example, while each interviewee had the official right to submit reports (although of different lengths) for review by CSD delegates, several respondents indicated that informal conversations with CSD personnel played a central role in the types of reports and/or resolutions their organizations presented at the meeting. Personal ties with IGO personnel allowed them to learn where various countries stood on issues they were concerned about. This allowed them to construct proposals and initiate lobbying actions in a very targeted fashion.

These interviews made clear that holding consultative status and developing informal ties were distinct strategies—each offering different benefits. However, they also work together. One co-chair of a prominent NGO advocacy network in the Southern Hemisphere provided this comparison.

> I think we have made a lot of headway in the UN in terms of being able to get on-going drafts of things and to be able to be physically present during the negotiations, so that you are actually in the process, and watching, and influencing. But. . . with the MAI campaign, for example, the documents were all secret. . . . So, with that kind of work, you really need to have contacts inside, outside . . . getting the right information out at the right time, to have a sense of what are the politics of some of these things going on, and that means having personal contacts. (Interview B)

Another respondent, a UN liaison for one of the largest environmental TSMOs, also expressed the advantages that informal ties bring to participation at IGO meetings.

> I think it helps us to be more targeted in our work, so that we can come to these meetings with recommendations that have a flying chance of being adopted—instead

of coming in from left field completely. It all helps us to have a better political sense of what the opportunities are and to exploit those opportunities more effectively. Because, otherwise, you think "well, here's a meeting on freshwater coming up," instead of a set of recommendations that belong somewhere else. There certainly have been some NGO recommendations like that floating around. (Interview A)

Another explanation for why informal alliances with UN agencies are so important for TSMOs is related to the subjective nature of such relationships. While relatively strict and rational criteria have been developed to regulate which TSMOs receive consultative status, no such criteria govern the formation of informal relationships between TSMOs and UN agencies. Instead, they are forged to meet participants' mutual interests. The type of information that passes through informal channels is often more privileged, because sharing is more likely to be based on trust and shared goals.

An unanticipated finding of this study is that the model predicted betweenness centrality as well as it predicted Freeman's simple count centrality. Although research suggests that these forms of centrality represent different structural characteristics of network actors (Gould and Fernandez 1989), Diani (1995) has reported strong correlations between various measures of centrality. My results suggest that informal alliances with elites facilitate both forms of structural position equally. However, given that the sample was slightly biased toward higher simple count (Freeman's) centrality, this finding should not be overstated.

Of course, the most important implication of this research pertains to how elite alliances are conceptualized by social movement scholars. Theoretically, I have argued that elite alliances should be seen as strategic ties between individual political elites and movement actors. Clearly, some organizations pursue these relationships and others do not, either because of resource limitations or because of a conscious rejection of institutionalized politics. My findings indicate that movement groups gain considerable advantage if they incorporate political "networking" into their collection of tactics. Such SMOs are more likely to obtain structural positions among their peers that provide influence and enable them to engage more fully in sector activity. Also, my data suggest that formal associations with elite organizations provide insufficient information to increase the structural positions that facilitate success.

One limitation of this project is that it was unable to assess the effect that organizational budget has on centrality. Future research should evaluate the extent to which financial resources influence centrality and ability to build and maintain alliances with elites. It is quite possible that elite political organizations (e.g., UN agencies and IGOs) build informal alliances with organizations that they know are financially capable of carrying out joint projects and rallying a significant support base.

Regardless of this limitation, the current project has clearly demonstrated that alliances with elites are characteristics of individual social movement actors. While the presence of sympathetic elites certainly affects social movement success, a better conceptualization of elite alliances must include diadic relationships between individual movement actors and elites. When elites are present and sympathetic to movement aims, movement actors must strategically decide whether to forge relationships with them. Those movement organizations that invest in this strategy become influential, central actors within their movement.

NOTES

1.   Transnational social movement organizations comprise a subset of a larger nongovernmental organization (NGO) population.

2.   Simple count centrality is also commonly referred to as *degree centrality* in the network literature. I have chosen to use the term simple count centrality because it better represents what the concept is measuring.

3.   I define elite agencies as organizations that possess institutionally legitimate authority to grant or deny social movement demands. Typically, such organizations include local, state, or federal agencies and political parties; however, if the social movement is advocating changes with transnational implications, elite organizations may also comprise regional or global intergovernmental institutions, such as the Organization of American States (OAS) or agencies of the United Nations (UN).

4.   Organizations in consultative status with UN agencies are subject to periodic reviews. On occasion, governments have used this review process as an opportunity to scrutinize particular TSMOs — especially those that have criticized them. Therefore, one reason some TSMOs may pursue informal ties in lieu of formalized consultative ties is to avoid the politics of the review process.

5.   These comments were collected during the Sixth Session of the UN Commission on Sustainable Development as part of my dissertation research (Caniglia 2000).

6.   Blau (1965: 125) notes that "number of different locations where the organization operates" is a measure of complexity rather than size.

7.   These results are further bolstered when the control variables are dropped, in which 138 cases are analyzed. When simple count centrality is regressed onto consultative status and informal ties the R2 is .65; when betweenness centrality is substituted, the R2 is .64. Only informal ties is significant in each of these models.

REFERENCES

Aldrich, Howard, and David A. Whetten. 1981. "Organization-Sets, Action-Sets, and Networks: Making the Most of Simplicity." Pp. 385-408 in *Handbook of Organizational Design*, Paul C. Nystrom and William H. Starbuck, eds. Oxford: Oxford University Press.

Blau, Peter M. 1981 [1965]. "The Comparative Study of Organizations." Pp. 110-128 in *The Sociology of Organizations*, Oscar Grusky and George A. Miller, eds. New York: Free Press.

Boli, John, and George M. Thomas. 1997. "World Culture in the World Polity: A Century of International Non-governmental Organization." *Annual Sociological Review* 62): 171-190.

Borgatti, S. P., M. G. Everett, and L. C. Freeman. 1992. *UCINET IV VERSION 1.0*. Columbia, Md.: Analytic Technologies.

Boutros-Ghali, Boutros. 1996. "Forward." Pp. 7-12 in *NGOs, the UN, and Global Governance*, Thomas G. Weiss and Leon Gordenker, eds. Boulder, Colo.: Lynne Rienner Publishers.

Buechler, Steven. 1996. "New Social Movement Theories." In *Social Movements:Perspectives and Issues*. Mountainview, Calif.: Mayfield Publishing Company.

Calhoun, Craig, Marshall W. Meyer, and W. Richard Scott. 1990. *Structures of Power and Constraint*. Cambridge: Cambridge University Press.

Caniglia, Beth Schaefer. 2000. "Do Elite Alliances Matter? Structural Power in the Environmental TSMO Network." Ph.D. diss., University of Notre Dame.

Collins, Randall. 1979. *The Credential Society: An Historical Sociology of Education and Stratification*. New York: Academic Press.

Diani, Mario. 1995. *Green Networks: A Structural Analysis of the Italian Environmental Movement*. Edinburgh: Edinburgh University Press.

————. 2000. "Mobilization Forum: The Relational Deficit of Ideologically Structured Action." *Mobilization* 5(1): 17-24.

Donini, Antonio. 1996. "The Bureaucracy and the Free Spirits: Stagnation and Innovation in the Relationship between the UN and NGOs." Pp. 83-102 in *NGOs, the UN, and Global Governance*, Thomas G. Weiss and Leon Gordenker, eds. Boulder, Colo.: Lynne Rienner Publishers.

Edwards, Bob, and Sam Marullo. 1995. "Organizational Mortality in a Declining Social Movement: The Demise of Peace Movement Organizations in the End of the Cold War Era." *American Sociological Review* 60 (December): 908-927.

Edwards, Michael, and David Hulme, eds. 1996. *Beyond the Magic Bullet: NGO Performance and Accountability in the Post-Cold War World*. Bloomfield, Conn.: Kumarian Press.

Eisenger, Peter K. 1973. "Conditions of Protest Behavior in American Cities." *American Political Science Review* 67:11-28.

Fernandez, Roberto, and Roger V. Gould. 1994. "A Dilemma of State Power: Brokerage and Influence in the National Health Policy Domain." *American Journal of Sociology* 99(6): 1455-91.

Freeman, Linton C. 1979. "Centrality in Social Networks: Conceptual Clarification."*Social Networks* 1: 215-239.

Gale, Richard. 1986. "Social Movements and the State: The Environmental Movement, Countermovement, and Government Agencies." *Sociological Perspectives* 29(2): 202-240.

Gould, Roger V., and Roberto M. Fernandez. 1989. "Structures of Mediation: A Formal Approach to Brokerage in Transaction Networks." *Sociological Methodology* 19: 89-126.

Haas, Peter, ed. 1992. "Knowledge, Power, and International Policy Coordination." *International Organization* 46 (winter 1992).

Higley, John, and Richard Gunther. 1992. *Elites and Democratic Consolidation in Latin America and Southern Europe*. Cambridge: Cambridge University Press.

Jenkins, Craig J., and Craig Eckert. 1986. "Channeling the Black Insurgency: Elite Patronage and the Development of the Civil Rights Movement." *American Sociological Review* 51: 812-830.

Jenkins, Craig J., and Charles Perrow. 1977. "Insurgency of the Powerless: Farm Worker Movements (1946-1972)." *American Sociological Review* 42: 249-68.

Keck, Margaret, and Kathryn Sikkink. 1998. *Activists beyond Borders: Transnational Advocacy Networks in International Politics*. Itheca, N.Y.: Cornell University Press.

Klandermans, Bert. 2000. "Must We Redefine Social Movements as Ideologically Structured Action?" *Mobilization* 5(1): 25-30.

Knoke, David. 1990. *Political Networks: The Structural Perspective*. Cambridge: Cambridge University Press.

Knoke, David, and James H. Kuklinski. 1982. *Network Analysis*. Beverly Hills, Calif.: Sage Publications.

Knoke, David, and Edward O. Laumann. 1982. "The Social Organization of National Policy Domains." *Social Structure and Network Analysis*, Peter Marsden and Nan Lin, eds. Beverly Hills, Calif.: Sage Publications.

Kriesi, Hanspeter. 1989. "New Social Movements and the New Class in the Netherlands."*American Journal of Sociology* 94:1078-1116.

Laumann, Edward O., Peter V. Marsden and David Prensky, eds. 1983. "The Boundary Specification Problem in Network Analysis." In *Applied Network Analysis,* Ronald S. Burt, and Michael J. Minor, eds. Beverly Hills, Calif.: Sage Publications.

Laumann, Edward O., and David Knoke. 1987. *The Organizational State*. Madison: University of Wisconsin Press.

Lipsky, Michael. 1968. "Protest as a Political Resource." *American Political Science Review* 62 (December): 1144-58.

Marsden, Peter. 1990. "Network Data and Measurement." *American Sociological Review* 16:

435-463.

McAdam, Doug. 1982. *Political Process and the Development of the Black Insurgency, 1930-1970*. Chicago: University of Chicago Press.

———. 1996. "Political Opportunities" Pp. 17-37 in *Comparative Perspectives on Social Movements,* Doug McAdam, John D. McCarthy, and Mayer Zald, eds. Cambridge: Cambridge University Press.

McAdam, Doug, John D. McCarthy, and Mayer Zald. 1996. *Comparative Perspectives on Social Movements*. Cambridge: Cambridge University Press.

Meyer, David, and Sidney Tarrow. 1998. *The Social Movement Society: Contentious Politics for a New Century*. Boulder, Colo.: Rowman & Littlefield.

Neidhardt, Friedhelm, and Dieter Rucht. 1993. "Auf dem Weg in die Bewegungsgesellshaft? Uber die Stabilisterbarkeit sozialer Bewegungen." *Sozialer Welt* 44: 305-326.

Nelkin, Dorothy, and M. Pollak. 1982. *The Atom Besieged: Extraparliamentary Dissent in France and Germany*. Cambridge, Mass.: MIT Press.

Parsons, Talcott. 1970. "Equality and Inequality in Modern Society, or Social Stratification Revisited." Pp. 14-72 in *Social Stratification and Theory for the 1970s,* Edward O. Laumann, ed. Indianapolis: Bobbs-Merrill.

Pfeffer, Jeffrey. 1978. "Who Governs?" Pp. 1-30 in *The Sociology of Organizations: Basic Studies*, 2nd ed. Oscar Grusky and George A. Miller, eds. New York: Free Press.

Piven, Frances Fox, and Richard A. Cloward. 1977. *Poor People's Movements: Why They Succeed, How They Fail*. New York: Vintage Books.

Putnam, Robert. 1976. *The Comparative Study of Political Elites*. Saddle River, N.J.: Prentice Hall.

Risse-Kappen, Thomas. 1994. "Ideas Do Not Float Freely: Transnational Coalitions, Domestic Structures, and the End of the Cold War." *International Organization* 48(2):185-214.

Rosenau, James N. 1993. "Environmental Challenges in a Global Context." Pp. 257-274 in *Environmental Politics in the International Arena: Movements, Parties, Organizations, and Policy,* Sheldon Kamieniecki, eds. New York: State University of New York Press.

———. 1993. "Environmental Challenges in a Turbulent World." Pp. 71-93 in *The State and Social Power in Global Environmental Politics,* Ronnie Lipschutz and Ken Conca, eds. New York: Columbia University Press.

Rucht, Dieter. 1996. "The Impacts of National Contexts on Social Movement Structures: A Cross-Movement and Cross-National Comparison." Pp. 185-204 in *Comparative Perspectives on Social Movements*, Doud McAdam, John McCarthy and Mayer Zald, eds. Cambridge: Cambridge University Press.

Sikkink, Katherine. 1993. "Human Rights, Principled Issue-Networks, and Sovereignty in Latin America." *International Organization* 47(3): 411-441.

Smith, Jackie, Ron Pagnucco, and Winnie Romeril. 1994. "Transnational Social Movement Organizations in the Global Political Arena." *Voluntas* 5(2): 121-154.

Smith, Jackie. 1997. "Characteristics of the Modern Transnational Social Movement Sector." Pp. 42-58 in *Transnational Social Movements and Global Politics: Solidarity beyond the State,* Jackie Smith, Charles Chatfield and Ron Pagnucco, eds. Syracuse, N.Y.: Syracuse University Press.

Smith, Jackie, Charles Chatfield, and Ron Pagnucco, eds. 1997. *Transnational Social Movements and Global Politics: Solidarity beyond the State*. Syracuse, N.Y.: Syracuse University Press.

Stinchcombe, Arthur L. 1965. "Social Structure and Organizations." Pp. 142-93 in *Handbook of Organizations*, James March, ed. Chicago: Rand McNally.

Tarrow, Sidney. 1988. "National Politics and Collective Action: Recent Theory and Research in Western Europe and the United States." *Annual Review of Sociology* 14: 421-40.

Taylor, Verta, and Nancy E. Whittier. 1996. "Collective Identity in Social Movement Communities: Lesbian Feminist Mobilization." In *Social Movements: Perspectives and*

Issues. Mountainview, Calif.: Mayfield Publishing Company.

Tilly, Charles. 1978. *From Mobilization to Revolution.* Reading, Mass.: Addison Wesley.

Union of International Associations (UAI). 1993. *Yearbook of International   Associations.* Munich, Germany: K. G. Saur.

Wasserman, Stanley, and Katherine Faust. 1994. *Social Network Analysis.* Cambridge: Cambridge University Press.

Weber, Max. 1947. *The Theory of Social and Economic Organizations.* New York: Oxford University Press.

Weiss, Thomas G., and Leon Gordenker, eds. 1996. *NGOs, the UN, and Global   Governance.* Boulder, Colo.: Lynne Rienner Publishers, 1996.

Willetts, Peter. 1996. *The Conscience of the World.* Washington, D.C.: Brookings Institution.

Zald, Mayer N., and John D. McCarthy. 1987. *Social Movements in an Organizational Society.* New Brunswick, N.J.: Transaction Publishers.

———. 2000. "Ideologically Structured Action: An Enlarged Agenda for Social Movement Research." *Mobilization* 5(1): 1-16.

Chapter 10

BUILDING NETWORKS FROM THE OUTSIDE IN: JAPANESE NGOs AND THE KYOTO CLIMATE CHANGE CONFERENCE

Kim D. Reimann

On December 7, 1997, 20,000 people gathered at Heian Shrine in Kyoto to show their support for an ambitious international protocol for the reduction of greenhouse gases worldwide. Organized by Students' Action for COP3 and Kiko Forum, an umbrella group of 225 Japanese NGOs, the event was a culmination of 688 NGO-sponsored workshops, events, and symposiums held in Japan throughout 1997 to raise awareness about global warming and to challenge Japan's international environmental policies. During the Third Conference of Parties to the UN Framework Convention on Climate Change (COP3) held in Kyoto from December 1-11, 1997, Japanese NGOs lobbied for higher greenhouse gas emission reduction targets, issued press statements, and harshly criticized the Japanese government's policy.

This relative success of Japanese NGOs in mobilizing a movement around the international issue of climate change contradicts what one might have expected in a country where environmental groups have traditionally been weak and generally uninterested in global issues. Prior to 1997, in fact, only a handful of Japanese NGOs closely followed international climate change politics. Have things changed in Japan in the 1990s? If so, why and how?

This chapter looks at changing patterns of Japanese environmental NGOs active in the international sphere and argues that in the early 1990s changes in the international realm provided activists new opportunities and frameworks that allowed them to overcome steep domestic organizational barriers and participate in new activities focused on global environmental issues. Building upon recent work done by sociologists and political scientists, it outlines how international opportunity, transnational diffusion, and international socialization of state actors have encouraged the growth of NGOs and new forms of social action.[1]

INTERNATIONAL ENVIRONMENTAL ADVOCACY NGOS IN JAPAN

Scholars of Japanese environmental organizing have all noted that although local environmental protests and activism proliferated in the 1970s, these activities never fully congealed into a national movement with national associations as they did in many other industrialized countries (Broadbent 1998; McKean 1981; Schreurs 1996). Moreover, after tough antipollution measures were enacted by the Japanese government in the early 1970s, the movement's focus shifted from protest to everyday environmentalism such as recycling, organic farming, and educational activities. In general, the mid-1970s and 1980s were periods of less politically visible activity by environmentalists in Japan, and environmental advocacy NGOs active in global issues were practically nonexistent (McKean 1981; Schreurs 1996).

Since the late 1980s, however, advocacy groups interested in various aspects of global environmental politics have emerged in Japan. Some new groups focus on particular environmental problems such as tropical forest destruction, while others with a domestic focus have expanded their interests to include international concerns. As figure 10.1 illustrates, since the late 1980s, the number of advocacy groups focusing on global environmental issues or involved in a campaign with international dimensions has dramatically grown.[2]

This recent emergence of international environmental NGOs in Japan is puzzling because domestic barriers to organizing advocacy groups have been formidably high. Consistent with strong state theory and social movement theory (Krasner 1995; Skocpol 1985; Risse-Kappen 1995; McAdam, McCarthy, and Zald 1996; Kriesi,

Figure 10.1. Japanese Advocacy NGOs Involved in Global Environmental Issues

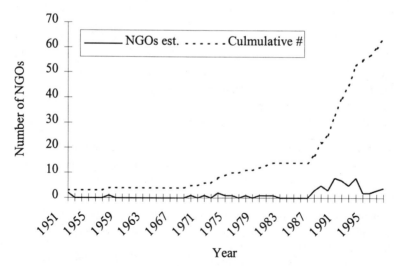

Sources: Honnoki USA 1992, JACSES 1994, JANIC 1996a and 1998a, Kansai Association for International Exchange 1994, and Internet search.

Koopmans, Duyvendak, and Guigni 1995), which argue that state policies and domestic opportunity structures strongly influence how society organizes, rigid domestic policies and political institutional structures have made it very difficult to organize an advocacy NGO in Japan.

First, state policies such as legal frameworks and fiscal regulations regarding NGOs strongly affect activists' ability to organize, mobilize resources, and form legitimate groups (Fremont-Smith 1965; McCarthy, Hodgkinson, and Sumariwalla 1992). In Japan, such state policies have posed serious obstacles to the emergence of an active advocacy NGO sector. NGO legal status has been a contested issue and it was only in 1998 that a system of registration for nonprofit organizations was passed in the Japanese Diet. Until then, complicated requirements for establishing a "public interest corporation" discouraged activists from officially incorporating themselves, especially since this special legal status often implied bureaucratic control and a loss of freedom (Broadbent 1998; Pekkanen 2000; Imata, Leif, and Takano 1998; Yamamoto 1998). In terms of fiscal incentives, the standard tools of mobilizing funds and membership found in other countries such as tax deductible contributions and special bulk mail rates were not available (Pekkanen 2000; Imata, Leif, and Takano 1998).

Government funding policies for NGOs also affect their size and development. Scholars of international NGOs have noted that availability of state funds for international projects provide one source of financial support that affects group formation and development (Smillie and Helmich 1993; Smith 1990). Government funding of international NGOs involved in advocacy issues is more common in Europe and Canada than it is in the United States (Smith 1990), but until very recently it was absolutely unheard of in Japan.

Finally, key aspects of the political opportunity structure in Japan have been highly unfavorable to advocacy NGOs. Two important factors often mentioned by social movement scholars as determining political opportunity structure for group organizers, for example, are the degree of openness of the political system and the existence of elite allies (Kriesi, et al. 1995; McAdam, McCarthy, and Zald 1996; Jenkins 1987). Japan's highly centralized political system and the limited access to channels of influence for outsiders have meant that the political opportunity structure for advocacy environmental NGOs has been highly unfavorable, discouraging formal organizational formation. It has also been hard for NGOs in Japan to cultivate elite allies at the national level—thereby limiting political opportunities. Until recently, bureaucrats were seen as very antagonistic and paternalistic toward NGOs (Yonemoto 1994). The ruling Liberal Democratic Party generally held this view as well, and its long hold on power until 1993 meant that NGOs with ties to opposition parties would not necessarily have any influence or access to the policy-making process.

INTERNATIONAL EXPLANATIONS FOR RISING NGO ACTIVISM

If domestic political factors have been so unfavorable to NGO formation and growth in Japan, how does one account for the growth of global environment advocacy NGOs since the late 1980s? I argue that answers lie in international-level processes and their domestic-level effects on the NGOs' ability to mobilize. In particular, since the late 1980s three factors have provided new resources for societal actors interested in international issues: more international opportunities, transnational diffusion of ideas among NGOs, and the international socialization of state actors.

International Political Opportunities

International relations scholars interested in nonstate actors (Risse-Kappen 1995; Keck and Sikkink 1998) and social movement scholars interested in the international movement dimensions (della Porta and Kriesi 1999; McAdam 1998; Kriesi, et al. 1995) have called attention to the importance of international arenas, networks, and actors in stimulating political changes at the domestic level. According to these theories, the international arena can provide domestic actors with outside opportunities that help them gain voice and circumvent the limits imposed on them by the domestic context. Specifically, the international realm can aid otherwise "blocked" societal actors through two mechanisms: (1) participation in international governmental organizations (IGOs), and (2) alliances with international actors.

International governmental organizations (IGOs). These potentially provide activists whose domestic opportunities are closed with several key resources: legitimacy, an alternative access channel to governmental officials, financial resources, and media coverage. Since NGOs are included in UN and other international conferences and meetings, activists who have difficulty establishing legitimacy at home can form an NGO and turn to the international arena for official international recognition and access to an alternative political process (Passy 1999; della Porta and Kriesi 1999; Smith 1999). IGOs thereby provide NGOs a new space for lobbying their national representatives. IGOs have also on occasion provided grants to NGOs for participation in conferences, and they have supported NGO networking projects with funding, meeting spaces, and equipment. Finally, media coverage of international events provides activists with a new sort of public relations tool which reaches not only domestic but international audiences (Lahusen 1999; della Porta and Kriesi 1999).

International actors. These can also help NGOs and activists circumvent domestic resource and political opportunity problems. Materially, foreign actors such as private foreign foundations, foreign governments, and wealthy international NGOs can provide needed financing for NGO projects and activities (Keck and Sikkink 1998; Passy 1999). In terms of nonmaterial resources, international allies can help groups get international attention through their public relations efforts and media ties that in turn provide possible benefits at home such as greater domestic legitimacy and more media coverage. When they include powerful foreign governments, transnational alliances can provide groups with heightened domestic importance in the eyes of their own government (Keck and Sikkink 1998; McAdam 1998; Brysk 1993).

Transnational Diffusion

Writing about the international spread of ideas among nonstate actors, a new and growing literature on transnational social movements has turned to the concept of diffusion to examine how movements in one part of the world can activate similar movements in other parts of the world (McAdam and Rucht 1993; Snow and Benford 1999; Kriesi et al. 1995; McAdam 1995; Tarrow 1998).

Diffusion is defined as the acceptance by one set of actors of an object or idea through external channels of transmission. Such diffusion channels take one or a combination of two forms: (1) relational channels: direct, interpersonal contact between transmitters and adopters, and (2) nonrelational channels: indirect transfers of information through the mass media (McAdam and Rucht 1993: 59; Kriesi, et al. 1995: 184-186; Snow and Benford 1999).

Diffusion can involve a variety of objects of diffusion, ranging from the content of a campaign or a movement (e.g., the diffusion of the antinuclear movement in the 1970s) to organizational forms used by social actors (e.g., umbrella organizations) to forms of action (e.g., demonstrations, sit-ins, petitions, etc.) (Kriesi, et al. 1995: 185-186). Although *transnational* diffusion was traditionally viewed by scholars as less common than diffusion within a country due to the obvious obstacles of geographical and cultural distance, recently processes of globalization have made the diffusion of movement ideas and strategies across borders more common and easier to trace.

IGOs increasingly are spaces for the transnational diffusion of ideas among societal actors and global training grounds for activists. As the number of international conferences and international treaties has increased and allowed for greater NGO participation, IGOs have become a hotbed of NGO activity where social activists from various nations meet and learn from one another. This has been true at the UN and to a limited degree at the European Union when its institutions have become targets of social movements that spread to other nations (Imig and Tarrow 2001). Whether it is a "spin-off" movement following ideas of an "initiator" movement (McAdam 1995) or an adoption of new organizational forms or strategies, transnational diffusion at IGOs is one potentially powerful explanation of advocacy NGO growth and NGO-organized movements in new parts of the world.

International Organizations and the Socialization of State Actors

Diffusion of new ideas and practices, however, has not been restricted to transnational exchanges between NGOs and social movements. As sociological institutionalists have argued, international organizations and arenas are also the mechanisms through which *state* actors learn international norms and are socialized (McNeely 1995). In the case of NGOs, the emergence in the 1980s and 1990s of an international norm among Western nations recognizing the role of NGOs in international politics has pushed many states to reexamine and/or justify their own relations with society.

Recent international relations and sociological institutionalist scholarship have looked at how international structures help shape domestic level behavior and beliefs (Katzenstein 1996; Finnemore 1996; Meyer, Boli, Thomas, and Ramirez 1997; McNeely 1995; Risse, Ropp and Sikkink 1999). These scholars emphasize the causal importance of international structures and describe a socialization process by which international norms and ideas spread to far-flung corners of the world. In essence, as states become members of international organizations, they enter a process of socialization which requires them to recognize a set of international rules, expectations, and concepts. This process leads to domestic transformation as states adopt new policies promoted by international institutions and actors.

Regarding state policies toward NGOs, the 1980s and 1990s brought about a new level of interaction and cooperation between NGOs and governments in world politics. In the area of international development, NGOs were promoted by IGOs and activist Western states as a more effective and democratic way of providing foreign aid. In the area of advocacy and participation in world politics, the increasing openness of the UN and other international organizations to NGO participation in conferences, meetings, and other forums beginning from the late 1980s also gave NGOs a positive image as "global citizens." When the Cold War ended, a new focus on "civil society" by Western powers as a desirable part of democracy also provided international normative

Table 10.1.   Types of International Processes and Their Effects on NGOs at the Domestic Level

	Domestic Level Effect	Domestic Actors Involved	International Actors Involved
International Opportunity	Domestic-level obstacles are circumvented through use of new international resources	—NGOs, activists as initiators of action —state actors present at international organizations as responders to NGOs and international actors	—IGO as alternative access to state officials —International NGOs, IGOs, and third party states as alternative funding sources and external sources of legitimacy and pressure
Transnational Diffusion	Domestic societal actors and organizations are transformed through new ideas and forms of actions	—NGOs, activists as idea adopters (spin-offs)	—international NGOs as idea transmitters (initiators) —IGO as spaces of societal interaction and diffusion
International Socialization of State Actors	State structures and state actors are transformed (new state policies, opening of political structures)	—state actors as adopters (bureaucrats, politicians)	—IGO and states as transmitters of norms and ideas

support and legitimacy for NGOs.

This new pro-NGO international environment has provided domestic-level opportunities and political space for activists and groups in countries with weak NGO sectors. Although such effects vary from country to country, international-level activities have been a potential source of change in the domestic political opportunity structure for NGOs. Debates and new norms about NGOs found in international organizations and the international environment are sometimes reflected in changes at the domestic level: changes in government policies toward NGOs, greater numbers of politicians who are interested in international affairs and more willing to support NGO causes, the appearance of government officials seeped in the language of NGO-participatory democracy, and greater media attention.

COP3: GLOBAL WARMING COMES TO JAPAN

The Third Conference of Parties (COP3) to the UN Framework Convention on Climate Change (FCCC) was held December 1-11, 1997 in Kyoto. When Japan was announced as the COP3 host, a small group of Japanese NGOs previously active at global climate conferences decided that as the "NGO hosts" they needed to make extra efforts in COP3 organizing. These efforts included: coordinating logistical arrangements and events for hundreds of international NGOs that would be participating in COP3, lobbying the Japanese government for ambitious CO_2 reduction targets, raising public awareness about COP3 and global warming, and getting maximum visibility for NGOs in the press. All of this required resources beyond the budgets of most small NGOs in Japan. When Kiko Forum was set up in December 1996 as an umbrella organization for Japanese NGOs participating in COP3, its organizers were far from sure that they would be able to achieve this ambitious agenda (Hayakawa interview 1998; Asaoka interview 1998).

In the end, however, Kiko Forum was successful in many of its efforts to mobilize public interest, create a national support network, and have its voice heard by the government. Kiko Forum membership grew from 46 to 225 NGOs by the time COP3 opened in December 1997 (Kiko Forum 1998a). In addition to coordinating more than 750 public workshops and talks on global warming in 1997, Kiko Forum organized numerous mobilization events and campaigns to raise awareness of global warming and public support for tougher government policies (Kiko Forum 1998a; see table 10.2). Kiko Forum and its NGO members actively lobbied and met with the three key ministries responsible for formulating Japan's COP3 policies and were visible participants in public debates. They also attracted considerable media attention, and their position was well represented in the press.[3]

International Opportunity, Diffusion, and Socialization

Changes in international opportunity, the expanding transnational diffusion of movement ideas, and the international socialization of political elites provide important clues about how Kiko Forum came to be and why it was able to achieve many of its goals. This section traces the ways in which these three international processes helped Kiko Forum surmount what in 1996 seemed like serious barriers to organization.

1. International Events as Political Opportunities

International institutions and international actors provided essential resources for Kiko Forum and NGOs that allowed them to circumvent obstacles they faced at home.

Funding. Forty percent of Kiko Forum's funding came from foreign sources, and such funding was key in helping Japanese NGOs get their campaign off the ground (Asaoka interview 1998).[4] Foreign governments such as Germany, Denmark, and Norway sought dramatic cuts in greenhouse gas emissions at COP3, and they pursued this policy goal in part by providing substantial funding for Kiko Forum in order to encourage popular mobilization for a stronger treaty. Foreign foundations, including the Alton Jones Foundation and the Rockefeller Brothers Fund, provided funding in part out of concern that Japanese NGOs would be too weak to properly fulfill their role as NGO hosts.

Access to the political process. International organizations provided Japanese NGOs with access to policy makers and a new channel for lobbying the government, enabling them to overcome problems of access they faced in Japan. Accreditation for NGOs at FCCC-related UN meetings has been easy to obtain, allowing for a relatively large and broad inclusion of NGOs as observers in the FCCC process. Using this easy

Table 10.2. NGO-Organized Public Events in Japan in 1997 Related to COP3

Event or Activity	Date	Description
"100-Day-Before Campaign"	August 23	Symposium in Kyoto attended by 200 NGOs and the general public and a "human chain" of 1,500 people joining hands on Suma Beach in Kobe to show support for COP3. Organized by Kiko Forum and 22 groups in the Kobe region.
Petition to the Prime Minister	October 13	Petition delivered by Kiko Forum with 750,000 signatures collected nationwide calling on Prime Minister Hashimoto to show stronger leadership for COP3.
Eco-Relay	October 21 – November 30	A nationwide bicycle "eco-relay" organized by Kiko Forum that starts in 6 separate cities in Japan in October and ends with 600 cyclists in Kyoto on the day before COP3. A total of 10,000 participate in one of the various stages and more than 1,400 signatures of heads of local government are collected by the cyclists.
International Postcard Project	December 2	Gathering of 21 youth from 21 countries at Heian Shrine at start of COP3 to present 7000 postcard messages supporting global warning from 50 countries. Organized by the Group of 21.
COP3 Rally	December 7	A rally of about 20,000 in Kyoto during COP3 organized by Kiko Forum and Student Action for COP3, including Diet members Kan Naoto (Democratic Party of Japan), Ikenobo Yasuko (Shinshinto), and Nishiyama Tokiko (Japan Communist Party).

Sources: Kiko Forum, 1998a; Asahi Shimbun, 8.24.97; Asahi Evening News, 12.1.97; Daily
Yomiuri, 12.3.97; Asahi, 12.8.97; Japan Times, 12.8.97.

access, Japanese NGOs conducted their first lobbying activities in the mid-1990s at the international level. By 1996, they convinced Japanese officials to meet with them regularly at FCCC ad hoc meetings and main conferences. Lobbying that Kiko Forum was able to do for COP3 was thus built on a history of interactions with state officials working in UN policy arenas. Instead of starting their lobbying at the national level in Tokyo, NGOs began first at the international level where they enjoyed legitimacy and then worked their way down to the national level.

Establishing legitimacy and getting press coverage. In addition to funding support, international NGOs (INGOs) and UN offices provided valuable nonmaterial support to NGOs that gave them greater legitimacy, media coverage, and access to the government in Japan.

International NGOs (INGOs) like the Climate Action Network (CAN)[5] were very important allies for Kiko Forum, since foreign NGOs have tended to attract greater government and press attention in Japan. By publicly associating itself with INGOs, Kiko Forum was able to use INGOs' higher public profile to gain legitimacy in the eyes of both government officials and the press, which also proved useful for fund-raising and public relations. For example, a three-day conference in March 1997 held jointly by Japanese NGOs and sixteen foreign INGOs and NGOs was a turning point that provided Japanese NGOs greater access to state officials and high levels of media coverage.[6] Immediately after this conference, Kiko Forum found fund-raising and membership expansion were suddenly much easier (Asaoka interview 1998; Hayakawa interview 1998).

Since COP3 was being held in Japan, Kiko Forum also secured help from the UN and the FCCC secretariat. In addition to giving Kiko Forum advice on how to organize the NGO aspects of the conference, FCCC official Janos Pasztor and UN NGO liaison officer Azza Taalab participated in Kiko Forum conferences to educate the public on the FCCC process and the role of NGOs. Observing this cooperation from the UN, Ministry of Foreign Affairs (MOFA) officials also became much more cooperative with Kiko Forum (Asaoka interview 1998). In addition, the Global Environment Information Center (GEIC), a center run jointly by the UN University and the Japanese Environment Agency, actively supported Kiko Forum and individual Japanese NGOs by sponsoring a series of public information programs on COP3 and the role of NGOs, providing NGOs free Internet space on its web page, and providing free meeting space for NGO events related to COP3.

2. Transnational Diffusion

Beyond being opportunities for overcoming domestic barriers, international experiences also provided new models of behavior and organization for Japanese NGOs that helped them achieve their goals. Transnational diffusion of ideas and models were particularly powerful in the case of mobilizing for COP3.

The Klima Forum model. Kiko Forum consciously modeled its goals and campaigns on Klima Forum, a German NGO network which lobbied the German government and organized NGO events for the First Conference of the Parties (COP1), held in Berlin in 1995.[7] Kiko Forum took its name from Klima Forum (both mean "Climate Forum") and invited Klima Forum's leader Sasha Mueller-Kraenner to Japan for consultations during its early organizational stages in autumn 1996. Based on Mueller-Kraenner's experience and suggestions, Kiko Forum formulated the basic concept of its mobilizing role in the COP3 process (Asaoka interview 1998). This initial contact was followed up in December 1996 with meetings with other former Klima Forum organizers who helped Kiko Forum plan specific events and campaigns and estimate costs (Kiko Forum 1998a; Asaoka interview 1998). The Klima Forum model thus provided many key organizational and conceptual frameworks for Kiko Forum.

Lobbying. Through their contacts with INGOs and CAN at international conferences, Kiko Forum and its core NGO members also learned how Western NGOs lobby and pressure their home governments. Until relatively recently, lobbying at the national level by NGOs was rare in Japan. As some activists have mentioned in interviews, for many years NGOs were closed out of the policy process and it had never even occurred to them to try to lobby (Kuroda interview 1998; Hayakawa interview 1998). For Japanese NGOs interested in climate change, the FCCC process provided repeated exposures to lobbying and consultation with government officials. In the mid-1990s, Japanese members of CAN participated in CAN meetings with the Japanese government and learned how Western NGOs used these opportunities to promote their causes. Lobbying efforts by Kiko Forum and other NGOs during the COP3 process were thus based on previous learning experiences with INGOs.

Media training. Media coverage is a crucial element in any NGO advocacy campaign for building public support and interest, gaining name recognition and legitimacy, and putting public pressure on the state to adopt certain policies. Since the 1980s, media-targeted activities such as issuing press releases, staging press conferences, conducting interviews, and cultivating personal contacts with the media have become quite common among INGOs in the West (Lahusen 1999). In the case of COP3, Kiko Forum had a very conscious media strategy that involved the active use of foreign models. In order to raise public awareness about global warming and pressure the Japanese government, Kiko Forum decided it wanted to conduct an "American-style" media campaign (Asaoka interview 1998, Riggs interview 1998). To learn more about using the media effectively, Kiko Forum's executive director, Asaoka Mie, went to New York to learn the press strategies used by INGOs and to make the rounds with a Western INGO press relations officer during a UN international conference.

3. International Socialization of State Actors

Although in the early 1990s Japanese NGOs faced many of the same formal organizational barriers they had earlier, they found greater support for international-related NGOs among some state officials. This final section briefly looks at a few of these domestic changes and how more "internationalized" government officials and politicians provided Kiko Forum and Japanese NGOs with a more favorable environment for organizing.

Japan Fund for the Global Environment. Hosting a major international conference is a prestigious national event that puts pressure on the host country to not only show its guests a good time but also to produce concrete diplomatic results. As the official host, Japan's Environment Agency was very concerned about achieving an ambitious protocol on greenhouse gas reductions, and therefore the agency tended to view participation of NGOs favorably. It also knew that Japan would look bad internationally if its NGOs were excluded from such an important event.

Given this context, Kiko Forum was able to secure substantial state funds through the Japan Fund for the Global Environment (JFGE), a semi-public fund that provides grants to Japanese NGOs conducting international environmental projects. The director general of JFGE, Matsushita Kazuo—a man with extensive international conference experience who was sympathetic to NGOs—worked with Kiko Forum and put together a generous 40 million yen grant package under a new, separate budget called the "Global Partnership Program" (Shindo interview 1998). JFGE funds comprised nearly 30 percent of Kiko Forum's 1997 budget.

The creation of JFGE itself is an example of how international actors and institutions have helped bring about unexpected shifts in state policies toward NGOs. JFGE was one of several Japanese global environmental initiatives launched by then-prime minister Takeshita in the period leading up to the 1992 UN Conference on Environment and Development (UNCED), which were meant to showcase Japan's new commitment and global leadership on environmental issues. The idea for JFGE, however, was not a domestic one—Takeshita was a conservative who disliked NGOs—but rather an international one that resulted from discussions between Takeshita and UNCED secretary general Maurice Strong during preparations for UNCED (JANIC, *Kokoro*, July 1993). Maurice Strong was a longtime and very active promoter of NGO participation at both the UN and national level (Morphet 1996), and his imprint on Japanese policies toward NGOs is a clear example of how activist international actors and norms can override countervailing domestic practices and create small new windows of opportunity for previously marginalized actors.

The global environment politicians. In the late 1980s and early 1990s several Diet members took an interest in global environmental issues (Schreurs 1996: 268). The most environmentally active politicians are members of GLOBE (Global Legislators Organization for a Balanced Environment), an international parliamentary NGO formed in 1989 with sub-sections in the United States, the EU, Japan, and Russia.

As they have become involved in international exchanges and global conferences, some Japanese GLOBE parliamentarians have adopted more sympathetic views toward NGOs. House of Councilors member Domoto Akiko, GLOBE Japan's president during COP3 and the current head of GLOBE International, is one of the most active Diet members promoting both the environment and NGOs in Japan. She has formed her own environmental NGO, Mori no Kai. Domoto, and three other GLOBE Diet members are also on the board of directors of People's Forum 2001, a core member of Kiko Forum that has been following global warming since COP1. GLOBE Japan also took a big interest in COP3 and tried to include NGOs in its COP3 events. Generally, NGOs saw Domoto as an ally because of her contacts with them and her criticisms of Japan's global warming policies (Ogura interview1998).

Non-GLOBE Diet members also showed support for Kiko Forum by joining its public mobilization activities such as the eco-relay or the rally and parade during COP3. In particular, the election of Tsujimoto Kiyomi as a lower house Diet member in October 1996 was very timely for NGOs. A founder herself of an NGO called Peace Boat, thirty-seven-year-old Tsujimoto had participated at UNCED in 1992 as an NGO representative and was very familiar with the Japanese NGO world. Upon taking office, Tsujimoto took an active interest in COP3 by attending FCCC meetings and serving as an information "pipe" for NGOs (Tsujimoto interview 1997). Since information from government officials is often hard to obtain without insider connections, NGOs were able through Tsujimoto to get information they would not have gotten otherwise (Ogura interview 1998).

CONCLUSION

Synthesizing previous work by political scientists and sociologists into a single model, I have shown how international factors can affect the domestic environment for social activism by either providing alternative resources or by transforming domestic structures and actors themselves. In particular, I have emphasized the importance of IGOs as the space and medium through which new opportunities, transnational diffusion of ideas, and transformation of state actors takes place. Although these three types of international effects are not always at work, their relevance for NGOs and social movements has grown as the number of international conferences open to NGO participation has increased in the past decade.

Japan provides a fascinating case for the study of NGOs and the emergence of new social movements in non-Western settings. Compared with many other industrialized nations, it has been difficult in Japan to establish NGOs and mobilize the necessary resources for large-scale social activism. In some ways, Japanese activists face similar domestic obstacles as do those in many Southern developing countries. As the case of Kiko Forum and COP3 has shown, the traditional distinction of rich Northern and poor Southern NGOs is not always a clear one: despite Japan's status as a Northern nation, Japanese NGOs have clearly benefited from and turned to external resources.

Beyond providing external resources and ways of circumventing domestic limitations, international institutions and actors have also played a role in slowly transforming Japanese domestic structures and patterns of behavior. Through their participation in international conferences, Japanese activists have learned new forms of organization and action, have picked up new issues to champion, and have increasingly set up new NGOs. Japanese state actors such as bureaucrats and politicians, on the other hand, have gradually been socialized internationally to accept NGOs as legitimate actors and have given NGOs more access to the political process than was the case before the late 1980s. Although many tensions remain and NGOs still face much official resistance, state-NGO relations at the national level in Japan today are far more cooperative than they were a decade ago.

On a final note, however, a few limitations and qualifications to the international factors model should be noted. First, while external factors and conditions have clearly played a role in supporting the emergence and growth of *international*-oriented NGOs, it is unclear the extent to which they have done so for *all* NGOs. In general, one ought to expect international factors to have a greater and more direct effect on activists interested in issues debated in the international arena. Similarly, in terms of the state's changing attitude toward NGOs, one should also expect to find varying levels of international influence on the state depending on the degree to which a ministry or politician is integrated into global policy arenas (Risse-Kappen 1995). State actors that more actively participate in IGO politics are far more likely to be "socialized" and to take NGOs seriously than those who do not. Further refinements of the international model as well as additional investigation into its usefulness in other parts of the world provide fruitful avenues for future research.

NOTES

1.   As a preliminary note of clarification, this chapter focuses on NGO formation and mobilization and will not deal with the influence of NGOs on policy outcomes.

2.   These are conservative estimates. The data for figure 10.1 are taken from several NGO directories, a report on Japanese NGO participation in the UN Conference on Environment and Development, and an extensive Internet search. There are in fact more groups than those included in the figure because many of the NGOs located through my Internet searches did not provide their establishment dates on their web pages and had to be left out of the total count.

3.   Kiko Forum's *'97 New File,* contains 236 pages of newspaper clippings on NGOs and COP3 (Kiko Forum 1998b).

4.   NGOs also benefited from international funding for their COP3 related activities. Greenpeace Japan received support from Greenpeace International and WWF Japan received Japanese staff support for COP3 through WWF U.S. People's Forum 2001 received substantial funding for its COP3 activities from the National Wildlife Federation.

5.   CAN is a global network of NGOs (dominated by several large Western INGOs) and is dedicated to the issue of climate change.

6.   According to Kiko Forum executive director Asaoka, after this conference, officials at both the Ministry of International Trade and Industry (MITI) and the Ministry of Foreign Affairs (MOFA) began to take Japanese NGOs more seriously as part of a larger international movement.

7.   One Kiko Forum publication (1998a: 2) plainly states: "Without the prior existence of Klima Forum, the idea to form Kiko Forum might never have materialized."

REFERENCES

Asaoka Mie, 1998. Executive Director, Kiko Forum, interview August 5, 1998.

Broadbent, Jeffrey. 1998. *Environmental Politics in Japan, Networks of Power and Protest.* Cambridge: Cambridge University Press.

Brysk, Alison. 1993. "From Above and Below: Social Movements, the International System, and Human Rights in Argentina." *Comparative Political Studies* 26 (3): 259-85.

della Porta, Donatella and Hanspeter Kriesi. 1999. "Social Movements in a Globalizing World: An Introduction." Pp. 3-22 in *Social Movements in a Globalizing World,* Donatella della Porta, Hanspeter Kriesi, and Dieter Rucht, eds. London: Macmillan Press.

Finnemore, Martha. 1996. *National Interests in International Society.* Ithaca, N.Y.: Cornell University Press.

Fremont-Smith, Marion. 1965. *Foundations and Government: State and Federal Law and Supervision.* New York: Russell Sage Foundation.

Hayakawa Mitsutoshi. 1998. Managing Director, Citizens' Alliance for Saving the Atmosphere and the Earth (CASA), interview August 8, 1998.

Honnoki USA, 1992. *Japanese Working for a Better World—Grassroots Voices and Access Guide to Citizens' Groups in Japan.* San Francisco: Honnoki.

Imata, Katsuji, Elissa Leif, and Hiroyuki Takano, 1998. "Structural Impediments of Japan's Nonprofit Sector: Overcoming the Obstacles to Increased Nonprofit Collaboration with Japan." Paper presented at the Association for Research on Nonprofit Organizations and Voluntary Action 27th Annual Conference, Seattle.

Imig, Doug, and Sidney Tarrow. 2001. "Mapping European Contention: Evidence from a Quantitative Data Analysis." Pp. 27-52 in *Contentious Europeans: Protest and Politics in an Emerging Polity,* Doug Imig and Sidney Tarrow, eds. Lanham, Md.: Rowman & Littlefield.

Japan Center for a Sustainable Environment and Society (JACSES). 1994. *Report of a Survey on the Earth Summit Follow-up Activities in Japan.* Tokyo: JACSES.

Japanese NGO Center for International Cooperation (JANIC) 1998a. *NGO Dairekutori- '98.* (NGO Directory 1998) Tokyo: JANIC.

————. 1996. *NGO Dairekutori- '96.* (NGO Directory 1996) Tokyo: JANIC.

————. 1993. *Kokoro* (Newsletter), July.

Jenkins, J. Craig. 1987. "Nonprofit Organizations and Policy Advocacy." In *The Nonprofit Sector, A Research Handbook,* Walter W. Powell, ed. New Haven, Conn.: Yale University Press.

Kansai Association for International Exchange. 1994. *Interpeople Directory.* Osaka: Kansai Association for International Exchange.

Katzenstein, Peter J., ed. 1996. *The Culture of National Security: Norms and Identity in World Politics.* New York: Columbia University Press.

Kiko Forum. 1998a. *Activities of Kiko Forum in 1997 and Goals for the Future.* Kyoto: Kiko Forum '97.

————. 1998b. *Kiko Forum '97 News File.* Kyoto: Kiko Forum '97.

Keck, Margaret E. and Kathryn Sikkink. 1998. *Activists beyond Borders.* Ithaca, N.Y.: Cornell University Press.

Krasner, Stephen D. 1995. "Power Politics, Institutions and Transnational Relations." Pp. 257-279 in *Bringing Transnational Relations Back in: Non-state Actors, Domestic Structures and International Relations,* Thomas Risse-Kappen, ed. Cambridge: Cambridge University Press.

Kriesi, Hanspeter, Ruud Koopsmans, Jan Willem Duyvendak, and Marco G. Giugni. 1995. *New Social Movements in Western Europe, A Comparative Analysis.* Minneapolis: University of Minnesota Press.

Kuroda Yoichi, 1998. Research Fellow, Institute for Global Environmental Strategies (IGES), interview August 13, 1998.

Lahusen, Christian. 1999. "International Campaigns in Context: Collective Action between the Local and the Global." Pp. 189-205 in *Social Movements in a Globalizing World,* Donatella della Porta, Hanspeter Kriesi, and Dieter Rucht, eds. London: Macmillan Press.

McAdam, Doug. 1998. "On the International Origins of Domestic Political Opportunities." In *Social Movements and American Political Institutions,* Anne N. Costain and Andrew S. McFarland, eds. Lanham, Md.: Rowman & Littlefield.

————. 1995. "'Initiator' and 'Spin-off' Movements: Diffusion Processes in Protest Cycles." In *Repertoires and Cycles of Collective Action,* Mark Traugott, ed. Durham, N.C.: Duke University Press, 1995.

McAdam, Doug, and Dieter Rucht. 1993. "The Cross-National Diffusion of Movement Ideas." *Annals of the American Academy of Political and Social Science* 528: 56-74.

McAdam, Doug, John D. McCarthy, and Mayer N. Zald, eds. 1996. *Comparative Perspectives on Social Movements: Political Opportunities, Mobilizing Structures, and Cultural Framings.* Cambridge: Cambridge University Press.

McCarthy, Kathleen D., Virginia A. Hodgkinson, and Russy D Sumariwalla, eds. 1992. *The Nonprofit Sector in the Global Community, Voices from Many Nations.* San Francisco: Jossey-Bass.

McKean, Margaret A. 1981. *Environmental Protest and Citizen Politics in Japan.* Berkeley: University of California Press.

McNeely, Connie L. 1995. *Constructing the Nation-State, International Organization and Prescriptive Action.* Westport, Conn.: Greenwood Press.

Meyer, John W., John Boli, George M. Thomas, and Francisco O. Ramirez. 1997. "World Society and the Nation-State." *American Journal of Sociology* 103 (1): 144-181.

Morphet, Sally. 1996. "NGOs and the Environment." Pp. 116-146 in *The Conscience of the World. The Influence of Non-governmental Organizations in the UN System,* Peter Willetts, ed. Washington, D.C.: Brookings Institution.

Ogura Tadashi, 1998. Japan Tropical Forest Action Network (JATAN), interview June 26, 1998.

Passy, Florence. 1999. "Supranational Political Opportunities as a Channel of Globalization of Political Conflicts: The Case of the Rights of Indigenous Peoples." Pp. 148-169 in *Social Movements in a Globalizing World,* Donatella della Porta, Hanspeter Kriesi, and Dieter Rucht, eds. London: Macmillan Press.

Pekkanen, Robert. 2000. "Japan's New Politics: The Case of the NPO Law." *Journal of Japanese Studies* 26 (1): 111-143.

Riggs, Peter, 1998. Program Officer, Rockefeller Brothers Fund, interview March 19, 1998.

Risse, Thomas, Stephen C. Ropp, and Kathryn Sikkink. 1999. *The Power of Human Rights: International Norms and Domestic Change.* New York: Cambridge University Press.

Risse-Kappen, Thomas, ed. 1995. *Bringing Transnational Relations Back in: Non-state Actors, Domestic Structures and International Relations.* Cambridge: Cambridge University Press.

Schreurs, Miranda A. 1996. "Domestic Institutions, International Agendas and Global Environmental Protection in Japan and Germany." Ph.D. diss., University of Michigan.

Shindo Kaoru, 1998. Japan Environment Corporation, Japan Fund for the Global Environment, interviews November 11, 1997 and June 29, 1998

Skocpol, Theda. 1985. "Bringing the State Back In: Strategies of Analysis in Current Research." In *Bringing the State Back In,* Peter Evans, Dietrich Rueschemeyer, and Theda Skocpol, eds. Cambridge: Cambridge University Press.

Smillie, Ian, and Henny Helmich, eds. 1993. *Non-governmental Organizations and Governments: Stakeholders for Development.* Paris: OECD.

Smith, Brian H. 1990. *More than Altruism: The Politics of Private Foreign Aid.* Princeton: Princeton University Press.

Smith, Jackie. 1999. "Global Politics and Transnational Social Movements Strategies: The Transnational Campaign against International Trade in Toxic Wastes." Pp. 170-188 in *Social Movements in a Globalizing World,* Donatella della Porta, Hanspeter Kriesi, and Dieter Rucht, eds. London: Macmillan.

Snow, David A., and Robert D. Benford. 1999. "Alternative Types of Cross-National Diffusion in the Social Movement Arena." Pp. 23-39 in *Social Movements in a Globalizing World,* Donatella della Porta, Hanspeter Kriesi, and Dieter Rucht, eds. London: Macmillan Press.

Tarrow, Sidney. 1998. "Fishnets, Internets, and Catnets: Globalization and Transnational Collective Action." Pp. 228-244 in *Challenging Authority, the Historical Study of Contentious Politics,* Michael P. Hanagan, Leslie Page Moch and Wayne te Brake, eds. Minneapolis: University of Minnesota Press.

Tsujimoto Kiyomi, 1998. House of Representatives, interview, November 13, 1997.

Yamamoto, Tadashi, ed. 1998. *The Nonprofit Sector in Japan.* Manchester, U.K.: Manchester University Press.

Yonemoto, Shohei. 1994. *Chikyu kankyo mondai to wa nani ka.* (Explaining global environmental problems) Tokyo: Iwanami Shinsho.

Part V

Protest and the Global Trade Regime

Chapter 11

TRANSNATIONAL POLITICAL PROCESSES AND CONTENTION AGAINST THE GLOBAL ECONOMY

Jeffrey M. Ayres

Social movements scholars have rightly pointed out that neither globalization nor transnational activism are new phenomena (Tarrow 1998; McAdam 1998; Hanagan 1998). The world economy had interlocking trade and investment patterns as early as the nineteenth century. Similarly, transnational activism has flourished for over a century. The antislavery and workers' solidarity movements come to mind, as do the recent antinuclear, anti-apartheid, and international peace movements. Yet what is distinct about today's global economy is its neoliberal character, which structures contemporary transnational contention.

Proponents of neoliberalism argue that an economy is best organized by markets free of government intervention. Recent trade and investment accords such as the North American Free Trade Agreement (NAFTA) help define the neoliberal perspective globally. Three transnational economic institutions promote the neoliberal agenda by enhancing deregulation, unfettering free trade, and increasing the mobility of capital and multinational corporations. The World Trade Organization (WTO) oversees trade agreements. Unlike its predecessor, the General Agreements on Tariffs and Trade (GATT), the WTO can sanction countries that do not abide by global trade rules. The International Monetary Fund (IMF) and the World Bank are the other two global institutions fostering neoliberalism. Both emerged from the Bretton Woods discussions during World War II about the world economy's future, and they have expanded their roles in recent years.

Anecdotal evidence abounds linking this evolving neoliberal architecture and recent protests. Indonesian students and South Korean workers have protested the structural adjustment policies of the IMF. The Zapatista-led indigenous rebellion in the remote Mexican state of Chiapas targeted the January 1994 start of NAFTA. French strikers have resisted the wage and benefit cutbacks implicit in the European Union's "Maastricht orthodoxy." Finally, activists mobilized transnationally to stop the MAI, or Multilateral Agreement on Investment (Castells 1996; Schulz 1998; Ayres 1999). While protests against neoliberal structures continue, the impetus for challenging these arrangements boils down to several basic themes.

First, activists protesting these agreements object to the hierarchical character of negotiations. As affairs reserved primarily for business and government elites, the unrepresentative and undemocratic nature of negotiations alienate activist groups and their constituencies. Second, activist groups bemoan these negotiations' inattention to social concerns, and they frequently rally to demand that trade agreements include considerations about labor rights, food safety, and health and environmental standards. This occurred during the NAFTA debate when protests called for the insertion of labor and environmental side agreements. Protests are also aimed to educate and rally the public against the accords.

Third, activists have presented broad alternatives to the neoliberal thrust of the agreements. Frequently, activists hold counter-gatherings during economic trade summits and issue press releases that outline alternative development models. Imbedded in these protests are fears, expressed by both the Left and the Right, over loss of national sovereignty. In particular, those on the Left see that the accord's enforcement mechanisms are often at odds with national representative institutions, and they fear a weakening of democracy. This is often referred to as the "democratic deficit," a view that economic policy making has become straightjacketed by the constraints of neoliberal arrangements.

NAVIGATING RESEARCH ON TRANSNATIONAL CONTENTION

Contentious politics is defined as "collective activity on the part of claimants or those who claim to represent them relying at least in part on noninstitutional forms of interaction with elites, opponents, or the state" (Tarrow 1996a: 874). It is widely accepted that recent global transformations such as growing economic integration, emerging issues that transcend national borders, the proliferation of international institutions, conferences, and treaties, and the communications revolution have given rise to contentious politics that transcend national borders (Rucht 1999; Kriesberg 1997). Social movement scholars have increasingly globalized their studies by recognizing that "social movements are not just prisoners of their national boundaries, but are profoundly shaped by their international environments"(Jenkins 1995: 33). Thus, a transnational focus on contentious politics encompasses diverse instances of sustained movement activity across multiple states. It covers a broad spectrum of activities that typically embraces several social movements, coalitions, protests, campaigns, petitions and declarations, and other noninstitutionalized activities.

Certainly, an analytical focus on neoliberal economic institutions is in line with the globalization of contentious politics. The arrangements, regulations, and ministerial meetings that are integral to globalization processes stimulate transnational activism. Tarrow (1996b: 61) is close to the mark when he asks whether the "global economy and supranational institutions that have been developing around it over the past few decades have so thoroughly escaped the state as to create transnational movements." In fact, the question seems not whether neoliberal arrangements encourage transnational contention, but how and what kind.

Neoliberal arrangements promote varieties of transnational contention by virtue of their impact on political opportunities. The link between political institutions and social movement activity has been extensively documented, with an array of work highlighting how the national constellation of elites, political parties, and institutions structure or constrain opportunities for contention (McAdam 1982; Kitshelt 1986; Ayres 1998). Recently, scholars have considered how global changes affect opportunities, and how international trends not only shape domestic alignments and institutions, but also structure international opportunities (McAdam 1996; Oberschall 1996).

Specifically, neoliberal accords represent signposts to activists for new avenues of protest. Tarrow's refined definition of political opportunity structure is instructive: "consistent but not necessarily formal, permanent, or national signals to social or political actors which either encourage or discourage them to use their internal resources to form social movements" (1996b:54). Arguably, neoliberal arrangements create multiple levels of opportunity for contention. On the one hand, they shape domestic alignments and institutions, facilitating or constraining domestic opportunities for protest actions. On the other, these arrangements create new international opportunities, shaping the strategy and availability of transnational allies who find solidarity in mobilizing across borders against common targets. In particular, neoliberal integration has produced opportunities for activism at the headquarters of international organizations and around the international conferences and meetings where agreements are negotiated and signed.

In addition to political opportunities, mobilizing structures support and sustain transnational activism. Mobilizing structures are the organizations, networks, and coalitions that sustain contentious activity over time. McAdam, McCarthy, and Zald define mobilizing structures as "those collective vehicles, informal as well as formal, through which people mobilize and engage in collective action" (1996: 3). Smith, Pagnucco, and Chatfield have helped to internationalize the concept of mobilizing structures. They have devised a framework, adapted from McCarthy (1996), which classifies a variety of formal and informal movement and non-movement structures as important influences on transnational social movement mobilization (Smith, Pagnucco, and Chatfield 1997: 62).

Smith, Pagnucco, and Romeril (1994) have argued that successful transnational contention depends upon the availability of a transnational resource base, from which activists can draw material and human resources and in which they strategically interact to coordinate activities. The development of transnational mobilizing structures, therefore, can be assumed to have bolstered opposition to neoliberalism (della Porta, Kriesi, and Rucht 1999; Rucht 1999). National mobilizing structures can be expected to have merged with other national structures, creating supportive transnational organizational and resource bases.

Della Porta, Kriesi, and Rucht (1999: 5-13) divide the research on transnational contention into two categories. One highlights how global transformations affect national movements, or what is referred to as "national mobilization within a globalizing world." The other examines the emergence and spread of transnational movements focusing on transnational problems, or "mobilization beyond the nation state." In their reading, the bulk of transnational research falls into the former camp. The present research is a longitudinal case study that documents a pattern of contentious activity that bridges and overlaps with both groups. My analysis focuses primarily on Canadian activists and their successive protest campaigns against neoliberal economic agreements from the mid-1980s until 1999.

My methodology uses a variety of qualitative research techniques, including eight months of fieldwork in Canada, January-August 1992, and several return visits in 1993, 1996, and 1999. I gathered much of the data on various movements and organizations through semi-structured interviews with political activists, organizational leaders, and politicians (N=39), followed more recently by less numerous phone interviews. I also had the opportunity to visit many movement organization headquarters, including the Council of Canadians, the Action Canada Network, Common Frontiers, and the Ecumenical Coalition on Economic Justice.

During these visits I collected campaign literature, strategy documents, memorandums, minutes of meetings, and other documents germane to understanding movement activities. Finally, I have gleaned additional data on the more recent transnational campaigns against the Free Trade Agreement of the Americas (FTAA) and the MAI from the Internet. Many of the movement organizations studied maintain web pages that provide up-to-date information on their activities. By joining several organizations' e-mail lists, I gained access to daily information including press releases and other types of strategy communication related to ongoing campaigns. Together, this package of qualitative data provides a valid and reliable counterweight to the images that other secondary sources, including the news media, have provided on these movements and their supportive organizations.

TRANSNATIONAL CONTENTION: A VIEW FROM CANADA

Canadian activists have continuously struggled against neoliberalism since the mid-1980s. The pattern of activism emerged first with the national movement against the Canada-U.S. Free Trade Agreement (CUSFTA), but it has since evolved in an increasingly transnational direction. Figure 11.1 provides a listing of the mobilization forms according to the transnational accords they targeted which moves left to right along a continuum of increasing transnational scope. The longitudinal case study that follows demonstrates how transnational protest campaigns have evolved out of the experiences of activists in successive mobilizations against neoliberal policy initiatives. The early campaign against the CUSFTA epitomized a national movement affected by and reacting against an early offshoot of neoliberalism. The national umbrella coalition held together through the Pro-Canada Network (PCN) that opposed the CUSFTA also played a key role in the diffusion of strategies, including cross-border political exchange across North America during the NAFTA debate. The anti-FTAA mobilizations, in turn, relied upon the resourcefulness of the TSMO Common Frontiers, while the campaign against the MAI saw the transnationalization of dissent through an international coalition and the Internet.

This study highlights how, through a long period of contention, activists' policy targets changed over time, as did their mobilizing structures and strategies. Activists paired each policy realm, from the bilateral CUSFTA to the continental FTAA, with different protest strategies. At the same time, each successive trade liberalization measure targeted by activists shaped the political context for action. Restricted to exploiting national opportunity structures during the CUSFTA campaign, Canadian activists have since then targeted a multilevel national and international opportunity structure, and they have drawn from an expansive transnational mobilizing structure.

Figure 11.1. Transnational Accords and Mobilization Forms (by increasing transnational scope moving left to right)

CUSFTA	NAFTA	FTAA	MAI
National Umbrella Coalition (PCN)	Cross-Border Diffusion and Political Exchange	TSMO (Common Frontiers)	Transnational Coalition

Domestic Contention: The Mobilization against the Canada-U.S. Free Trade Agreement

Many social activist groups in Canada had already been articulating early criticisms of neoliberal economics before the tumultuous national debate over the CUSFTA. One distinct grouping, dubbed the "popular sector" (Cameron and Drache 1985), constituted a critical part of the national mobilizing structure for the nascent movement against the CUSFTA. Various churches, women's groups, farmers, trade unions, Native peoples, and other social agencies fell under this rubric, all sharing a counter-discourse on Canada's political economy. Popular sector groups rejected market-oriented responses to economic problems and felt marginalized from Canada's political elite and their decision-making institutions at that time.

Nationalist groups in Canada also complemented this activist work. Historically suspicious of any policies that smacked of closer economic ties between Canada and the United States, Canadian nationalists played a key role in mobilizing Canadian public opinion against the CUSFTA. For nationalists, a free trade agreement signaled a dramatic departure from tradition, and free trade had already played a role in the outcomes of two previous federal elections. Moreover, to nationalists, a CUSFTA threatened to undermine Canada's cultural distinctiveness, its social safety net, including its national health care system, and its sovereignty. The prospect of such an accord, therefore, carried enough historical baggage to spark the development of the Council of Canadians (COC), a pan-Canadian nationalist group, which would prove influential in contesting the CUSFTA negotiations.

Despite these precursors, the brunt of anti-CUSFTA mobilization began during the nearly two years it took for Canadian and U.S. trade representatives to negotiate the accord, between December 1985 and October 1987. By that time, various provincial and regional coalitions had formed, including the Ontario-based Coalition against Free Trade and La Coalition Québécoise d'Opposition au Libre-échange. Disagreements between Canadian and U.S. negotiators over the substance of the proposed CUSFTA delayed its completion, providing opposition groups with ample time to mature and develop their anti-CUSFTA message and solidify cross-sectoral ties.

The birth in April 1987 of the Pro-Canada Network (PCN) at the Maple Leaf Summit, a demonstration-event staged to counter the summit in Ottawa between then U.S. president Reagan and Canadian prime minister Mulroney, crystallized these various regional coalitions. Claiming to represent over ten million Canadians by the spring of 1988, the PCN emerged as the national vehicle for the communication and coordination of strategy among over twenty national organizations and provincial coalitions that had emerged to challenge the CUSFTA. Composed of different committees geared toward pooling resources, coordinating strategy, and directing action among affiliated organizations, the PCN orchestrated numerous protests during 1988 in an effort to turn the Canadian public against the CUSFTA. The PCN issued sectoral-wide critiques of the accord, oversaw a national petition drive against the deal, directed a cross-country National Day of Action, and worked with the Liberals and New Democratic Party, the two parliamentary parties opposed to the CUSFTA.

The PCN's greatest impact came during the fall 1988 reelection period when it coordinated a protest that pushed the CUSFTA debate to the center of the election campaign. It created easily recognizable lawn signs, T-shirts and "no, eh" campaign buttons and anti-CUSFTA election kits which it distributed to NDP and Liberal candidates. The PCN also participated in a televised debate against prominent supporters of the deal, and it developed a well-received cartoon booklet, *What's the Big Deal,* which it distributed in newspapers throughout Canada. Ultimately, the PCN played an unprecedented role for an extra-parliamentary actor in popularly educating and mobilizing Canadians against the CUSFTA.

Nonetheless, despite advantageous domestic political opportunities during the anti-CUSFTA protest, including the support of both parliamentary opposition parties and the electoral volatility that preceded the election, the efforts of the anti-CUSFTA coalition fell short. Mulroney's Progressive Conservative Party was reelected to a second governing majority in November 1988, ensuring the easy ratification of the CUSFTA shortly thereafter. Yet most social activist groups that had worked through the PCN to oppose the CUSFTA felt invigorated by the struggle and remained critical of the deal. More important, most groups remained committed to maintaining a cross-country network structure to educate and mobilize in the hopes that a future government might withdraw Canada from the accord.

In short, while activists failed to prevent CUSFTA's 1989 implementation, an extensive national mobilizing structure had developed which would help sustain contentious activity against neoliberalism into the 1990s. Canadian activists developed multisectoral networks of like-minded people with sharpened critiques of neoliberalism. Prominent national organizations with large Canadian constituencies such as the Canadian Labour Congress and the National Action Committee on the Status of Women remained supportive of protest actions. Additionally, Canadian activists could draw human and material resources from two strong national vehicles— the COC and the PCN umbrella coalition.

Continental Contention: Trilateral Mobilizing against NAFTA

If the cross-sectoral, cross-country mobilization against the CUSFTA marked a turning point in contentious politics in Canada, the debate over NAFTA encouraged further shifts in the form and strategy of the struggle against such neoliberal accords. Specifically, the process of negotiating NAFTA encouraged Canadian activists to target an increasing number of their claims outside of Canada. Instead of relying solely on those domestic opportunities for sustained mobilizations, Canadian actors found transnational avenues for continuing their protests against neoliberal principles. NAFTA in fact encouraged a shift in strategy toward greater transnational activism, which included the cross-border diffusion of protest and numerous instances of transnational political exchange.

Canadian activists sought to take advantage of these transnational openings in part because they perceived that postelection domestic political opportunities that had sustained anti-CUSFTA mobilization had shriveled. Faced with less-committed parliamentary opposition parties, and a Progressive Conservative government dedicated to neoliberalism, activists explored other ways of advancing popular education and dissent outside the parliamentary realm. Groups working through the PCN would continue to press the federal government to abandon the NAFTA talks, and seek to educate the public through demonstrations, petitions, and other actions. But attention also shifted to the United States and Mexico in an effort to derail the impending continental trade deal.

If political opportunities include the existence of supportive groups and allies (Tarrow 1989), then NAFTA dramatically enlarged the number of groups and sites available for coordinating transnational contention. NAFTA presented a common target—and the accord's negotiation process provided openings for influence—to those social activist groups in Canada, the United States, and Mexico that were concerned about possible negative effects on jobs, health, and the environment. If Canadian groups found fewer opportunities for mobilizing in their own country, then, they could exploit openings that were available in the United States and Mexico.

One significant outcome from the different types of cross-border exchanges that took place occurred with the diffusion of the PCN coalition structure. The meetings that took place between Canadians and Mexicans helped Mexicans develop a more critical perspective on free trade by learning from the Canadian experience of mobilizing against the CUSFTA. PCN's structure provided a model for the education and mobilization of Mexican civil society and political culture (Torres 1996, 1997), influencing the creation of la Red Mexicana de Acción frente al Libre Comercio (Mexican Action Network against Free Trade, or RMALC) in April 1991. Ultimately, the RMALC evolved into a vehicle representing over 100 activist organizations across Mexico critical of NAFTA. The development of the RMALC hinted that the mobilizing structure of organizations opposed to neoliberalism was expanding across the continent.

Transnational political exchanges also spread across North America both cross-sectorally and multisectorally. Women's environmental and labor groups set important precedents in their interactions and their opposition to both the process and the form that post-CUSFTA economic restructuring was taking (Kidder and McGinn 1995; Carr 1996; Dreiling 1997; Williams 1999). Because many women worked in occupations hardest hit by such economic restructuring, and racial and gender concerns and analyses were absent from the formal CUSFTA and NAFTA negotiations, women's groups and coalitions from all three countries regularly consulted and strategized through exchanges, study groups, and conferences (Gabriel and Macdonald 1993). Trilateral opposition to NAFTA thus helped to consolidate a transnational mobilizing structure to coordinate continental actions against the agreement.

In retrospect, Canadian activists played an important role in the development of continental protest against NAFTA. Notably, by both its cross-sectoral network form, and by the theme of its former target—opposition to the CUSFTA—the PCN provided the key "structure of affinity" (Giugni 1998) for anti-NAFTA mobilization that other groups, particularly in Mexico, adopted. The prospect that a neoliberal trade accord might bind the continent certainly encouraged Mexican activist groups to apply the lessons learned by their Canadian counterparts. The creation of RMALC in particular demonstrated how Canadian groups influenced the tactics adopted by others in the expanded, albeit unsuccessful, continental mobilization against NAFTA.

Hemispheric Contention: Transnational Networking against the FTAA

Despite the passage of NAFTA, the emerging debate over possibly expanding NAFTA into a hemispheric-wide free trade zone helped to sustain contention against neoliberal principles. Again, an implicitly neoliberal arrangement, the FTAA, if implemented, would remove barriers to trade and investment without putting in place a corresponding charter for mapping progress in social welfare and development. However, in the case of the FTAA, the dynamics of contention changed perceptively. The national movement in Canada that sprung up to oppose the CUSFTA was clearly shaped by the broad elite move to implement neoliberalism via the free trade deal. The NAFTA protests certainly illustrated numerous cross-border protests and strategizing by still nationally rooted collective actors. But the protest against the FTAA changed the dynamics of mobilization against neoliberalism with the emergence of hemispheric TSMOs. These TSMOs arose to coordinate strategy and disseminate information to activist groups from several different countries, clearly expanding further the base for countering hemispheric neoliberal restructuring.

The Toronto-based TSMO Common Frontiers formed an important part of the emergent transnational mobilizing structure postured against the FTAA. Common Frontiers evolved out of the Pro-Canada Network in 1989 in the aftermath of the Canadian federal election as a vehicle for sharing the experiences and lessons of the anti-CUSFTA mobilization. Since that time, Common Frontiers had increasingly provided information and analysis to activist groups across the hemisphere opposed to the evolving neoliberal agenda and its possible entrenchment in the FTAA. Notably, during the early stage of anti-FTAA protest, Common Frontiers remained composed of Canadian labor, church, environmental, and development groups seasoned by past mobilizations against the CUSFTA and NAFTA. Yet Common Frontiers evolved to include as working international partners the U.S.-based Alliance for Responsible Trade, the RMALC, the Brazilian Network for a People's Integration (REBRIP), and the Chilean Network for Fair Trade. Dedicated to building opposition against the FTAA and the wider neoliberal agenda, Common Frontiers stated goals included "identifying opportunities for the organizations of civil society in the Americas to confront the exclusionary, free-market model of economic integration in the Americas" (Common Frontiers 1999). In other words, Common Frontiers set out to help hemispheric groups exploit available opportunities conditioned by the FTAA debate.

FTAA-influenced international opportunities emerged, for instance, in the divisions that arose between political elites within different countries. These divisions played an important role in encouraging the development of common strategies, highlighting again the importance that shifting domestic alignments in one country can hold for the mobilization potential of groups in another. The stalemate in the U.S. Congress, for example, over whether to extend to President Clinton "fast-track" authority provided hemispheric groups with valuable time to consolidate links and strategies for further protests against the extension of NAFTA. For five years since the December 1994 meeting of various leaders of the Western Hemisphere at the First Summit of Americas in Miami, Florida, President Clinton had lobbied the U.S. Congress for such fast-track authority. This power would have provided him with the ability to negotiate new trade agreements, while prohibiting the U.S. Congress from amending any such deals. The stalemate resulted in part from a refusal on the part of Republicans in Congress to permit the inclusion of labor or environmental concerns in trade negotiations. Congress had renewed fast-track authority five times since first granting it to President Nixon in 1974. Yet in the fall of 1998, in a significant defeat for President Clinton's trade agenda, Congress voted against such a renewal.

During this time extensive transnational collaboration evolved between hemispheric organizations, as Canadian groups further diffused their experiences battling the CUSFTA and NAFTA to mobilizing against the FTAA. Common Frontiers developed, in particular, strong working links with groups in Chile, laying the groundwork for a public education campaign against admitting Chile into NAFTA or a new FTAA. It played an important role in the formation of the Canada-Chile Coalition for Fair Trade, composed of Canadian and Chilean organizations seeking to promote alternatives to the economic policies favored by both governments. It also supported the Steelworkers Humanity Fund's Chile-Canada worker exchanges and collective bargaining workshops.

The official meetings of trade and hemispheric political leaders negotiating the FTAA also turned into important opportunities for hemispheric activist groups. Both the preparatory meetings held prior to the official launch of the FTAA negotiations in Santiago, Chile, in April 1998 as well as the official meetings served as mobilization points, providing avenues to counterdemonstrate, network, strategize, and gain visibility around FTAA opposition. For instance, hemispheric groups held the Third Trade Union Summit parallel to the Trade Ministers' Meeting on the FTAA, in Belo Horizonte, Brazil, on 12-13 May 1997. At this summit, Common Frontiers helped to coordinate the participation of the Canadian delegation, where, together with other hemispheric groups, they issued a joint declaration on building a hemispheric alliance to confront the FTAA.

Building on the Brazil experience, hemispheric groups convened a People's Summit of the Americas in Santiago, Chile, on 15-18 April 1998. This summit ran counter to the second Summit of the Americas meeting, which had drawn over thirty political leaders from hemispheric countries to Santiago to launch the official start of the FTAA negotiations. Workshops stimulated cross-sectoral dialogue and reflection to identify cross-border commonalities and opposition to the FTAA. Beyond dialogue, the summit attempted to jump-start a transnational movement against the FTAA, as Common Frontiers noted:

> The Peoples' Summit in Santiago brought to the light of day the fact that there is a rising movement of resistance. This movement is one of the peoples of the Americas telling those political leaders, financial speculators and the transnational corporations who promote neoliberalism that their agenda is unacceptable. It is a movement of the peoples of the Americas demanding their very humanity. (Common Frontiers 1999)

Groups participating in the People's Summit also helped to draft the document *Alternatives for the Americas: Building a People's Hemispheric Agreement.* Hemispheric activists and scholars collaboratively produced this document out of dialogue over possible alternatives to the FTAA. *Alternatives* provided an in-depth critique of neoliberal economics and its impact on various social sectors, and alternatives for trade and development throughout the region. Common Frontiers, which played a key role in organizing the Peoples' Summit, continues to host *Alternatives for the Americas* on its website, where it is open to further updating through e-mail commentary.

Going Global: Contentious Politics against the New Trade and Investment Regimes

The global expansion of the neoliberal agenda, particularly through the proposed MAI, prompted Canadian groups increasingly to emphasize transnational strategies. This shifting context had a noticeable impact on the activities of the Council of Canadians, a group that since the CUSFTA debate had watched its membership swell to over 100,000. Once a stalwart of the Canadian nationalist Left, the COC in the 1990s became an active SMO and a leading practitioner of transnational economic activism against what it called the "corporate agenda." Its once-tentative ally and parliamentary opposition party, the Liberals, entered their second consecutive governing mandate in June 1997, having already reversed the party's trade policy in 1993, and became unabashed cheerleaders of the CUSFTA, NAFTA, and FTAA. Moreover, the other once-dependable opposition party, the NDP, fell on hard times, reduced to barely official parliamentary status, with little effective clout. Thus, with a vacuum on the Canadian political left, and with fewer avenues remaining for influencing Parliament, Canadian groups, including the COC, sought additional international openings for activism.

The focal point for the COC's new transnationalist outlook has been the "Citizen's Agenda for Canada." This new mission statement emerged out of the COC's 1994 annual meeting, in which the council reevaluated its approach to battling the CUSFTA and NAFTA. The agenda reflected a change in the council's strategy, from lobbying the federal government to abrogate these accords, to demonstrating against multinational corporations and cultivating transnational alliances. The COC further buttressed its commitment to greater transnational activism in its 1997 annual meeting, "The Citizen's Agenda in the Global Economy." This meeting included workshops, lectures, and strategy sessions on countering neoliberal economics both domestically and cross-nationally (Gibb-Carsley 1997).

Further illustrating its commitment to transnational networking, the COC, in November 1997, cosponsored an International Symposium on Corporate Rule in Port Elgin, Ontario. Attracting eighty-five delegates from Asia, Africa, Europe, Latin America, and North America, this symposium served as a forum for the development of international strategies to target four pillars of the global economy: the proposed MAI; mobile, fast-moving capital; the WTO; and the IMF. Delegates also agreed to hold an annual International Day of Resistance to target the activities of multinational corporations at the national and international levels. Following this symposium, the COC cohosted a global teach-in on "Challenging Corporate Rule: A Citizen's Politics for the 21st Century," at the University of Toronto. This conference drew nearly 2,000 activists from around the world to share stories and discuss responses to the effects of neoliberal economics on their countries (Gibb-Carsley 1998).

Also in November 1997, the COC held a forum at the People's Summit, a protest event staged parallel to the meeting of the leaders of the Asia Pacific Economic Cooperation (APEC) forum being held in Vancouver, British Columbia. This People's Summit continued the tradition of countersummits that had been held in prior years to coincide with the official APEC talks that had brought together leaders of Asian and Pacific countries to discuss trade-liberalization strategies for that region. Prior People's Summits, held in Seattle, Kyoto, and the previous year in Manila, had included days of workshops that brought women, trade unionists, environmentalists, indigenous peoples, and human rights advocates together to critique the effects of neoliberal economics. The COC's issue forum in Vancouver, "Unmasking Transnational Corporations," instructed activists on how to develop international links and strategies to expose the practices of multinational corporations in the global economy (Rowels 1997).

The 1997-1998 campaign against the MAI illustrated just how far these practitioners of transnational contention had advanced their craft. Through its tactics, the campaign managed to do what previous mobilizations against the CUSFTA and NAFTA had failed to do—it played a pivotal role in the decision by MAI negotiators to suspend indefinitely discussions on the accord. In fact, trade ministers for the Organization for Economic Cooperation and Development (OECD) were wholly unprepared for the transnational activism and public backlash that confronted their efforts to conclude MAI negotiations in the spring of 1998. For one, the OECD's secretive, closed-door approach to the negotiations was badly outdated. There was little tolerance for this approach to trade and investment negotiations in the eyes of activists who had experienced similar rebuffs through the CUSFTA, NAFTA, and FTAA negotiations. Also, OECD negotiators failed to appreciate that years of experience in cross-sectoral, transnational networking against neoliberalism had created an extensive transnational resource base from which activists could draw to contest the MAI.

The meetings of the OECD ministers in Paris also became important strategic venues for activists to protest the MAI. On the one hand, an international, multisectoral collection of activists met parallel to the OECD meetings to engage in direct communication and strategizing. On the other hand, OECD ministers consented to a meeting with activists. This NGO forum provided an opportunity for activists to press their case for reforms to the proposed MAI face-to-face with OECD ministers.

In addition, the activists' skilled use of the Internet and the public relations fiasco that resulted from it caught the OECD negotiators off guard. The Internet was crucial in linking anti-MAI activist groups into an international anti-MAI coalition. This informal network, while buttressed by a series of face-to-face meetings between activists in Paris and nationally affiliated coalitions, thrived through the exchange of information over the Internet that was critical of the MAI. OECD negotiators were unprepared to deal with the Internet's impact, while media outlets dubbed activists "network guerrillas" for their surprising and skilled attacks against the accord (Kobrin 1998). The Internet clearly added a new element to the strategies available to activists challenging neoliberalism. It sped up and eased the exchange of information across boundaries. It was not a substitute for the meetings held in person, especially in Paris, where activists gathered to build trust and exchange views. Yet it provided activists with a tool for creating opportunities for the rapid diffusion of anti-MAI protest.

Again, Canadian groups, including the COC, played a key role in unmasking the MAI and in derailing the negotiations. Having weathered the previous free trade battles, the COC was well prepared to challenge the MAI, and its efforts fell on a receptive audience in a Canadian public wary of the supposed benefits of another neoliberal accord. With the negotiations held in secret and the Canadian government failing to adequately educate the public on the nuances of the accord, the COC and dozens of national organizations filled the void. Across localities in Canada, a barrage of public teach-ins, street protests, petitions, and letter-writing campaigns unfolded into the spring of 1998 under the rubric of a national anti-MAI network. The COC's web page became an important clearinghouse of anti-MAI information. It contained up-to-date discussions, papers, press releases, and links to numerous anti-MAI e-mail lists and Internet sites throughout the world. The COC web page also provided information on how to create an "MAI-free" zone in a local community, and encouraged citizen feedback in the interactive development of a "Citizens' MAI."

The combined efforts of the various national coalitions and the international coalition against the MAI gave the appearance that the tide in contention against neoliberal globalization had shifted. The outcome of this transnational activism was groundbreaking: it represented the first time that activists mobilizing against a significant proposed addition to the neoliberal architecture had succeeded in banishing it from the world stage. The French government, whose decision to pull out of the negotiations irrevocably damaged the possibility of their success, credited the national and international coalitions, and the resulting public outcry with the accord's demise. The French report on the failed negotiations read in part

> The MAI thus marks a step in international economic negotiations. For the first time we are witnessing the emergence of a "global civil society" represented by non-governmental organizations, which are often active in several countries and communicate across borders. This is no doubt an irreversible change.[1]

CONCLUDING REFLECTIONS: GETTING TO SEATTLE

The data marshaled in this study provides background for understanding the larger and more recent mobilizations against neoliberal trade issues. Clearly, this study identifies a trend: the mobilizing structures and strategies propelling protest against neoliberalism have become increasingly transnational, matching the growth in multilateral policy targets. This dramatically altered political context for mobilization, composed of domestic and international political opportunities, paved the way for the groundbreaking transnational "mobilization against globalization" protests at the Seattle WTO ministerial meetings in fall 1999.

This study also more generally reaffirms the important supporting role played by transnational mobilizing structures in a successful international protest. While the first two cases of protest against the CUSFTA and NAFTA drew primarily from national mobilizing structures in the form of organizations, SMOs, and national coalitions, the anti-FTAA and MAI campaigns clearly thrived on an expanded transnational resource base. In particular, the counterarenas in Latin America and Europe where activists met provided the time for networking and coordinating activities outside of any national base. Granted, further research should be conducted before any conclusions can be made as to the long-term durability of these transnational alliances. However, evidence suggests that the alliances from the FTAA and MAI campaigns were not temporary exchange relations, but they were solidified through both TSMOs and routinized through transnational contacts and interactions through the Internet.

In addition, this study emphasizes that international processes structure both domestic and international protest opportunities. The neoliberal international trade agreements, from the CUSFTA to the MAI, successively influenced how, when, and where Canadian activists would mount campaigns to target the state, multinational corporations, and the trade agreements. Clearly, these trade arrangements were signals to actors to mobilize and use resources to form both national and transnational coalitions and SMOs. This transnational activism illustrates that actors' interests and claims are no longer framed solely by domestic political opportunities and constraints but by international opportunities as well.

In fact, it is clear with regard to this still-evolving transnational activism that states and domestic political institutions are no longer the dominant targets for political protest. Rather, activists increasingly are accessing international opportunities for influence outside the state. In particular, with regard to the protests against the FTAA and MAI, activists focused more on intergovernmental arenas, such as the hemispheric trade ministers' summits or the meetings of the OECD. These international settings provided activists with opportunities to sometimes personally confront the negotiators, while at the same time attend countersummits and strategy sessions. These international arenas were especially attractive, since it was unlikely that the FTAA or MAI accords were going to be placed before national legislatures for debate and passage. This further limited the attractiveness of domestic institutions for protest, necessitating transnational campaigns in international arenas.

For the near term, activism against neoliberal institutions in the global economy promises to remain an important part of the recent upswing of transnational contention. Activists clearly have continued to target multilateral institutions, such as the WTO, IMF, and World Bank, and the brewing public doubts universally expressed about the equity and supposed benefits of corporate globalization add fuel to this hotly contested debate. From this vantage point, more work needs to be done to assess the permanence of these transnational organizations and coalitions, as well as the claims that we have entered on the dawn of a global civil society. Nonetheless, the preceding case should remove doubt that what we have witnessed over these past several years is the coalescing of a transnational social movement against neoliberal globalization.

NOTE

1. See the French original of *Rapport sur l'accord multilateral sur l'investissement (AMI)* at: http://www. finances.gouv.fr/pole_ecofin/international/ ami0998/ami0998.htm.

REFERENCES

Ayres, Jeffrey, M. 1998. *Defying Conventional Wisdom: Political Movements and Popular Contention against North American Free Trade.* Toronto: University of Toronto Press.
———. 1999. "From the Streets to the Internet: The Cyber-Diffusion of Contention." *Annals of the American Academy of Political and Social Science* 566: 132-143.
Cameron, Duncan, and Daniel Drache, eds. 1985. *The Other Macdonald Report: The Consensus on Canada's Future That the Macdonald Commission Left Out.* Toronto: James Lorimer.
Carr, Barry. 1996. "Crossing Borders: Labor Internationalism in the Era of NAFTA." Pp. 209-233 in *Neoliberalism Revisited: Economic Restructuring and Mexico's Political Future,* Gerardo Otero, ed. Boulder, Colo.: Westview Press.
Castells, Manuel, Shujiro Yazawa, and Emma Kiseljova. 1996. "Insurgents against the Global Order: A Comparative Analysis of the Zapatistas in Mexico, the American Militia and Japan's AUM Shinrikyo." *Berkeley Journal of Sociology* 40:19-59.
Common Frontiers. 1999. Retrieved 2 August 1999 (www.web.net/comfront/aboutus/aboutus. html).
della Porta, Donatella, Hanspeter Kriesi, and Dieter Rucht, eds. 1999. *Social Movements in a Globalizing World.* New York: St. Martin's Press.
Dreiling, Michael. 1997. "Remapping North American Environmentalism: Contending Visions and Divergent Practices in the Fight over NAFTA." *Capitalism, Nature, Socialism* 8(4): 65-98.

Gabriel, Christina, and Laura Macdonald. 1993. "NAFTA, Women, and Organizing in Canada and Mexico: Forging a Feminist Internationality." *Millennium: Journal of International Affairs* 23(3): 535-562.

Gibb-Carsley, Victoria. 1997. "Building International Solidarity: Fighting Back against the Global Corporate Agenda." *Canadian Perspectives*: 10.

———. 1998. "Challenging Corporate Rule: A Report from the Global Teach-In." *Canadian Perspectives*: 11.

Giugni, Marco. 1998. "The Other Side of the Coin: Explaining Crossnational Similarities between Social Movements." *Mobilization: An International Journal* 3(1): 89-105.

Hanagan, Michael. 1998. "Irish Transnational Social Movements, Deterritorialized Migrants, and the State System: The Last One Hundred and Forty Years." *Mobilization: An International Journal* 3(1): 107-126.

Jenkins, J. Craig. 1995. "Social Movements, Political Representation and the State: An Agenda and Comparative Framework." Pp. 14-34 in *The Politics of Social Protest: Comparative Perspectives on States and Social Movements*, J. Craig Jenkins and Bert Klandermans, eds. Minneapolis: University of Minnesota Press.

Kidder, Thalia, and Mary McGinn. 1995. "In the Wake of NAFTA: Transnational Workers Networks." *Social Policy*: 14-21.

Kitschelt, Herbert. 1986. "Political Opportunity Structures and Political Protest: Anti-nuclear Movements in Four Democracies." *British Journal of Political Science* 16: 57-85.

Kobrin, Stephen. 1998. "The MAI and the Clash of Globalizations." *Foreign Policy* 112: 97-109.

Kriesberg, Louis. 1997. "Social Movements and Global Transformation." Pp. 3-18 in *Transnational Social Movements and Global Politics: Solidarity beyond the State*. Jackie Smith, Charles Chatfield, and Ron Pagnucco, eds. Syracuse, N.Y.: Syracuse University Press.

McAdam, Doug. 1982. *Political Process and the Development of Mass Insurgency, 1930-1970*. Chicago: University of Chicago Press.

———. 1996. "Conceptual Origins, Current Problems, Future Directions." Pp. 23-40 in *Comparative Perspectives on Social Movements: Political Opportunities, Mobilizing Structures, and Cultural Framings*, Doug McAdam, John McCarthy, and Mayer Zald, eds. Cambridge: Cambridge University Press.

———. 1998. "The Future of Movements." Pp. 229-245 in *From Contention to Democracy*, Marco Giugni, Doug McAdam, and Charles Tilly, eds. Lanham, Md.: Rowman & Littlefield.

McAdam, Doug, John D. McCarthy, and Mayer N. Zald. 1996. "Introduction: Opportunities, Mobilizing Structures, and Framing Processes—Toward a Synthetic, Comparative Perspective on Social Movements." Pp. 1-22 in *Comparative Perspectives on Social Movements: Political Opportunities, Mobilizing Structures, and Cultural Framings*, Doug McAdam, John McCarthy, and Mayer N. Zald, eds. Cambridge: Cambridge University Press.

McCarthy, John. 1996. "Mobilizing Structures: Constraints and Opportunities in Adopting, Adapting and Inventing." Pp. 141-151 in *Comparative Perspectives on Social Movements: Political Opportunities, Mobilizing Structures, and Cultural Framings*, Doug McAdam, John McCarthy, and Mayer N. Zald, eds. Cambridge: Cambridge University Press.

Oberschall, Anthony. 1996. "Opportunities and Framing in the Eastern European Revolts of 1989." Pp. 93-121 in *Comparative Perspectives on Social Movements: Political Opportunities, Mobilizing Structures and Cultural Framings*, Doug McAdam, John McCarthy, and Mayer Zald, eds. Cambridge: Cambridge University Press.

Rowels, Mary. 1997. "The Human Impact of Free Trade: A People's Summit." Retrieved 7 July 1999. (http://www.igc.org/dgap/oav1n4.html).

Rucht, Dieter. 1999. "The Transnationalization of Social Movements: Trends, Causes,

Problems." Pp. 206-222 in *Social Movements in a Globalizing World*, Donatella Della Porta, Hanspeter Kriesi, and Dieter Rucht, eds. New York: St. Martin's Press.

Schulz, Markus. 1998. "Collective Action across Borders: Opportunity Structures, Network Capacities, and Communicative Praxis in the Age of Advanced Globalization." *Sociological Perspectives* 41(3): 587-616.

Smith, Jackie, Charles Chatfield, and Ron Pagnucco, eds. 1997. *Transnational Social Movements and World Politics: Solidarity beyond the State*. Syracuse, N.Y.: Syracuse University Press.

Smith, Jackie, Ron Pagnucco, and Winnie Romeril. 1994. "Transnational Social Movement Organizations in the Global Political Arena." *Voluntas* 5(2): 121-154.

Tarrow, Sidney. 1989. *Struggle, Politics, and Reform: Collective Action, Social Movements, and Cycles of Protest*. Cornell Studies in International Affairs Western Societies Papers. Cornell University. Ithaca, N.Y.

———. 1996a. "Social Movements in Contentious Politics: A Review Article." *American Political Science Review* 90(4): 874-883.

———. 1996b. "States and Opportunities: The Political Structuring of Social Movements." Pp. 41-61 in Doug McAdam, John McCarthy, and Mayer Zald, eds. *Comparative Perspectives on Social Movements: Political Opportunities, Mobilizing Structures, and Cultural Framings*. Cambridge: Cambridge University Press.

———. 1998. "Fishnets, Internets, and Catnets: Globalization and Transnational Collective Action." Pp. 228-244 in Michael Hanagan, Leslie Page Moch, and Wayne T. Brake, eds. *Challenging Authority: The Historical Study of Contentious Politics*. Minneapolis: University of Minnesota Press.

Torres, Blanc. 1996. "Redes y Coaliciones en el Proceso de Negociación y Aprobación del Tratado de Libre Comercio de América del Norte." Pp. 431-470 in *Regionalismo y Poder en América: Los límites del Neorrealismo*, Arturo Borja, Guadalupe Gonzalez, and Brian J. R. Stevenson, eds. San Andel, Mexico: Centro de Investigación y Docencia Económicas.

———. 1997. "La Participación de Actores Nuevos y Tradicionales en las Relaciones Internacionales de México." Pp. 119-145 in *La Política Exterior de México*. El Colegio de México: Instituto Matías Romero De Estudios Diplomáticos.

Williams, Heather. 1999. "Mobile Capital and Transborder Labor Rights Mobilization." *Politics and Society* 27(1): 139-166.

Chapter 12

GLOBALIZING RESISTANCE: THE BATTLE OF SEATTLE AND THE FUTURE OF SOCIAL MOVEMENTS

Jackie Smith

On the evening of November 29, 1999, Seattle business and political leaders hosted an elaborate welcoming party in the city's football stadium for delegates to the World Trade Organization's Third Ministerial Conference. At the same time, thousands of activists rallied at a downtown church in preparation for the first large public confrontation in what became the "Battle of Seattle."[1] Protesters emerged from the overflowing church and joined thousands more who were dancing, chanting, and conversing in a cold Seattle downpour. They filled several city blocks and celebrated the "protest of the century." Many wore union jackets or rain ponchos that proclaimed their opposition to the World Trade Organization. Several thousand marchers (police estimates in local newspapers were 14,000, activists estimated 30,000; see Njehu 2000) progressed to the stadium, and around it formed a human chain—three or four people deep—to dramatize the crippling effects of the debt crisis. The protest deterred more than two-thirds of the expected 5,000 guests from attending the lavish welcoming event. The human chain's symbolism of the "chains of debt" was part of an international campaign (Jubilee 2000) to end Third World debt. It highlighted for protesters and onlookers the enormous inequities of the global trading system, and it kicked off a week of street protests and rallies against the global trade regime.[2]

The Seattle protests revealed a broad and diverse opposition to the recent expansion of neoliberal global economic policies. The "Battle of Seattle" and its predecessor campaigns against the Multilateral Agreement on Investment (MAI) and "fast track" authorization represented some of the first major popular challenges in the

United States to these policies. Indeed, these campaigns may mark a turning point in economic globalization by demonstrating a capacity for mass challenges to international trade agreements and high levels of popular concern about global human rights, labor rights, and environmental protection.[3] The Seattle protests challenge our understanding of state-social movement relations because they demonstrate how global-level politics affect a wide range of local and national actors. Scholars must ask how global economic, political, and social integration affect both *mobilization* and *collective action.* In terms of mobilization, Seattle raises questions about processes across national boundaries, and across class and cultural divides. Can social movements transcend local and national identities and interests to coherently oppose state and corporate elites? (see e.g., Tarrow 2001; Fox 2000; Smith 2000).

In terms of collective action, scholars must ask how global processes affect social movement repertoires that are forged primarily through nationally oriented contention. Global integration clearly alters traditional, state-level politics. If interstate relationships are becoming more important, then state decisions and practices are constrained by their relationships with other states and economic elites. How do global agreements alter domestic political structures? How do differences in power and interests among states affect challengers' leverage? To date, relations among social movements and intergovernmental organizations such as the UN have been largely accommodative, but Seattle points to a more contentious relationship.

What does this contrast tell us about today's global political system and of the role social movements within it? This chapter traces the origins and mobilizing structures behind the Seattle protest, and analyzes its tactics and their relevance to international institutional contexts. By asking both *who* and *what* constituted the Battle of Seattle, this analysis advances understandings of how global integration affects social movement mobilization and action.

BACKGROUND: THE SEATTLE MINISTERIAL

The original 1994 WTO agreement committed member states to a Millennium Round of talks that would expand trade liberalization policies under the WTO. The United States and other Western nations were strong advocates of WTO expansion, and they extensively tried to advance these goals before the Seattle meeting. For many states in the global South, however, the WTO was a disappointment. Although initially attracted by the promise of greater access to Western markets and greater influence in the IMF and World Bank, Southern governments found themselves left out of important WTO decisions.[4] Key deliberations were held in closed-door, "Green Room" meetings organized at the behest of the United States, Canada, European Union, and Japan (referred to as "the Quad"). Secret agreements were then presented to Southern members who were most vulnerable to pressure from the powerful Quad states (Vidal 1999; Zoll 1999). Southern governments also realized fewer economic rewards from expanded trade under the WTO than they had expected. Their agenda in Seattle was therefore to review existing agreements and to make them more equitable rather than to support a Millennium Round that would expand the WTO regime under rules they saw as highly skewed toward Western and corporate interests. This division among states was an important cause of the ultimate breakdown of talks in Seattle. In addition to this North-South split, there were divisions between European and U.S. interests over food safety standards and agricultural issues. In short, governments faced difficult prospects for staging a successful meeting in Seattle. All hope of bridging the North-South gap was effectively lost when President Clinton succumbed to pressure from protesters and called for labor protections within the WTO.

Social movement forces allied against the WTO expansion also contributed to these difficulties. Strong European resistance to genetically modified foods made it difficult for European governments to liberalize regulations on agricultural imports. Farmers' movements, which are strong in many European countries, also fought against cuts to subsidies and other agricultural supports. Southern governments benefited from analyses of researchers who were intellectual leaders of the anti-WTO movement.[5] Certainly, Southern challenges to Quad dominance in the WTO were bolstered by massive protests of Quad states' own citizens. It would be hard to argue that the Seattle Ministerial would have failed as miserably as it did without tens of thousands of protesters surrounding the meeting site.

The major protest slogan was "No WTO" (or "Hell no, WTO" if you were a steel worker or Teamster), but there was no clear consensus among protest groups about whether the WTO itself should be abolished or reformed. What was clear was that virtually all protesters in the streets of Seattle sought to democratize and incorporate values other than profit making into global economic institutions.

These goals could not be promoted effectively in national contexts for a number of reasons. First, for citizens of countries with small markets and little economic power, attempting to influence domestic policies is useless because these governments carry little weight in international negotiations. Second, in countries like the United States (as well as in global economic institutions), economic policies are considered technical, not political, decisions. They are formulated by bureaucrats in the U.S. Treasury Department and in the Trade Representative's Office, and they are not open to democratic scrutiny for reasons of trade-secret protection and competitiveness. Most citizens know very little about these offices and are deterred by the technical language. Third, the WTO agreement has removed key decisions from national policy debates. WTO limits on citizens' ability to affect even national policies have made the WTO agreement itself a target. Even in the United States, which wields the strongest influence in the WTO, citizens cannot simply work within domestic contexts to affect changes. They may seek to influence WTO policies domestically, but they gain more leverage as collective actors at the multilateral level where they can exploit differences among states.

MOVEMENT ORIGINS: STRUCTURES AND IDENTITIES

The Seattle resistance grew from earlier local, national, and transnational mobilizations against trade liberalization agreements, World Bank and IMF policies, and failures to protect human rights and the environment. The Seattle protests were novel because of substantial participation by citizens from the United States and other advanced industrialized countries against an international organization. They also involved a web of transnational associations and movement networks that developed out of activist streams of the 1980s and 1990s. This web facilitated cooperation and exchange across national boundaries.

The organizations most prominent in Seattle had previously mobilized against global trade and multilateral financial policies. Labor organizations, consumer groups (most notably Nader's Public Citizen), and major North American environmental organizations began focusing on trade liberalization especially during negotiations around the Canada-U.S. Free Trade Agreement and subsequent North American Free Trade Agreement (see, e.g., Audley 1997; Aaronson 2001; Ayres 1998; Shoch 2000; Naím 2000). Seattle's neoliberal trade opposition had even earlier roots. Perhaps the earliest resistance began in the global South with resistance to IMF-imposed structural adjustment policies (Walton and Seddon 1994). Environmental and human rights campaigners increasingly tried to curb World Bank lending for projects that threatened peoples and ecosystems in the global South (Rothman and Oliver in this volume; Fox and Brown 1998; Keck and Sikkink 1998; Rich 1994). These efforts drew the attention of Northern peace activists in the 1980s. Many of the older activists in Seattle, particularly those mobilized around "Jubilee 2000" or affiliated with peace movement organizations like the Women's International League for Peace and Freedom, traced their opposition back to the 1980s mobilizations around Third World debt and its relationship to conflict and economic justice in Central America and other developing regions (see, e.g., Smith 1994; Marullo, Pagnucco, and Smith 1996). Partly as a result of these struggles, the annual World Bank/IMF meetings became sites of protest rallies in the late 1980s (Scholte 2000; Gerhards and Rucht 1992). An international "Fifty Years Is Enough" campaign emerged in the mid-1990s to mobilize against the 1995 "celebration" of the fiftieth anniversary of the Bretton Woods conference and the founding of the World Bank and IMF (Foster 1999:145-153; Cleary 1996: 88-89).

Research on social movements has shown that formal social movement organizations play important roles in framing movement agendas, cultivating collective identities, and mobilizing collective actions. At the same time, churches, community organizations, friendship networks, and professional associations provide resources for movements and often engage in similar kinds of protest-oriented activities, even though these are not their principal purpose. Because these "extra-movement" groups have routine contacts with broad segments of society, they promote wider social movement participation and legitimacy (McCarthy 1996; C. Smith 1996). The anti-WTO protests included many of these "extra-movement" organizations and informal networks as important participants. For instance, many churches and unions with standing committees on social justice or solidarity issues had at least some regular contact with social movements. Many U.S. labor unions provided logistical and financial support so that their members could participate in an entire week of protest and educational activity.[6] Also, churches played an important role by disseminating information about the protests and by providing meeting spaces, legitimacy, and other resources. Jubilee 2000 was based largely in churches and faith-based social justice organizations, and the event drew many protesters to Seattle. School groups, in particular those opposing sweatshop labor, also helped raise awareness of protests and mobilize participation. In addition, protest organizers worked consciously to cultivate ties with community groups and with an active social movement sector in the Pacific Northwest.[7]

But the Seattle protests also were built upon transnational mobilizing structures that shaped leadership and strategies. For instance, the rapid expansion of transnational social movement organizations (TSMOs) during the past fifty years provided many activists with substantive knowledge of the political views of groups from different parts of the world, opportunities to gain skills and experience in international organizing work, expertise in international law, and familiarity with multilateral negotiations (Sikkink and Smith 2002). TSMO growth promoted transnational dialogue and helped organizers to coordinate interests and propose policies that accounted for the needs of people in both the global North and the global South. By facilitating flows of information across national boundaries, organizations with transnational ties helped cultivate movement identities, transcend nationally defined interests, and build solidary identities with a global emphasis (cf. Gamson 1991).[8] These identities are crucial for long-term mobilization and alliances across national boundaries where routine face-to-face contact is rare. They require deliberate efforts to define "who *we* are" in order to sustain activists' commitment.

TSMOs must demonstrate wide geographic representation if they are to be effective in multilateral political arenas. Engaging participants from many different countries lends credibility to an organization's agenda and, until recently, it was a central criterion for official UN accreditation. It also provides an organization with first-hand information on conditions in a variety of countries, facilitating efforts to link local examples to global policy debates. To cultivate a diverse membership these organizations must create spaces for transnational dialogue on common goals and strategies (Smith, Pagnucco, and Chatfield 1997). While most protesters in Seattle were from the United States and Canada, there were many from other parts of the world, particularly among the speakers at protest rallies and teach-ins. Southern activists and scholars comprised 30 to 40 percent of the panelists at the largest protest rallies and the People's Assembly. Many of the activists from poor countries traveled to Seattle as a consequence of their participation in transnational associations. Data on TSMOs show a trend toward greater participation of global South countries (Smith 2000). The Ministerial's location in Seattle meant underrepresentation of Southern activists, but when UN conferences are held in the South they draw many Southern representatives (Clark, Hochstetler, and Friedman 1998; Smith, Pagnucco, and Lopez 1998)

In the process of building coalitions and joint strategies, activists learn each other's positions and, where conditions favor it, build relationships and trust that are crucial for ongoing cooperation (Rose 2000). For instance, while Western environmental and labor activists might accept a policy of promoting environmental and labor protections through existing WTO mechanisms, dialogues with their counterparts in developing countries led to a position opposing the extension of WTO authority into other areas. As a result, the common statement endorsed by nearly 1,500 citizens' organizations from eighty-nine countries called on governments to adopt "a moratorium on any new issues or further negotiations that expand the scope and power of the WTO." It also called for review of existing agreements to address their negative effects on human and labor rights, health, women's rights, and the environment.[9] While it is difficult to determine the effects of these kinds of joint statements, the process of preparing them and, for many groups, the decisions about whether or not to sign them, can involve extensive group deliberations about shared interests and identities.

Table 12.1 maps the major organizational participants in the Seattle anti-WTO actions. We hope to learn whether the participants are principally national or transnational organizations, and whether transnational groups differ from the others in their mobilization roles. Prevalent TSMO roles suggest that globalization processes, like consolidation processes of the modern nation-state, affect how people associate for political purposes.

While the table is not an exhaustive list of organizations protesting in Seattle, it does include those most directly involved. The table clarifies an important division of labor between groups with formalized transnational ties and those with diffuse ties. Groups with no ties or with diffuse transnational ties and groups with informal and

Table 12.1. Mobilizing Structures behind the "Battle of Seattle" and "N30"

Type of Transnational Tie	Movement[a]	Extra-Movement
No formal TN ties	Local chapters of national SMOs (e.g., NOW) Neighborhood no-WTO Committees United for a Fair Economy	School groups Friendship networks
Diffuse TN ties	Direct Action Network Reclaim the Streets Ruckus Society Coalition for Campus Organizing	Union Locals Some churches
Routine TN ties	Public Citizen Global Exchange Rainforest Action Network United Students against Sweatshops Council of Canadians Sierra Club	AFL-CIO United Steel Workers of America International Longshore and Warehouse Union Some churches
Formal transnational organization[b]	Greenpeace Friends of the Earth International Forum on Globalization Third World Network Peoples Global Action 50 Years Is Enough Network Women's Environment and Development Organization	International Confederation of Free Trade Unions European Farmers Union

[a] This list is illustrative, not comprehensive. The organizing scheme draws from McCarthy's (1996) distinction between social movement structures, which are explicitly designed to promote social change goals, and "non movement" (here extra-movement) mobilizing structures. The latter group is important for social movements but their basic organizational mandates encompass goals beyond those of social movements.

[b] Organizations may vary in formalization and hierarchy: Friends of the Earth and Greenpeace have defined organizational structures and institutional presence; groups like People's Global Action resist forming an organizational headquarters; and Reclaim the Streets sustains a loose, network-like structure relying heavily on electronic communication and affinity groups.

decentralized organizations were principally involved in mobilizing and education, as well as in efforts to "shut down" the meetings.

Groups with formalized transnational connections were also involved in education and mobilization, but they played more important roles in framing and informing protester critiques of the global trading system. They also lobbied government delegations and relayed information from official meetings to protest groups that lacked official accreditation. They supported other groups' mobilization efforts by developing educational materials, speaking at rallies and teach-ins, and bringing in speakers from the global South. These groups were the international specialists that had ready access to detailed information about WTO processes and regulations. They could produce examples of the effects of global economic policies, and frequently they had privileged access to official documents and delegations. As in national contexts where the different foci of local versus national groups create rifts in group identities and perceptions, there is some evidence of conflict across this division of labor, although it does not appear to have seriously detracted from protest efforts.

Groups without formal transnational ties are principally local chapters of national groups and local groups formed around the anti-WTO mobilization. United for a Fair Economy, for instance, is a national group focusing on inequalities in the U.S. economy. These groups were important in local participant mobilization in Seattle, and they often worked with or were mobilized because of groups like Direct Action Network, Public Citizen, or others with more extensive transnational ties. Groups with diffuse ties include regional organizations whose memberships cross the U.S.-Canada border and/or groups with other transnational ties that grow out of their organizing efforts. For instance, the Berkeley-based Ruckus Society (whose leaders include former Students for a Democratic Society organizers) primarily brings together Canadians and Americans for nonviolence training. The Coalition for Campus Organizing does progressive organizing on college campuses, and recently it has focused on sweatshops and educational issues, including issues raised by the WTO General Agreement on Trade in Services (GATS).[10] Its international work has led to cooperation with student organizations in Canada.

Organizations listed as having "routine" transnational ties typically are national organizations which have staff devoted to international organizing or solidarity building, have standing committees to work on international issues (e.g., Sierra Club, AFL-CIO, Public Citizen), or have sustained cooperation with activists from other countries (e.g., Global Exchange, USAS). In practice, these organizations' transnational interpersonal and inter-organizational contacts can substantially affect their agendas and frames.

Organizations with formal transnational structures incorporate transnational cooperation into their operational structures. Groups like Greenpeace and Friends of the Earth have a federated structure with national-level branches that disseminate information on global campaigns but often tailor it to national needs. Their headquarters facilitate research and information exchange and, in the some cases, conduct global-level direct action protests and lobbying. The International Forum on Globalization (IFG) is a cadre organization made up of international experts on globalization. Founded in 1994, it produces educational materials and organizes teach-ins about global financial integration. IFG leaders have been called "paradigm warriors" because they advance public debate about globalization. Third World Network has a similar structure, although it consists entirely of scholars and experts from the global South. People's Global Action (PGA) is a loose coalition of mostly grassroots organizations with a website, but no headquarters. PGA includes many groups from India and other parts of the global South that came together after Zapatista organizers issued an electronic call for an international meeting (PGA 2000). It has convened several international meetings on globalization since the mid-1990s and supported protests at earlier meetings of the WTO and G-7 countries. The 50 Years Is Enough Network is one example of what may be an increasingly common coalitional form. Rather than having national branches, groups sharing the network's views to join as partners to participate in joint statements and actions. This maintains local groups' autonomy while keeping them informed about global issues and offering flexibility about campaign participation. The important point is that these organizations have formal mechanisms for sustained transnational communication and cooperation (see Nepstad's chapter in this volume).[11]

Extra-movement mobilizing structures for the Seattle protests also demonstrate transnational linkages. The International Confederation of Free Trade Unions (ICFTU) held its annual conference in Seattle just prior to the WTO gathering, attracting labor leaders from over 100 countries. These international exchanges promote labor solidarity and force U.S. labor leaders to confront their isolationist and nationalist positions. Churches also often promote transnational exchanges and solidarity (C. Smith 1996), such as missions, solidarity work in support of affiliated churches, and fact-finding visits. Because they help link global identities and interests with routine social activities, both religious and labor alliances can advance transnational mobilization to a general audience.

This overview demonstrates that globalization processes affect how social movements mobilize and organize. Substantial transnational ties among key organizations lie behind the Seattle protests, suggesting a transnational-national (or local) division of labor. Transnational ties can be diffuse, growing out of shared purposes, or formal. In between, we find numerous innovative mechanisms for transnational cooperation. Groups with routinized transnational structures seem to be more involved in lobbying and information gathering than national and local groups, which disseminate information and mobilize protesters. Although this chapter is only a snapshot of a single protest episode, the data show that social movements have developed formalized, integrated, and sustained organizational mechanisms for transnational cooperation around global social-change goals (see also Smith 2000). This development is reinforced by the political demands of the global policy process, political socialization, and globally oriented identity construction.

GLOBAL POLITICAL PROCESSES AND MOVEMENT TACTICS

Changes in global politics parallel earlier changes in national polities (cf. Tilly 1984). They involve both cooperative and conflictual interactions among states, citizens, and challengers. Global institutions are formally controlled by states, but historical analyses show that social movement challengers can influence them through interventions in domestic and multilateral policy processes (Chatfield 1997; Finnemore 1996; Meyer, Boli, Thomas, and Ramirez 1997; Smith 1995). States are more vulnerable to social movement challengers because multilateralism creates new arenas to question state agendas, draw international attention to domestic practices, and cultivate alliances with powerful actors outside the domestic political arena, including other states. At the same time, the centralization of political authority at the global level raises the costs of effective political challenges. Contenders seeking to shape local policies governed by global political arenas must mobilize resources in a broader political arena.

As political authority moves toward global institutions, we should expect changes in social movement repertoires similar to those Tilly observed with the rise of nineteenth-century national polities, such as special-purpose associations and the targeting of then-remote national structures. These changes paralleled the rise of national electoral politics:

> The distinctive contribution of the national state was to shift the political advantage to contenders who could mount a challenge on a very large scale, and could do so in a way that demonstrated, or even used, their ability to intervene seriously in regular national politics. In particular, as electoral politics became a more important way of doing national business, the advantage ran increasingly to groups and organizers who threatened to disrupt or control the routine games of candidates and parties. (Tilly 1984: 311)

By the late twentieth century, the growth of international institutions imparted political advantages to transnational contenders who could intervene regularly in intergovernmental political processes. Social movements and corporate actors have found that they must develop capacities to monitor and participate in transnational political processes.[12]

Does Seattle provide evidence to support this interpretation? Table 12.2 categorizes some of the major protest activities according to their relationship to established protest forms. We would expect protest repertoires to overlap substantially during periods of transnational restructuring, just as "old," pre-national protest coexisted during the rise of national protest repertoires. Moreover, because global institutions are based on constitutional forms consistent with Western state institutions, they further reinforce repertoire overlap. However, we should also expect adaptations in national protest forms to challenge a state's international policies as well as the policies of international institutions.

Adapting the Repertoire

The left-hand column of table 12.2 lists adaptations of older protest forms. Many simply represent a change in target from the nation-state to the international policy arena. Thus, the age-old blockade is used to prevent international meetings from taking place. Similarly, street protests and rallies are widely evident. Both dramatize the worthiness, unity, numbers, and commitment of groups supporting social movement goals—as they do in national protests (see McAdam, Tarrow, and Tilly 2001). The "N30" protests called as part of an "International Day of Action," (to coincide with the WTO conference opening on November 30) nicely demonstrate how old forms are applied to transnational targets. "N30" protests occurred at urban financial centers and U.S. embassies, and they dramatized the global character of WTO opposition. One account reported demonstrations in over twenty countries, including Australia, Canada, Colombia, Czech Republic, Germany, Greece, India, Pakistan, the Philippines, Spain, and Turkey (www.n30.org). Protests in London, France, Mexico, and India were among those resulting in property damage and/or other violence.

Education and Mobilization. An important part of the protests in Seattle and elsewhere were educational actions, which included speaker panels and other events to inform the public about economic globalization and its effects on local policies and democratic institutions. "Teach-ins," first used in the anti-Vietnam war protests (Gamson 1991), were employed throughout the United States and Canada (and elsewhere) to educate citizens about the global policy process and the rules and consequences of the WTO. They served as important low-cost and low-risk opportunities for sympathizers to begin or reinforce their involvement in the movement. In Seattle, many of these teach-ins brought together labor activists with

Table 12.2.   Globalization and Protest Repertoires: Selected Anti-WTO Protest Forms

Adaptations of Existing Forms	Innovations in Traditional Forms[a]
Education and Mobilization • Cultivating organizations and "affinity groups" • Public demonstrations at global site • Teach-ins and speaker forums • Coordinated "N30" protests around the globe • Polity-bridging–Local MAI-Free Zones • Nonviolence training/medic training	*Organization/ Mobilization Actions* • Transnational organization • Producing NGO newspaper at global conferences

Framing and Symbolic Mobilization
• Press Center and conferences for mainstream media
• Global witnessing / Transcontinental Caravan
• Satirical newspaper wraps
• Dramaturgy
  -Street theater and puppets
  -Greenpeace's condom drop
  -Banner hangs
  -Boston WTeaO Party
  -Bové's Roquefort resistance
	Borrowing Official Templates
	• Global Peoples' Assembly
	• Participation in government delegations to multilateral forum
	• People's Tribunal versus corporate crimes
	
	Electronic Activism[b]
	
	• Information exchange: Internet, list serve
	• Independent Media Center
	• Rapid response action networks
	• Virtual sit-in
	• Mirror websites
	• E-mail and fax jams

Disruption • Blockade of international conference site • Civil disobedience • Legal observers • Vandalism against corporate sites	

[a] These activities are innovative in that they have been introduced to social movement repertoires more recently, although some have been used to some degree for many decades. Most of these forms had been used frequently before the Seattle protests by actors targeting global institutions.

[b] For details on these activities, see "Electronic Civil Disobedience" *Car Busters* 1, no. 7 (winter 2000): 22-23 (www.antenna.nl/ayafa/cb), "Fax Off, Bastards," *Car Busters*, 1, no. 7 (winter 2000): 23; *Seattle Times*, November 30, 1999, A1.

other groups, enabling dialogues that were unlikely to happen elsewhere. These events constituted spaces where participants' commitment and identity with a growing movement and with other victims of "corporate-led globalization" were cultivated. Rather than focusing on U.S. policies, the speakers emphasized the global trade regime and how state policies shape it. While mass media focused on street protests, more long-term damage to official trade policies may have been done in the churches, union halls, and schools where activists and the public engaged in global civic education.

Activists furthered mobilization efforts by drawing new sympathizers from schools, churches, and other social movement groups. A tactic used by the Direct

Action Network was to develop "affinity groups," which coordinated activists while preserving the benefits of local participation, such as flexibility, responsiveness, and protection from police repression. Affinity groups resembled strategies used in earlier U.S. movements (see Epstein 1991) and are characteristic of the large anarchist contingent in the Seattle protests. Also assisting efforts to resist police repression were efforts by groups like the Ruckus Society and DAN to educate activists about nonviolent action and prepare them for confrontations with police. Training workshops in nonviolence, first aid, and legal observation supplemented others promoting skills like puppet making and banner hanging.

Public protests also served to generate awareness of issues and to encourage sympathizers to become involved in the movement. Although protests typically rely upon media coverage to help spread their message, they also serve movement-building functions by motivating and encouraging movement sympathizers and adherents (see, e.g., Lipsky 1968). Mass rallies and protests create a relatively (in many Western contexts) low-cost means for people with limited knowledge of an issue to learn about and begin movement involvement. Moreover, the act of protesting builds activist identities by dramatizing conflict and creating "us-versus-them" identities. It can generate new levels of commitment on the part of both new and long-term activists (see McAdam 1988; Gamson 1991). When protesters face state repression—particularly the extreme physical violence and large numbers of arrests used in Seattle—this effect is amplified.

Protest also disseminates information about movement goals to a wider public. Protest participants affect the ways their own organizations and informal networks of family and friends perceive the protests and interpret media frames. They provide alternative sources of information from mainstream media frames, and activists encourage friends and kin to pay greater attention to the public discourse on the protests than they otherwise would. In addition, when protesters interact with bystanders, they convey humanized interpretations of the protest purposes and goals distinct from those in the mass media.

Another strategy for mobilizing new sympathizers was adapted from the 1998 "MAI free zones" campaign. This was an effort to block a Multilateral Agreement on Investment, a "bill of rights for investors" that would have liberalized international investment rules and restricted the ability of local governments to control local economic decisions (see Barlow and Clarke 1998). Seattle activists argued that governments were seeking to revive the MAI in WTO negotiations. Using nuclear-free-zone tactics of the 1980s, movement organizers educated local legislators and the public about how MAI elements of WTO agreement impinged on local authority and democracy. It was a strategy that won over some influential and credible allies. The Seattle city council declared the Ministerial site an "MAI-free zone," which set an ominous tone for trade delegates facing an agenda full of MAI elements within the WTO framework.

Symbolic Mobilization. Seattle protesters also took extensive efforts to mobilize symbols and to frame their messages. Public Citizen and other well-resourced organizations sponsored an NGO press center and organized press conferences. More provocative groups wrapped copies of the *Seattle Post Intelligencer* with a satirical headline page titled *The Voice of the People.* Headlines like "Jordan Gives Nike the Boot, Joins Worldwide Boycott," "Mumia Freed," and "Monsanto Patents Food Chain" (by Dolly Bah) greeted those purchasing papers from vending machines near delegates' hotels and conference sites.

Speakers at teach-ins and other educational events engaged in what might be called "global witnessing" about the effects of global economic policies. Tactics emphasizing such witnessing were the transcontinental "caravans" across the United States and Canada that brought international representatives of citizens' organizations to protest at the outlets and headquarters of U.S. corporations and to speak in local communities about how globalization affects their countries.[13] These events gave human faces to global interdependencies and implicated Western industry and consumption practices in world suffering. Some caravan speakers brought word of victories of local resistance against corporate globalization. Others provided tangible testimony to counter officials' claims that the WTO's principal aim is to help poor countries.[14] Speakers from the global South expressed willingness to share their knowledge and experience in order to help their American counterparts understand corporate globalization and how to resist it. One panel included both Third World activists and legislators from the United States and Canada, who remarked that the accounts they heard from Southern activists would help them face their neoliberal opposition in future legislative battles.[15]

Guerilla theater played an important role in the Seattle protests and took several forms. Greenpeace activists showered government delegates with condoms bearing the slogan "practice safe trade" from a balcony of an official meeting venue. A "Boston WTeaO Party" demanded "no globalization without representation" and dumped into Seattle's harbor rejected products such as shrimp caught with nets that kill endangered sea turtles and steel imported at prices below U.S. production costs. At the same time, a hero of global protesters, José Bové, resisted globalization—this time not by smashing McDonald's restaurants—but by distributing nearly 500 pounds of embargoed Roquefort cheese amid a chorus of protesters' cheers.[16] A group of U.S. and Canadian activists calling themselves "Art and Revolution" practiced "puppet-ganda" and street theater on WTO issues. The Direct Action Network promoted puppet making, contributing to the festive atmosphere while providing opportunities for creative, irreverent, and often humorous activism. Finally activists risked arrest and safety by scaling buildings and scaffolding to display massive banners. One Seattle banner that survived a few hours before police removed it displayed "WTO" with an arrow pointing in one direction followed by "DEMOCRACY" with an arrow pointing in the opposite direction.

Disruption. Disruption and confrontation were important tactics in Seattle, and certainly they left lasting media impressions. The main protest website and many mobilizing flyers called upon activists to "Shut Down Seattle." The direct-action training focused on blocking access to the meeting site. Using "lock down" and "tripod"[17] strategies in which activists risked serious physical harm in order to complicate police efforts to remove them, protesters occupied key intersections and forced delegates to stay in their hotels for much of the first day. When activists encountered delegates in the streets, they presented critiques of the WTO to them. The use of the decentralized, affinity-group strategy complicated police efforts to respond to protest actions, contributing to both their diversity and their effectiveness (Gillham and Marx 2000).

On mid-morning, November 30, blockades rather than property damage actually triggered the first indiscriminate use of tear gas by police (Author's observation notes; Ackerman 2000: 63). Apparently frustrated by their inability to guarantee delegates' access to the opening ceremony, police used tear gas to clear a path for delegates for the opening session. Anarchist groups, who had announced over protest electronic list servers their intentions to target downtown shops, did not use violence first. The authorities began the cycle of violent confrontation, which escalated into what was essentially a police riot.

Other forms of nonviolent civil disobedience abounded throughout the week. Some was directed at communicating protester messages to delegates. Some of the first arrests were Global Exchange organizers who—wearing their NGO badges to enter the opening ceremony—took the podium and addressed the handful of delegates who managed to pass through the barricades. Outside the hall, delegates from the People's Tribunal against Corporate Crimes were arrested as they crossed police lines to deliver their "indictment" to the leaders of G-7 countries. Many more protesters were moved by police crackdowns to engage in disruptive protest against police violence and denial of First Amendment rights. Clogging up jails and hampering police booking procedures through "jail solidarity" (refusing to give names until all arrestees were guaranteed reduced sentences), protesters adopted some classic forms of civil disobedience developed in civil rights and anti-Vietnam war protests.

Innovative Repertoires

Although many tactics used in Seattle are adaptations of earlier repertoires, others are innovative in the sense that they target multilateral arenas and that they often involve TSMOs. Transnational associations are not new, but the last half-century has seen an explosion in their numbers. Their tactics often rely on new technologies, ironically the same ones that have fueled the global economic expansion the protesters resist.

Organization and Mobilization. One of the most basic innovations is the creation of transnational associations. Others include the creation of transnationally oriented movement media, such as the NGO newspapers at intergovernmental conferences. These papers present counterhegemonic interpretations of negotiations and highlight the proposals and activities raised by challenger groups. Such newspapers have proved important in pressing governments to take up concerns of challenger groups and in providing alternatives to great-power dominated conference frames. They have been used at many inter-governmental conferences, including those on nuclear disarmament, Law of the Sea, human rights, and women's and environmental issues (Atwood 1997; Clark, Friedman, and Hochstetler 1998; Levering 1997; Willetts 1996).[18]

Borrowing Official Templates. Activists in Seattle and other multilateral contexts structure their collective action around official templates. For example, one of the Seattle coalitions organized a "Peoples' Assembly" to parallel official deliberations. Daily panels centered on a different agenda item such as environment and health, women, human rights, labor, and agriculture.

Another way that challengers borrow official forms is by getting sympathetic experts or even movement activists onto national delegations to international meetings. Because international negotiations are highly technical, governments look beyond their diplomatic corps to fill their delegations. In some fields, such as human rights, environment, and women's issues, some of the most widely respected experts are social movement activists. Their expertise and familiarity with the international negotiation processes make them a rich resource for governments seeking to influence negotiations. While they are obviously not likely to appear on delegations of countries opposing their views, activist experts may sit on delegations of sympathetic countries. Or they may force their way onto a delegation by using national laws such as the U.S.

Federal Advisory Council Act that requires government advisory panels at international meetings to represent a fair balance of viewpoints.[19] When movement sympathizers serve on delegations, they are often conduits of information between official and popular forums.

Another form of official template borrowing involves dramaturgy in the application of international legal principles. In Seattle, the Program on Corporations, Law, and Democracy and the National Lawyers Guild Committee staged a "Global People's tribunal on Corporate Crimes against Humanity." Its purpose was to dramatically "bring to trial" corporate practices around the world. "Witnesses" included a former sweatshop worker from the Philippines who had worked for a Gap subcontractor until she was fired for promoting union activities, a farmers' organization representative from India discussing the effects of Monsanto's seed marketing practices on Indian farmers, and an Indian medical doctor who treated victims of Union Carbide's 1984 chemical disaster in Bhopal. The lawyer-activists facilitating the event educated the audience and "jury" on the relevant international law and tribunal procedures, and the Tribunal issued an "indictment" for crimes against humanity of the governments under whose laws the guilty corporations were established.[20] The appeal to international law against state and corporate practices serves to emphasize the legitimacy or worthiness of the protesters' cause even in the authorities' own terms.

Electronic Activism. Perhaps the most significant innovations result from the same technological innovations that have advanced economic globalization, namely, electronic communications and exchange. These were likely introduced simultaneously to both national and transnational protest repertoires as technologies facilitating inexpensive transnational communications became widely available. Both national and transnational social movement groups make extensive use of Internet sites and electronic list serves to expand communication with dispersed constituencies and audiences. These communication networks allow organizers to almost instantaneously transmit alternative media accounts and images of protests to contrast those of mainstream, corporate-owned media outlets. Alternative electronic media networks also rapidly disseminate information about resistance against economic globalization in the global South, such as the Mexican student strikers. This conflict escalated shortly after Seattle as students rallied in solidarity with jailed Seattle protesters. New technologies also allowed transmission of police radio communications during the protests that undermined authorities' legitimacy.

Rather than rely solely on the mainstream media to convey the images of the protests to the general public, activists organized an "Independent Media Center" (IMC) in Seattle, issuing press badges to volunteer photographers, video recorders, and reporters (no formal credentials necessary) wanting to cover the protests. IMC volunteers had access to a press office and could post their reports, pictures and video (some for direct cable broadcast) onto a website linked to other movement sites.

Electronic civil disobedience also becomes possible as commerce and other essential activities are linked to the flow of electronic information. Anti-WTO protesters who could not get to Seattle could satisfy their desire to join in the protests by engaging in electronic "sit-ins" at the WTO Internet site to block other information-seekers' access to the site. At least one hacker developed a "mirror" site that drew in unwitting information seekers who thought they were viewing the official WTO web page. The site was subtly different from the official one, and carried criticisms of the WTO (*Seattle Post Intelligencer*, November 29, 1999, A1). More confrontational "e-protest" takes the form of e-mail and fax jamming, where large faxes (e.g., protest letters written one word per page) and e-mail messages are sent to disrupt routine flows of information to targets.

Reviewing the tactics employed in Seattle, we find a protest repertoire that both adapts forms that have been typical of national social movement repertoires and expands the repertoire to address multilateral institutional arenas. This protest repertoire can be attributed to the global-level reorganization of political and economic relations in which challengers themselves play a role. Events in Seattle should be examined as part of a more continuous process of evolving forms of contentious politics that began late in the nineteenth century, but gathered momentum especially during the latter half of the twentieth century, through which challengers have increasingly sought to influence international policy and processes (see, e.g., Chatfield 1997; Keck and Sikkink 1998). The Battle of Seattle, then, was not the first, nor likely the last, in the contest to shape global economic, political, and societal integration. It is part of an interactive process of contention between elites and popular challengers that will have implications for the course of future conflicts and institutional changes.

CONCLUSION

This examination of the Battle of Seattle reveals that protests around global trade liberalization involve extensive transnational mobilizing structures that are likely to develop further as a consequence of the Seattle mobilization. It also shows that tactical repertoires are altered and that a shift from nation-states to transnational actors is under way. While nation-states remain a focus, challengers face an emerging system of "multi-level governance" (Marks and McAdam 1996) or "complex multilateralism" (O'Brien et al. 2000) whereby the relations among states become resources or obstacles to movement goals. For instance, U.S. trade policy depends upon support from European allies. Mobilizations against trade in genetically altered foods challenged the unity of Western positions and made the U.S. insistence on unlimited trade a threat to its alliance with other Western states.

When considering globalization's impact on popular protest, however, the crucial question is not whether globalization diminishes the power of states or the importance of national political processes, but rather *how* international institutions affect abilities of states, corporations, and challengers to influence political processes. Indeed, many international campaigns seek to change international policy by shaping individual state decisions, and therefore urge participants to target their own (or sometimes other states') domestic policies. The rifts between the United States and European governments over agricultural and safety issues, and among rich and poor countries over trade liberalization rules, were important contributors to Seattle's success. So while states indeed control international institutions, they cannot control all aspects of day-to-day operations. Moreover, they do not stand together as a united front against all challengers. Some states may serve as movement allies on particular issues, or they may see their strategic interests served by movement opposition to other governments' policies. Global activists exploited these divisions among states to prevent agreement at the Seattle Ministerial meeting.

There are other important questions about the effects of globalization on protest. The repression faced by protesters should raise warning flags for scholars of social movements about how globalization affects democracy (see, e.g., Markoff 1999). In the United States where free speech and assembly are staunchly defended, officials successfully enforced an illegal "no-protest zone." Moreover, agents in support of the neoliberal trade regime revealed a blatant disdain for democracy. For instance, Slade Gorton, the Republican U.S. senator from Washington State, appeared on the local television news on the night of the N30 protests and vandalism, arguing that Mayor Schell should have declared the entire city a "no-protest zone." This comment produced no immediate discussion despite its obvious disregard for the democratic process. Further contempt for democratic principles is apparent in a document from a pro-trade think tank, the Institute for International Economics. It suggests advancing U.S. trade interests by eliminating public participation and democratic accountability by obfuscating references to "fast track" executive authority. Such authority essentially eliminates a meaningful congressional role in trade negotiations by forcing the legislative branch to either reject or approve the whole of agreements (Institute for International Economics 1999).[21] Former World Bank chief economist Joseph Stiglitz highlights this problem in his critique of the IMF: "Economic policy is today perhaps the most important part of America's interaction with the rest of the world. And yet the culture of international economic policy in the world's most powerful democracy is not democratic" (Stiglitz 2000).

Beyond infringements of democratic rights, states also retain the ability to inhibit mobilization by denying visas to activists (as the U.S. government did for some Seattle protesters) and by scheduling global meetings in remote locations where democratic rights are not recognized. Singapore was the site of the 1996 WTO ministerial, and future meeting sites are likely to be considerably less open and accessible than Seattle. For instance, the Middle Eastern kingdom of Qatar was selected as the site of the next WTO Ministerial in 2001. These and other tactics raise the costs of protest through repression, countermobilization, and outright exclusion of activist groups. They must be considered as we continue to explore the effects of globalization on democracy and contentious politics.

The Battle of Seattle has triggered broad public appreciation for the need of expanded public discourse about globalization and for greater transparency and accountability in multilateral institutions. Activists outside the United States have been inspired by seeing protesters in what one of my informants called a "politically underdeveloped nation" stand up—even in the face of brutal repression—to resist the neoliberal expansion that their own government has been championing for decades. The Battle of Seattle is one of the most significant recent episodes of collective action, and it points to a future of social movements that is increasingly global in both target and form and that finds itself in more direct confrontation with global institutions than its historical predecessors.

NOTES

1. During the weekend prior to the WTO meeting, a number of smaller street protests and other events took place, beginning on Friday afternoon with a regularly scheduled "critical mass" bicycle ride through the streets of downtown Seattle and an evening "teach-in" organized by the International Forum on Globalization.

2. This account and other details about the Seattle protest events are drawn from participant observation research which included observation at Seattle marches and rallies; attendance at teach-ins, lectures, cultural events, press conferences, and strategy sessions organized by various

factions of the antitrade liberalization movement; informal interviews with participants; observation of the single pro-trade Seattle rally held by the local Christian Coalition chapter and the Chamber of Commerce; and analysis of organizational literature and electronic communications in addition to local, national, and some international media coverage.

3. Evidence of the impact of the Seattle protests on at least the discourse of neoliberalism's advocates abounds. For instance, early in 2000, reports were released by the WTO, World Bank, IMF and OECD attempting to bolster the case that more trade is needed in order to address the needs of the world's poor. A report by the Canadian Security Intelligence Service (2000) noted the need for advanced security measures at international financial meetings. And the discourse at a meeting of the world's bankers and economists revealed elite attempts to respond to widespread "antipathy toward free market competition" (Stevenson 2000).

4. The WTO rules, for instance, progressively liberalize tariffs and other trade restrictions over a set period. Rules for different categories of goods vary, so that tariffs on primary commodities—that is, those that are exported from the South to the North—remain high until the end of the WTO phase-in period, while those on manufactured goods are reduced more rapidly. Moreover, most of the rules take 1994 tariff and subsidy levels as the starting point, so the Southern countries that typically had less extensive sets of tariffs and minimal agricultural subsidies were prevented from adding new ones, even as they were forced to compete in a market dominated by countries that had relatively high tariffs and subsidies to protect their domestic industries (see Khor 1999). Voting in the WTO provides one vote per country member, but in the IMF and World Bank it is weighted according to a government's financial contribution, and the United States enjoys the largest voting share (nearly 20%).

5. For instance, members of the International Forum on Globalization's board of directors, including Laurie Wallach and Martin Khor, among others, reported providing analyses of trade issues for government officials.

6. Labor organizations have typically been considered outside at least the contemporary U.S. social movement sector because of their historical association with institutionalized politics and their tendency to focus on member services and contract negotiations rather than class struggle. In practice, some U.S. labor organizations resemble SMOs in their approach to struggle, most notably the International Longshore and Warehouse Union, which has traditionally emphasized radical confrontation and class solidarity (Levi and Olson 2000). The experience of labor in the Battle of Seattle and contemporary debates within the AFL-CIO suggest a possibility that labor issues could take a more contentious turn vis-à-vis political institutions. Social movement scholars may find need to rethink their assumptions about relationships between the social movement sector and organized labor in the United States.

7. People for Fair Trade (supported and initially staffed by Ralph Nader's Public Citizen/Global Trade Watch) provided tools for community organizers and organized neighborhood working groups on the WTO in preparation for the Ministerial meeting (www.peopleforfairtrade.org/).

8. According to Gamson (1991), organizational identities result from activists' association of their personal identity with a particular SMO. Such identification can precede or lead to movement and solidary identities. Movement identities refer to the association of the goals and values of a movement with one's own, and solidary identities involve the inclusion of the individual or group in a wider community of fate. Examples of the latter would include class identities or identities such as victims of corporate exploitation.

9. The "Statement from Members of International Civil Society Opposing a Millennium Round or a New Round of Comprehensive Trade Negotiations" can be found at: www. citizen.org/pctrade/mai/Sign-ons/WTO Statement.htm.

10. The GATS agreement progressively opens trade in services just as traditional trade agreements served to open markets for trade in goods. Such services range from banking and finance to public education, utilities, and health, which were on the agenda for the failed Seattle talks.

11. With the exceptions of Greenpeace and Friends of the Earth (both formed in 1971) and Third World Network (formed in 1984), the transnational SMOs listed here were formed during the 1990s.

12. The advantage of transnational mobilization certainly varies according to issue. Whereas human rights and some environmental activists find natural and necessary connections to multilateral processes, other areas, such as the abortion debate, are less directly affected by multilateral policies and require more local and national emphases.

13. The caravans were organized by groups associated with Peoples' Global Action. The U.S. caravan suffered minor setbacks when U.S. officials denied visas to several participants.

14. Despite the ambiguous evidence of trade's effects on poor countries (see UNDP 1998, 1999), in the wake of the failed Seattle talks, WTO director general Mike Moore stated: "I feel particular disappointment because the postponement of our deliberations means the benefits that would have accrued to developing and least-developed countries will now be delayed. . . . The longer we delay launching the [WTO expansion] negotiations, the more the poorest amongst us lose" (http://www.wto.org/wto/new/ press160.htm). For details on discrepancies between economic data and the claims of trade advocates, see Weisbrot (2000), Smith and Moran (2000).

15. The November 29 panel, "Environment and Health Day" featured a "People's Tribunal" on "The Human Face of Trade: Health and The Environment." U.S. representatives George Miller and Maine Waters and Canadian MP Bill Blaikie participated, plus Magda Aelvoet, the Belgian minister of consumer protection. Activists from Mexico, Malaysia, the Philippines, Trinidad, Pakistan, and Ghana addressed the tribunal.

16. The United States had outlawed the importation of Roquefort cheese and other luxury products after the WTO backed its claim that the EU ban on the import of hormone-treated beef violated trade laws.

17. "Lock-downs" involve the use of chains, bicycle locks, clamps, and PVC pipes to link activists' limbs, making the involuntary removal of any one of the lock-down participants hazardous. The tripod involves three tall poles that are arranged in a tripod and secured by three activists. One activist climbs the poles and sits on or hangs from the tripod. To remove the barricade without causing injury, authorities must bring in a crane or fire truck.

18. Many of these cases show that government delegates from some (especially poor or less central) states have come to rely on movement publications, particularly the newspaper, for information on technical aspects of the problems under negotiation and/or the political processes surrounding the negotiations.

19. Environmentalists sued the U.S. Trade Representative's Office in order to have this law respected and their viewpoints reflected in the makeup of trade advisory panels on paper and wood (*World Trade Observer,* November 18, 1999,1; also available at www. worldtradeobserver.org). As a result of the decision, Friends of the Earth-U.S. president Brent Blackwelder joined the U.S. delegation as a Trade Advisory Council member.

20. People's Tribunals were also used during anti-Vietnam War protests and at UN conferences. Their use of international human rights law and international legal proceedings make them tactical innovations.

21. Movement pressure twice defeated Clinton's earlier efforts for "fast track" negotiating authority.

REFERENCES

Aaronson, Susan Ariel. 2001. *Taking Trade to the Streets: The Lost History of Public Efforts to Shape Globalization.* Ann Arbor: University of Michigan Press.

Ackerman, Seth. 2000. "Prattle in Seattle: Media Coverage Misrepresented Protests." Pp. 59-66 in *Globalize This! The Battle against the World Trade Organization and Corporate Rule,* edited by Kevin Danaher and Roger Burbach. Monroe, Maine: Common Courage Press.

Atwood, David. 1997. "Mobilizing Around the United Nations Special Session on Disarmament." Pp. 141-158 in *Transnational Social Movements and Global Politics: Solidarity beyond the State*, edited by J. Smith, C. Chatfield, and R. Pagnucco. Syracuse, N.Y.: Syracuse University Press.

Audley, John J. 1997. *Green Politics and Global Trade: NAFTA and the Future of Environmental Politics*. Washington D.C.: Georgetown University Press.

Ayres, Jeffrey M. 1998. *Defying Conventional Wisdom: Political Movements and Popular Contention against North American Free Trade*. Toronto: University of Toronto Press.

Barlow, Maude, and Tony Clarke. 1998. *The Multilateral Agreement on Investment and the Threat to American Freedom*. Washington D.C.: Public Citizen's Global Trade Watch.

Canadian Security Intelligence Service. 2000. "Anti-Globalization: A Spreading Phenomenon." Report #2000/08, Canadian Security Intelligence Service (August 22). Available at: http://www.csis-scrs.gc.ca/eng/miscdocs/200008e.html.

Chatfield, Charles. 1997. "Intergovernmental and Nongovernmental Associations to 1945." Pp 19-41 in *Transnational Social Movements and World Politics: Solidarity beyond the State*, edited by J. Smith, C. Chatfield, and R. Pagnucco. Syracuse, N.Y.: Syracuse University Press.

Clark, Ann Marie, Elisabeth J. Friedman, and Kathryn Hochstetler. 1998. "The Sovereign Limits of Global Civil Society: A Comparison of NGO Participation in UN World Conferences on the Environment, Human Rights, and Women." *World Politics* 51:1-35.

Cleary, Seamus. 1996. "The World Bank and NGOs." Pp. 63-97 in *The Conscience of the World: The Influence of Non-governmental Organisations in the UN System*, edited by P. Willetts. Washington, D.C.: Brookings Institution.

Epstein, Barbara, 1991. *Political Protest and Cultural Revolution: Nonviolent Direct Action in the 1970s and 1980s*. Berkeley: University of California Press.

Finnemore, Martha. 1996. *National Interests in International Society*. Ithaca, N.Y.: Cornell University Press.

Foster, John. 1999. "Civil Society and Multilateral Theatres." Pp. 129-195 in *Whose World Is It Anyway? Civil Society, the United Nations, and the Multilateral Future*, edited by J. W. Foster and A. Anand. Ottawa: United Nations Association of Canada.

Fox, Jonathan, and L. David Brown. 1998. *The Struggle for Accountability: The World Bank, NGOs, and Grassroots Movements*. Cambridge, Mass.: MIT Press.

Fox, Jonathan. 2000. "Assessing Binational Civil Society Coalitions: Lessons from the Mexico-U.S. Experience." Working Paper Number 26, Chicano/Latino Research Center, University of California, Santa Cruz (April).

Gamson, William A. 1991. "Commitment and Agency in Social Movements." *Sociological Forum* 6:27-50.

Gerhards, Jürgen, and Dieter Rucht. 1992. "Mesomobilization: Organizing and Framing in Two Protest Campaigns in West Germany." *American Journal of Sociology* 98: 555-595.

Gillham, Patrick F., and Gary T. Marx. 2000. "Complexity and Irony in Policing and Protesting: The World Trade Organization in Seattle." *Social Justice* 27 (2): 212-236.

Institute for International Economics. 1999. "International Economics Policy Issues." Institute for International Economics, Washington D.C.

Keck, Margaret, and Kathryn Sikkink. 1998. *Activists beyond Borders*. Ithaca, N.Y.: Cornell University Press.

Khor, Martin. 1999. "How the South Is Getting a Raw Deal." Pp. 7-53 in *Views from the South: The Effects of Globalization and the WTO on Third World Countries*. San Francisco: International Forum on Globalization.

Levering, Ralph A. 1997. "Brokering the Law of the Sea Treaty: The Neptune Group." Pp. 225-242 in *Transnational Social Movements and Global Politics: Solidarity beyond the State*, edited by J. Smith, C. Chatfield, and R. Pagnucco. Syracuse, N.Y.: Syracuse University Press.

Levi, Margaret and David Olson. 2000. "The Battle of Seattle." *Politics and Society* 28: 309-329
Lipsky, Michael. 1968. "Protest as a Political Resource." *American Political Science Review* 62:1144-1158.
Markoff, John. 1999. "Globalization and the Future of Democracy." *Journal of World Systems Research* http://csf.colorado.edu/wsystems/jwsr.html 5:242-262.
Marks, Gary, and Doug McAdam. 1996. "Social Movements and the Changing Structure of Political Opportunity in the European Community." Pp. 95-120 in *Governance in the European Union*, edited by G. Marks, F. W. Scharpf, P. C. Schmitter, and W. Streeck. Thousand Oaks, Calif.: Sage.
Marullo, Sam, Ron Pagnucco, and Jackie Smith. 1996. "Frame Changes and Social Movement Contraction: U.S. Peace Movement Framing after the Cold War." *Sociological Inquiry* 66: 1-28.
McAdam, Doug. 1988. *Freedom Summer*. New York: Oxford University Press.
McAdam, Doug, Sidney Tarrow, and Charles Tilly. 2001. *Dynamics of Contention*. New York: Cambridge University Press.
McCarthy, John D. 1996. "Mobilizing Structures: Constraints and Opportunities: Adopting, Adapting and Inventing." Pp. 141-151 in *Political Opportunities, Mobilizing Structures and Framing: Social Movement Dynamics in Cross-National Perspective.*, edited by D. McAdam, J. McCarthy, and M. Zald. New York: Cambridge University Press.
Meyer, John W., John Boli, George M. Thomas, and Francisco O. Ramirez. 1997. "World Society and the Nation-State." *American Journal of Sociology* 103:144-181.
Naím, Moisés. 2000. "Foreign Policy Interview: Lori's War." *Foreign Policy* 118: 28-55.
Njehu, Njoki Njoroge. 2000. "Building the Movement: Johannesburg, Seattle, and Beyond." Economic Justice News 2: 2,18.
O'Brien, Robert, Anne Marie Goetz, Jan Aard Scholte, and Marc Williams. 2000. *Contesting Global Governance: Multilateral Economic Institutions and Global Social Movements.* New York: Cambridge University Press.
PGA. 2000. "The Accelerating History of PGA" *Worldwide Resistance Roundup Inspired by Peoples Global Action* Bulletin 5, February (UK Edition). On file with the author.
Rich, Bruch. 1994. *Mortgaging the Earth: The World Bank, Environmental Impoverishment and the Crisis of Development*. Boston: Beacon Press.
Rose, Fred. 2000. *Coalitions across the Class Divide: Lessons from the Labor, Peace, and Environmental Movements*. Ithaca, N.Y.: Cornell University Press.
Scholte, Jan Aart. 2000. "Cautionary Reflections on Seattle" *Millennium: Journal of International Studies* 29:115-121.
Shoch, James. 2000. "Contesting Globalization: Organized Labor, NAFTA, and the 1997 and 1998 Fast-Track Fights." *Politics and Society* 28:119-150.
Sikkink, Kathryn, and Jackie Smith. 2002. "Infrastructures for Change: Transnational Organizations, 1953-1993." In *Restructuring World Politics: The Power of Transnational Agency and Norms*, edited by S. Khagram, J. Riker, and K. Sikkink. Minneapolis: University of Minnesota Press.
Smith, Christian. 1994. *Resisting Reagan*. Chicago: University of Chicago Press.
———. 1996. "Correcting a Curious Neglect, or Bringing Religion Back In." Pp. 1-25 in *Disruptive Religion: The Force of Faith in Social Movement Activism*, edited by C. Smith. New York: Routledge.
Smith, Jackie. 1995. "Transnational Political Processes and the Human Rights Movement." Pp. 185-220 in *Research in Social Movements, Conflict and Change*, vol. 18, edited by L. Kriesberg, M. Dobkowski, and I. Walliman. Greenwood Conn.: JAI.
———. 1997. "Characteristics of the Modern Transnational Social Movement Sector." Pp. 42-58 in *Transnational Social Movements and World Politics: Solidarity beyond the State*, edited by J. Smith, C. Chatfield, and R. Pagnucco. Syracuse, N.Y.: Syracuse University Press.

————. 2002. (forthcoming) "Bridging Global Divides?: Strategic Framing and Solidarity in Transnational Social Movement Organizations" *International Sociology.*

Smith, Jackie, and Timothy Patrick Moran. 2000. "WTO 101: Myths about the World Trading System" *Dissent* (spring): 66-70.

Smith, Jackie, Charles Chatfield, and Ron Pagnucco. 1997. *Transnational Social Movements and Global Politics: Solidarity Beyond the State.* Syracuse, NY: Syracuse University Press.

Smith, Jackie, Ron Pagnucco, and Charles Chatfield. 1997. "Transnational Social Movements and Global Politics: A Theoretical Framework." Pp. 59-77 in *Transnational Social Movements and Global Politics: Solidarity beyond the State*, edited by J. Smith, C. Chatfield, and R. Pagnucco. Syracuse, N.Y.: Syracuse University Press.

Smith, Jackie, Ron Pagnucco, and George Lopez. 1998. "Globalizing Human Rights: Report on a Survey of Transnational Human Rights NGOs." *Human Rights Quarterly* 20:379-412.

Stevenson, Richard W. 2000. "Trade Support Is Dwindling, Fed Chief Says: Policy Makers Note Globalization Protests." *New York Times*, August 26, 2000, C1, C14.

Stiglitz, Joseph. 2000. "What I Learned at the World Economic Crisis." *The New Republic,* April 17. At http://www.tnr.com/041700/stiglitz041700.html .

Tarrow, Sidney. 2001. "Transnational Politics: Contention and Institutions in International Politics." *Annual Review of Political Science* 4:1-20.

Tilly, Charles. 1984. "Social Movements and National Politics." Pp. 297-317 in *Statemaking and Social Movements: Essays in History and Theory*, edited by C. Bright and S. Harding. Ann Arbor: University of Michigan Press.

UNDP (United Nations Development Programme) Annual. *Human Development Report.* New York: Oxford University Press.

Vidal, John. 1999. "The Trade Talks Collapse: Real Battle for Seattle." *The Observer* (London), December 5, 20.

Walton, John, and David Seddon. 1994. *Free Markets and Food Riots: The Politics of Global Adjustment.* Cambridge, Mass.: Blackwell.

Wallach, Lori, and Michelle Sforza. 1999. *Whose Trade Organization?: Corporate Globalization and the Erosion of Democracy.* Washington, D.C.: Public Citizen.

Weisbrot, Mark. 2000 "Globalization for Dummies" *Harper* 300 (May): 15-19.

Willetts, Peter. 1996. *The Conscience of the World: The Influence of NGOs in the United Nations System.* London: C. Hurst.

Zoll, Dan. 1999. "Developing Nations Complain of Being Shut Out of Ministerial Planning Process." Pp. 1, 8 in *World Trade Observer.* www. worldtradeobserver.org.

Chapter 13

FROM LUMPING TO SPLITTING: SPECIFYING GLOBALIZATION AND RESISTANCE

Sidney Tarrow

Modern biologists are divided into the two camps of the splitters and the lumpers.
The first are in favour of making a species out of every petty variety; the second are
all for lumping unimportant minor forms into a single species.
Cornhill Magazine, no. 295, March 1894

In August 2001, a group of Christian aid workers from an American organization
called Shelter Now International was arrested by the ruling Taliban on charges of
spreading Christianity among the country's Muslim population. Alongside a large
number of their Afghan helpers, two Americans, four Germans, and two Australians
were taken into custody. "An investigation is being conducted," said a representative
of the then-Ministry for the Promotion of Virtue and the Prevention of Vice, "and"—
he added forebodingly—"it will be decided according to Sharia" (*New York Times,*
August 7, 2001). Efforts to free the captives by their respective governments, their
families, and international organizations were to no avail in a country where the
promotion of any religion other than Islam was punishable by death.

The September 11 bombing of the World Trade Center by the Al Qaeda organization pushed that story off the front pages, while the American-inspired war against
the Taliban that followed left the captives' fate in question. But in November, as the
American-backed Northern Alliance swept southward toward Kabul, the aid workers
were taken from their jail cells by fleeing Taliban forces and transported southward.
There was fear that they would be made hostages, but as the Taliban retreat became
a rout, they were left behind to be dramatically freed by Northern Alliance fighters
and spirited out of the country by American helicopters a few days later. Two of the

young women among the ex-prisoners soon appeared on American television. Poised and radiant, they might as easily have emerged from their college Christian societies as from the squalor of an Afghan prison. We all know what happened next: as the liberated Christian aid workers were appearing on American morning television, the Taliban dissolved into the Afghan countryside and many foreign-born Al Qaeda fighters sought refuge in nearby Pakistan and began to trickle out to more distant places.

These so-called Afghan Arabs were not just Arab nationals but were also Filipinos, Chinese Uighurs, Indonesians, Malaysians, Bosnians, and Chechens. Some had been in the country since the anti-Soviet war of the 1980s; others arrived only when the Taliban took control in the mid-1990s. Some formed the core of groups like the Egyptian Islamic Jihad, the Abu Sayyaf in the Philippines, and Algeria's Islamic Salvation Front; others were recent recruits against the American-led war. Will members of this ragtag transnational army melt back into their own societies just as easily as the young Christian aid workers blended into middle America? Not likely: As one news analysis predicted,

> an extremist rise in most of the various host countries should be expected as the evacuation from Afghanistan continues. The fighters will return with experience, training and a renewed network of contacts in other countries. One side effect of this dispersal may be the foundation of a second network of Islamic extremists. Just as the Soviet war against Afghanistan—and the subsequent scattering of fighters—produced a worldwide network of extremists, the American war in Afghanistan will produce a secondary network, one that might not be centered around Osama bin Laden.[1]

Two transnational groups—one so service-oriented that some would hesitate to include it in the universe of transnational contention, the other violently contentious; one Northern, the other predominantly Southern; one Christian and one Muslim—both operated across borders and came into contact on the soil of the beleaguered Afghan state, triggering the vengeance of the most powerful state in the world. Their story suggests that understanding the relations between globalization and resistance will be complicated, contradictory, and contested. The first effort of this chapter will be to hold both of these "lumpy" terms up to a more exacting conceptual light; the second will be to call for a sociology of transnational contention that disaggregates such general concepts into less-aggregated ones; and the third will be to examine some specific mechanisms from the study of political contention.[2]

GLOBALIZATION AND RESISTANCE

Globalization and Resistance, an inviting title for a book which comes at the turn of a new millennium that has seen antiglobalization movements exploding all over the world. Some have taken the form of unconcerted but simultaneous protests against international institutions—like the anti-debt movement in Latin America against the IMF (Walton and Seddon 1994)—what I have elsewhere called domestication (Tarrow 1998: chap. 11); others take concerted form—like the transnational campaigns at Geneva, Prague, Davos, and Genoa; still others take the form of deliberate legal campaigns to extradite and punish former authoritarians and torturers through a transnational "justice cascade" (Lutz and Sikkink 2001); still others take the form of the savage blows of a transnational terrorist organization against individual states;

and some may take the form of resistance to various forms of authority at the state level that are connected causally to globalization.

To many observers, it seems that these protests cohere in a panoply of responses to the master process of globalization, which I define, with Charles Tilly, as "an increase in the geographic range of locally consequential social interactions, especially when that increase stretches a significant proportion of all interactions across international or intercontinental limits" (1994: 1-2). But as the examples above suggest, there are a number of forms of transnational contention and it is not always clear that the actual targets of these actions—as opposed to their framing by activists—can be usefully connected to globalization. Consider first the anti-WTO campaign at Seattle: it found its strongest support from local trade unionists against American trade policy. For them, though not for all the anti-WTO protesters, the meetings were a pretext for domestic protest. Activists are keenly aware of the international role of various states, and they focus their energies to encourage sympathetic ones to support them and press recalcitrant ones to change their policies. Next, think of the "justice cascade" against Latin American torturers and dictators: its catalyst was a Spanish judge using local laws who tried—and failed—to extradite Alfonso Pinochet from a reluctant British state. Finally, though Al Qaeda's attack on the World Trade Center targeted a symbol of neoliberalism, it would be a stretch to link that movement to globalization except in the most metaphorical way. Besides, it triggered a revival of the United States's hegemonic national project (Ayres and Tarrow 2001). In these examples and in many others, there is somewhat less globalization than meets the eye, and a wider range of collective action than what is well captured with the term "resistance." Let me turn to each concept in turn before suggesting some ways of disaggregating them and specifying their links to one another.

Globalization

As the concept emerged in the 1990s, globalization said perhaps too much, since it lumped together the international free trade regime, domestic economic deregulation and privatization, the rise of a global communication system, the internationalization of public authorities, and the growth of transnational ties among nonstate actors. With respect to contentious politics, it said too little because it led many observers to lump together virtually all forms of collective action that cross national boundaries (see the critique in Yashar 2002): from the sedate lobbying by NGO coalitions of international institutions to the contentious campaigns that ATTAC and Global People's Action mount to the dramatic actions of French farmers and environmentalists against McDonalds. That there is something new, and profoundly transnational, in these interactions is beyond dispute; that they are different in their implications from intranational contention is also true (*pace* Gay Seidman 2001); but that they can usefully be reduced to the products of globalization for analytical (as opposed to political) purposes is another matter.

That globalization can be linked to so many different kinds of contention results in part from the concept's multiple origins, some of them analytical and others political. It derived from four positions that are more prone to the positing of general covering laws than to the kind of empirical work represented in this volume or to the specification of concrete mechanisms and processes:

- from enthusiasts for globalization like the *Economist*, who see it solving many of the problems of both North and South in the world economy;
- from a plethora of domestic activists who are trying to frame their claims in global terms;
- from world systems and neo-Polanyan theorists who habitually see the world in core/periphery terms and tend to combine the political and the economic (Arrighi 1994; McMichael 1996, 2002);
- and from the academic models of sociological institutionalists who posit the formation of a world polity from the diffusion of Western norms (Meyer, Boli, and Thomas 1998).

These divergent academic and activist origins have given "globalization" an intellectual and ideological magnetism—both positive and negative—similar to the attraction and repulsion that "modernization" and "development" had during earlier decades. This has brought together activists working in a wide variety of areas; but it had done so at the cost of lumping together numerous forms of interstate and transnational connections that may not have much to do with one another and has obscured the differences among the many forms of transnational contention that we see in the world today.

Resistance

This takes us to our second umbrella term—resistance. When James Scott adopted the term in the 1980s, it had had a clear empirical referent in the efforts of occupied peoples to oust their foreign oppressors (i.e., the French Resistance against Nazism; the Palestinian Intifada against Israeli occupation). Scott appropriated the concept to mean individual acts of surreptitious contention against local power holders in autocratic rural societies (Scott 1985). His followers expanded it to cover all kinds of contentious politics—especially in the South. More recently it has been shifted again to encompass the activism of transnational NGOs that specialize in information, lobbying, and service provision.

Applying the term "resistance" to every collective act in transnational space has produced a common language for scholars and activists from North and South from divergent theoretical perspectives. But unless it is disaggregated, it can create confusion among Scott's individual weapons of the weak, collective forms of contention, and the more contained transnational advocacy networks that have taken root around international institutions (Keck and Sikkink 1998a). If the term is applied to such different forms of collective action as domestically organized strikes against corporations whose management happens to be foreign, attempts of minority ethnic groups to gain certification as "indigenous" at the United Nations, foundation-sponsored NGO forums around international conferences, and farmers' protests against genetically modified seeds that happen to be produced abroad, how will it help us to understand the logic and dynamics of these various forms of protest and their relationship—if any—to global economic integration? From an analytical point of view, the links between the global economy and such forms of collective action need to be better specified.[3]

Eastern Europe (Arato and Cohen 1992). Dissidents in Poland and elsewhere developed the concept both to indicate the kind of society they wished to develop—a pluralistic Western one—and the fact that they wished, not to organize opposition parties, which would have been promptly smashed, but to develop resistance within their societies. The comparison helps us to understand the weakness of the concept's global application. In the earlier episode of political/intellectual construction, civil society had both a historical antecedent in Western societal development and a clear strategic target—the overweening power of state socialism and its tendency to strangle all forms of autonomous social organization. In contrast, the global civil society project found neither the historical antecedent nor such an overweening target in the international system.

The global civil society theorists launched their project with panache and enthusiasm. But with respect to transnational contention, their work suffered from four major flaws that prevented them from providing an effective bridge from globalization to resistance.

- *First,* it concatenated forms of transnational contention that have a great deal to do with globalization with those whose connection to globalization is indirect and with those whose connection to it is improbable. Struggles against oppression of virtually any variety were indifferently gathered under the same umbrella, as long as the actors involved claimed to find shelter under it. The problem with this move was that the polemical unity of the target (e.g., globalization) was used to claim—rather than demonstrate—the transnational unity of movements. Many of these movements had very little in common, and often had conflicting logics.

- *Second,* and related to the first point, seldom were the concrete causal mechanisms connecting globalization to contentious outcomes specified theoretically or demonstrated empirically. Thus, the human rights movement, which aims its efforts mainly at dictators, torturers, and abusers of women and children—and whose behavior would have been familiar before anyone thought of the term globalization—has sometimes been framed as part of the struggle against globalization (Lynch 1998).[4]

- *Third,* and related to the second point, the role of states and international institutions remained problematic in plotting the causal relations between globalization and resistance through global civil society. While some noted that states were losing their grip or framed them as the major impediment to the formation of a global civil society, others wisely pointed out that "a return to the state is in all probability necessary to meet the dislocations and poverty generated by the latest round of globalization" (Lynch 1998:164). As for international institutions, which are often framed as the targets of transnational contention, their role as facilitators to and occasional allies of transnational NGOs received remarkable little attention (but see O'Brien, et al. 2000).

- *Fourth,* most of the work in the global civil society tradition focused on four areas in particular: the international human rights movement, the environmental movement, indigenous people's rights, and, most recently, campaigns against the international free trade regime. These campaigns are made up of actors who are largely secular, mostly progressive, and usually linked to Northern sources of funding, expertise, and political influence. There is nothing wrong with this focus on secular, progressive, and Northern-supported campaigns as long as it is made explicit that they are but one peak in the transnational archipelago of transnational interactions, many of which are not secular, not progressive, and would be profoundly hostile to the groups supporting the global civil society project.

SPLITTING THE BIGGEST LUMPS

The contributors to this volume take us well beyond this first generation of scholarship on globalization and resistance. But starting from the foundation that they provide, we can go further: first, by disaggregating these two umbrella concepts into more manageable mechanisms and processes; and second, by applying to transnational contention some recent developments from the more familiar world of domestic social movements. The second argument will be illustrated in the next part of this chapter. The first can be illustrated from the case with which I began.

Back to Afghanistan

The Al Qaeda network and the Christian aid workers who converged on Afghanistan in the 1990s were both parts of transnational organizations and movements that go well beyond that unfortunate country. While the first was the emanation of a vast transnational spectrum of Islamist groups, the second is a latter-day development of the first transnational wave of activism—the missionary efforts of Western Christian churches (Keck and Sikkink 1998a). The story illustrates not only the profound differences between these two groups but also the differences between them and the organizations typically studied in the global civil society tradition.

For a start, both groups were inspired by religion—a driving force in today's transnational activities that scholars have largely ignored, faced by the secular, progressive organizations that are the stock-in-trade of the global civil society project (Bush 2001). Moreover, they differed in the practices through which they expressed their religious convictions: Shelter Now combined its service activities with proselytizing, while Al Qaeda sought to protect Islam against perceived threats by training militants for the most violent forms of contention. Each had obscure relations with states, challenging the idea of global civil society as a more or less autonomous public sphere: Al Qaeda, to hear the Afghans talk about it today, literally taking over the Taliban state; and the Shelter Now workers working under the protection of the German government and literally plucked out of Afghanistan by the United States.

Most important for our purposes, these two organizations, with financial and activist sources from opposite sides of the globe, cannot in any meaningful sense be traced to globalization unless we are willing to stretch that concept to cover forms of missionary activity that began in the sixteenth century and Islamist reactions to the corruption of the West. That would be quite a stretch even for an umbrella concept like globalization. Moreover, the term "resistance" hardly begins to capture either the activities of each group or their interaction without more careful specification of these concepts. Though the young women who were arrested by the Taliban were indeed proselytizing for Christianity,[5] their major activity was service to the impoverished people of Afghanistan, while the Al Queda fighters were using the country to prepare attacks on the West and the corrupt regimes of the Middle East—aggression, not resistance.

If a single episode in Central Asia can reveal such a conundrum of causes and processes of transnational conflict and interaction, the simple dichotomous pairing "globalization" and "resistance" should be refined into a finer set of orienting concepts. We need not, however, retreat to the opposite pole—giving up classification for telling tales of the activities of individual movements. We can begin by breaking down globalization and resistance into broad component processes, and then examining some concrete mechanisms within those processes.

Disaggregating Globalization

Let us begin by disaggregating the globalization metaphor into two of its component parts that are most relevant to transnational contention: economic integration and internationalization.

By *global economic integration* I mean, with Tom Friedman, "that loose combination of free-trade agreements, the Internet and the integration of financial markets that is erasing borders and uniting the world into a single, lucrative, but brutally competitive marketplace" (Friedman 1996, quoted in Lynch 1998). There is a strong version of the concept (e.g., the thesis that all significant forms of economic activity today are governed by a neoliberal international economic project. That, in turn, divides into a structural version, according to which all states are losing autonomy, faced with the inexorable drive of world financial markets, and a political version whereby the United States, or more broadly, the North, directs the globalization project, while weaker states fall into line. Note that both of these strong versions depend on a not-always-articulated assumption of the identity of political and economic power (but see McMichael 2002). Since states are still very much with us, and since their international policies are not easily reduced to their economic projects (e.g., U.S. policy since September 11), then it is analytically more secure to begin with the weaker version that I quoted from Tilly earlier. This does not imply that states are the only actors worth studying in the international system, but that state's international policies only partially, if importantly, intersect with the globalization of world markets, production, and regulation.

By *internationalization,* I mean the appropriation or construction of organizations, networks, and institutions across national boundaries. Here too, scholars have produced a strong and a weak variant: *substitutive* internationalization, which holds that international institutions grow up at the cost of the state; and *supplementary* internationalization, the extension of state and societal networks across boundaries. In the case of European integration, these two views translate into the two main theses that have guided researchers, supranationalism and multilevel governance (Sweet and Sandholtz 1994; Hooghe and Marks 1999). Nonstate forms of internationalization follow similar lines: some transnational organizations operate primarily at the international level, accreting to international institutions and their operations like a coral reef; while others operate primarily within the ambit of national states, extending their activities to other states and to international institutions on a case-by-case basis.

These distinctions between economic integration and internationalization make a difference for the student of transnational contention. For example, the main source of the anti-WTO agitations of the past few years was primarily the negative aspects of economic integration, although protesters' targets were both states and international institutions. Scholars like Philip McMichael are therefore correct to see this movement as part of a new Polanyian countermovement (McMichael 2002). But other movements, like the human rights movement, have internationalized in response to no visible force of economic integration, but to the rise of international norms and regimes and of the institutions that govern it (Risse, Ropp, and Sikkink 1999; Lutz and Sikkink 2001).

It could be argued that globalization has secondary effects in facilitating the formation of such international regimes and of the networks that surround them, but this is very different from the stronger claim that globalization is the cause of these movements (cf. Lynch 1998: 152-153). Consider the anti-landmine treaty that resulted from the interaction of nonstate actors and a few key states. We could ignore the considerable role that states played in the passage of the treaty and say that cultural globalization brought these agents together around a common project to rid the world of landmines (Price 1998), but it would be reductive and diverting to say that globalization was either the cause or the target of their efforts.

It can also be argued that there are other facets of globalization that facilitate transnational activism: like the denser and more rapidly moving communication system that makes it possible for protesters to speak the same language, make claims on the same targets, and organize coordinated demonstrations; or the global migration flows that have given rise to new forms of "transnational communities" of activists; or even the standardization and integration of scientific and technical standards. I do not claim that these are unimportant channels for transnational contention; only that we will make more analytical progress by focusing on observable processes and mechanisms than on master processes like globalization.[6]

By according internationalization an analytical space distinct from economic integration, we can sort out the mechanisms and processes that produce transnational social movements, *some of which* have their origins in economic integration, others in internationalization, while others may follow different causal trajectories. We are also helped to understand the framing of transnational contention as an autonomous process, in which concrete actors with political agendas draw on the symbols of globalization but are not determined by it. Further, we can examine different forms of resistance by asking what people are resisting *against*—which may be economic integration, or something very different. And this will help us, in turn, to specify within these broad processes the concrete mechanisms that link the sources of contention to their actors, their forms or contention, and their outcomes.

Disaggregating Resistance

The first decade of research on transnational activism tended to absorb all forms of transnational advocacy and activism under movement-like language. Consider the excellent study of O'Brian and his collaborators, *Contesting Global Governance* (2000): these authors provide a vigorous definition of what they take to be their main subject, namely, global social movements. But when they operationalize that broad concept, their attention centers only on the activities of international NGOs (pp. 13-15). The problem is that, while some of these groups are indeed engaged in contentious interaction with international targets, many others are engaged primarily in service work, still others in lobbying and information flow, while others resemble more closely the more contentious and sustained forms of interaction that many people mean by the term "social movements."[7] (Of course, in some international institutions, lobbying is not accepted as legitimate activity by member states).

In their lucid comparison of social movements and transnational advocacy networks, Margaret Keck and Kathryn Sikkink point to many similarities among the two forms of activism—for example, their dependence on external opportunity structures and their use of framing; but, they are careful to underscore that, while movements engage primarily in contentious interaction with opponents, transnational activist networks engage primarily in information exchange (1998b). The advocacy work done by NGOs and advocacy coalitions in New York, Washington, Geneva, and Brussels is important and dedicated; so is the service work of such groups as Doctors without Borders and Save the Children. But such forms of activism are worlds apart from the "days of action" we saw in Seattle, Quebec, Prague, and Genoa (Smith, this volume; Lichbach 2001).

From Seattle on, scholars became sharply aware that the forms of transnational activism range from the highly transgressive and even violent to the routine and bureaucratic, and that this difference has major implications for the future of the movement against economic integration (Lichbach 2001). Activists became grimly aware of these differences as conflicts developed between such groups as the anarchist black block in Genoa and more moderate advocacy groups that opposed their tactics and when the police and the Berlusconi government made no distinction between the two (della Porta and Tarrow 2002). Even within generally institutional groups like the labor movement, there are both contentious and more constrained forms of activism.

Disaggregating these forms and the actors who chose them is important not only for sociological accuracy but also it will help us to understand three important dynamic factors:

- *First, coalition formation:* how do different sectors of transnational activity relate to one another? Are the coalitions we saw at Seattle among contained unions and NGOs and the more contentious antiglobalization groups merely conjunctural, or can they produce an enduring alliance?
- *Second, action repertoires:* Is there an action dichotomy between the groups emerging from the two main forms of globalization—economic integration and internationalization—such that the former are more likely to engage in more contentious forms while the latter are more likely to become involved in routine transactions with their targets? Similarly, are groups that have their origins in the North less contentious and groups from the South more so?
- *Third, dynamics:* Is there a secular trend from the more contained to the more transgressive contentious forms, a routinization of contention along classical Michelsian lines, or a tendency to polarization between more radical and more moderate groups?

While there may be no clear answers to these questions, posing them as empirically testable hypotheses will help us to trace the dynamics of transnational contention. So will the attempt to go beyond broad processes and specify specific causal mechanisms of contentious politics.

LEARNING FROM DOMESTIC CONTENTION

Students and advocates of transnational contention have often chided Western social movement scholars for the fact that we often obsessively focused on national politics and ignored both the international roots of domestic movements (McAdam 1999: xv) and the transnational visions of many movements (Seidman 2001: 345-346). When we did turn to transnational factors it was often only to look at their most familiar and most traditional forms: the diffusion of a domestic movement to other countries through structural equivalence, ideological affinity, or interpersonal ties among activists (McAdam and Rucht 1993). Not even learning was carefully specified and studied, as Sean Chabot shows in his contribution to this volume.

There is much truth in these criticisms. However, though social movements have most often been studied at the national level, there is little in the conceptual canon of social movement studies that is *inherently* parochial. Consider the fruitful expansion of resource mobilization theory from the domestic to the transnational realm in Jackie Smith's work on international NGOs (1997), or the appropriation by Margaret Keck and Kathryn Sikkink of network theory (1998a). Although they use the term in its less technical sense than most sociologists would do, there are clear parallels between the key concepts of social network theory and the transnational advocacy networks they study in their important book.[8] Concepts like social networks, opportunity structures, and framing are not inherently domestic or Northern, just as concepts like resistance, revolution, or subaltern groups are not inherently either transnational or Southern. They can be adapted to the world of transnational contention.

From Static to Dynamic Contention[9]

The broader weakness in the canon of domestic social movement studies is the static way in which some of its central building blocks have been specified. During the 1960s and 1970s, much of the best North American and European work concerning contentious politics concentrated on social movements, then assimilated other forms of contention to prevailing explanations of social movements. Attention focused on four key concepts: *political opportunities*, sometimes crystallized as static opportunity structures, sometimes as changing political environments; *mobilizing structures*, both formal movement organizations and the social networks of everyday life; *collective action frames*, both the cultural constants that orient participants and those they themselves construct; established *repertoires of contention,* and how these repertoires evolve in response to changes in capitalism, statebuilding, and other, less monumental processes (McAdam, McCarthy, and Zald 1996).

This line of thought grew from a quadruple critique of prior research traditions. First, social historians had launched what many of them called "history from below" as an intellectual rebellion against the emphasis on elites and high politics that prevailed in earlier historical writing. Second, in a similar vein, many social scientists rejected the prevailing conception of mass movements and similar phenomena as collective behavior, as a confusion of common sense by fads, delusions, demagogues, and crowd influence. Third, the historians and social scientists in question commonly combated official interpretations of civil rights activism, student movements, worker mobilization, and other popular politics of the 1960s as impulsive, irresponsible outbursts of self-indulgence. Fourth (and in partial reaction to the first three lines of thought), Mancur Olson (1965) and other rational action theorists countered simple assertions of rationality on the part of protesters. They made two telling observations about analysts of popular protest. Those analysts (a) ignored the fact that many—perhaps most—sets of people who share a grievance or interest fail to act on it, and (b) lacked a plausible theory of the conditions or process under which people who do share an interest organize and act on it.

In an academic version of identity politics, scholars sometimes drew boundaries among themselves, observers sometimes detected separate schools of thought, while still other observers attended only to the boundary separating these related lines of thought from other perspectives. But by the 1980s most North American students of social movements had adopted a common social movement agenda, and they differed chiefly in their relative emphasis on different components of that agenda—opportunities, mobilizing structures, framing, and repertoires of contention. That agenda stimulated much empirical work, but it provided only a structural and static baseline model of social movements. By packing more of its cause-and-effect relations into its underspecified arrows among these concepts than in its labeled boxes it provided only still photographs of contentious moments rather than dynamic, interactive sequences.

To move to a more dynamic approach to the study of transnational contention, we must first distinguish among episodes, processes, and social mechanisms:

- *Episodes* are continuous streams of contention including collective claims making that bears on others' interests. The Battle of Seattle was an important episode in transnational contention.
- *Processes* are regular sequences of mechanisms (listed below) that produce similar, generally more complex and contingent transformations of those elements. Economic integration and internationalization are complex processes that in turn are made up of mechanisms.
- *Mechanisms* are a delimited class of events that alter relations among specified sets of elements in identical or closely similar ways over a variety of situations. Scholars in the global civil society tradition assume a mechanism in the notion of identity shift that would be necessary in order for people to cohere in solidarity across states.

Within contentious politics, we can impose a rough distinction among environmental, cognitive, and relational mechanisms.

- *Environmental mechanisms* mean externally generated shifts in some connection between the structure or process of concern and surrounding structures and processes that shift the context within which people interact. For example, climate change or population shift are environmental mechanisms with profound implications for contentious politics.
- *Cognitive mechanisms* operate through alterations of individual and collective perception; words like recognize, understand, reinterpret, and classify characterize such mechanisms. For example, identify shift is one cognitive mechanism that is frequently deduced by scholars of global civil society as the source of international solidarity.
- *Relational mechanisms* alter connections among people, groups, and interpersonal networks. Brokerage is a typical relational mechanism relating groups and individuals to one another in stable sites, but it can also become a relational mechanism for mobilization in transnational contention, as groups impacted by economic integration discover their common interests through the intervention of a third party or site of interaction.

Environmental, cognitive, and relational mechanisms combine. In the best-studied episode of contentious politics in the United States, the civil rights movement is widely held to have resulted from a combination of environmental, cognitive, and relational mechanisms: the environmental shift of vast numbers of African

Americans from the rural South to the cities of both North and South; the cognitive shift in the meaning of blackness in their own, and white peoples' mentalities; the relational role of the black churches as fora for mobilization; and the new forms of innovative collective action that the movement developed (McAdam 1983, 1999).

In the world of transnational contention, we can find similar concatenations of mechanisms, processes, and episodes. The Rio process revealed the depth of the environmental threat of climate change; this combined with identity shift and the brokerage of both transnational NGOs and some states to produce a vast national and international mobilization to control greenhouse emissions. It has also produced some innovative forms of collective action, like the grassroots groups in the United States that are beginning to "self-produce" compliance with the Kyoto accords in the absence of their government's agreement to the treaty.[10]

In related work, Doug McAdam (1999: preface) has developed a mobilization model that McAdam, Charles Tilly, and I have adopted in our *Dynamics of Contention* (2002: chap. 2). Its intention is both to transcend the static nature of the domestic social movement paradigm and to specify a number of links among dynamic mechanisms that we see as crucial to the mobilization process:

- Rather than look upon political opportunity structure as an objective factor, we focus on the attribution of opportunity and threat and on the different mix of opportunity and threat that different contenders face.
- Instead of focusing on preexisting mobilizing structures, we call attention to the active appropriation of sites for mobilization.
- Instead of limiting our attention to frames as strategic tools of social movement leaders, we expanded our view of framing to involve the interactive construction of disputes among challengers, their opponents, elements of the state, third parties, and the media.
- And instead of merely counting the action repertoire of challenging groups, we focused on innovative collective action by challengers and their opponents.

The transformation from a set of static features of social movements to a dynamic model is summarized in the model in figure 13.1. Let us illustrate how it can apply to the dynamics of transnational contention.

THE DYNAMICS OF TRANSNATIONAL MOBILIZATION

The attribution of opportunity and threat, the appropriation of institutional sites for mobilization, the framing of episodes of contention, and innovative collective action: none of these mechanisms is inherently limited to domestic contention. Although the cases that illustrate this mobilization model in *Dynamics of Contention* are domestic, if the mechanisms it specifies are indeed robust, we should find them in transnational processes of mobilization as well. In what follows, no attempt to demonstrate this assertion can be offered. But by ranging broadly over the recent literature on trans national contention, I hope to illustrate how a dynamic mechanism-and-process approach can take us beyond both the static structuralism of the domestic social movement model and the poorly specified approach of globalization theorists in understanding the dynamics of transnational mobilization.

Figure 13.1. A Dynamic, Interactive Framewrok for Analyzing Mobilization in Contentious Politics

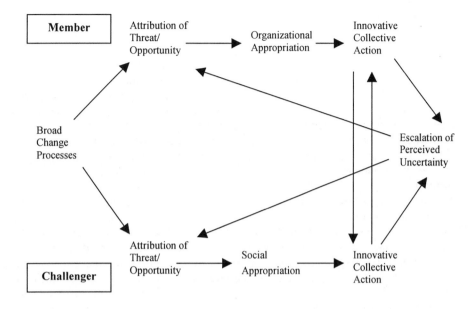

Attribution of Threats and Opportunities

In a recent article, Jack Goldstone and Charles Tilly argue that threats and opportunities are the dual sources of social movement activism (2001). They are seconded by David S. Meyer's distinction between the effects of good news and bad news on mobilization (2002). If students of domestic social movements have overestimated opportunity structure, scholars of globalization have been better at pinpointing the threat side, especially by specifying the costs of neoliberalism to the subaltern peoples of the South (McMichael 1996). But they have been less attentive to the opportunity side of the equation. If people do not protest in response to threat alone and if mobilization depends on social networks, mobilizing frames, and on the attribution of opportunity (McAdam, Tarrow, and Tilly 2001: chap. 3), surely the same must be true of transnational mobilization.

Movement scholars have been properly criticized for specifying opportunity only domestically. The problem is how, in the absence of an encompassing structure of authority like the state, to operationalize it transnationally. Three ways of specifying opportunity internationally can be proposed:

International events. These offer opportunities for activists from a variety of countries to come together. The Chiapas insurgency, the Beijing Woman's Conference, the Rio Conference on the environment, the various G-7 and WTO summits both implicitly and explicitly offer opportunities to meet and forge ongoing ties with other activists, shape coalitions, and frame programs for the future. Many of these result in transnational campaigns, but others (like the U.S. government's rejection of the Kyoto process) are visibly producing an increase in domestic environmental organizing.

Initiatives of state allies. While states are most often framed in the globalization literature as the targets of transnational contention, in fact, states or state actors frequently provide institutional allies for transnational campaigns. Some states may be reluctant to voice their opposition to major power initiatives for fear of being isolated internationally, a situation in which protest groups can exercise marginal power (Knopf 1993). As the debates over the Kyoto protocol, FTAA, and MAI demonstrated, the ultimate actors in reining in neoliberal globalization are states, not transnational NGOs or social movements. Currently the most impressive roadblock to the successful completion of the FTAA is not the notable transnational educational and lobbying activities of the Hemispheric Social Alliance, but the formidable and growing objections of Brazil to U.S. domestic trade policies (Ayres 2001; Ayres and Tarrow 2001). Within the transnational activist networks of Keck and Sikkink, the role of state actors must be better specified and operationalized: are they integral parts of these networks, or do they provide the external opportunities on which they are built?

International institutions as "coral reefs." A third way of specifying opportunity transnationally is through the inducement to transnational activism offered by the activities of international institutions (O'Brien et al. 2000). The World Bank, the United Nations, the WTO: these institutions do not willingly aim at empowering nonstate actors. But for reasons of their own—or because the states that created them wish them to do so—they invite input and offer targets for nonstate actors. Such opportunities allow nonstate actors to travel abroad, encounter and learn from one another, and form more enduring ties that can eventually challenge the international actors who bring them together. In a language I have used elsewhere, international institutions are like coral reefs in the oceans of global anarchy, attracting both contained forms of contention that attach themselves to the reef and transgressive actors who peck at their edges and often attack their enemies from within their recesses (Tarrow 2001).

Different kinds of transnational organizations face different combinations of opportunity and threat. Opportunity structures faced by more militant groups will differ from those faced by less militant ones; groups with close organizational links to domestic movements or parties can rely on their support in the international arena; and domestic threats (for example, from menacing authoritarian regimes) can be turned into opportunities for support from transnational allies. The converse is also the case: groups that become too dependent on international allies may become divorced or alienated from domestic sources of support.

Appropriation of Organizational Sites

If the attribution of the threat of global inequality were sufficient to explain transnational action, we ought to find that equally threatened actors across the globe organize equally effectively against the institutions that govern the global economy. But they do not. Why not? There are a number of answers to the question, ranging from the difficulty of organizing concerted collective action to the high transaction costs in doing so to the dispersion and differences in the claims of different collective actors. This problem is more complex in the case of transnational contention, where the collective action problem is more severe, transaction costs are higher, and populations are both socially and geographically more dispersed.

The study of domestic contention has produced a number of answers to this problem. One that has received remarkably little attention in the study of transnational contention is the availability of organizations and institutions to link dispersed and distinct national groups to one another. Using the differential availability of institutional venues for nonstate actors as an intervening variable between threat and collective response, we can do a better job of understanding who mobilizes and who doesn't and which institutions offer more tempting and more responsive targets to their claims.

For example, the World Bank—far more welcoming to nonstate actors than either the IMF or the WTO—has stimulated the formation of nonstate coalitions (O'Brien et al., 2000: chap. 2) and responded to environmental protests with the creation of an Inspection Panel (Fox and Brown 1998). In its desire to increase transparency, the European Union encourages and finances transnational civil society groups and lobbies (Imig and Tarrow 2001). Whether these become tame puppets of the Eurocrats or develop an autonomous capacity for mobilization varies from sector to sector and over time (for example, compare Guiraudon 2001 with Kettnaker 2001); but it is certainly a fertile field for transnational research.

Students of global civil society look naturally to transnational organizations as the logical sources for transnational mobilization. Such venues are important, and scholars like Jackie Smith (1997) and John Boli and George Thomas (1998) have done heroic work plumbing the depths of the *Yearbook of International Associations* to chart their development. But if we believe—as I do—that much of transnational activism is rooted in domestic resources and networks (Tarrow 2002), we should also examine the social appropriation of domestic institutions and organizations for transnational purposes. Just as scholars of the American civil rights movements showed how the religious institutions of the black church could be appropriated for contentious purposes (Morris 1984; McAdam 1999), researchers should examine the appropriation of both domestic and international institutions for transnational purposes.

Framing Transnational Contention

Globalization as a process is too poorly specified, too ambivalent, and too multivocal, a symbol to help us in explaining the sources of transnational contention; but these very characteristics make it a fertile symbol in *framing* contention (Kertzer 1988: chap. 1). We can employ the contributions of David Snow and Robert Benford (1986; 1992) to better understand the extraordinary success of the globalization frame—not only in the academic community but also in the social movement world—as a way of understanding the outpouring of transnational activism in the last decade. Not since the centrality of the rights frame emerged in the United States in the 1960s and 1970s has an image been so widely framed as both the source of people's claims and an element that brings them together around attributed common goals. In four ways, Snow and Benford's categories help to underscore why globalization seems to have succeeded so brilliantly as a social movement frame; but a fourth category, frame transformation, illustrates its major problem:

- *First,* globalization is an effective device for bringing together material claims and what international relations scholars call principled issue groups. Lichbach's research underscores this when he estimates the wide variety of protesters in transnational coalitions (Lichbach 2001).
- *Second,* globalization has an extraordinary frame-bridging capacity, bringing together opponents of free trade, supporters of a cleaner environment, those who

demand access for Third World farmers to Western markets, opponents of neo-liberalism and supporters of global democracy (Lichbach 2001:ms. 25-34).

- *Third,* the fact that the hegemonic state in the world today is also the core of the global financial system governed by international institutions makes it possible to condense the target of globalization, the target of anti-American nationalism, and the target of internationalization into one apparently unified super-target.
- But, *fourth,* globalization as a mobilizing frame so far has lacked the capacity of frame transformation—the most far-reaching and most difficult of Snow and Benford's categories for a movement to achieve. Especially the North-South tensions that lie just beneath the surface of the anti-free trade movement suggest the difficulty of transforming region-specific claims into a new global collective identity (Wood 2001). And in the wake of September 11, when so many of the movement's supporters at least temporarily slipped away—or shifted their focus to the reborn antiwar movement—the transformative effect of the globalization frame remains an open question.

Innovating with Collective Action

From the 1970s on, the systematic study of forms of contention, the social actors who employ them, and the reaction of elites, authorities, and third parties to their actions has been part of the stock-in-trade of the study of social movements.[11] Yet until quite recently, this tradition has been poorly mined by students of transnational contention. Part of the reason is the technical difficulty of assembling data on protest events that span a number of countries and finding sources from those countries that are comparable in coverage (Imig and Tarrow 2001: chap. 1); another part is due to the dominance of the case study tradition in the first decade of work in the study of transnational contention; but an important part is almost certainly due to the fact that research has focused predominantly on groups that engage in routinized forms of interaction with officials—lobbying, information sharing, organizing, and attending conferences—and not in protest activities. Only in countries of the European Union, with its robust traditions of farmers' and ecological protests, has systematic protest event analysis begun to flourish.[12]

Since the Battle of Seattle, the questions of who protesters are, how they behave, and how these forms of action compare to domestic activism have grown in importance. New methods of analysis, like the use of activist Internet sites, have joined more traditional methods in providing systematic evidence of groups' participation in different international events (Almeida and Lichbach 2001). As might be expected, who the protesters are and much of what they do are not very different from what scholars have been finding over the past three decades of empirical research on domestic protest events.

For example, Mark Lichbach estimates that that between 20,000 and 25,000 of the Seattle protesters came from Seattle and Washington state and that only 1,000 to 3,000 came from outside Canada or the United States (2001: 55). With respect to forms of action they use, Jackie Smith finds that many of them are adaptations of familiar forms of domestic collective action. She enumerates six familiar forms of education and mobilization, eight routine forms of framing and symbolic mobilization, and four forms of disruption that are well known by domestic social movements (Smith, this volume). Imig and Tarrow (2001) found that the vast majority of protests against the European Union took place on native soil and were aimed against domestic targets. Not only that: many of the actions that Smith observed in Seattle were not new; rather, they were innovations in traditional protest forms, like the production of NGO newspapers at global conferences, mounting anti-conferences at or near the sites of official intergovernmental meetings, and various forms of electronic activism (Smith, this volume).

On the other hand, some people traveled considerable distances to participate in the Seattle protests—like the Indian members of People's Global Action. Lichbach also found cognate Seattle protests all over the world (Lichbach 2001: 44-48). In Europe, farmers, environmentalists, and industrial workers have been learning to coordinate their protests against the EU and even cooperating against multinational targets (Imig and Tarrow 2001). In sectors of activity that are inherently international—like the marketing and certification of genetic seeds, European activists have mounted both national protests and transnational campaigns to influence the European Union (Kettnaker 2001). And many of the actions of these protesters have innovated around the core of the social movement repertoire (Smith, this volume).

These studies focused predominantly on the actions of protesters; none of these scholars were able to analyze the interactions of protesters, police, and EU and national officials. The next phase of research will have to go beyond enumeration of protest events to try to understand which kinds of actors are using which forms of action, how they interact with opponents, allies, and authorities, and whether—as movement activists claim—we are witnessing the rise of a global cycle of transgressive politics. We also need to study the strategy of states vis-à-vis transnational protest campaigns; here, the evidence from Genoa is chastening as a police riot met a largely peaceful mass protest against the G-7 meetings and a bloody roundup at a protesters' residence reminded Italians of fascist *rastrellamenti* (della Porta and Tarrow 2002).

Jeffrey Ayres (2001) has studied a number of these meetings. He sees evidence that the institutionalization of protest policing that has been documented over the past twenty years is being reversed by repression of transnational protests (compare with McPhail, Schweingruber, and McCarthy 1998; della Porta and Reiter 1998). Whether the police and political reaction to September 11 will tighten the repressive vice still further against transnational protesters is a key question for students of both national and transnational contention, as well as for activists (Ayres and Tarrow 2001).

CONCLUSION

These examples show only a few of the ways in which the domestic social movement tradition can help scholars of transnational contention to move toward a new phase of research and theorizing. There are, of course, many others: coalition theory may help to understand the conditions in which advocates for the environment, indigenous groups, development rights, and antiglobalization protesters can come together in enduring alliances. The sociology of religion can help scholars to recognize the tremendous importance of religious-based transnational groups under the apparent "secularizing" trend of world polity formation (Bush 2001). And the tools that have been developed for the study of political activism can help us to understand the relationships between domestic and international involvements in transnational contention (Dalton 2002; Tarrow 2002).

Is there a new stratum of individuals and groups that can reasonably be characterized as transnational in its identity, its ways of life, and its commitments? Or is transnational activism merely an occasional extension of the forms and channels of activism that we have become familiar with from the study of domestic contention? We will not learn the answer to this question by declaring that the world has become a global civil society and deducing from that a new class of citizens. While a global civil society may be the ultimate outcome of economic integration and internationalization, I agree with Jeffrey Ayres that beginning from that construct as if it already existed would be an odd way to conduct research (Ayres 2001).

In a world in which people still live in states and states have shown an unbridled capacity to both facilitate and deal brutally with movements, there is a surer way to proceed: examining the mechanisms that trigger transnational activism, studying the organizational networks that sustain it, understanding how the framing of meaning draws on international symbols, and examining how transnational involvement affects the innovation of collective action forms. Discovering that these mechanisms derive causally from globalization would be a major social scientific achievement. But even if they do not, shifting from the broad canvas of globalization to the finer fabric of the mechanisms of activism is a step that will take us far in understanding the dynamics of transnational contention. That step has been mightily advanced by the contributions to this book.

NOTES

1. www. stratfor.com/asia/commentary/0111212045.htm.

2. This chapter draws on the theoretical perspective outlined in a joint program of Doug McAdam, Charles Tilly and myself (2001) and on two other efforts: Tarrow 2001 and Ayres and Tarrow 2002, available at www. ssrc.org/sept11.

3. I have made this argument in greater detail in Tarrow 1998:chap. 11 and 2001. For a clear-headed analysis of the genetic modification conflict in India, which shows that it cannot be reduced to "the people vs. the transnational corporations," see Herring 2001.

4. In a private comment, Evelyn Bush notes that "the conceptual relationship between human rights and globalization is complex and has changed over time. Initially, it was argued that human rights was a strong indicator, if not a cause, of globalization, insofar as it embodied the rights of an international body or movement to interfere in the domestic affairs of certain states. More recently, we have started to think of human rights as response to, instead of a beneficiary of globalization." See Bush 2001.

5. See the transcript of Katie Couric's interview with two of the American aid workers on the *Today Show* at www. msnbc.com/news/663829.asp?cp1=1.

6. The dogged wisdom of my collaborators, Doug McAdam and Charles Tilly, have led me away from a single-minded emphasis on integration and internationalization.

7. This touches on a fundamental—but respectful—difference I have had with one of the editors of this volume: in the best resource mobilization tradition, in her many works, Jackie Smith defines transnational social movements largely in terms of their organizations' social change goals (see Smith 1997); in contrast, in the political process tradition, I have defined social movements in terms of their action forms and their sustained conflictual interactions with opponents, elites, and authorities (Tarrow 1998: chap.1).

8. Devotees of social network analysis will be surprised to discover that Keck and Sikkink take their start from the more popular meaning of the word "network" and do not draw explicitly on the more analytical meaning of the term used in social network analyses.

9. The following section follows closely the argument in McAdam, Tarrow, and Tilly 2001: chap. 2.

10. I am grateful to Bogdan Vasi for pointing this out to me from his research on climate change.

11. See the reviews in Rucht, Koopmans, and Neidhardt, eds. 1998, and Klandermans and Staggenborg, eds. 2002.

12. See the contributions to Imig and Tarrow, eds., 2001; Reising 1998; and Roederer 2000.

REFERENCES

Almeida, Paul D., and Mark I. Lichbachap. 2001. "To the Internet; From the Internet: Sources of Data about Antiglobalization Protest," unpublished paper, University of Maryland Political Science Department.

Arato, Andrew, and Jean Cohen. 1992. *Civil Society and Political Theory.* Cambridge, Mass.: MIT Press.

Arrighi, Giovanni. 1994. *The Long Twentieth Century: Money, Power, and the Origins of Our Times.* London: Verso.

Ayres, Jeffrey M. 2001."Global Civil Society and Transnational Protest: No Swan Song Yet for the State," unpublished paper, St. Michael's College.

Ayres, Jeffrey M. and Sidney Tarrow. 2001. "The Shifting Grounds for Transnational Activism." In *After September 11th: Perspectives from the Social Sciences.* New York: SSRC (www.ssrc.org/sept11.)

Boli, John, and George Thomas. 1997. "World Culture in the World Polity." *American Sociological Review* 62: 171-190.

Bush, Evelyn. 2001. "Transnational Religion and Secular Institutions," unpublished paper, Cornell University Department of Sociology

Dalton, Russell. 2002. *Citizen Politics: Public Opinion and Political Parties in Advanced Industrial Democracies.* 3rd ed. Chatham, N.J.: Chatham House.

della Porta, Donatella, and Herbert Rieter. 1998. *Policing Protest: The Control of Mass Demonstrations in Western Democracies.* Minneapolis: University of Minnesota Press.

della Porta, Donatella, and Sidney Tarrow. 2002. "After Genoa." SSRC Items, winter.

Falk, Richard. 1995. *On Humane Governance: Towards a New Global Politics.* University Park: Pennsylvania State University Press.

Fox, Jonathan, and L. David Brown, eds. 1998. *The Struggle for Accountability: The World Bank, NGOs, and Grassroots Movements.* Cambridge, Mass.: MIT Press.

Friedman, Tom. 1996. "Revolt of the Wannabees," *New York Times.* February 7, A15.

Goldstone, Jack A., and Charles Tilly. 2001. "Threat (and Opportunity): Popular Action and State Response in the Dynamics of Contentions Action." Pp 179-194 in *Silence and Voice in the Study of Contentious Politics*, Ron Aminzade, ed. New York: Cambridge University Press.

Guiraudon, Virginie. 2001. "Weak Weapons of the Weak: Transnational Mobilization Around Migration," in *Contentious Europeans: Protest and Politics in an Emerging Polity.* Doug Imig and Sidney Tarrow, eds., Lanham, Md.: Rowman & Littlefield.

Hellman, Judith. 1999. "Real and Virtual Chiapas: Magic Realism and the Left." *Socialist Register* 2000. London: Merlin.

Herring, Ronald. 2001. "Promethean Science, Pandora's Jug: Conflicts Around Generically Engineered Organisms in India." The 2001 Mary Keatinge Das Lecture, Columbia University.

Hooghe, Liesbet, and Gary Marx. 1999. *Multi-Level Governance and European Integration.* Lanham, Md.: Rowman & Littlefield.

Imig, Doug, and Sidney Tarrow, eds. 2001. *Contentious Europeans: Protest and Politics in an Emerging Polity.* Lanham, Md.: Rowman & Littlefield.

Keck, Margaret, and Kathryn Sikkink. 1998a. *Activists beyond Borders: Transnational Activ-ists in International Politics.* Ithaca, N.Y.: Cornell University Press.

———. 1998b. "Transnational Advocacy Networks in the Global Society," in David S. Meyer and Sidney Tarrow, eds., *The Social Movement Society.* Lanham, Md.: Rowman & Littlefield.

Kertzer, David. 1988. *Ritual, Politics and Power.* New Haven, Conn.: Yale University Press.

Kettnaker, Vera. 2001. "The Campaign Against Genetically Modified Foods in Western Europe," In *Contentious Europeans: Protest and Politics in an Emerging Polity.* Doug Imig and Sidney Tarrow, eds. Lanham, Md.: Rowman & Littlefield.

Klandermans, Bert, and Suzanne Staggenborg. 2002. *Methods in Social Movement Research.* Minneapolis: University of Minnesota Press.

Knopf, Jeffrey W. 1993. "Beyond Two-Level Games: Domestic-International Interaction in the Intermediate Range Nuclear Forces Negotiations." *International Organization* 47: 599-628.

Lichbach, Mark I. 2001. "Global Order and Local Resistance: Structure, Culture and Ration-ality in the Battle of Seattle," unpublished paper, University of Maryland Political Sci-ence Department.

Lipschutz, Ronnie D. 1992. "Restructuring World Politics: The Emergence of Global Civil Society." *Millenium* 21: 389-411.

Lutz, Ellen, and Kathryn Sikkink. 2001. "The Justice Cascade: The Evolution and Impact of Foreign Human Rights Trials in Latin America." *Chicago Journal of International Law* 2: 1-33.

Lynch, Cecilia. 1998. "Social Movements and the Problem of Globalization." *Alternatives* 23:149-173.

McAdam, Doug. 1983. "Tactical Innovation and the Pace of Insurgency." *American Socio-logical Review* 48: 735-754.

———. 1999. *Political Process and the Development of Black Insurgency, 1930-1970.* 2nd ed. Chicago: University of Chicago Press.

McAdam, Doug, John D. McCarthy, and Mayer Zald. 1996. *Comparative Perspectives on Social Movements: Political Opportunities, Mobilizing Structures and Cultural Fram-ings.* New York: Cambridge University Press.

McAdam, Doug, and Dieter Rucht. 1993. "The Cross-National Diffusion of Movement Ideas." *Annals of the American Academy of Political and Social Science* 528: 56-74.

McAdam, Doug, Sidney Tarrow, and Charles Tilly. 2002. *Dynamics of Contention.* New York: Cambidge University Press.

McPhail, Clark, David Schweingruber and John d. McCarthy. 1998. "Policing Protest in the United States, 1960-1995," Pp. 49-69 in *Policing Protest.* Donatella della Porta and Her-bert Reiter, eds., Mineapolis and St. Paul: University of Minnesota Press.

McMichael, Philip. 1996. *Development and Social Change: A Global Perspective.* Thousand Oaks, CA: Pine Forge.

———. 2002. "Globalization Countermovements," unpublished paper presented to the Workshop on International Studies in Planning, Cornell University, January.

Meyer, David S. 2002. "Opportunities and Identities," In *Social Movements: Identity, Culture and the State.* David S. Meyer, Nancy Whittier, and Belinda Robnett, eds. New York: Oxford University Press.

Meyer, David S., and Sidney Tarrow, eds. 1998. *Towards a Movement Society?.* Lanham, Md.: Rowman & Littlefield.

Meyer, John, John Boli, and George Thomas. 1998. "World Society and the Nation-State." *American Journal of Sociology* 103: 144-181.

Morris, Aldon. 1984. *The Origins of the Civil Rights Movement: Black Communities Organ-izing for Change.* New York: Free Press.

O'Brien, Robert, Anne Marie Goetz, Jan Aart Scholte, and Marc Williams. 2000. *Contesting Global Governance: Multilateral Economic Institutions and Global Social Movements.* Cambridge: Cambridge University Press.

Price, Richard. 1998. "Reversing the Gunsights: Transnational Civil Society Targets Landmines." *International Organization* 52: 613-644.

Reising, Uwe. 1998. "Domestic and Supranational Political Opportunities: European Protest in Selected Countries, 1980-1995," *European Integration Online Paper 2:* http://eiop.or.eiop/.

Risse, Thomas, Stephen C. Ropp, and Kathryn Sikkink. 1999. *The Power of Human Rights: International Norms and Domestic Change.* New York: Cambridge University Press.

Roederer, Christilla. 1998. "Popular Struggle and the Making of Europe's Agricultural Policy." Unpublished PhD dissertation, University of South Carolina Department of Government and International Studies.

Rosenberg, Justin. 1993. *The Empire of Civil Society.* London: Verso.

Rucht, Dieter, Ruud Koopmans, and Friedhelm Neidhardt. 1994. *Acts of Dissent: New Developments in the Study of Protest.* Berlin: Sigma.

Scott, James C. 1985. *Weapons of the Weak: Everyday Forms of Resistance.* New Haven, Conn.: Yale University Press.

Seidman, Gay. 2001. "Adjusting the Lens: What do Globalizations, Transnationalism, and the Anti-Apartheid Movement Mean for Social Movement Theory?" Pp. 339-358 in *Globalizations and Social Movements,* John A.Guidry, Michael D. Kennedy, and Mayer N. Zald, eds. Ann Arbor: University of Michigan Press.

Smith, Jackie. 1997. "Characteristics of the Modern Transnational Social Movement Sector," In *Social Movements and Global Politics,* Jackie Smith, Charles Chatfield and Ronald Pagnucco, eds. Syracuse, N.Y.: Syracuse University Press.

Snow, David, and Robert Benford. 1992. "Master Frames and Cycles of Protest." Pp. 133-155 in *Frontiers of Social Movement Theory*, Aldon Morris and Carole McClurg Muleller, eds. New Haven, Conn.: Yale University Press.

Snow, David A., E. Burke Rocheford Jr., Steven K. Worden, and Robert Benford. 1986. "Frame Alignment Processes, Micromobilization, and Movement Participation." *American Sociological Review* 51: 464-481.

Stone Sweet, Alec, and Wayne Sandholtz. 1994. "European Integration and Supranational Governance." *Journal of European Public Policy* 2: 297-317.

Tarrow, Sidney. 1998. *Power in Movement.* Cambridge: Cambridge University Press.

———. 2001. "Transnational Contention and International Institutions." *Annual Review of Political Science* 4: 1- 20.

———. 2002. "Rooted Cosmopolitans in Transnational Politics," unpublished paper, Cornell University.

Tilly, Charles. 1993. "Globalization Threatens Labor's Rights." *International Labor and Working Class History* 47:1-23.

———. 1994. *Popular Contention in Great Britain, 1758-1834.* Cambridge, Mass.: Harvard University Press.

Walton, John, and David Seddon. 1994. *Free Markets and Food Riots: The Politics of Global Adjustment.* Cambridge, Mass.: Blackwell.

Wapner, Paul. 1995. "Politics beyond the State: Environmental Activism and World Civic Politics." *World Politics* 47: 311-340.

Wood, Lesley. 2001. "An Oppositional Transnational Coalition: The Case of People's Global Action", unpublished paper, Columbia University.

Yashar, Deborah. 2002. "Globalization and Collective Action: A Review Essay." *Comparative Politics.* forthcoming.

INDEX

About the Contributors

Jeffrey M. Ayres is associate professor of political science at Saint Michael's College in Colchester, Vermont, and an adjunct professor of Canadian studies at the University of Vermont. He is the author of *Defying Conventional Wisdom: Political Movements and Popular Contention against North American Free Trade* (1998), and several articles on Canadian politics, political economy, and social movements.

Beth Schaefer Caniglia is assistant professor of sociology at Oklahoma State University, where she also serves on the faculty of the Environmental Institute and the School of International Studies. Her areas of interest focus on international aspects of environmental sociology, especially those that concern international environmental policymaking and the role of nongovernmental organizations at the United Nations. Her current projects explore the role of nongovernmental organizations in the construction of world models of nation-state behavior, and she is currently part of an interdisciplinary groundwater research and development project in South Africa.

Sean Chabot is a Ph.D. student of the Amsterdam School for Social Science Research at the University of Amsterdam. His dissertation examines the Gandhian repertoire's transnational diffusion from the Indian independence movement to the American civil rights movement. He has recently published articles on this subject in *Mobilization, Passages,* and *Peace Research,* and is currently focusing on the nexus among globalization, transnational diffusion, and social movements.

Marco G. Giugni is a researcher at the Department of Political Science at the University of Geneva, Switzerland. He has published several books and articles on social movements, including *Entre stratégie et opportunité* (1995), *New Social Movements in Western Europe* (co-authored, 1995), *Histoires de mobilisation politiques en Suisse* (co-authored, 1997), *From Contention to Democracy* (co-edited, 1998), *How Social Movements Matter* (co-edited, 1999), and *Political Altruism?* (co-edited, 2001). His current research focuses on political claims-making in the fields of immigration, unemployment, and social exclusion.

Michael Hanagan teaches at the New School University in New York City. He is the author of several books on labor history and has also co-edited a number of books, most recently, *Expanding Rights, Reconfiguring States* and *Challenging Authority: The Historical Study of Contentious Politics*. He is a senior editor of *International Labor and Working-Class History*. He is currently collaborating on a world history textbook and on a comparative study of the welfare state in England, France, and the United States.

Hank Johnston is editor of *Mobilization: An International Journal,* Department of Sociology, San Diego State University. He teaches courses in globalization theory, social psychology, and ethnic mobilization there, and has written widely on ethnic-national movements, political and religious resistance against repressive regimes, and framing and discursive aspects of social movements. He is currently researching collective action repertoires in newly industrializing states.

Tammy L. Lewis is assistant professor in the Department of Sociology and Anthropology at Muhlenberg College. Her current research includes analysis of trends in international environmental aid. She is also working on a project examining coalitions between labor activists and environmental activists. She is the co-author of *Environment, Energy, and Society* (with Craig Humphrey and Fred Buttel, 2002).

Gregory M. Maney is assistant professor in the sociology and anthropology department at Hofstra University. His research focuses upon transnational dimensions of protest, ethnic conflict, and social change. He has recently published articles on these topics in *Social Problems, Mobilization,* and *Political Opportunities, Social Movements, and Democratization*. He is currently researching strategic responses of the global justice movement to changes in the international political context.

Sharon Erickson Nepstad is assistant professor of sociology at Duquesne University, where she also teaches in the Graduate Center for Social and Public Policy's program in peace studies and conflict resolution. Her current research is on the Catholic Left and the Plowshares Movement.

Pamela Oliver is professor of sociology at the University of Wisconsin, Madison. Her current research in social movements focuses on diffusion models of the inter-relation between repression and protest, and the interplay between protest and news coverage. She is also working on racial disparities in imprisonment and arrest.

Kim D. Reimann is currently an advanced research fellow at the Program on U.S.-Japan Relations at Harvard University and will be an assistant professor of political science at Georgia State University beginning August 2002. Her work examines the evolution of international NGOs across industrialized nations, with a particular focus on Japan. She is the author of "Building Global Civil Society from the Outside In? Japan's Development NGOs, the State, and International Norms," in *The State of Civil Society in Japan* (Frank J. Schwartz and Susan J. Pharr, eds., 2003).

Franklin D. Rothman is associate professor in the Departamento de Economia Rural of the Universidade Federal de Viçosa, Minas Gerais, Brazil, in the postgraduate program in rural extension. He coordinates research and extension projects on the social and environmental impacts of hydroelectric dams in his home state of Minas

Gerais, Brazil, and has served as advisor to the regional movement of dam-affected people. His most recent publication is "A Comparative Study of Dam-Resistance Campaigns and Environmental Policy in Brazil," which appeared in the *Journal of Environment and Development* in December 2001. He has also written about the landless workers movement in Brazil.

Jackie Smith is associate professor of sociology at the State University of New York at Stony Brook. She is co-editor of *Transnational Social Movements and World Politics: Solidarity beyond the State*, and she is currently editing (with Joe Bandy) *Coalitions across Borders: Negotiating Difference and Unity in Transnational Struggles against Neoliberalism* (2003). Her current research examines transnational organizations and the dynamics of contemporary mobilization against global trade liberalization.

Sidney Tarrow is Maxwell Upson Professor of Government and Sociology at Cornell where he teaches social movements, European politics, and transnational contention. The author of *Power in Movement* and *Democracy and Disorder,* Tarrow has recently collaborated with Doug McAdam and Charles Tilly on *Dynamics of Contention* and with Doug Imig on *Contentious Europeans.*